The Gambia

THE BRADT TRAVEL GUIDE

THE BRADT STORY

The first Bradt travel guide was written by Hilary and George Bradt in 1974 on a river barge floating down a tributary of the Amazon in Bolivia. From their base in Boston, Massachusetts, they went on to write and publish four other backpacking guides to the Americas and one to Africa.

In the 1980s Hilary continued to develop the Bradt list in England, and also established herself as a travel writer and tour leader. The company's publishing emphasis evolved towards broader-based guides to new destinations – usually the first to be published on those countries – complemented by hiking, rail and wildlife guides.

Since winning *The Sunday Times* Small Publisher of the Year Award in 1997, we have continued to fill the demand for detailed, well-written guides to unusual destinations, while maintaining the company's original ethos: that adventurous travel is more enjoyable if the wishes of the local people are taken into consideration.

Travel guides are by their nature continuously evolving. If you experience anything which you would like to share with us, or if you have any amendments to make to this guide, please write; all your letters are read and passed on to the author. Most importantly, do remember to travel with an open mind and to respect the customs of your hosts – it will add immeasurably to your enjoyment.

Happy travelling!

Hilary Bradt

Hilary Bradt

19 High Street, Chalfont St Peter, Bucks HP9 9QE, England
Tel: 01753 893444 Fax: 01753 892333
Email: info@bradt-travelguides.com
www. bradt-travelguides.com

The Gambia

THE BRADT TRAVEL GUIDE

Craig Emms and Linda Barnett

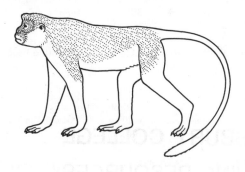

Bradt Travel Guides Ltd, UK
The Globe Pequot Press Inc, USA

First published in 2001 by Bradt Travel Guides Ltd,
19 High Street, Chalfont St Peter, Bucks SL9 9QE, England
Published in the USA by The Globe Pequot Press Inc,
246 Goose Lane, PO Box 480, Guilford, Connecticut 06437-0480

Text copyright © 2001 Craig Emms and Linda Barnett
Maps copyright © 2001 Bradt Travel Guides Ltd
Photographs © 2001 Individual photographers

The author and publisher have made every effort to ensure the accuracy of the information
in this book at the time of going to press. However, they cannot accept any
responsibility for any loss, injury or inconvenience resulting from
the use of information contained in this guide.

British Library Cataloguing in Publication Data
A catalogue record for this book is available from the British Library
ISBN 1 84162 040 8

Library of Congress Cataloging-in-Publication Data applied for

Photographs
Front cover Woman in wedding outfit (Ariadne Van Zandbergen)
Text (Linda Barnett (LB), Ariadne Van Zandbergen (AVZ)

Illustrations Annabel Milne
Maps Alan Whitaker

Typeset from the authors' disc by Linden Sheffield
Printed and bound in Italy by Legoprint SpA, Trento

Authors

Craig Emms and **Linda Barnett** are professional ecologists who have travelled extensively around the world in pursuit of and working with wildlife. They are currently resident in The Gambia and are based at the Research and Development Unit of the Department of Parks and Wildlife Management.

In 1999 and 2000 they co-authored a weekly column called 'Focus on Wildlife' in the Gambian national newspaper, the *Daily Observer*. This established an avid readership amongst Gambians and did much to highlight the cause of wildlife conservation within the country. Their official duties include researching various aspects of the wildlife, writing grant proposals, training the staff of the protected areas in research techniques and removing troublesome cobras, mambas and pythons from people's compounds, to name just a few.

While researching and writing this guidebook they shared their home at Abuko Nature Reserve with orphaned or injured baboons, antelopes, genets, squirrels, giant pouched rats, pelicans, birds of prey, owls, parrots and other birds, before rehabilitating them back into the wild.

In their spare time they like to have a few beers with friends and swim in the sea.

Contents

Acknowledgements

We are very grateful for the help and support of the entire team at Bradt Travel Guides, especially Tricia Hayne, without whom, of course, this guidebook would never have been published.

We would also like to thank all of our friends and colleagues in The Gambia, especially our good friends Mike and Sheelagh Fowler for their useful comments and good sense of humour. In addition we are extremely grateful to Dr Almamy Camara, the Director of the Department of Parks and Wildlife Management (DPWM), for looking over and commenting on the drafts of the protected areas. Thanks also to the individual managers of the protected areas – Alpha Jallow, Alhagie Manjang, Amadou Camera and Fabala Kinteh – for their useful comments. Many thanks also to Dr Janice Carter of the Chimpanzee Rehabilitation Project, for setting us straight on a few points.

Jackie Gorman, formerly a technical assistant with the Irish-based Agency for Personal Service Overseas (APSO) and the Ecotourism Unit of the DPWM provided us with lots of useful details and contacts – thanks Jackie, we hope that Ireland is not too cold and wet! We are very grateful for the help received from Jato Silla, the Director of the Forestry Department; Hali Abdoulie Gai and Bakary M K Houma of the Gambian Public Transport Corporation (GPTC); Yahya Sanyang of APSO; and Patrick Southern, chairman of the Ground Operators' Association.

Many thanks, too, to Lyn Mair, for information regarding Classical Cruises. We met Lyn by chance one sunny afternoon in Abuko Nature Reserve, and it turns out that she is the author of the Bradt guide to the Seychelles – it's a small world!

We are grateful to Badara Bajo and Kebba Bajo of the Gunjur Environmental Protection and Development Group, who showed us around their many projects, of which they are rightly proud, and to the many birding guides who shared their intimate knowledge of the best sites to see birds in The Gambia.

We also acknowledge our debt of gratitude to all the owners, management and staff of the various hotels, camp, restaurants etc, throughout the country, and to the numerous fellow travellers who knowingly or unknowingly helped us with our research.

Last, but by no means least, we would like to give a big 'thank you' to our good friend Findy Kujabi, who helped us to unravel the intricacies of bush taxi travel, as only a true Gambian can – *abaraca* Findy.

Introduction

The Federal Republic of The Gambia has been called 'the gateway to Africa', and in many ways this is true. First and foremost, it is a tiny country, one of the smallest in Africa, and every part of it is easily accessible even during the shortest of visits. Secondly, the official language is English, which makes it very easy for anglophone visitors to get along. Thirdly, it possesses an amazing diversity of landscapes and habitats for such a small place. These range from shady, lush forests festooned with creepers to mile upon mile of golden, sandy beaches; from vast areas of brooding mangroves to the broad expanse of the river, which defines the country physically. Alongside this, there is also a rich variety of wildlife, some of which is easy to see and can hardly be missed, such as the troops of monkeys which crash through the treetops or swagger across the roads, or the huge monitor lizards that stalk the grounds of hotels. Other wildlife needs to be searched for, like the secretive hippos that live up-river or the beautiful genets (see *Small carnivores* in *Chapter 4*) that hunt by night. Perhaps the best-known feature of this country for many visitors, are the hundreds of species of birds. Many are familiar to Europeans, such as the flocks of waders and warblers that visit from Europe during the winter, but most of them are truly African and, being African, are bright, colourful and loud.

West Africa is a beautiful part of the world, but unfortunately it has also recently become one of the most violent, in human terms. We've all heard horrific stories of civil wars and strife, killings and mutilations. Countries such as Liberia and Sierra Leone must surely be the last places that visitors will want to go to these days. Who needs all of that when all you want is to get away and have a peaceful and relaxing break? The Gambia is different. Sure, it does have its troubles, as every country does. There is crime and sometimes there is civil unrest. However, on a relative scale there is nothing like we get back home in Europe or North America and The Gambia has never suffered from the same scale of violence as other West African countries. The Gambia is a hodgepodge of different peoples and different religions, yet they all seem to get along with each other and to tolerate one another. The people are also extremely friendly and pleased to see visitors to their country, and this is particularly so the further that one travels from the heavily populated urban and mass-tourist areas near the coast. It is here, as you travel inland, that you suddenly realise that you are in Africa – the real Africa, away from the hotels and air conditioning, the fancy restaurants and the hassle. Cattle, goats and chickens wander across the pot-holed roads, small wheeled carts plod along lethargically, drawn by donkeys or bullocks, while their drivers sit relaxed and their passengers sprawl, often asleep. Small villages of rounded mud-walled huts with grass roofs sit astride the roads. Men sit beneath huge shady trees, brewing pots of green tea, while brightly-dressed women walk elegantly by carrying huge bundles or pots on their heads with seemingly no effort at all, and crowds of smiling children wave and shout. Everywhere people are working in the fields, not with tractors and machinery, but with their hands and simple hand-tools. This is the real

Africa. A land and people that doesn't appear to have changed in centuries.

Yet The Gambia is more than this. There is a modern airport and new roads are being built. There are new hospitals, clinics and schools. Despite its small size and poor economy, The Gambia is forging ahead to improve the lot of its people. All of this in a country of beauty, peace and stability. As the Gambians are fond of saying: 'No problem'.

On a more personal note, we have chosen The Gambia to be our home, at least for the foreseeable future. Our work (and our hobby) involves researching the wildlife of this small, unique country. As such, we make no apology about writing so much about its natural heritage. Recent government surveys have revealed that over a third of all visitors to The Gambia come here because of its birdlife, and another third because of its landscape and wildlife. So we have felt free to indulge ourselves a little and write about what we enjoy doing the most – spotting wild birds and animals. If you are not an independent traveller and prefer the comfort and reassurance of package holidays in good hotels, then we hope that we have provided lots of useful information for you, too. Maybe we might even inspire you to get out and about and explore this fascinating country a little. We certainly hope so.

LIST OF MAPS

Part One

General Information

Striped ground squirrel

THE GAMBIA AT A GLANCE
Location West Africa
Size 11,300km² (7,022 square miles)
Time GMT. No daylight saving time
Electricity 220-240 volts
International telephone code + 220
Status Federal Republic
GDP US$324 million, US$352 per capita in 1991/91
Currency Gambian dalasi (100 bututs per dalasi)
Population 1,038,175 in 1993. Annual growth rate of 4.2%
Economy Major earners are agriculture, trade and tourism
Capital Banjul (1993 population 42,326)
Language Official language is English. Local languages include Mandinka, Wolof, Jola, Fula and others.
Religion 90% Muslim, 10% Christian, and some traditional religions such as Animism
Flag Three horizontal stripes - red, blue and green from top to bottom. Each colour separated by a narrow white stripe.
National anthem 'For The Gambia our Homeland'
National motto 'Progress, Peace and Prosperity'

Gambian epauletted fruit bat

Background Information

FACTS AND FIGURES
Location and size
The Federal Republic of The Gambia lies on the western coast of tropical Africa. It is shaped like a long, crooked finger extending inland and is surrounded on its northern, eastern and southern borders by the French-speaking, and much larger, country of Senegal. To the west of The Gambia lies the Atlantic Ocean, while the country itself lies on a latitude that is almost equal distance from the Equator and the Tropic of Cancer. From north to south, The Gambia extends for a maximum of 48km, though the coastline with its bays and promontories, is 80km in length. Moving inland from west to east, the country roughly follows the route of the River Gambia inland for 480km. With a total land area of only 11,300km² The Gambia is one of the smallest countries in Africa and is less than half the size of Wales. Or, to put it another way, Washington State is 15 times bigger than The Gambia.

Climate
The Gambia has a wonderfully warm climate that is characterised by a long dry season from mid-October to early June, followed by a short rainy season from mid-June to early October. July and September are the hottest months of the year with average daytime maximum temperatures of around 30°C. During this period there are frequent and magnificent rainstorms that cool everything down for a while, before the humidity shoots up to almost 100%. From December to mid-February the average daytime temperature falls to around 24°C, which is fairly comfortable, especially if you are coming here from the cold and wet of a European or North American winter. After February the days get steadily hotter until the rains come in June. By the coast temperatures are generally slightly lower due to cooling offshore winds, but remember that these figures are only average and some days the temperatures can be a lot higher. We have often encountered days when the temperatures are in the high 30s or even as high as the mid 40s. Average rainfall per year is around 1020mm, but in the west it can be much higher – up to 1700mm – while in the drier east it can be as low as 800mm. Over the past 40 years or so there has been a slight warming in the average temperatures experienced in The Gambia and a decrease in rainfall. The latter has badly affected the livelihoods of farmers who are heavily dependent on rain-fed crops.

The capital and other principal urban centres
The capital of The Gambia is Banjul, which was formerly known in colonial times as Bathurst. This small city is situated on an island located at the southern tip of the River Gambia's mouth, where it empties into the Atlantic. Banjul is by no means the largest urban concentration in The Gambia but is still the administrative centre for the country. Its population stood at just over 42,300 in 1993. The largest

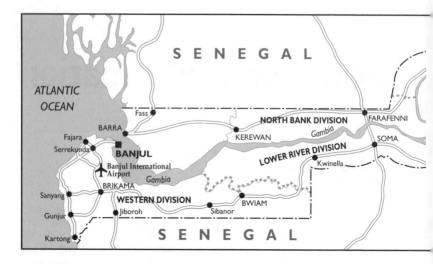

urban centre in The Gambia is without doubt the vast unplanned sprawl of Serrekunda, including Kanifing, which had an estimated population of over 228,214 in 1993. However it has grown a lot since then. Other large towns, in descending order of size, are Brikama, with a population of 234,917; Kerewan, with 156,462; Basse, with 155,059; Georgetown – which has recently been renamed as Janjangbureh – with 88,247; Kuntaur, with 67,774; and Mansa Konko, with 65,146. All of the preceding population estimates are based on the census figures of 1993.

Administrative divisions

The Gambia is divided into five administrative sectors whose names are fairly self-explanatory, and these were established in 1935 at the time when the British ruled in the country. In addition to these divisions the Greater Banjul Area is administered separately. A divisional commissioner – located at divisional headquarters – supervises each division. The Western Division (WD) is located south of the River Gambia and covers the Atlantic coast, Banjul, Serrekunda and Brikama (where the divisional headquarters is located), right through to the town of Kalagi in the east. Its eastern border follows the natural curves of the Bintang Bolon (a *bolon* is a creek or tributary). The North Bank Division (NBD) covers the north bank of the River Gambia from Jinack Island, which comprises the whole of its Atlantic coastline, through Barra, Kerewan (where the divisional headquarters lies), and Farafenni, to just beyond the town of Ngeyen Sanjal. The Lower River Division (LRD) composes of the south bank of the river east of WD and includes the major towns of Mansa Konko (where the divisional headquarters is), and Soma. Its eastern border is found just beyond the town of Pakali Ba. The next two divisions – Central River Division (CRD – formerly known as MacCarthy Island Division) and Upper River Division (URD), both cover parts of the north and south banks of the river within their territories. The Central River Division stretches east to Sami Wharf Town on the north bank and Cha Kunda on the south. It contains the major towns of Kau-ur, Kuntaur and Bansang. Janjangbureh is the divisional headquarters of CRD and is located on MacCarthy Island. The town is still often called by its former name of Georgetown. The Upper River Division is at the far end of the country and extends eastwards to the border with Senegal. Major towns within this division include Alohungari, Basse Santa Su (where the

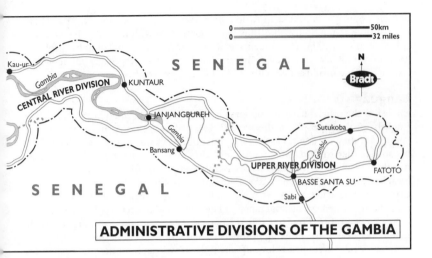

ADMINISTRATIVE DIVISIONS OF THE GAMBIA

divisional headquarters is based), Sabi and Fatoto.

Each of the administrative divisions is further split into smaller districts, of which there are, at present, 35. A chief, known as a *seyfo*, heads each of these districts and the chiefs are elected into their position by the village heads, who are known as *Alkalos*.

Time

Being almost directly south of Britain, The Gambia is on GMT. Thus British visitors experience no change in time when visiting The Gambia except during the summer months when Britain is on daylight saving. The eastern coastline of the USA is five hours behind The Gambia, while most of Europe is one hour ahead.

National flag

The national flag is made up of three horizontal stripes – red, blue and green – running from top to bottom. Each of the colours is separated by a narrow white stripe. A director of a government department gave the following account of the national flag to us but we have no way of telling whether it is the official view (which we have failed to find anywhere) or just his personal view. The blue stripe represents the River Gambia, which regulates all life within the country. The green stripe represents agriculture, which is the most important income generator in the country, and the red stripe indicates the ability of The Gambia to defend itself. The whole flag is held together by the white stripes which represent peace.

Population

In 1983 the population of The Gambia was 687,817, but this had grown by almost 51%, to 1,038,175 in 1993, giving an annual growth rate of 4.2%. Much of the increase is due to migration into the country, especially from other strife-torn countries in West Africa, by people who are looking for somewhere peaceful to settle down. However, the fertility rate is also persistently high, standing at 6% in 1993. Taking into account the annual growth rate the population figure for 2001 must be closer to 1,443,000. This gives an average of about 128 people per km² (compare this to the much higher figure in England, which had an average of around 354 people per km² in 1981). This makes The Gambia one of the most densely populated countries in Africa, after Rwanda, Burundi and Nigeria. There is a continuing rapid growth of the urban population with over 40% based in the urban centres in 1993. The percentage of the urban based population has probably grown even higher since then as more and more people – especially young people – have become disillusioned with village life and have drifted into the towns.

Language

English is the official language of The Gambia. You will have no problem locating English-speaking people in the western areas of the country and being able to communicate with them. However, as you go further upcountry English speakers become harder to find. We have noticed that there are also a few guides, based mostly at the hotels, who can speak passable German or Dutch as well. The main local languages are Mandinka, Wolof, Jola and Fula, though there are several others that are not as widespread. As more and more West Africans from other states migrate into The Gambia, the range of languages and dialects spoken is bound to increase even more. French as a first language is becoming much more common, mainly because of the growing numbers of Senegalese living in the country.

Literacy rates were just below 40% in 1994. However, a continuing programme focused on improved education has sought to positively improve this situation and now many more children have access to education. Gambians also have a natural ability to pick up different languages very easily which could be a result of living in such a multi-lingual society.

Religion

The main religion in The Gambia is Islam and around 90% of the population are Muslim. The remaining 10% are Christian and there's also a small minority of people who still believe in traditional forms of religion such as animism. As with most things Gambian, there is a distinct lack of inter-religious animosity within the country, and everyone is free to worship how and who they want, without prejudice. We have personally found that Christians and Muslims mix very well and there is nothing but a healthy curiosity about each other's methods of worship and beliefs. Some traditional beliefs are still widely held throughout the population. These include the protective power of *jujus*, which are worn by nearly everyone. There are also strong beliefs in the continuing existence of dragons and witches, etc. This may well sound medieval to Westerners but we should remember that we were still burning witches at the stake a few hundred years ago. On the African continent these beliefs are still very potent and are an integral and important part of the way of life and The Gambia is no exception.

A HISTORICAL BACKGROUND
Prehistory

There is very little evidence available to tell us when man first settled in West Africa, though it is thought that the earliest settlers were here around 1.6 million years ago. Before the Stone Age the inhabitants of the region appear to have been nomadic hunter-gatherers who made only temporary settlements before moving on to follow the herds of wild animals that sustained them.

The first definite proof of people living in the area now called The Gambia, comes from Stone Age tools found under the sand-dunes at Fajara and Cape Point. These have been dated to around 2000BC. During the Stone Age the lifestyle of the people changed dramatically and they stopped following wild animal herds to settle down and grow vegetable and cereal crops. Cattle were also domesticated during this period. All of this change led to a sudden increase in the size of the human population.

The next major development in West Africa was the coming of the Iron Age (there appears to be a complete lack of a Bronze Age in the region). The discovery of iron was very significant and heralded the clearance of large areas of forest for agriculture, as iron tools proved to be much more durable than stone tools (and sharper too).

Arabs and the beginnings of Islam

Trade became increasingly important for West Africans as the whole structure of society slowly changed. Some people gave up being farmers and herdsmen and branched out into other occupations such as traders, smiths, artisans, artists and administrators. Alongside these of course, came the first soldiers and rulers. During the 1st century AD another major event began to change the region. This was the introduction of the camel into North Africa from Arabia. The 'ship of the Sahara', as camels became known, allowed traders to cross the great Saharan Desert for the first time in history. This meant that long trade routes were opened up between West Africa and Europe and Asia, via Arabia. Many goods were then transported north across the Sahara, including gold, ivory and slaves, much of it in return for rock salt imported from the Berber-controlled Saharan salt mines. It appears that by AD500 many settlements were well established in The Gambia. Evidence for their existence is plentiful and can be seen in the form of burial sites, stone circles and shell mounds that are scattered widely across the country.

It was in AD620 that one of the most significant events to shape humankind happened in Arabia. This was the birth of the Islamic religion, founded by the prophet Mohammed. This new religion proved very popular amongst Arabs and slowly spread from its birthplace into northwest Africa. At first, Islam was the religion of only the wealthy classes and the rulers, but its spread into the general population of West Africa was aided by a group of religious teachers who were called *marabouts*. The *marabouts* were attached to the chiefs as secretaries to their courts. As a reward for good service many of the *marabouts* received land from the chiefs and were allowed to found their own villages. These villages had Koranic schools, followed Islamic dietary laws and kept fast during the Holy Month of *Ramadan*, and soon they became islands of Islam amongst the traditional beliefs still held by many West Africans.

Another important event now took place, and this was the sudden growth of the slave trade. Up until this point in time most of the slaves taken by the Arab nations came from the Berber people of North Africa. However the Berbers had also converted to the Islamic religion and it was against Islamic laws for one Muslim to take another as a slave. This meant that a new source of slaves had to be found and eventually a new source was located in sub-Saharan Africa.

The Kingdom of Manding (Mali)

From the 5th century AD, West Africa became divided into several kingdoms. The three main kingdoms up until the 15th century were Ghana, Manding (known as Mali by the Europeans) and Kanem Borno. Present day Gambia was situated within the Kingdom of Mali, which was itself a sub-state of the vast Kingdom of Ghana, and was known in Baghdad as 'the land of gold'. The Kingdom of Mali achieved its own independence in the 13th century, under the kingship of Sunjatta Keita, the leader of the Malinké people. By the 14th century the kingdom had become huge and encompassed all of The Gambia and Senegal in the west and stretched east as far as Nigeria and Niger. At this time trade with the Arab nations reached a peak and Mali became very rich and prosperous. Slaves were traded for salt, which was in short supply in the region, as well as horses and weapons. Huge armies were raised to protect the trade routes and to further extend the kingdom through conquests. Apart from Islam, the Arabs also brought with them books. Many Arabs settled in the region and built mosques, introducing their religion to the lower classes of people until Islam slowly established itself as the main religion. As more West Africans became able to read and write they were also empowered to increase their trade and therefore their wealth. Thus it was not long before the powers of Europe began to hear of the wealth of West Africa from Arab traders.

The Kingdom of Mali began to subside in the mid-15th century and many people began to move around the sub-region as it disintegrated. The Serer people moved from south of the River Gambia onto the north bank of the river and created the kingdoms of Siné and Saloum, which remained powerful until the 19th century. A group of Malinké people also migrated south into the valley of the River Gambia, taking Islam with them, where they joined the Jola people, who were already present. These invaders became known as the Mandinka people.

The Kingdom of Kaabu

This kingdom started as a westward extension of the Kingdom of Mali, but as the Kingdom of Mali declined the Kaabu Kingdom gradually took over the reins of power. Stretching from the River Gambia in the north to Guinea in the south and ruled by Mandinkas, it was a great centre for trade. However, as time passed, Fula states and kingdoms surrounded Kaabu, and many Fulas, who were nomadic pastoralists, migrated onto Mandinka lands, which were fertile and well watered. By the mid-19th century the Fula formed the largest single ethnic group in the region. However they were still governed by the Mandinkas, who ruled them with a rod of iron and treated them very harshly. The situation remained the same until after the Soninke–Marabout Wars of the 1880s (see *The Soninke–Marabout Wars* on page 11) when the *marabouts* were defeated.

The arrival of Europeans

At this time many stories of the untold wealth of West Africa began to reach the ears of the royal houses of Europe. The first nation to strike out for West Africa was Portugal; the Portuguese reached Cape Verde (where the city of Dakar was later built) in 1447. Here, explorers heard about the River Gambia and the gold that was reputed to be found in large quantities along its banks. In 1455, Prince Henry of Portugal sent Luiz de Cadamosto and three ships to search for this river. When they eventually found it they managed to sail only four miles up river before being attacked by local tribesmen in canoes and giving up. The next year they returned again to The Gambia and this time managed to sail 20 miles up river. Along the way one of their crewmen died and was buried on an island in the river that still retains his name to this day: James Island (also known as St Andrew's). The Portuguese eventually achieved a foothold in the country amid other European nations who were also becoming interested in the region. Many trading posts were established along the coast which traded brandy, guns and salt for gold, ivory and leather. The incomers also built forts to protect their trading posts from hostile local inhabitants and from marauding pirates.

Unfortunately for them, the Europeans soon found that the tales of untold wealth to be found in West African gold were vastly exaggerated. They cast about for another source of easily accumulated wealth to be gleaned from these lands and it wasn't long before they realised the vast possibilities of profit that could be gained from the trade in slaves.

The slave trade

Slavery had existed in West Africa for many years before the Europeans arrived. Warring tribes had often raided each other's villages and taken prisoners, who were then kept on as slaves. However, unlike the slaves of later years these people were often treated as one of their new master's family and many had a chance to eventually earn their freedom. When the Europeans arrived in West Africa, they were hungry for vast numbers of slaves to work in the cotton fields and plantations of their colonies in the New World. Even so, it was not the Europeans who captured the slaves for this growing trade but the Africans themselves. Many African kings and chiefs soon realised how much wealth they could accumulate from the sale of slaves to the Europeans.

It is interesting to note that in 1620 a British explorer, Captain Richard Jobson, was offered some young women as slaves. He refused, saying that these people were 'of his own shape' and should not be enslaved. He went on to write that the English were a people who did not deal in any such commodities, but unfortunately this noble observation was later proved untrue and England became one of the largest dealers in slaves within West Africa.

As the demand for slaves began to grow, inter-tribal warfare became much more common, and attacks on villages more frequent, in order to feed this demand. Some of the African leaders became very rich by selling their captured enemies into slavery. For the slaves themselves, life was hard and dangerous. Many of them would not survive the voyages taking them to the New World, as the conditions on board the European slave ships were atrocious (it has often been said that a slave-ship could be recognised by its awful smell, even from many miles away). Once they reached their destination, most of the slaves would go on to die within the first three years, and very few of them lived as long as ten years. The slave masters soon realised that it was cheaper to work their slaves to death and replace them with new ones, than to treat them well, let them live longer and bear children. Children would have to be fed for years before they became productive workers and were therefore not economically viable. At the height of the slave trade in the 18th century, over 100,000 slaves were transported from Africa every year. Nobody knows for sure the total number of slaves taken from the region in the four centuries of trade, but it has been estimated to be an astonishing 10–15 million people.

The Portuguese were the first to develop the slave trade, monopolising it on a massive scale until the mid-16th century, when the English joined in, later followed by the French and the Dutch. The River Gambia became a major route into the interior of West Africa and became strategically very important. Over the time of the slave trade there were lots of skirmishes between traders of different nationalities over ownership of the fortified trading stations along the river. Fort James for example, changed hands eight times in violent clashes over a 60-year period before being finally secured by the British. At around the same time the trading station at nearby Albreda became French controlled.

The West African kingdoms eventually declined. There followed a period of great instability throughout the region and the balance of power moved to the coastal states. European influence and their introduction of firearms into the region led to even more instability. Islam flourished in the area and the *marabouts* became very powerful figures among the local people. It was believed that many of the *marabouts* had divine powers and could communicate directly with Allah. The Fula people were strong believers in the Islamic faith and were widespread throughout the region. Through their influence Islam became the dominant religion.

In the early 19th century another major event occurred that would change the world: the industrial revolution soon took hold of all Europe. Increased mechanisation reduced the need for vast numbers of slaves and increased the need for raw materials and markets for goods manufactured from those raw materials. Europe gradually came to see the colonies both as sources of raw materials and as markets for manufactured goods; and so the relationship between some Europeans and the West Africans changed accordingly. Thus slavery was banned by the British in 1807. The Royal Navy became increasingly active in the region, chasing and capturing French slavers and their ships, then releasing the cargoes of slaves and resettling them onto the mainland. The captured slavers were usually hanged. This may make the British seem to be the good guys at this time, but such activity appears to have been carried out primarily for economic reasons: the slave trade was damaging the rest of their trading enterprises. The French eventually followed with their own ban on slavery, but not until 1848. Such policies did not put an end to the slave trade, however, which carried on up-river of Albreda and Fort James. The trade was mainly perpetuated by Gambians who had found it very profitable and viewed the change in policy by the Europeans with strong disapproval. In the 1880s Muslim leaders in The Gambia were still taking slaves and exporting them and it was not until new laws were introduced in the late 1890s that this trade became illegal. Some slavery carried on in The Gambia until at least 1911. However this should be put into some historical perspective: slavery was not abolished in nearby Mauritania until 1980.

The colonial period

In 1816 Britain bought the island of Banjul from a local chief (see *Chapter 6*) and the British began to exert more influence over The Gambia. The British renamed the island Bathurst and built a large fort there to protect their traders and to deny access to the river for slavers. Four years later the River Gambia was declared a British Protectorate, and in 1826 Fort Bullen was built on the mouth of the river at Barra, opposite Bathurst. In 1828 the British also built another fort up-river at Georgetown. In the early 1830s there was a short and limited war between the British and the people from the state of Niumi on the north bank of the river, which resulted in British and French troops retaking Barra Point, which had been captured by the army of Niumi. After a brief and bloody conflict the people of Niumi capitulated to the British.

When the slave trade was officially ended the British and the French found that they needed to establish another source of wealth in West Africa. They decided to introduce groundnuts (peanuts), as there was a huge international market for this crop. In 1829, large areas along the River Gambia and elsewhere in Senegal were planted with this new crop. However, in the 1870s unforeseen European political and economic events led to increased competition between foreign traders and the growers of groundnuts in West Africa. This poor state of affairs led to the Berlin Conference of 1884–85. At this conference the major European powers split the whole continent of Africa into a number of colonies to be ruled by them. It was at this time that The Gambia became a colony of Great Britain and her boundaries were set into their present-day position. It is said that the borders of The Gambia, which to a great extent follow the twists and curves of the River Gambia, were set by a British gunboat that sailed the length of the river. The gunboat was supposed to have fired its gun both north and south, and the border was placed where the shells landed. However this is probably just a fanciful tale as there is no historical evidence to support it.

The Soninke–Marabout Wars

In the late 19th century the Fula people, led by their *marabouts*, attempted to overthrow their traditional Mandinka rulers by the use of force. The Fula wanted to extend the Islamic faith to displace the traditional beliefs and indifferent Islamic beliefs practised by the *Soninke*, a Mandinka group to which the local rulers and their courts belonged. This was called a *jihad*, or 'holy war', and the fierce and bloody fighting, especially near Bathurst, became known as the 'Soninke–Marabout Wars'. Eventually the *marabouts* were overthrown by the colonial powers and the years that followed were peaceful and quiet.

The World Wars

The Gambia became just a small colony, with no inherent wealth in the form of mineral resources, so nobody really knew what to do with it. The main aim of the British rule in The Gambia appeared to be to create peace in the area with the minimum of expense. The administration raised enough revenue to run itself but not to provide any social services. Britain's financial policy up to World War II was that her colonies had to be self-supporting, so this resulted in very little attention being paid to the socio-economic development of The Gambia. During World War II the situation improved slightly as Britain assumed direct responsibility for development in her colonies. However, in spite of a few projects that were set up in The Gambia to try and diversify agricultural production, and a few more resources being directed towards health and education in the country, nothing really changed that much.

During both World Wars many Gambian soldiers fought on the side of the Allies, as did a lot of other West Africans, and many were killed in action. The brave men who died in the service of their country are remembered in the Fajara War Cemetery which is located along Kairaba Avenue in Fajara (see *Chapter 7*).

Independence

It wasn't until the early 1960s that The Gambia again entered the international arena. In 1962 the Gambian parliament – the House of Representatives – was formed. A popular young man by the name of David Jawara, from upcountry, had founded a political party called the People's Progressive Party (PPP) at the start of the decade. This party easily won the elections to form a majority in the House of Representatives. Following this the country gained its independence from British colonial rule in 1965. David Jawara was inaugurated as Prime Minister, though the Queen of England still remained as titular head of state. One of the first things to change was the name of Bathurst, which reverted to its former name of Banjul. Also around this time Gambia was renamed as *The* Gambia, due in no small part to the fact that it was often getting confused with the African state of Zambia.

From 1965 to 1975 The Gambia prospered. World groundnut prices increased three-fold and the tourist industry grew from just 300 visitors during 1966 to over 25,000 ten years later. Initially most of the tourists came from Sweden, but gradually more and more came from the United Kingdom. It was during this period, in 1970, that The Gambia became a fully-fledged independent republic. Prime Minister Jawara became president and also changed his name from David to the local equivalent, Dawda.

However this high couldn't last forever and groundnut prices began to fall sharply in the late 1970s, making most Gambians worse off than they had been before independence. In 1980 a group of disillusioned soldiers staged a coup but President Jawara asked for help from the Senegalese and the coup failed. Later in 1981 there was another coup attempt while Jawara was away in London, and his family were taken as hostages and held prisoner in the Medical Research Council buildings in Fajara. Again the Senegalese army helped, along with special forces soldiers from Britain who secured the release of the president's family, and the coup failed again. At this time the tourist industry was still growing and became a vital source of income for the Gambian government. Politics became more volatile and support for opposition parties grew, especially the 'Movement for Justice in Africa' (MOJA). Eventually the leaders of MOJA were arrested or were forced into hiding.

In 1982 President Jawara announced that The Gambia and Senegal armed forces would be fully integrated and the Senegambian Coalition came into being. This policy lacked popular support amongst the Gambian population, especially amongst the Mandinka who saw the coalition as a take over bid by the Wolof (who are the predominant ethnic group in Senegal), and tensions flared in the country. However, Jawara won the elections in the same year, and the following elections in 1987, as he still had a large popular backing. In the late 1980s things went from bad to worse in The Gambia as groundnut prices continued to fall. At the same time the International Monetary Fund, on whom The Gambia relied heavily, restructured its agricultural subsidies and spending on public services were cut. The remote upcountry areas were hit the hardest and there were cases of malnutrition and even starvation in the poorest areas. There were two more failed coup attempts during this period.

In 1989 tensions became strained between Senegal and The Gambia and the coalition was dissolved. Senegal imposed severe border restrictions between the two countries, but by 1991 things had again cooled down and a new treaty of friendship and cooperation was signed between the two countries. In 1992 the PPP was re-elected for its sixth term in power.

The Gambia today

Following his re-election in 1992, popular support for Jawara began to decline. On July 22 1994 there was an angry protest by soldiers. This was mostly about their salaries, which were being paid several months late, but also about their poor treatment by Nigerian officers during peacekeeping duties in Liberia and Sierra Leone. Surprisingly this protest turned into yet another coup d'état. This time though, the coup did not fail and Jawara was ousted from power, though he managed to escape to a US warship that happened to be in Banjul harbour. He was later granted asylum in Senegal. The leader of the successful coup was a young lieutenant in the Gambian army named Yahya Jammeh. A new military government was formed called the Armed Forces Provisional Ruling Council (AFPRC), consisting of several senior military officers as well as civilian ministers from the previous government.

The coup had immediate and serious repercussions for The Gambia. On the advice of the British Foreign and Commonwealth Office (FCO), many thousands of British tourists cancelled reservations and several of the major tour companies halted all flights to The Gambia. The annual number of visitors dropped by over 65% to less than 40,000. The USA went one stage further and cut all aid to The Gambia. There was also an exodus of non-government organisations and charities from the country. It was not until March 1995 that the FCO relented and said that travel to The Gambia was safe again. But even then it still took a while for the number of visitors to pick up and the poor 1994–95 tourist season hit the industry very hard, forcing many businesses to close down and lay off workers.

In September 1996 national elections were held and a new constitution was voted in. In the Presidential elections Yahya Jammeh won 56% of the vote.

Elections for National Assembly Members were held in January 1997, and the AFPRC, now renamed as the Alliance For Patriotic Reorientation and Construction, won 33 of the 45 seats. President Jammeh appointed four more members from his party including the speaker. In August 1997 the government released several opposition members that had been imprisoned immediately after the coup and granted amnesty to several other detainees.

Since the coup in 1994 the country has been fairly stable, despite a few more attempted coups by army officers, and the country has high expectations for what the future may bring. There have, inevitably, been some complaints about the misappropriation of government funds and the infringements of some individuals' human rights, but these have been overshadowed by the many positive benefits that have occurred in The Gambia. Opposition parties are allowed in the country, as is a free press. You only have to read any one of the national newspapers to see that the opposition and the press can be quite openly critical of the government, as befits a democracy. The country is now nearing the point of becoming almost self-sufficient in rice production (thanks to technical help from the Republic of China) and starving people are a thing of the past. Of course The Gambia is not rich in natural resources that can be exported and still relies heavily on the groundnut crop which is sometimes badly affected by wildly fluctuating world prices. But other resources such as mangoes and smoked fish are now being exported, and overseas aid from many countries is actively sought, especially from other Islamic states such as Kuwait and Libya. A new international airport has been constructed, new roads have been built and old roads that are in a bad state of repair are being resurfaced. A national television station has opened and new health clinics have been built upcountry, with more promised, thus improving primary health care. New hospitals are also being built and all areas now have access to schooling thanks to new schools being opened upcountry. All in all, The Gambia appears to bucking the trend of other West African countries, and doing well. The future is looking positive for The Gambia.

ECONOMY AND INFRASTRUCTURE

As natural resources are scarce in The Gambia, agriculture has become one of the mainstays of the economy. Nearly 75% of the rural population are employed in agriculture and farming contributes between 20–25% of the country's gross domestic product (GDP). Production is for two main markets, the first of which is local. Rice, millet, maize, sorghum, findo (a cereal belonging to the grass family), fruits and vegetables are all grown for home consumption. Rice is an important component of the average Gambian's diet. Despite the fact that rice yields have risen dramatically during the last decade and the country is closer to being self-sufficient in rice production, vast amounts are still imported. Food is not in short supply in The Gambia, as it is in many African countries. People do not starve here, though they may temporarily have to go without in some cases and many Gambian manual workers spend a large proportion of their wages on buying rice. Other foodstuffs tend to come in gluts during their growing periods. For example, during the rainy season there are vast amounts of mangoes for sale everywhere, and at the beginning of the dry season you begin to see huge piles of water melons for sale on most street corners.

Groundnuts, cotton and sesame are the principal cash crops. Groundnuts have been the chief cash crop since the British introduced them in 1829 and have remained so even with recent attempts to diversify agriculture. There has been a significant reduction in growing groundnuts during the last two decades (from 147,320 tonnes in 1974–75 to 76,381 tonnes in 1995–96), but this is due mostly to low, erratic rainfall and declining world market prices.

Livestock farming is also an important contributor to the GDP (between 10–11% in 1983). Everywhere you go in The Gambia you will see herds of *ndama* cattle, sheep and goats, most of which are trypano (sleeping sickness) tolerant. Most of these animals are grazed in the bush during the day, where herdsmen stop them from wandering onto farm crops (most of the time), and they are staked out at night. Draught animals such as bullocks, donkeys and horses are also important to rural communities and carts drawn by these animals form the most common transport in such areas.

The Gambia lies within one of the richest fishing zones in the world and the natural productivity of Gambian waters is further enhanced by the flow of nutrients from the River Gambia, so it comes as no surprise that fishing is an important industry here. It is estimated that between 22,352 and 30,480 tonnes of fish are caught off the coast each year, with the majority of this being taken by fishermen using locally constructed fishing canoes, or *pirogues*, powered by outboard motors. Most of the catch is destined for home consumption as fresh fish, but much is also smoked at special centres along the coast. Fish is one of the main sources of protein in The Gambia. Both frozen and smoked fish are becoming increasingly important in the export market.

Forests are also an important resource in The Gambia, providing fuel, food, medicine and materials for the construction industry. However unlike fish, which appear to be under-exploited at the moment, forests are over-exploited and have declined in both quantity and quality over the last few decades. Many people within the country now understand how important forests are, especially in the protection of soil against desiccation and erosion (a problem that is affecting much of the land in The Gambia), as well as for wildlife and recreation.

There is a fair network of roads within the country, although much of it suffers from a lack of maintenance. For example it is possible to drive from Banjul to Basse along a paved road all of the way, but often the road is pot-holed and some parts become flooded during the rainy season. These problems often add a considerable time to the journey. On the north bank of the River Gambia the situation is worse. A good paved road extends from Barra to Kerewan. This then gives way to a dirt road that can be absolutely atrocious to travel along. We have ended up almost seasick after a journey along this road, being thrown about so much by the uneven surface. The road along the south coast from Bakau to Kartong is also bad at the moment, due to heavy trucks ruining the road as they carry sand from the Kartong sand mines into the north. However, all is not doom and gloom. In some areas, such as along the main highway north and east of Brikama, the road surface is being replaced and in some parts widened. Recently, many of the worst pot-holed sections of the main highway were resurfaced, although the sections in between are now as bad as the old ones were, and desperately need some work. A new road, no doubt built because of complaints from the tourist industry, now leads from south of the airport towards the coast and then north into the area where most of the large hotels are. This means that nowadays tourists do not have to face the culture shock of landing and then being immediately driven to their hotels through the urban sprawl of Serrekunda. They have a much more pleasant drive through farmed countryside (and on a smooth road). This new road crosses the coast road, which will join Kartong to the coastal resorts in the north. Work has recently started on it, and the road extends as far south as Tanji at the time of writing. However, it should be finished soon.

Many villages in rural areas can only be reached along sandy dirt tracks. These are fine during the dry season but some of them become impassable during the heavy downpours of the rainy season, for example the road from Kanuma through Niumi National Park towards Jinack Kajata. It is unlikely that many of these roads will be paved in the near future.

Public transport is adequate at the moment. The Gambian Public Transport Corporation (GPTC) runs regular buses along the main highways, and also operates ferries across the river. In the main though, ordinary people rely upon bush taxis to travel from town to town, and shared taxis to travel within towns. This is fine but taxis are often full and do not always run late in the evenings, so it can be difficult to get around, especially at odd hours. Many people turn up late for work simply because the transport is so irregular.

One transport source that seems to be totally under utilised is the River Gambia itself. Ferries have plied the river in the past and at least one of them has sunk with a terrible loss of life. However the river appears to be such an outstanding resource that we are really surprised it does not get used more. Perhaps the length of time that it takes to travel by ferry from one end of the country to the other, compared to the shorter time it takes by road, is the limiting factor here. This is Africa though, not Europe or the USA, and not everyone is in a hurry to get from one place to another.

Education in The Gambia appears to be the best it has been since independence began, but there are still big problems to overcome. Most areas of the country now have schools although many teachers are unqualified and poorly paid. Many schools also have a lack of teachers, which means that they have to be run on a shift basis, with one set of pupils being taught in the morning and another set in the afternoon. Even so, many classrooms are very crowded, with high pupil to teacher ratios, and have poor resources. The school system is state run but there are also a number of Islamic schools that are run in conjunction with the state system by local mosques. Most children in the country get an education up to primary level, but then the number falls dramatically for a number of reasons. Many pupils do not pass their exams and therefore cannot go on to secondary level. Also many families are so poor that they cannot afford secondary school fees, school uniforms and books. Many children, especially girls, are also kept out of school to work in the fields or gardens. The literacy rate in The Gambia was just over 37% in 1994.

Industry is not that important to the Gambian economy, comprising only about 6% of the GDP in 1994–95 and employing less than 2% of the national labour force. The sector can be split into small, medium and large-scale industries. Small-scale industries include poultry production, metal working and welding, repair workshops, and various crafts such as pottery, carving, jewellery making and tie die and batiks. Most medium and large-scale industries are involved in fish processing and exportation. Mining operations for sand and gravel are operated throughout the country, for the most part supplying the local construction industry. Clay is also mined in some areas for use in pottery.

Tourism is the largest single industry in The Gambia and dates back to 1964 when Scandinavian tour operators first launched charter flights to the country. Since then the number of tourists has steadily risen, although the coup of 1994 temporarily reduced numbers due to Britain's negative travel advice. The vast majority of the tourists are British, followed by the Swedes, Germans, French and Danes. However, the recent addition of a new direct air-route to The Gambia may bring more American tourists to The Gambia in the future. Direct and indirect benefits created by tourism are estimated to be around 12% of the GDP. Nearly 10,000 people are employed by the industry, although it has to be said that many of these jobs are insecure, poorly paid, and only persist during the tourist season. Many tourists appear to visit The Gambia just for the sun, sea and sand of the

Atlantic coast, and are happy to sit on beaches or around hotel swimming pools. However many go on at least one organised trip away from the hotels during their stay. This is fine and people should be allowed to do just what they want to do, especially as they have worked hard to save up for their holiday. However, these days, the government is realising that this form of tourism largely benefits only the hotel owners, tour operators and the businesses around the hotels, rather than the whole community. Therefore it is trying to encourage more community-based 'eco-tourism' ventures away from the coast, where the local communities can feel more of the benefits of tourism. A prime example of this sort of operation is Tumani Tenda (see *Chapter 8*), where local villagers have developed a camp for tourists which employs local people, and where the profits go directly back into projects to improve village life. This arrangement is a two-way process and we feel that the tourists who benefit from it get more out of their holiday by being able both to interact with real Gambians and have a relaxing holiday at the same time. Hopefully there will be many more projects like this one in the future, giving much more choice to people who choose to spend their holidays in The Gambia.

Planning and Preparation

WHEN TO GO

The best time to visit The Gambia really depends on the reason for your visit. The dry season (mid-October to early June) covers the main tourist season (October to April) and corresponds with the winter in the northern hemisphere. If it's sun and relaxation you're after, this is probably the best time for you to visit as you are almost guaranteed cloudless skies and blazing sunshine (at least most of the time). If you want to travel around the country and see different places then again this will be the best time as all of the roads will be passable after the end of the rainy season. At this time of the year another major advantage is that mosquitoes and other annoying biting things, such as tsetse flies, will be lower in number. So your chances of catching malaria, etc will also be lower. There are also financial advantages to travelling to The Gambia in the period from October to April (apart from the Christmas period and New Year) since there are regular package flights during the tourist season and it's possible to pick up some very good deals and get here cheaply.

In contrast, during the rainy season there are far fewer flights into the country and prices can be quite high. At this time of the year the flights (from Europe) often take longer. You may have to change at Brussels, stopover at Dakar on the way here, and again at Dakar or perhaps even Conakry on the way back. Many tourist facilities, such as restaurants, are also closed during the summer months. Obviously there is a lot of rain in this season, though some of it falls at night time and the storms can be pretty spectacular to watch, better than many firework displays. The high rainfall leads to very humid conditions and it can also be very hot, making it physically very uncomfortable. There is also the added risk from malaria as mosquitoes can be very abundant, and tsetse flies can be a painful nuisance in some areas. If you plan to travel around during your visit be aware that many of the smaller roads and dirt tracks can be impassable during the rains, and sometimes even the major roads can be flooded and pretty atrocious to drive on. We often joke that the Banjul to Basse Highway, where it passes through Serrekunda, becomes more like the River Serrekunda during bad storms.

If the main purpose of your visit is to watch wildlife then you face a dilemma, since each of the seasons has its own highlights and short-comings. The dry season brings huge numbers of migrant birds to The Gambia, especially from September to December. At this time of year the wetlands are full of water and teeming with life. Most of the migrants pass through on their way further south and east, though a significant number stay on throughout the winter. The return passage of the migrants to the north is less spectacular as many of the wetlands have dried up by March and April. This means that the migrants don't tend to stop for long. However, by the latter half of the dry season, most of the vegetation will have died back or even have been burnt away, so many animals, especially birds, will be much more visible. They also tend to concentrate in certain areas, especially where there is a supply of freshwater, for example at the crocodile pools in Abuko Nature Reserve. As the dry season progresses there is less wildlife around. Butterflies, dragonflies, chameleons, etc all tend to become much less conspicuous, while many creatures will pass these dry months away in a torpid state hidden inside termite mounds or hollow trees.

The beginning of the rainy season is the time when life starts to show itself again. After the first light rains, much of the ground will be cloaked in a covering of lush green grass and herbs. After a couple of months the grass will be so tall and thick that you can hardly see through it and by the end of the wet season many areas of bush will be almost impassable as the grass grows to two or three metres high. Butterflies, dragonflies and a myriad of other insects fill the air. Lizards take on their breeding colours, agamas (the lizards you are most likely to see, even around the hotels) becoming bright blue with yellow heads and black tips to their tails, while orange-flanked skinks become so bright that they really catch your eye when they scuttle across the roads. Birds too take on their breeding colours, and every species looks brighter and fresher. Some, such as the bishops, change from drab browns into coats of gorgeous reds or yellows. This is the time of year when other migrant birds also appear in The Gambia. Some of them come from within Africa itself, and include species such as the splendidly marked cuckoos (some of which are bright iridescent green). As well as the African birds that migrate here during the summer months, we also see straw-coloured fruit bats, *Eidolon helvum*, that visit in huge numbers to take advantage of the bountiful supply of flowers and fruits, especially mangoes. Of course watching the birds and other wildlife becomes difficult during the rainy season because the vegetation is so thick.

PAPERWORK

Ensure that your **passport** will not expire for a while. Immigration officials prefer an expiry date of at least three months after the end of your visit but make it six months to be on the safe side. **Visas** to enter The Gambia are not required by nationals of Commonwealth countries (including the UK) and some European countries which include Belgium, Denmark, Finland, Germany, Italy, Luxembourg, the Netherlands, Norway, Spain and Sweden. All other nationalities need a visa. Visas are available from Gambian embassies and consulates in other parts of the world. The process normally only takes two or three working days to complete, though of course this may be longer if you are applying by post. You will need to take along two passport photos. In the USA visas cost US$45 and are available from the Gambian Embassy in Washington (see page 19 for address). It is also possible to print off and fill in a visa application form straight from the website at: www.gambia.com.

If you are travelling from a country that does not have a Gambian embassy or consulate, then you should be able to obtain a visa directly upon landing at Banjul International Airport or at major immigration posts along the border. However this is not always guaranteed so our advice is not to rely on it. If you are travelling from a country that has yellow fever, ie: other African countries including Senegal, then you may be asked to show an **international certificate of vaccination or revaccination against yellow fever**. If you do not have such a certificate you may be refused entry.

Visa extensions can be obtained from the Immigration Office in The Gambia (Macoumba Jallow Street, Banjul; tel: 228611).

If you want to drive or hire a vehicle whilst you are in The Gambia, then invest in an **international driver's licence**, which you can get from the offices of most automobile associations in your own country for a small fee.

For your own peace of mind, as well as for sound security reasons, we would advise you to photocopy your passport and other travel documents, and make a list of all important bits of information on a separate sheet of paper. The list should include travellers' cheques numbers and refund information, credit card details and the telephone numbers to cancel them if they are stolen, travel insurance policy details including their 24-hour emergency numbers, bank details, driving licence number, passport number and the details of your next of kin to be contacted in an emergency. You should also include things like the serial numbers of video cameras, other cameras and lenses, telescopes etc. If you do this and then distribute copies of these details around your person and your luggage (not forgetting to leave a copy with someone back home), then you will find life a whole lot easier if you lose anything or have anything stolen.

If you are planning a short trip into **Senegal** whilst on holiday in The Gambia, then you will require a visa unless you are a national of Belgium, Denmark, France, Germany, Italy, Ireland, Luxembourg, the Netherlands, UK or USA. A one month tourist visa costs about US$20 and is available from Senegalese embassies, high commissions and consulates around the world. Multiple entry and three month visas are also available.

EMBASSIES, HIGH COMMISSIONS AND CONSULATES
Gambian embassies, high commissions and consulates
Belgium 126 Ave Franklin-Roosevelt, Brussels 1050; tel: 02 640 10 49.
Canada 102 Bloor Street West, Suite 510, Toronto, Ontario M5S INI; tel: 416 923 2935.
France Rue Saint-Lazare, 75008 Paris; tel: 01 42 94 09 30.
Germany Kurfurstendamm 103, Berlin; tel: 030 892 31 21.
Senegal 11 Rue de Thiong, Dakar; tel: 821 72 30 or 821 44 76.
UK 57 Kensington Court, London W8 5DG; tel: 0171 937 6316.
USA 1155 15th Street NW, Washington DC 20005; tel: 202 785 1399; fax: 202 785 1430.

The Gambia also has embassies located in Vienna in Austria, Montréal in Canada, Abidjan in Côte d'Ivoire, Accra in Ghana, Bissau in Guinea-Bissau, Tokyo in Japan, Lagos in Nigeria, Lisbon in Portugal, Freetown in Sierra Leone, Stockholm in Sweden and Zürich in Switzerland.

Embassies, high commissions and consulates in The Gambia
Many of these addresses swap and change frequently, since some consulates are volunteers, although this list is as full and accurate as we could make it at the time of writing. It may be worth your while to look up the address or telephone number in *The Gambia Business Directory*, which can be found in most supermarkets, or to telephone directory inquiries on 151.

Austria SOS Kinderdorf International, PMB 28, Banjul.
Belgium Bakau New Town.
Brazil c/o Gamsen, Kanifing.
Canada 14 Jally Nyama Street, Fajara.
Denmark Karaiba Avenue, Serrekunda.
France Alliance Français, Karaiba Avenue.
Ghana Radio One FM, Kairaba Avenue, Fajara.
Guinea Liberation Street, Banjul.
Guinea-Bissau Liberation Street, Banjul; tel: 228134.
Israel Taf Construction, Kanifing Industrial Estate.
Ivory Coast (Côte d'Ivoire) Tobacco Road, Banjul.

Japan c/o Shyben A Madi & Sons Ltd, Russel Street, Banjul.
Liberia Garba Jahumpa Road, Bakau New Town.
Libya Independence Drive, Banjul.
Mali c/o VM Company Ltd, Cotton Street, Banjul.
Mauritania Just off Kairaba Avenue, Fajara; tel: 496518.
Netherlands c/o NTC Building, Ecowas Avenue, Banjul.
Nigeria Garba Jahumpa Road, Baukau New Town.
Norway Saitmatty Road, Bakau.
Pakistan Picton Street, Banjul.
Republic of China Kanifing South.
Senegal Kairaba Avenue, Fajara; tel: 373752.
Sierra Leone Daniel Goddard Street, Banjul.
Spain Kotu.
Sweden Saitmatty Road, Bakau.
UK 48 Atlantic Road, Fajara; tel: 495133 or 495134; fax: 496134.
USA Kairaba Avenue, Fajara; tel: 392856, 392858 or 39197; fax: 392475.

GETTING THERE AND AWAY
By air

There are flights to The Gambia throughout the year. During seven months of the dry season (October to April), chartered flights are available from Europe. During the whole of the year there are a number of scheduled flights from Europe and America. Before reading this section please remember that travel details can and do change fairly regularly. Therefore we have not included prices here except to say whether flights are relatively cheaper or more expensive at different times of the year.

If you are intending to travel from Europe to The Gambia during the main tourist season (mid-October to April), then you can find some very cheap deals if you shop around. This is because there are a lot of chartered flights at this time of year (as well as being cheap, chartered flights are usually direct flights, which equates to a shorter time in the air). On the downside planes can be cramped and with little legroom. The deals can be even better if you are flexible about which dates you wish to travel. It is worth approaching any travel agent (rather than an airline, which can be more expensive) and asking about either flight-only deals or deals offering accommodation as well. Even if you are intending to travel around the country during your stay, flights with accommodation thrown in are normally only a little more expensive. Such an arrangement can provide you with somewhere to stay on the first and last nights of your holiday.

There are a number of scheduled flights throughout the year but they are more expensive than chartered flights unless you are intending to stop for longer than the normal one- or two-week holiday, in which case they can work out cheaper. However, some of these flights, at least from Europe, are not direct and may stopover at Dakar, leading to a longer period aboard the aircraft. The airlines operating flights to The Gambia include Air 2000, Monarch, Sabina, International Airlines Ltd, Air Namibia, Belview Airlines, Condor, Air Ghana, Air Afrique, GIT and Airfrot. Air Ghana has direct flights from New York to Banjul.

Banjul International Airport is increasingly used by a number of airlines and is thus becoming a gateway into other West African countries within easy reach of both Europe and North America: Gambia Airways flies directly to Praia in the **Cape Verde Islands** weekly; Air Guinea and Guinea Air Service each have two weekly flights into **Guinea Conakry**, while Gambian Airways has three flights per week to the same destination; Ghana Airways flies direct from Banjul to Abidjan in **Côte d'Ivoire**, twice a week; there is a daily shuttle service between Banjul and Dakar in

Senegal with either Gambia Airways or Air Senegal; Air Bissau operates two weekly flights to **Guinea Bissau**; Gambia Airways flies directly to Bamako in **Mali** once a week; both Gambia Airways and Ghana Airways fly to Freetown in **Sierra Leone**, with four flights operated per week and Ghana Airways has two flights to Accra in **Ghana** each week.

Specialist tour operators
Birdwatching
The following run organised birdwatching holidays for small groups to The Gambia:

Naturetrek (Cheriton Mill, Cheriton Alresford, Hampshire SO24 0NG, UK; tel: 01962 733051; fax: 01962 736426; email: info@naturetrek.co.uk; web: www.naturetrek.co.uk)
The Travelling Naturalist (PO Box 3141, Dorchester, Dorset DT1 2XD, UK; tel: 01305 267994; fax: 01305 265506; email: jamie@naturalist.co.uk; web: www.naturalist.co.uk)

Other
Bicycle Africa (4887 Columbia DRS, Seattle, WA 98108-1910, USA; email: ibike@ibike.org) run a variety of bicycle tours in Africa which includes 'West Africa – people to people' which has a two-week programme in The Gambia.
Explore Worldwide (1 Frederick Street, Aldershot, Hants GU11 1LQ, UK; tel: 01252 760100; web: www.explore.co.uk) currently offer a two-week programme in The Gambia for small groups (no more than 16 people). The tour consists of a river cruise upcountry, some nature treks and cultural performances.
Gambia Experience (Kingfisher House, Rownhams Lane, North Baddesley, Hants SO52 9LP; tel: 02380 730888; fax: 02380 731122; email: holidays@gambia.co.uk; web: www.gambia.co.uk) specialises in The Gambia with a wide choice of flights and accommodation, including package trips.
Ornitholidays (20 Straight Mile, Romsey, Hants SO51 9BB; tel: 01794 519445; fax: 01794 523544; email: ornitholidays@compuserve.com; web: www.ornitholidays.co.uk
Spector Travel (2 Park Plazza, Boston, Massachusetts, 02116, USA; email: africa@spectortravel.com) specialises in Africa and offers at least four 'black history' trips every year to The Gambia.
Tribes (12 The Business Centre, Earl Soham, Woodbridge, Suffolk IP13 7SA, UK; tel: 01728 685971; fax: 01728 685973; email: web@tribes.co.uk; web: www.tribes.co.uk) are a worldwide eco and cultural holidays company with a programme in The Gambia focused on Tumani Tenda Camp in the Western Division.
West African Tours Ltd PMB 222, Serrkeunda, The Gambia; tel: +220 495258/495532; Fax: +220 496118; email: watours@gamtel.gm; web: www.westafricantours.com.

Cruises
Classical Cruises (132 East 70th Street, New York, NY 10021; tel: (212) 794 3200 or (800) 252 7745; web: www.classicalcruises.com) market a cruise called 'The road to Timbuktu and the rivers of West Africa'. The cruise is aboard the *Harmony* and takes 35 passengers. The trip starts off in Mali and then on to Dakar by air where the passengers join the *Harmony*. From here the ship sails south to the Casamance, visiting Cap Skirring, Elinkire and M'Lomp. It then sails north to The Gambia and upriver to Albreda and Juffureh, then on to Tendaba, where the passengers visit Kiang West National Park for a day. Then it's back to Banjul at the mouth of the River Gambia where the birdwatchers amongst the passengers can visit Bund Road and Abuko Nature Reserve, while non-birders can visit the markets and National Museum. The *Harmony* then sails north again into the Saloum Delta, before returning to Dakar, where the passengers get a chance to visit Gorée Island and have a tour of the city.

Overland from Europe

To travel overland from Europe is fairly straightforward, although you will have to cross the Sahara, so you will need to have a reliable four-wheel-drive vehicle. You start in Morocco and head south through Mauritania and Senegal. Remember that some African countries are not always peaceful or even friendly to foreigners so always check with your home country's foreign office before attempting the journey. Overland travel can be done two ways. One is by the seat of your pants, where you have an old unreliable vehicle, little money, no technical expertise or experience, but a lot of faith. This can be a fun way to travel or it can be an unmitigated disaster. We would not recommend this method to anyone. The second way is to have a reliable vehicle, carry spares and learn how to fix it when it breaks down. If you don't have experience of overland travel then at least read up on it or try to meet someone who has and make sure you have enough money to cover most eventualities. Remember the old adage: prior preparation and planning prevents poor performance (see also *Appendix 2: Further Information*).

MAPS

The only reliable place to buy maps in The Gambia is Timbooktoo along Kairaba Avenue in Fajara, although sometimes you can also pick them up at the various tourist shops dotted around the coastal resorts. If you want a good map it is probably sensible to visit your local bookshop in your home country before leaving for your holiday.

The most useful maps that we have found are *The Gambia; 1:300,000 scale*, published by the Government of the UK (Directorate of Overseas Surveys) for The Gambia Government in 1980; *An International Travel Map – Gambia; 1: 350,000 scale*, published by International Travel Maps, 345 West Broadway, Vancouver, B.C. Canada, V5Y 1P8; and *Gambia; 1:400,000 scale*, published by the Cartographic Department, Macmillan Education Ltd, Houndmills, Basingstoke, Hampshire, RG21 2XS, UK (this also has some interesting text in both English and German). However, all of the maps to The Gambia have certain drawbacks, most notably that most are out of date and do not include many new villages, sites etc. You may also find problems with some place names, due to the phonetic spelling in local languages, eg: Jinack Island may also be spelt as Jinnack or Ginack. To date, we have not found the ideal up-to-date map for use in The Gambia and many of the smaller tourist-types maps contain only basic information.

WHAT TO TAKE

There is virtually nothing that you will need that you cannot buy from somewhere in The Gambia, either in the markets, general stores or supermarkets. When people come to visit us here they always ask if we would like them to bring anything and we always have trouble trying to think of things that we need but can't buy here. There are a few things that we have not managed to find, like decaffeinated teabags and re-chargeable batteries, but there's always someone who knows where you can get hold of even these things in The Gambia. Of course, they won't necessarily be cheap. There is a curious price-structuring here that means that some things (such as fresh mushrooms) are enormously expensive when compared to Europe while other things are very much cheaper (petrol and diesel for example).

Basically, what you bring with you will depend on what you want to do in The Gambia. If you are planning to camp, you will need to bring a tent and camping equipment. If you are planning to travel but to stay in available accommodation then you will need to keep your luggage fairly light but make sure that you have indispensables like mosquito bednets. If you are planning to stay in a hotel and grab some sunshine on the beach or by the swimming pool, then all you really need is suncream and your swimming kit: the choice is yours. If you come here intending to camp in the bush, for example, you will probably have camped before and so will have a fair idea of what you need. However, the following section does contain some hints that may be useful.

Carrying luggage

If you are going to stay in a hotel, it doesn't matter what you bring as your luggage, unless you are intending to bring fragile items. If this is the case you'll find you need one of the rigid-type suitcases and the items need to be carefully packed, perhaps in towels or clothes.

If you are travelling around the country or camping then you will, of course, need a backpack of some description. There are thousands of makes and styles of packs so we are sure that you will find one to suit you. Be aware that if you are using public transport, you will have to do a fair bit of walking to and from drop off/pick up places, camps and hotels etc, so make sure that you have a comfortable pack before you come to The Gambia.

If you want to travel around in the daytime from a base location (such as a camp) then a day-sack (with water bottle) is almost essential as you will always need to have water on your person in The Gambia. It will also be useful for carrying lunch, bird books, binoculars etc.

Clothes

Always wear a hat in the sun, preferably one with a wide brim. You will feel much more comfortable and will also reduce the likelihood of sunstroke and sunburn.

There are a few important points to remember when deciding on clothes to bring to The Gambia. First, it gets very hot during the day and you will sweat a lot, especially during the rainy season. Second, it gets a little cooler during the late evening and night. Thirdly, if you are walking in the bush you are likely to get stabbed and scratched by numerous thorns and there is always the risk of a snake-bite around the feet and lower parts of the leg. Lastly, there are lots of little insects that enjoy biting people, especially in the evening and during the night (including the numerous kinds of ants that you will find just about anywhere). Bearing all this in mind, decide what activities you will be doing on your holiday and take the appropriate clothing.

Natural fabrics such as cotton are the best, and light-coloured clothing reflects more of the heat and keeps you cooler. For walking around town in the tourist areas, a pair of shorts (or a knee-length skirt), T-shirt and sandals are fine. If you are walking around towns and villages upcountry, please remember that this is a predominantly Muslim country, so wear long trousers or a longer skirt so as not to cause offence (see *Etiquette* in *Chapter 3*). Women should preferably not wear tight trousers, but a loose skirt or wrap. In the bush you will need to wear fairly thick long trousers and a good pair of walking boots. There are numerous types of boots sold in high-street shops. Many are so light that they feel like shoes and are very comfortable. It is important to wear ankle-length boots, socks and trousers because there are snakes out there and they do bite people. Most snake-bites occur on the feet and lower legs and many of them will not penetrate clothing, so be sensible, just in case. Do not believe the books that tell you snakes are rare and snakebites almost unheard of. It's simply not true, though you are still unlikely to see a snake during your visit, since they usually disappear as soon as they hear heavy-footed humans clomping through the bush. Cobras in particular are fairly common in most habitats within The Gambia and taking simple precautions means that you can wander about without having to watch where you place every footstep. Tucking the bottoms of your trousers into your socks will also help to prevent attack by that other great nemesis of the tropics – the driver, or army ant. Step into a column of these nasty little devils and within seconds they will swarm up your legs. If you haven't tucked your trousers in then the swarm will be up the inside of your trousers and will be very painful. Many times we have had to step smartly into cover and do a quick strip to get the ants off!

In the evenings wear clothes that cover your legs, ankles and arms to reduce your chance of getting bitten by mosquitoes. You may also find it a bit cool at this time of the day so bring a light sweater or sweatshirt with you.

We frequently see tourists wandering about in nothing but the briefest of shorts or bikini-tops. Time and again they are so sunburnt that they look like lobsters. In the tourist areas they are often ignored by Gambians who are used to such stupidity from visitors. Away from the tourist areas this behaviour can be highly offensive to Gambians and reinforces the idea held by some, that most tourists are helping to lower the morals of the country. If you are determined to go out looking like this then it is perhaps worth knowing that to a Gambian, only seriously mentally ill people wander about undressed on the streets.

If you find that you have forgotten some vital piece of clothing once you have arrived in The Gambia, don't worry; you will be able to buy replacements for most things, especially in the tourist and urban areas of Western Division. You may want to bring the absolute minimum amount of clothing with you anyway, as there are some great bargains to be had (especially in locally produced shirts, dresses and wraps), in the markets and craft markets.

Camping equipment

There is no compelling reason why you should want to camp in The Gambia, as accommodation is readily available and fairly cheap. Even if you are caught away from a tourist area or camp it is always possible to ask local villagers to put you up in their 'compounds' (a 'compound' is a collection of houses around a central yard – normally shared by one extended family), for a night or two, usually at a very cheap rate. On the other hand, some people just love to camp. If you include yourself in this group of people it's likely that you have done this type of thing before and know what you are doing. If you haven't then here are just a few important hints. Keep your equipment light as there is nothing as exhausting as carrying lots of heavy stuff around on your back all day, especially when its very hot. Also keep it simple; there is really no need for all of the fancy gadgets you can buy in camping shops. Most just add unneeded bulk and weight to your kit. Your main requirements are a tent (with an integral mosquito net), a roll-mat, a light summer-type sleeping bag, a stove, and cooking and eating utensils. Anything else is probably superfluous, though there will no doubt be plenty of people out there who will throw their hands up in terror at the prospect of leaving behind their battery-powered GPS or satellite telephone. Food for camping can be bought with you to The Gambia if you prefer the less weighty dehydrated form. Otherwise, tins of food can be purchased at the supermarkets, or you may wish to ask villagers to cook local food for you if you are camping close by.

Other useful items

The content of this list will depend on what you intend to do on your holiday. A must for most people, even if you are a sun-worshipper, is a good solid, leak-proof **water bottle** to carry with you even when just lying on the beach. Also **suncream** and **insect repellent** are very useful items to carry around. These are readily available from most high-street camping shops. If you're a birdwatcher or otherwise interested in wildlife and natural history, then don't forget the **binoculars**, whatever you do. Serious birders will of course bring their **telescope** and **tripod**.

A small **medical kit** might be useful (see *Personal first aid kit* in *Chapter 5*). If you are really worried about AIDS etc, then carry a medical pack that contains sterile equipment such as syringes and needles, so that local medics can use your equipment on you if they should need to. **Sterile medical kits** are again readily available in the highstreet. If you are on prescription medication don't forget to bring an adequate supply with you since not all medicines are available once you are in The Gambia. A nice gesture would be to donate your medical kit either to a local health clinic or to a hospital at the end of your holiday. Medicines and equipment are always in short supply and much needed.

One vital piece of equipment we have found you will need, if you intend to wander about in the bush, is a small basic **compass**. It is amazingly easy to lose your way and sense of direction in the bush, even if you step from the path for a distance of only a few metres. Keep your eye on the direction you are travelling in as you go along or you can too easily get lost and be faced with a long walk to get where you want to go.

Other sundry items include **tampons** or **sanitary pads**, as they are not always easy to get hold of up-country. **Loo paper** cannot always be found when you most need it so carry a roll in your bag. A good **torch** or **flashlight** is a must if you are camping or a nature-lover and intend to hit the bush after dark to see those owls, nightjars and bushbabies (you'll need a torch to keep an eye open for snakes anyway). Another good item to carry is an **alarm clock** so that you can get yourself up in time to catch your transport.

Photographic equipment

Unless you are a dedicated wildlife photographer, a large number of the photographs you are likely to take in The Gambia will be of people, national monuments, buildings and landscapes. On the whole a point and shoot or compact autofocus camera will be fine for this job. A 28–70mm zoom lens will allow you greater flexibility in the type of picture you are able to take.

The best type of film to bring with you is low speed 50, 64 or 100 ISO. These types of film are ideal for most of the light conditions you will encounter and produce a much less grainy picture than 400 ISO if you want to enlarge any of your photographs later on.

Print film at speeds of 100, 200 and 400 ISO is readily available in The Gambia, but many shops store film at ambient temperature making results variable. Slide film is only available at the **Photo Express** shop on Kairaba Avenue. There are many shops here that process films. They are relatively expensive and the results can again be variable. If you are only staying for a few weeks, it is best to take your films home for processing.

One of the most important aspects of photography in The Gambia is caring for your camera. During the dry season the air is full of dust and a thin layer of it settles everywhere. Make sure that you bring a cover for your camera, and keep it in it when it's not in use. Replace or close your lens cap when you are not using your camera. Change films in your hotel room rather than on the beach or in the bush, even if you miss some great shots. Keep used films in the containers they come in to prevent dust contamination. Your lens is the most important part of your camera. Loose dust and debris is best puffed away with a blower brush, which can be purchased at a specialist photography shop before leaving home.

In the rainy season the atmosphere becomes very humid, and it is a good idea to include a small bag of silica gel with your camera to absorb excess moisture.

MONEY
Organising your finances
The first thing you should think about is security. There can be nothing worse than coming on holiday only to have all of your money stolen in the first few days and not being able to replace it. We suggest you carry a mixture of cash and travellers cheques, together with a credit card. Keep the bulk of it either locked away in the hotel safe or hidden away on your person in a discreet money belt. Hide your money belt beneath your clothing and don't keep lots of cash in one of those highly visible belts that go outside of your clothing, as they just act as irresistible targets for pickpockets and other thieves (see *Theft* in *Chapter 3*). You should keep some small notes and coins in your pockets for general use so that you don't have to constantly delve into your money belt, especially in view of potential thieves. Above all, use your common sense and don't flash great wads of cash around in front of people. You can carry cash in two forms, either as local money (dalasis) or as foreign currency (French francs, US dollars, German Marks or pounds sterling), all of which can be exchanged for local currency quite easily.

Travellers' cheques in the above currencies can be exchanged easily too. Keep a record of the cheque numbers, and which ones you have already changed or spent, so that you can get the unused ones refunded or replaced if they are stolen or lost. Take travellers' cheques of fairly small denominations with you (say a mixture of US$20–100) as the smaller ones can be much more useful and you will find times when you need to spend or change only a small amount. Also try and get your travellers' cheques from large, well-known companies as these are recognised much more quickly by cashiers. Carry a credit card as a back up.

You have a choice of places to exchange your cash and travellers' cheques. Most of the hotels will happily carry out this service but will charge the earth or will offer you very bad exchange rates. Banks in Banjul, Serrekunda and the Atlantic resorts will also exchange your money, at better rates, and there are also many foreign exchange bureaux in the tourist areas. Your last resort is to exchange cash with street vendors, who can be found outside Banjul post office and at Westfield Junction. Remember though, to exchange money this way is illegal in The Gambia. You might get a good deal but you are also putting yourself at risk, either of being arrested, conned or targeted by watchful thieves. If you're travelling across the border into Senegal then you will normally be able to exchange cash from street vendors at border posts or in towns.

You can use your MasterCard or Visa to draw cash at all Standard Chartered Banks for a standard charge.

Remember that once away from the coastal areas banks are few and far between, so try and exchange your money or cheques before travelling upcountry.

Costs and budgeting
The Gambia is not an expensive country, but for those of you who think everything here is going to be dirt cheap, forget it, especially if you stay in and around the hotels and the tourist areas, where everything is obviously

more expensive.

Travelling around the country on a shoestring budget, using local transport such as bush taxis, eating street food, staying in the cheapest accommodation, and relying on well water to drink, you are probably looking at a budget of around a maximum of US$15 per person per day. This includes extras such as entrance fees to museums and national parks etc, which are generally not expensive.

If you're after a bit more comfort, like using shared taxis to get around and eating in a restaurant or bar at least once a day, staying in decent accommodation and drinking only tap water, bottled water and soft drinks, then you're looking at a maximum of around US$50 per person per day. However this budget doesn't include extra money for the odd organised trip which can be quite expensive.

If you plan to stay in good quality accommodation, eat solely at restaurants and use tourist taxis or hire a privately operated jeep and driver to travel around, then you should budget for up to US$150 per person per day. If you don't use the tourist taxis and take an organised trip every day then it will cost about the same.

If you've got money to burn then don't worry, you can spend it all here and have all the luxury you want. There is excellent upmarket accommodation at Mandina River Camp at Makasutu Culture Forest, Sindola Camp, the Coconut Residence or Ngala Lodge. You can also eat at their top-notch restaurants, and hire a flash four-wheel-drive with air conditioning and a driver to see a bit of the countryside.

Common warthog

Travelling in The Gambia

TOURIST INFORMATION AND SERVICES

There is very little information available to tourists actually within The Gambia itself. There are no official tourist offices and only a very few old leaflets doing the rounds, such as the one about James Island. However, there is an official Republic of The Gambia web site at: www.gambia.com, where some information can be gleaned, but most of it is quite old. You could try getting in touch with the Gambia National Tourist Office in London (The Gambia High Commission Building, 57 Kensington Court, London W8 5DG; UK tel: 020 7376 0093; fax: 020 7938 3644; email: info@thegambia-touristoff.co.uk).

When it comes to nature reserves and national parks, the Department of Parks and Wildlife Management have produced a small booklet: *A Guide to the Protected Areas of The Gambia, West Africa*. This is usually available from the entrance booth at Abuko Nature Reserve or, if they do not have a copy, you could try going to the department's headquarters which is located up the driveway by the exit to the same reserve. There is also an excellent guide to the history and historical sites: *Historic Sites of The Gambia – an Official Guide to the Monuments and Sites of The Gambia*. This is available from many of the tourist shops and can even be found in many supermarkets, as well as at the National Museum in Banjul, the Slavery Museum at Albreda and the Stone Circle Museum at Wassu.

Most Embassies, Consulates and High Commissions of The Gambia will be pleased to give advice to tourists before you visit the country (see *Chapter 2* for a list).

PUBLIC HOLIDAYS

There are a number of public holidays in The Gambia throughout the year, but none of them should affect your stay as a tourist, except for the obvious fact that banks and offices will be closed. Sometimes there is a reduction in the number of taxis and some tourist destinations may close early or for the whole day.

During the Holy Month of *Ramadan*, you should refrain from smoking, eating or drinking when in the presence of Muslims between dawn and dusk, as they fast during this time. Apart from being impolite, it is also a bit cruel to imbibe in front of someone who may not have eaten or drunk for some hours, never mind having gone without a cigarette all day!

Some of the holidays have dates that vary with the year, and some cannot be officially recognised until the state of the moon has been decided. The holidays that vary are *Koriteh* (which is the end of the Muslim fasting period – *Ramadan*), *Eid El Adha* (or *Tobaski*), Good Friday, Easter and *Tamxarit* (Muslim New Year). In addition there are the following fixed-date holidays:

January 1	New Year's Day
February 18	Independence Day
May 1	Workers' Day

July 22   Army Takeover Day
August 15   Assumption of Mary
December 25   Christmas Day

MONEY

The unit of currency in The Gambia is the dalasi, which is divided into 100 *bututs*. The value of the dalasi has undergone a slow reduction for the past decade or so, but has not devalued as much as some African currencies. The current rate of exchange in early 2001 was around D14.7 per US$1, depending of course on where and how you change your money, and whether you exchange cash or travellers' cheques (see *Money* in *Chapter 2*). It is impossible to say what the exchange rate will be when you read this guide.

The unit of currency in neighbouring Senegal is the CFA, or *Communauté Financière Africaine*, also called the *seefa* by English-speaking travellers. This is a currency that is used in many of the French-speaking countries in West Africa and is supported by the French Government at a fixed rate of 100:1 against the French franc. This may sound good but in reality means that this currency is at the mercy of the French who could (and have in the past) suddenly devalued it. In *Chapter 13* we have calculated the current rate of exchange for the *seefa* (in early 2001) at around CFA 732 per US$1.

Foreign exchange

Many European currencies, and of course US dollars, are recognised in The Gambia. These can all be exchanged for the local currency in Banjul, Serrekunda, Brikama and the Atlantic coast resorts, where there are dozens of bureaux de change. Once you move away from these areas the task becomes more difficult because of the lack of banks in the rural areas, although it is sometimes possible to change money in Farafenni and Basse. If you are caught short upcountry then you may be lucky and find someone who is willing either to exchange currency directly or to except foreign money. Try asking around, especially in local shops, but don't rely on this as you will not always be able to find someone. The answer is to change all the money you think you will need before travelling upcountry.

Small change

Try to keep a fair selection of different sized notes and coins in your pockets. Particularly useful are the 5 dalasi (D5) and 10 dalasi (D10) notes, as no one, anywhere, ever seems to have change for larger notes. The cynics amongst you who have already visited The Gambia and have come across this problem before, may well say that this is very convenient for the vendor, as many Europeans when faced with the lack of a few dalasis change will often say 'keep it and don't worry'. We, of course, wouldn't dare to agree with this. Dalasi coins are also very handy for giving out to the beggars who grace the doorsteps of every supermarket or shop, or who poke their heads into your taxi every time you stop moving. Of course, it's up to you if you want to give anything in this situation (see *Begging* in this chapter).

Prices

The Gambia is not as cheap as many African countries, but you will generally find that you get reasonable value for your money and just about everything can be paid for in the local currency.

Prices in this book are quoted in US dollars as this allows easier planning of finances before your visit, rather than trying to work out the local currency. All US dollars in this guide have been calculated at a rough conversion rate of D14.7 to

US$1 (and CFA 732 to US$1). To avoid too many fractions and the fact that exchange rates can vary quite a lot, even over a short time period, we have rounded everything off to the nearest 50 cents. Remember that all prices stated in this guide are intended as rough quotes and therefore should not be taken as written in stone, as they were assessed during the early months of 2001. They may or may not be subject to real inflation in terms of US dollars during the lifespan of this edition. In addition, some establishments automatically raise their prices from year to year, though many try to keep them at the same level.

Government taxes are included in most advertised prices. Some restaurants will also include the service charge on the bill, so check carefully before tipping.

MEDIA AND COMMUNICATIONS
Newspapers

There are several local newspapers that are sold in Banjul and the other major towns, both by the coast and upcountry, though upcountry they are likely to be out of date. The most popular of these is the *Daily Observer*, which combines a mixture of factual articles, news reports, letters, reviews, and features on music and entertainment. Sometimes the quality of the printing lets this otherwise excellent newspaper down, but on the whole it always makes for an interesting read. After being sold this newspaper really does the rounds (probably because there is such a dearth of *any* reading material in The Gambia) and is passed from person to person until the print is nearly worn off. For over a year we wrote a weekly column for the *Observer*, entitled *Focus on Wildlife*, and we would find people still reading our articles six months after we had written them. Some of the headlines are great, but would probably not pass a censor in Europe. We especially like ones such as 'Man kills talking owl', 'Shepherd shot dead, sheep blamed' or a recent headline which read '49 worms bow to herbalist' which doesn't really bear thinking about. There is also a weekend edition of this newspaper – the *Sunday Observer* – which is very good. The price of the *Observer* is less than US$0.50, which is great value for money, and we would advise you to buy at least one copy to take home with you as a memento of your visit.

Apart from the *Daily Observer*, there are also several other newspapers which are published less regularly and are mostly not of the same quality, though still interesting. These include the *Independent*, the *Forroyah* and the *Point*. In our view the best of these is probably the *Independent*, which is fairly new and has been set up by a former editor of the *Observer*. This newspaper is very political at times and often criticises the policies of the present government in very strong terms. This is probably the reason why its editor and reporters seem to be in constant trouble with the authorities and why the paper seems to be closed down fairly regularly by government bureaucrats. This is definitely worth a read if politics is your thing.

Most of the supermarkets and some of the hotels also sell European newspapers and periodicals, though most of them are slightly out of date. We've not checked, but we imagine that the US Embassy also has fairly up-to-date copies of the major US newspapers. It's worth asking there if you really want to keep up with what's going on back home.

Radio and television

The national television and radio company is GRTS (Gambian Radio and Television Service), and they broadcast throughout the country. GRTS television is a little different from European or American TV and has only the one channel. Each evening the news is broadcast around 20.00 and lasts half an hour, featuring not only international and national news, but also sports. Apart from this, the programming consists of a mixture of locally produced items, religious programmes, and cheap films and documentaries from around the world (many of them in English). You may be surprised at some of the programmes that are extremely popular here, like a South American soap opera and an English comedy, *Keeping up appearances*. Many of the hotels and restaurants receive international satellite TV and show a range of programmes like CNN and BBC News.

There are a number of local commercial radio stations, such as Radio One, West Coast Radio and Radio Syd, but many of them can only be picked up in the coastal area. Radio Gambia, which is operated by GRTS, can generally be picked up in most areas of the country. The BBC World Service is also very popular in The Gambia.

Post

Posting letters and postcards to the UK, Europe, USA and Australia is a very reasonable price (less than US$0.50). Post leaving the country during the dry season (when there are regular flights in and out) gets home very quickly and the service is reliable. During the rainy season it takes a little longer because there are less flights, but is still reliable.

Post coming into the country is another story and it is often delayed (for reasons that we do not fully understand). We have received parcels within days of them being posted in the UK and at other times we have waited months to get them. The newspapers are also full of complaints against postal workers who allegedly steal money and cheques from the mail, especially registered post.

If you intend to receive mail during your stay in The Gambia, then it's best to use the poste restante service at Banjul post office, which is reasonably good; mail should be addressed as in the example below:

Joe Bloggs
Post Restante
Banjul Post Office
Banjul
The Gambia

Make sure, if you are receiving money, that you get it as a cheque, preferably crossed, and for safety's sake get the sender to put it in a normal letter rather than a registered letter. Much safer still is to have your money transferred through a bank (ask at any bank for details of which service is currently the best and safest). Moneygram and Western Union Money Transfer are both commonly used in The Gambia.

Telephone

The telephone system in The Gambia is quite efficient and getting through from overseas can be fairly easy. The international country code for The Gambia is 220. Telephoning overseas from within The Gambia is also relatively easy.

Gamtel (the national telephone company) offices have small plywood cubicles that give a certain amount of privacy but do little to cut down the ambient noise levels. You will probably have to queue before making your call (this is where you find out that many Gambians have never heard of queuing). After making your call you need to speak to the person behind the counter who will be able to tell you how much it has cost. Private telecentres are found all over the country and offer the same service as Gamtel, but usually they are less efficient and more expensive (as they rent their phones from Gamtel, and then add their own profits on top), so our advice is to stick with Gamtel wherever possible. Making internal calls within

The Gambia is very easy and there are no area codes. The operator's number and directory inquiries is 151. As with most places in the world, calling a mobile telephone number is more expensive.

All of the big towns have Gamtel offices and phone booths, and there is also an ongoing programme of providing telephone services to many of the smaller towns and villages, so you are never likely to be more than a few hours away from a phone wherever you are.

Internet
The internet is becoming very popular in The Gambia, as is the case in the rest of the world. Recently a few internet and cyber cafés have opened up in Banjul and the coastal area (see the relevant chapters for more information). No doubt during the lifespan of this edition several more will open up around the country. Even a few of the upmarket hotels provide internet connections in their rooms. It is relatively easy to send and receive emails in The Gambia. The two main servers are Gamtel and Quantumnet.

ELECTRIC DEVICES
Electricity is 220–240V. If you intend to operate delicate electrical equipment then you should make sure you use a stabiliser or voltage regulator, as the voltage does tend to fluctuate quite a lot. Adapters are needed for appliances using 110V. A few three/two pin adapters could be useful. The power system in The Gambia is pretty dire at the best of times and demand often far outreaches the capacity to deliver. It is generally not so bad during the tourist season but you should still expect there to be irregular power cuts during your visit. In the rainy season power cuts (known locally as 'load sharing') are much more regular and some areas, even in the urban centres of the Western Division, may go many hours without electricity each and every day. Many of the large hotels and restaurants get over this problem by having their own generators so that they have a guaranteed 24-hour supply. Remember if you intend to travel upcountry, you will find many of the lodges and restaurants will not have any electricity, or only for a limited period during the day.

GETTING AROUND
Driving
Although this is a former British colony, Gambians drive on the right hand side of the road. If you intend to drive in The Gambia as a visitor be ready for a different experience from driving in Europe or the USA. The new roads are great. They are relatively smooth and straight, and they get you to where you want to go very quickly. The older roads are an entirely different story. Where they have been recently repaired they are mostly as good as the new roads, but if they haven't been repaired for a number of years they can be anything from bad to atrocious, depending on the number and frequency and depth of the pot-holes. Dirt roads can be even worse, though we find it's a toss-up between dirt roads (that buck and twist you about) and pot-holed roads (that jerk you violently) as to which ones are worse. There is a constant fight it seems to replace the old roads as quickly as they wear out but this is not helped by the rainy season, when construction of any kind is practically impossible. Considering the general lack of resources in the country its amazing that so much is actually being done, though a lot of the construction money for major projects has come from foreign donors like Kuwait.

Conditions for driving vary but you should be aware that lots of factors can make conditions bad, including heavy rain and high wind during the rainy season, and thick dust and blinding sun (especially early in the morning or late in the evening) during the dry season. Driving at night, especially in urban areas can be a nightmare, as there are no (or at least very few) streetlights in The Gambia. Like everywhere in the world the driving skills of taxi drivers can be seemingly non-existent but apart from this you will also face the common problem of dogs, donkeys, cattle, sheep and goats wandering across the road. Many Gambian children, and even adults, especially in the rural areas, also appear to have little road sense and will often wander out on to the road in front of you without looking to see what's coming their way (especially in the dark). Other problems include slow-moving donkey-, horse- and bullock-drawn carts, and bush taxis that speed along swerving madly to avoid the pot-holes. Many vehicles look extremely un-roadworthy and quite a few have cracked windscreens, faulty or no headlights and indicators that seem to be wired up the opposite way to what they are supposed to be. We've also noticed that a few vehicles, especially large lorries and trucks, appear to have barely survived some massive collision and have very twisted chassis. We call these twisted vehicles 'crabs', as they seem to almost travel sideways along the roads.

Our advice is to take it slow and easy when driving in The Gambia. This way you at least give yourself those vital extra milliseconds to make a decision before it gets serious. Do not be put off by the constant honking of car horns. They are used to greet people walking by the road and to get your attention when someone is intending to overtake you. Another common habit is to honk to warn off pedestrians that are standing too close to the edge of the road.

Cars can be hired (for which you need a valid national licence) from the **Novotel Kombo Beach Hotel** (tel: 465466 or 465468; fax: 465490; email: kombo@gamtel.gm) in Kotu and from **Julrental** (tel: 496896; fax: 990046) based at Tafbel Maisonettes Hotel at Kololi. At Julrental, half day jeep hire is from US$24, plus insurance and 10% government sales tax. Full day jeep hire ranges from US$30–3.50 per day depending on how long you hire it for, plus US$12 insurance daily and 10% sales tax. A refundable deposit of US$615 is required. Another car hire firm is **A & B Rent a Car** (tel: 460926), also based at Kololi, by the Senegambia Hotel. A & B has a range of cars for hire, with a minimum hiring age of 23, including automatics, Land Rovers, other four wheel drive vehicles and Mercedes vans, from US$22–58 per day, plus insurance (which ranges from US$8.50–13.50 per day) and 10% government sales tax. A refundable deposit of US$683 is also required. In addition they will hire out vehicles for a half day at between US$19–40.50, plus all the above-mentioned extras.

Motorbikes can be hired from **A & B Rent a Car** (tel: 460926) at Kololi. A half-day hire will set you back US$17, while a full day ranges between US$19–24 per day, depending on the length of the hire. These prices are exclusive of insurance (US$7.50 per day) and 10% government sales tax. **Mr Bass**, which is based outside the Kairaba Hotel in Kololi, also hires out motorbikes. These cost US$13.50 for one hour, US$32.50 for a half day and US$39 for a full day. These prices include a full tank of petrol and insurance. **Awa's Rental** (tel: 495005; mobile tel: 994521) in Kotu, rent out motorbikes for US$32.50 for a full day, US$22 for a half day and US$7 for one hour. These prices include a full tank of petrol.

Bicycles

Bicycles are a good way of getting around and have the great advantage that they let you see the towns and countryside at your own pace. Do be careful when out riding though, as Gambian drivers (especially taxi drivers) often seem to ignore bike riders and drive very close to them or cut them up. There's also the problem of the bad state of many of the roads, which are either full of pot-holes or have

ROAD SAFETY

The state of bush, shared and tourist taxis varies enormously. Some are extremely well maintained and often they will be good makes like Mercedes or BMW. At the other end of the spectrum, you have the old wrecks that shake and rattle as they roll along, usually on bald tyres. Our only safety suggestion is that you make a quick judgement call whenever getting on board a taxi. If you think it is an old wreck or that the driver is not up to much (you can usually tell by watching how he swerves around pot-holes and/or other vehicles as he approaches you) then don't get in. After all, it's your life. Most taxi drivers are good, though often their knowledge and use of indicators appears pretty limited, but they do work extremely long hours. If you catch a taxi at dusk the chances are that the same driver has been driving since before dawn, with little or no rest.

their edges worn unevenly away (or both). This often forces bike riders further out into the road and into the flow of traffic, so beware. Bikes can be hired from **Bicycle Safari Tours** (tel: 497935; email: bikesafari@qanet.gm) **Cape Point Hotel** (tel: 495005; fax: 495375), **Badala Park Hotel** (tel: 460400 or 460401; fax: 460402) **Kairaba Hotel** (tel: 462940, 462941 or 462942; fax: 462947; email: kairaba@gamtel.gm) also hire out bicycles as does **Mr Bass**, which is based outside the Kairaba Hotel in Kololi. His rates are US$1.50 for one hour, US$3.50 for half a day and US$5.50 for a full day. There is another small bicycle-hire business in Kololi that you will find on the street where the tourist taxis stand. Here the rental is US$1 for one hour, US$3.50 for half a day and US$5.50 for a full day. **Awa's Rental** (tel: 495005; mobile tel: 994521) at Kotu have mountain bikes for hire at US$7 for a full day, US$3.50 for a half day and US$1.50 for an hour. **Mr Bass Crocodile Pool Bike** at Kotu does a safari to the sacred crocodile pool at Bakau for US$3.50.

Public transport

All of the major routes through The Gambia are by road as there is no rail system in the country. Because the vast majority of the population cannot afford to run their own vehicles, public transport is the main method of getting from one place to another, though many people also rely on getting lifts. Compared to European prices, public transport costs in The Gambia can seem ridiculously low.

Public transport is split clearly into the following categories: public buses, bush taxis and shared taxis. There are only standard schedules for the buses and nothing is guaranteed. At busy times you could be waiting for a long time for a taxi with room in it or you may be lucky and get one straight away. At the weekends and late at night there are far fewer taxis around and catching one might be impossible, so plan ahead and arrange to be picked up if you think this may be a problem. Most towns and villages have one place from which all transport leaves and these are easily found by just asking. If in doubt in the big towns do the sensible thing, grab a taxi and ask him to take you to the place where bush taxis leave for your particular destination. This will cost a little more but will save the hassle.

Buses

The Gambia Public Transport Corporation (GPTC) runs buses between most of the large urban areas on the south bank and a section of the north bank of the River Gambia. It's even possible to take an express bus from one end of the country to the other (Banjul to Basse), sit in air-conditioned comfort and watch a movie. Most of the time, though, the buses are not that comfortable and, unless you arrive early at the main depot, you may not even get a seat. Buses leave for Basse from the station in Cherno Adama Bah Street in Banjul, about seven times daily. There are three types of service: ordinary; express and super express. Ordinary buses leave Banjul at 06.45, 07.30, 09.00, 10.00 and 13.00. These cost less than US$4.50 and take about eight or nine hours to reach Basse, stopping at all of the larger towns along the route. The express service leaves Banjul at around 08.00 and arrives at Basse at around 15.00, and the fare is around US$5. The express only stops at Serrekunda, Brikama, Soma, Kudang, Brikama Ba, Bansang, Sotuma and Basse. The super express leaves at 11.00, costs around US$7 and takes only around six hours to reach Basse, stopping at Serrekunda (on request), Brikama, Soma, Brikama Ba, Bansang and Basse.

On the north bank of the River Gambia there is an ordinary service running between Barra and Kerewan. The roads are too rough for buses to travel any further east than this at the present time.

GPTC also run a twice-daily express service to Dakar from Barra, leaving in the mornings when the ferry arrives from Banjul. This trip takes around five hours, costs about US$7 and only stops at the immigration post on the border, Kaolak and Dakar.

Bush taxis

Bush taxis are the most frequent and common form of transport in The Gambia, and consist of a great variety of minibuses. On the north bank of the River Gambia they also come as Peugeot 504s with a cover over the back for shade. Almost every village and town (at least those that are close to the main highways) has a bush taxi service running to and from it, and of course the larger the town the more frequently the bush taxis will run. Bush taxis generally run to and from a certain place in each town, which is normally, though not always, situated by the market. These are undoubtedly the best locations for catching a bush taxi to take you to a certain location, though you will often have to wait until the minibus is full before starting the journey. One way of getting around this is to purchase the empty seats in the minibus at their normal price if you are in a hurry. This is not normally expensive except for longer journeys. You can also catch a bush taxi by standing by the road and sticking your arm out to catch the attention of passing drivers. However this is not a guaranteed method as the taxi may already be full. The driver will usually flash his lights at you to let you know he has seen you but that he hasn't room for you. Prices are amazingly cheap compared to European fares but you usually travel sitting cramped up in a hot confined space, so you're not paying for comfort. If you do not know the area well just ask the driver or his fare collector to drop you off at the place you want to go.

Shared taxis

Shared taxis are easy to spot as they are all painted bright yellow with green stripes. They are extremely common within large towns, but much less frequent along the routes between towns and villages. These taxis normally ply a set route and pick up passengers along the way for a set fee. As a tourist it is wise to ask the fee before getting in the taxi as some of the more unscrupulous drivers may try to rip you off by charging you more. There is also the problem, if you are a white tourist (known here as a *toubab*), that a taxi will stop for you and expect you to want a 'town trip' rather than a shared ride. A town trip is where you hire the whole taxi and he will take you wherever you want for a larger than normal price, which of course is negotiable. Sometimes this is useful but often you may just want to be dropped off along the way as a normal passenger paying the normal fare. To make sure you

TOURIST TAXI TARIFFS

The table below shows the range of prices that can be charged (for 2001) and should only be used as a rough guide when planning ahead.

Destination	One-way journey (US$)	Return journey (US$)
Abuko		$12–15.50
Airport	$10–11	$15.50–16.50
Bakau	$4–5	$10
Banjul	$2.50–10	$6–17
Basse		$170–205
Bintang		$40.50–47.50
Brikama		$19–20.50
Brufut Beach		$24
Dakar		$170–205
Janjangbureh		$115.50–136
Juffureh	$81.50–102	
Kalagi		$68–81.50
Lamin Lodge		$15.50–20.50
Makasutu		$27–41
Pirang		$24
Sanyang		$37.50–40.50
Serrekunda	$3.50–5	$10
Sukuta	$4–5	
Tanji		$24–27
Tendaba Camp		$75–81.50
Wassu		$183.50–205

don't get caught up in any of this, set the price before he pulls away, preferably before you get into the taxi. If you wait until you're half way to your destination you run the risk of being overcharged. If in doubt about any of this, just take a few minutes to watch the locals and see how they handle getting a taxi, then do the same. If you are having problems and need help then just ask a local person and 99 times out of 100 they will be glad to help you for nothing but your thanks.

Tourist taxis

Tourist taxis are easily spotted because they are painted green, usually with a white diamond on the side. These are specially licensed vehicles (at least they should be) that you can find outside any of the tourist hotels. They will run you to any destination for a fixed price, but they are usually much more expensive than shared taxis. Most hotels have a board outside their entrance gates, which has a table of fixed prices on it for certain trips (see below). Often the prices will be for a two-way trip and will include a period of waiting, but check with your driver first. As with most things in The Gambia, these prices are often negotiable. You will probably find that the driver who first gives you a ride will stick with you throughout your visit and every time you leave the hotel grounds he will be there asking if you want a lift anywhere.

Ferries

Ferries are mainly operated by GPTC and ply the routes between Banjul and Barra, across the *bolon* before Kerewan, between Manso Konko and Farafenni, at Kuntaur,

MacCarthy Island and Basse Santa Su, as well as at a few other smaller sites.

The main ferry from Banjul to Barra and back again is an experience that you should not miss during your visit. You will find it hard to believe just how many vehicles and people can get on to one small ferry and get off the other side in safety. If you are travelling by car, fares can be fairly expensive, but if you are on foot they are very low. Although ferries generally run to a fixed timetable, in some parts of the country, especially upriver, they run only when there is enough traffic to fill them up, so you will have to wait, sometimes for a long time, to cross the river. It is best to plan ahead for these delays if you intend to use a ferry upcountry. If you are travelling on foot then this will not be a problem because there are always small boats and *pirogues* plying the ferry routes that will take you across.

River trips
The River Gambia is under-used regarding tourist trips and at the moment only one ground operator runs regular trips upriver using boats. This is **Gambia River Excursions** (contact through Lamin Lodge; tel: 497603; mobile tel: 996903; web: www.gre.gm). A three-day trip from Lamin to Janjangbureh costs around US$102, a shorter two-day trip to Janjangbureh costs US$68 and a one-day trip to Tendaba Camp costs US$34. These prices are all for full board.

Microlite flights
Madox Microlites (tel: 374259) are based at Banjul International Airport and offer hour or half-hour long flights (with an experienced pilot, of course). They are also thinking of extending this itinerary to include flights upcountry (to Tendaba Camp and possibly even further on to Cap Skirring and Niokolo Koba National Park in Senegal). They also offer full courses on piloting microlites.

ORGANISED EXCURSIONS
Organised excursions can be the best way to see a little of the country if money is not too tight but time is. Lots of ground operators, both small and large, offer excursions of varying lengths, from just a few hours to a few days. Most are aimed at the mass market of tourists staying in the hotels of the Atlantic resorts, and as such they can be a little jaded and biased, not giving you a true picture of life out there beyond the swimming pool and beach. However, if this is your first time to Africa and you're a little worried about going out on your own, or perhaps you just don't want the hassle of sorting out your own transport and food, etc (after all – you are on *holiday*) then going on an organised excursion, where you are in a group and it's all arranged for you, might just be right up your street.

Many of the ground operators listed below also offer longer excursions to places such as Tendaba and Janjangbureh as well as tailor made excursions.

Major ground operators
West African Tours Tel: 495258 or 495532; fax: 496118; telex: 2354 WAT GV
Discovery Tours Tel: 495551
Gamtours Tel: 392259
Gambia Tours Tel: 391041
Tropical Tours Tel: 460536

Other ground operators
North Bank Tours Tel: 494088; mobile tel: 995950; fax: 495950;
email: paradise@qanet.gm

Gambia River Excursions (contact through Lamin Lodge; tel: 497603; mobile tel: 996903; web: www.gre.gm
Lion Tours (mobile tel: 993145
Adventure Safaris Tel: 461261; mobile tel: 996451
Pleasuresports (Gambia) Ltd. Tel/fax: 462125
Janneh Boating and Fishing Ltd. Tel/fax: 497630
Ganscot Tel: 373091
Kairaba Tours Tel: 462101

The excursions

The excursions run by the ground operators are prone to changes from time to time, either in part or completely, so the short list below is only a guide to what is on offer.

Roots excursion This is a popular full-day excursion which includes lunch. It has been estimated that around 80% of all tourists who have visited The Gambia have been on this tour. After being picked up at the hotel you're taken to Banjul Port where you join a large boat which takes you on a pleasant trip up and across the River Gambia. Your first landing is at the old slaving station at Albreda on the north bank. Here you can visit the museum with its thought-provoking display on slavery and then take a cool drink under the *bantaba* (the traditional focal point of any Gambian community, a place to meet and talk, or simply to relax in the shade) while listening to the *kora*. (The *kora* is a large musical instrument with 21 strings, and is often played by the local griot, who is the oral-historian of a community.) After this brief interlude you're whisked away into the village of Juffureh, just a few hundred metres away. Here you get to meet the *alkalo* (chief) of Juffureh, who at the time of writing was one of only two female *alkalos* in all of The Gambia. After this you move on to meet an old lady by the name of Binta Kinteh, who is apparently a living relative of the famous Kunte Kinteh (of *Roots* fame). Then it's a quick whiz around the craft market and a walk back to the boat. We found ourselves wondering how many times the *alkalo* and Binta Kinteh had been through this experience and whether it meant anything to them apart from being a source of revenue. However, don't let our cynicism put you off, as this is a very relaxing tour and it is a good way to meet some very nice people in the villages. An excellent lunch is then served on the boat followed by a quick visit to James Island. It has to be quick as this island with its ruined fort is tiny, and getting smaller all the time through erosion (see *James Island* in *Chapter 9* for more details on the history of the fort). The ruins are quite extensive but don't be fooled by the guide's patter about the one room that is still complete. He will probably tell you it's a punishment room but we've heard on the grapevine that it was only a storeroom. Never mind. After this trip its back to Banjul on board the boat. This is a great way to spend a day, with the added bonus that you stand a very good chance, especially in December and January, of seeing a bottlenose dolphin (up to 20–30 have been seen together) in the river. They know the boats that do the roots tour very well and often come over for a bit of bow-riding and leaping about. The perfect end to a good day. This tour can be booked through the tour operators at your hotel, or alternatively you can contact the boat owners direct (tel and fax: 462125, 962125 or 964650), which will save you money though you'll probably have to find your own way to the port. The cost of the tour is around US$33–41, depending on which ground operator you choose to go with.

Treasure Island (also known variously as **Coconut Island** and other names). This excursion is to Jinack Island on the north bank of the River Gambia. Depending on which ground operator you choose to go with, you will have a

Previous page Senegal parrot (AVZ)

Above Village weaver (AVZ)

Above right Blackcap babbler (AVZ)

Right Red-cheeked cordon-bleu (AVZ)

Above Great white pelican (LB)

Above right Blue-bellied roller (LB)

Right African pygmy kingfisher (LB)

mixture of Land Rover and boat trips to get there, followed by lunch and a chance to relax on the 11km of unspoilt beach (with no bumsters – see page 53). Prices are around US$38.

Four-Wheel-Drive adventure/bush and beach safari A range of excursions will take you deep into the bush along sandy tracks, normally to the south of the coastal resorts. Some of them combine this with a drive back along the beach and visits to places of interest along the way, such as Tanje Village Museum. Prices are around US$38.

Birds and breakfast Just what it says – an early morning start will get you to Lamin Lodge just as dawn is breaking, where you will have a wonderful trip in a paddled *pirogue* among the mangrove creeks. This is followed by a pleasant breakfast at Lamin Lodge (normally a few callithrix monkeys drop by to try and pinch some food), then it's a walk around Lamin rice fields, which are a mecca for birds. You are escorted all the way by experienced birding guides. The price of this excursion is around US$31.50.

Champagne and caviar This is a very good excursion where you get the chance to totally chill out and relax, with absolutely no hassle (except getting on and off the bus at Denton Bridge where vendors will try to sell you anything from batiks to trinkets). The excursion is around Oyster Creek in the mangroves of Tanbi Wetland, aboard a large and comfortable *pirogue*. You can relax, or birdwatch, or sunbathe on the roof of the *pirogue*, the choice is entirely up to you. There is a wonderful lunch on board with, of course, champagne and caviar, and often a chance to cool off with a swim in the creek. The price of this excursion is around US$37.

Camel Safari This excursion is worth taking just because it is so different from anything else on offer in The Gambia. A short drive takes you down the new coast road to Tanji, where you board your camels (a pair of people sit in chairs on either side of the camel – so you don't get too bumpy a ride). There is a 45–50 minute camel ride along the beach to Solifor, followed by lunch at the seaside (BBQ chicken, sausage, potato salad etc). Then you can relax for a while and have a chance to swim before boarding the camels again for the return trip. The price of this excursion is around US$30.

Other excursions on offer include a visit to Abuko Nature Reserve, creek fishing, horse riding, a night cruise, a sunset cruise, a Creole night, a city tour, an orientation tour, a visit to Jerreh on the north bank of the River Gambia and a full day at Makasutu Culture Forest and Brikama.

CAMPING

There is no problem with camping in The Gambia. There are no campsites that cater just for campers though, as they all have accommodation as well. But saying that, none of them will mind you setting up your tent within their grounds and using their facilities, as long as they get something out of the arrangement. Perhaps you can buy your meals there or hire their transport for bush safaris for example. Almost anything can be arranged by negotiation. If you want to camp away from it all, then it should be OK to camp almost anywhere, providing the land is not under cultivation or is a part of someone's back yard. To be on the safe side, and to be polite, it is worth locating the nearest village to your intended campsite and approaching the *alkalo* of the village for his permission. There will very rarely be any problem, but it's best to make sure that the site is not a sacred one or that you may otherwise cause offence to someone by erecting your tent there. A small donation to the village development fund or to the landowner will always be a good idea. The only disadvantage to this is that once your campsite is known you will probably be descended upon by hoards of curious children, so privacy will become a problem. We have found that some villagers will recognise this as a problem right away and will order the kids off, but you may have to gently ask others to do it for you. Then again you may enjoy the company. Even if you are miles away from anywhere in the middle of the bush, it normally doesn't take long for someone to find you and for the word to go out amongst the kids. This is a very small country.

You may want to explore during the day and leave your tent standing; this can be a problem and your valuables, including your tent, may be stolen if unprotected. If you are in a campsite you can leave your tent as long as you ask the watchman or caretaker to keep an eye on things for you. If you are out in the bush then the best way is to ask the *alkalo* if you can hire someone to look after your things during the day, as there will always be somebody who is pleased to get some extra money for easy work like this. Of course you'll probably find that your watchman goes back to his village for lunch or something like that and leaves your tent unattended for at least a while, so make sure that you leave only the bare minimum behind and certainly nothing that is valuable. Generally though, if you are out in the bush and no one knows where you are, it's probably best to take everything with you on your back, rather than leave it.

If you are cooking your own food then please be aware of how dry the land can be during the dry season and be careful not to start a bush fire. It's best if you cook using a stove rather than firewood and make sure you clear all combustible material from the vicinity of your cooking area. Remember that in protected areas, forest parks and community forests, fires are not allowed and you must in any case seek permission to camp in these places from the relevant authorities before attempting to do so (Department of Parks and Wildlife Management; tel: 375888; email: wildlife@gamtel.gm; Department of Forestry; tel: 227307 or 224782; fax: 224765; email: forestry.dept@gamtel.gm). The Department of Forestry is planning to set up campsites in a few of their forest parks and can also direct you towards community forests that have existing camping facilities. Be aware also that there is always a danger that you can get caught in a bush fire that is not of your making, especially in the latter half of the dry season. Use your common sense, and make sure you do not camp in an area that looks like it may be a bush fire waiting to happen and ensure that you have a good escape route if you are caught unawares. This is *very important* as bush fires can and do kill people. In the rainy season make sure you do not camp in a spot where it looks like there may be a seasonal water flow, otherwise you may wake up several hundred metres away from where you originally pitched your tent!

Canned foods are readily available in the many supermarkets in Bakau, Fajara and Serrekunda and bottled water is not normally a problem to get hold of except in the most remote districts, where you may have to rely on water drawn from a well. In the latter case make sure you have an adequate supply of water purification or sterilisation tablets on hand before you come to The Gambia, as they are almost impossible to get hold of here. Bottled soft drinks are available in every village store so there is no problem there. These stores will also normally have rice and sugar and perhaps other food stuffs. Vegetables and fresh or smoked fish can be brought from village markets, and if you ever fancy a bit of fresh chicken then we're sure you'll be able to find someone who will be willing to sell you one of the chickens walking around their compound. Of course you'll probably have to kill and pluck it yourself.

One word of warning when camping out in the bush is to keep all food stored in a safe place, especially at night, preferably in sealed containers off the ground and away from your tent. In most places you will probably be visited by a harmless but inquisitive giant pouched rat, *Cricetomys gambianus*, or any of a dozen species of small rats and mice. Scraps of food, especially chicken, may also attract the attentions of genets or civets if you are in the right place. Remember also that there are hyenas in many parts of the countryside still, and the smell of food will attract them too. As well as all these nosy critters waking you up in the middle of the night, you may also attract some other, less welcome guests such as ants or termites, so be careful.

The best type of tent to bring with you is one that has a sewn-in groundsheet and a separate flysheet. The former because it will stop unwelcome guests such as snakes, scorpions, and especially ants, from entering the tent. The latter because you may find it very hot, even at night, and it will be a lot cooler to sleep just under the tent's inner sheet, rather than rigging the flysheet as well. You will need a flysheet if you are planning on camping during the rainy season. If your tent gets wet during the night (even in the dry season there can be a significant amount of dew around) move it to a sunny spot in the morning and it will dry out completely in half an hour or so.

ACCOMMODATION

The quality of accommodation in The Gambia is totally dependent on where you book your holiday and whether you come as a 'flight-only' visitor. Many chartered holidays do not state a specific hotel and you can end up in any of the Atlantic coast hotels from the Senegambia Hotel to Badala Park Hotel. Some of these hotels have less than the best accommodation and can be noisy, bawdy places, while others are more upmarket with nice rooms and classy entertainment. Getting a good hotel is often a matter of luck, but if you get a chance to choose your hotel, check the *Where to stay* section of the relevant chapter(s) before booking. If you come 'flight only' you have a broad spectrum of choice. If you want self-catering accommodation, there is a wide choice of apartments around the coastal resorts. Or you can choose a small hotel like the Safari Garden, which has a pleasant family atmosphere and is very relaxing, or a hotel like the Senegambia, which is larger but has lovely gardens and a variety of restaurants and bars. Or you can go very upmarket and choose the Coconut Residence or Ngala Lodge, which have very swish rooms and cracking restaurants in a pleasant environment, though you will pay through the nose for them. There is a whole range of standards and prices to choose from in The Gambia.

If you are looking for accommodation away from the coast and the main tourist areas, then again you have a wide choice, though the standard is generally lower. Many of the camps offer very basic accommodation in huts, with facilities ranging from almost nothing to having your own shower, WC and ceiling fan. In defence of these camps though, it is not the five-star facilities that most people visit them for. It is for the peace and quiet in out-of-the-way places, or the chance to meet real Gambians in the real Gambian countryside. Where, for example, can you find a better site than Madiyana Camp on the island of Jinack, where you have 11km of unspoilt beach and Niumi National Park all around you? Or Tumani Tenda on the banks of the Kafuta Bolon, where you can get involved in all sorts of traditional activities? Both sites lack constant electricity and the accommodation is fairly simple, but they also have a wonderful air of relaxation and timelessness, and what can be better than that? If you want the quietness of the bush but also want to be pampered a little, and of course if you can afford it, there are places that will suit you too. For example, Mandina River Camp in Makasutu Culture Forest, where there are five-star rooms in a wonderfully peaceful rural setting, together with personalised service.

If you want to stay for a longer period and finances are low, or you are visiting on a shoestring budget, then probably your best bet is to rent a room in an ordinary compound. Ask any *alkalo* in any village and he will be sure to know someone that will put you up for a very reasonable price. You can often join in with family meals or cook your own if you prefer, but you have to negotiate the deal that you want. This is probably the best way of getting to know real Gambian people and seeing and sharing how they live.

FOOD

Eating in the Gambia can be a varied experience, because of the number of established restaurants in the kombos (the administrative districts of Cape St Mary, Fajara, Bakau, Kotu, Kololi, Sukuta and Serrekunda) that offer different types of dishes such as European, Lebanese, Mexican, Indian and Chinese. There really is no shortage of international cooking, usually at very reasonable prices. Being so close to the sea, fresh fish is also on most menus and well worth trying. The Gambia also has its own version of McDonalds – called McFadi's – on Kairaba Avenue in Fajara/Bakau (see *Chapter 7*). You will also find that distinctive Gambian dishes are often available in many places.

In The Gambia the staple food is rice or millet served with a sauce which comes in three main types. There is *benechin*, which is a Wolof dish that literally means a one-pot meal (*bena* = one, *chin* = pot), where the sauce can be made with fish, chicken or beef. *Domada* is a dish where the sauce is made from groundnuts and chicken *yassa* is grilled chicken marinated in an onion and lemon or lime sauce. These dishes are served with a variety of local vegetables including cassava, potatoes, sweet potatoes, okra, green beans and a bitter tomato. The food is made spicier by using stock cubes and small red peppers. We can also recommend shrimps cooked in the Gambian style – fried with garlic and served with rice or chips: simply delicious!

Many restaurants will have Gambian dishes on their menus, although some may require some notice for their preparation. You can also find them in the local bars and restaurants along most streets. The best way to experience Gambian food however is to be invited to a friend's compound to sit and eat with their family. It is difficult not to feel welcome sitting around a communal bowl, where food is served on a large flat tray, the rice underneath and sauce and vegetables arranged over the top. You can eat from the bowl with the fingers of your right hand or you can ask for a spoon.

On the street you can also obtain a variety of food throughout the day. At breakfast time there are stalls selling coffee and various fillings for sandwiches including mayonnaise, margarine, chocolate spread and black-eyed beans pounded into a paste and deep-fried or roasted. The bread comes in two types: airy light French baguettes or the more heavy bread called *tapalapa*. Throughout the day you may also see vendors selling meat cooked on little portable grills. The evening is the time for the *afra* or 'meat grilling' bars to come alive. They sell a variety of grilled meat including chicken, beef and lamb.

Throughout the day fresh fruit, roasted peanuts and cashew nuts, Madeira cake and coconut pieces are readily available to snack on. Oranges, bananas, grapefruits, papayas and apples are available all year, whereas mangoes and watermelons are more seasonal. In the Lebanese bars you can also find *shawarmas*. These are similar to a shish kebab and contain thin slices of lamb with salad and humus in a pita bread. For around US$1 they are good value and filling.

DRINKS

Soft drinks are available almost everywhere in the Gambia. Even in the most remote village they will be able to sell you a can or bottle of coke from the local shop (most of these sell soft drinks very cheaply compared to the hotel prices). Bottled water can also be bought in most places.

Local drinks include *wonjo* (which is a sweet but very refreshing drink made from hibiscus flowers), ginger and baobab. They are often sold most unappetisingly in recycled oil and brake fluid containers. You can also buy them at some bars and restaurants, eg: the Village Art Gallery and Restaurant and the Bantang Bantaba at the Methodist Mission in Brikama. You will find fresh fruit juice on the beaches. Beware of these, though, as their high fruit content and freshness can have quite dramatic effects on the system! The local beer is *Julbrew*, which is an award-winning light lager-type beer.

You may also see men preparing a drink from green tea, at any time throughout the day, but mostly in mid-afternoon. The process takes about an hour when the brew is heated up on a charcoal fire, and prepared in small glasses with copious amounts of sugar. This drink is called *attire*, and is full of caffeine. It has a strong taste that becomes more refreshing on the third brew. The brewing of *attire* is almost a social ceremony and usually the men sit around and relax and chat while the pot is brewing.

GAMBIAN CULTURE
The people

The Gambia is a nation containing a myriad of different peoples from all over the world. However, the majority of the country's historical inhabitants are made up of eight different tribes. These are the Mandinka, Wolof, Fula, Jola, Sarahule, Serer, Aku and Manjango. Many recent immigrants from the surrounding countries including Senegal, Ghana, Guinea, Guinea-Bissau, Liberia and Sierra Leone have joined them. Many of these immigrants have fled from the civil wars and rebellions plaguing their homelands to seek peaceful co-existence in The Gambia. Mauritanians, intensely proud and dressed in their long, loose, sleeveless robes of blue, run many of the small shops in every village and town that seem to be open all hours. Businessmen from Ghana also run The Gambia's biggest fishery complex at Ghana Town. Alongside these there are also the ex-pat community which range from newly arrived Europeans to second and third generation Lebanese, many of whom opted to keep their Gambian passports when they were given a choice of nationalities at the time of independence in 1965.

Although it is not possible to tell the peoples of the different indigenous tribes apart by their appearance, each ethnic group has its own traditions, language and background. Conversely, the small size of the country, generations of intermarriage and the unifying force of Islam have also contributed to a great sharing of cultural heritage among the tribes and peoples of The Gambia.

The tribes

Mandinkas make up the largest proportion of the Gambian population. Traditionally they were farmers and even today they are engaged in business and farming, especially the production of groundnuts throughout the country. The Fulas are also farmers. Traditionally they were mainly cattle herders originating in the area north of the Senegal River, though it is thought by some that they came from much further north than this in earlier times – perhaps even from southern Europe. The Wolofs are thought to have originated in Southern Mauritania where droughts and raids forced them south into the area north of The Gambia in western Senegal. During the religious wars of the 19th century, Wolofs established themselves in Banjul and on the north bank of the river as traders and ship builders. Nowadays, Wolofs on the north bank are usually farmers, while those in Banjul are influential in business, commerce and the civil service. The earliest settlers in the area south of The Gambia River were the Jolas, who had migrated from Egypt. They bought palm seed, cotton and rice with them. Nowadays many live near the coastal areas in The Gambia and unlike many of the tribes in The Gambia they have generally retained more of their traditional practices and beliefs, due in part to their independent nature.

The Sarahules were rulers and merchants of the Kingdom of Ghana, and thus have a long history in the West African region. Those found in The Gambia arrived during the 19th century as refugees from the religious wars in Senegal. Nowadays many are farmers living along the eastern Gambian border, but remain famous for their gold and silver trading activities throughout West and Central Africa.

The Serers are among the oldest ethnic group in the Senegambia region, having migrated into the delta regions from north of Senegal. Today they are mainly found along the river mouth, with fishing as their main trade.

The Akus are a tribe that played an influential role in the Gambian economic and governmental life during the colonial period. They are the descendants of European traders and their African wives, as well as liberated slaves from Sierra Leone. Most are Christian and have European names and continue to figure prominently in Gambian commerce and the civil service.

The Manjangos are believed to have arrived in the Senegambia region as seasonal migrant workers from Guinea-Bissau. Today their main occupation is tapping the oil palms for wine.

Social structures

In the past the tribes of The Gambia organised their society along hierarchical lines with status determined by birth. Marriage between the various classes was uncommon.

The class structure consisted of three broad groups – the freeborn, the artisans and the slaves. At the top were the freeborn who consisted of nobles and commoners. The former were the royal lineages and great warrior families; the latter included farmers, traders and *marabouts*. Lower down the scale were the artisans who consisted of specialised workers such as blacksmiths, leather workers, wood carvers and weavers. Although not slaves, the artisan families were attached to the free born families in a patron-client relationship.

Musicians were also a lower caste but highly respected. A particular type of musician called a *griot* performed song and poetry, containing stories of a family, village or clan as a form of oral history.

The tribes of The Gambia today continue to organise their society along the hierarchical lines using the same structure as in the past. An individual's roles and behaviour in society are determined by his/her class. However, the inherent respect and reverence shown between the classes is being eroded by urbanisation and the higher level of education received by a higher percentage of the population. Western ideas and moral values are also spreading amongst the population, especially in the tourist areas where young Gambians are constantly exposed to foreign visitors, but also through TV, radio, videos and magazines. Many of the older generation of Gambians fear a morale decline in their teenage sons and daughters.

Festivals and ceremonies

During your stay in The Gambia, you are very likely to hear, before you see, a Gambian ceremonial occasion taking place. Occasions such as weddings, naming ceremonies, initiation ceremonies and other special Muslim and Christian festivals are celebrated by lavish feasting, drumming, music and dancing. A village will also celebrate the arrival of a special guest, the event being marked by the dancing of the *kanali* – a group of women dancers.

Festivals and ceremonies are loud and colourful events when participants have new clothes made and dress elegantly. Of course they are also costly affairs and so traditionally contributions are made to the host family in the form of money or food. If you are invited to a celebration, you will be expected to bring something. You should also expect to give a present or some money to the *griots* (musicians and oral historians) that come to these events.

Festivals and ceremonies are very important and much of African life is centred on social events, which help to reinforce the social structure.

Marriage

Traditionally, marriages in The Gambia are arranged. However, this practice is less common now in the urban areas. The marriage ceremony itself is the finale of a week's activities, involving the exchange of gifts and visits to relatives. The official ceremony takes place at the mayor's office and is followed by eating and dancing at someone's compound. The procession of cars from the office to the home is marked by much blowing of car horns and shouting, and by the decoration of the bride and groom's car, so much so that it's hard to miss this one!

Initiation ceremony (circumcision)

Traditionally, circumcision in many African countries is an event that marks the transition from childhood to adulthood. Boys and girls are circumcised separately in groups, usually between the ages of eight and 12, although it can occur at an earlier age. After the operation, the groups are taken into the bush and taught about their adult responsibilities and rules of behaviour whilst they are healing. When the children return to their villages, there is much feasting and socialising, and the initiated individuals are given new clothes and decorations by their parents. Special dancing with masquerades, eg: the *kankurang*, (a man dressed from head to foot in a costume made of grass – there is a life-size model outside the National Museum in Banjul, see *Chapter 6*) also marks the return of the initiate.

Today in the urban areas, children are circumcised at a hospital or clinic, and the bush school lasts for a shorter period. Female circumcision is a controversial subject which receives much attention and discussion in the media at certain times of the year. The practice, which is now referred to by some as 'female genital mutilation', is still perceived by many as an aspect of Islamic teaching. The operation causes extreme pain and distress to the individual concerned and may result in healing problems or even in death by infection. A local organisation in The Gambia, called Gamcotrap, which promotes customary health practices among women, also campaigns and lobbies to dissuade female genital mutilation. It is an uphill struggle.

Naming ceremonies

One week after a child is born, an important ceremony takes place when the child is named. An elder, who either shaves the baby's hair or cuts a lock

SUPERSTITIONS AND TABOOS

There are many superstitions in Gambian culture and here are a few examples of the more common ones: if a person dreams of seeing raw fish or a snake, it is a sure sign of pregnancy; anything that is done on a Saturday will be repeated in the future, so many people avoid visiting the sick and making condolences on this day. Even seeing a shooting star is a portent that a prominent person will die.

It is taboo to buy or sell items like soap, needles or charcoal etc at night, and it is also forbidden to whistle at night, since all these things will lead to bad luck. It is also taboo for a widow to go out of her home during her mourning period.

Many animals are also believed to have magical or special powers. Unfortunately many of these beliefs are less than positive, and impact quite negatively on the wildlife. An example of this is the Gambian's belief about owls. Most people, especially in the rural areas, still regard owls with superstitious dread. They fear them, believing that they are transformed local wizards and witches. They also believe that the call of the owl announces an impending death. Such cultural belief results in many injured owls being bought to the Department of Parks and Wildlife Management (if an owl puts in an appearance during the daytime it is instantly stoned and often killed unless someone intervenes and rescues the bird). Geckos and chameleons also live charmed lives, but only in the sense that they are very much feared and left alone. In contrast some people will not kill or eat certain animals because they believe they have some ancestral connection with them.

Dragons or ninki nanka are the most feared of all animals in the Gambia. They live in remote areas and are usually hostile beasts who are able to kill by merely looking at someone. Fortunately however in The Gambia there also exist professional dragon slayers who are immune to such effects, and who for vast sums of money will go and slay dragons. Since no one else can look at a dragon without dying, clients must rely on the word of the dragon slayer that the deed has been done.

Gambians are also great believers in the sanctity and holy power of certain places. The sacred crocodile pools provide examples, as do the many sacred sites scattered throughout the country. These sacred sites range from crocodile pools, groves, trees and stone altars through to tombs, burial sites and places where esteemed holy men have prayed. The sanctity of such places is a blessing in disguise as it is prohibited to cut down the trees or otherwise disturb the sites and so a small remnant of the natural Gambia remains untouched.

and says a silent prayer, performs this ceremony in the morning (around 10.00). The elder whispers into the infant's ear the name the parents have chosen which is proclaimed aloud by a *griot*. While the name is being whispered, a chicken, goat or sheep is slaughtered. A 'charity' of kola nuts, cakes or other special foods is distributed to the guests, and the baby's tuft of hair is buried. Guests bring small gifts for the infant and the *griots* as well. Later in the day, a meal is prepared followed by drumming and dancing. If you are informed of a naming ceremony, even in casual conversation, this is an invitation to attend. It is an informal invitation, and you will be most welcome.

Muslim and Christian holidays

As a predominantly Muslim country, the people of The Gambia celebrate many religious holidays (see *Public holidays* in this chapter).

Observance of these holidays usually involves special prayers and the offering of charity followed by feasting and dancing. They are also occasions for Gambians to dress up and visit with friends and relatives. On *Tobaski* day, all heads of families who can afford it slaughter a sheep, goat or cow and divide the meat among friends, relatives and the poor as charity. Christian ceremonies are also observed in The Gambia, particularly in cities where a large proportion of the population is non-Muslim, eg: Banjul.

Roots Homecoming Festival

The Roots Homecoming Festival, partly inspired by the success of Alex Haley's book, *Roots*, was first held in May 1996 and has now become an annual week-long event that is held in June. The festival is a celebration of the Gambian culture through music, dance, arts and crafts and also commemorates the enslavement and transportation of millions of Africans to the Americas. Many black people from the USA and Europe participate in the festival – even taking part in traditional ceremonies, and parts of the festival are also attended by the President of The Gambia. The Roots Homecoming Festival is organised by the Gambian Department of State for Tourism and Culture and a programme of events is available from the Gambia Tourist Office in London (see *Tourist information and services* page 28).

Traditional beliefs

Although there is a strong Islamic and Christian influence in The Gambia today, many practices originating from past animist beliefs remain. Indeed, much behaviour is still governed by superstitious beliefs that endow natural objects and phenomena, idols, fetishes and individuals with supernatural forces or the power to protect or to use such forces. Some might say that this is not so far removed from Westerners' point of view when one considers the number of people who consult a daily horoscope and avidly watch horror videos.

You will see that many Gambians, from tiny babies to old citizens, wear amulets, commonly called *jujus*, on their body around the waist, neck, arms or legs. The *jujus* are often leather packets, or cowrie shells, which contain writings from the Koran as a spell, or charm, which is said to protect the wearer. The *juju* will have been provided either at birth, naming or initiation ceremonies by the local *griot*, or animist priest. Alternatively the spell or charm may have been prescribed by a *marabout*. Gambians consult *marabouts* for a variety of reasons but the following are the most common: to protect against evil spirits; to improve one's status; or to remedy a situation. Such is the belief in these men that we were almost crushed in a human riot when a particularly famous *marabout* boarded the Banjul to Barra ferry, and all the passengers wanted to touch him.

In addition to the special powers of *jujus*, the Gambians also have quite rigid beliefs in taboos and superstitions, although there is much variation in these beliefs from tribe to tribe, and from village to village.

Art

Artwork is all around you in The Gambia. Not only in the market stalls, or *bengula* (meeting place), near the hotels or craft markets in Banjul but also in the metalworkers' yards, wood workers' and tailors' shops along every road.

At the markets you can buy all kinds of wood carvings, straw and wicker work, leather work, pottery, jewellery, textile work, including weaving and metalwork. Many of the woodcarvings are finished by the stall owners who sell them, but beware as their colour is a result of staining with shoe polish, and will fade with time without constant attention. Having said this, the carvings of African masks, bowls, male and female figures and animals make good purchases and gifts.

The woven cloth you see in the markets represents the most important cloth in The Gambia in the form of cotton. Cloth is made by '*marbos*', a caste of weavers who traditionally come to The Gambia in the rainy season and produce cloth on demand for clients. Traditionally these clothes were used for special occasions such as marriage ceremonies, circumcisions and burials. The dyes used for colours in the weaving were made traditionally from natural sources; for example the ironwood tree, *Prosopis africana*, gives a red colour while the mango tree produces black. Further details about weaving can be found in *Traditional Crafts in The Gambia* by Abdoulie Bayo (see *Appendix 2: Further Reading*).

Tie dye and colourful batiks also abound. You will also see clothes that have been made up in the traditional Gambian style – loose with embroidery, or made on more Western lines. You may want to bring pictures of clothes that you would like made up whilst staying here. Many of the tailors are able to turn a photograph into a made-to-measure designer dress or suit before your very eyes (or in a week at the most).

Away from the markets, other creative forces are at work. You only have to glance at the metalworkers' yards to see intricate gate designs, and the handiwork of the recycled metal workers. Goods range from spoons and ladles through to saucepans, brightly painted metal boxes and candleholders.

As well as seeing and buying arts and crafts in The Gambia a few visitors like to find out how such goods are made. It is possible to take part in a variety of workshops including batik, soap making and tie dye, through to painting and pottery (see, for example *Safari Garden Hotel* and *Gena Bes Batik Factory* in *Chapter 7*, *Tumani Tenda* in *Chapter 8* and *Alaka-Bung Lodge* in *Chapter 11*).

There are a few places where you can also see exhibitions of work from local artists. These are at the Alliance Franco-Gambienne in Fajara, Arch 22 and the African Heritage Gallery – both in Banjul – and the Village Gallery in Kololi.

Music and dancing

The Jim Reeves song 'I hear the sound – of distant drums' has become our theme tune since we arrived in The Gambia. Most nights of the week, and often during the day as we travel around, the beat of drums is the most frequent noise we hear. Sometimes for visitors staying at the hotels the noise can be quite overwhelming and keep you awake until the early hours of the morning.

Drumming is an essential part of West African traditional music, and the music itself is at the heart of their culture. It is through the music that history is passed from generation to generation, social structures are reinforced and traditional skills are perfected.

Traditional music is performed by a distinct social group of people – the *griots*, who are minstrels, musicians or praise singers. The local terms are *jali* (Mandinka), *gewel* (Wolof), or *gawlo* (Fula). In this way *griots* are well respected socially since they act as the historians for West African societies.

Music often accompanies traditional West African dances. The dances depict everyday scenarios including hunting, fishing and working in the fields, and include stories around a wedding or naming ceremony, for example. Traditional beliefs where innate objects come to life or spiritual powers enter an animal also find their way into the dances.

Griots play music on a variety of instruments. These include a selection of drums including the *tama, sabar, mblatt, djemba* and *gorong*; stringed instruments range from the single-string plucked lute, or *moolo*, and the *riti riti* or bowed fiddle, to the 21-stringed *kora*; wind instruments include the flute and trumpet, and percussion is represented by the *balafon* (a xylophone made out of hard wood), shake-shake and claves. There is an excellent selection of these instruments with more specialised varieties at the Tanje Village Museum (see *Chapter 8*).

Hotels, guesthouses and camps will often invite local villagers, dancers and musicians to entertain their guests. Alternatively you should look out for performances of the dynamic dance troop, Fantala Ballet, or book yourself into one of the many schools that offer dancing and drumming lessons (see, for example, *Tumani Tenda* in *Chapter 8* or *Juffureh Rest House* in *Chapter 9*).

Wrestling

This is the oldest sporting activity in the Senegambian region, dating from before the 13th century and probably originating in Mali. Successful wrestlers were and still are seen as extremely important and able men with great innate spiritual and physical powers.

Traditionally, the wrestling match is between contestants from two different villages. Each team is called a *kato*. The event is usually marked by a sense of progression with the youngest and least skilled wrestlers starting first. The entire match builds up towards a climax in which the final bout is between the champions of each team.

As with all Gambian ceremonial occasions, the events are colourful and noisy affairs and music is inseparable from traditional Gambian wrestling. The basic instrument is the drum, with each ethnic group having its own traditional wrestling tunes. Unlike Western wrestling there are no long drawn-out holds and techniques like arm, leg or arm locks; simply the first to be knocked down loses. After a particularly well-fought fight, friends and well-wishers, especially women, will rush into the arena to press coins into the hands of a favourite contestant and rush out again.

Successful wrestlers are believed to possess a superior endowment of spiritual strength, which Mandinkas call *nyamo*. Large numbers of amulets are worn on every part of their body and magic potions are taken to increase their power.

Wrestling was once the Gambian national sport. Today it is still popular but has to a large extent been replaced by soccer. Wrestling is no longer included on the school curriculum so there are fewer people able to take part in the sport. If you wish to watch a wrestling match, they still occur regularly in Serrekunda and a few other places throughout the country. The best way to see a match is to organise a visit through an official guide or a Gambian friend.

Soccer

Youngsters can be seen on any open patch of ground or on beaches playing soccer barefoot, and a few of them have gone on to be international stars in foreign teams. In the evenings you can often see crowds gathered around TV sets by the roads or in bars, to watch national and international matches. Occasionally matches also take place at the Independence Stadium in Bakau, where games against neighbouring countries draw large crowds.

Draughts and *warri*

You may often see small groups of men sitting under trees or in cosy areas around a large board. They will either be playing draughts or the national board game known as *warri*. A typical place to see this is the courtyard of the Serrekunda post office. *Warri* boards can be purchased at many of the craft markets and stalls in the coastal resorts and the stallholder will be only too glad to show you the rules of the game – though they are not simple.

Dressing and hairstyles

Much of the Gambian dress in the urban areas is wonderfully varied and colourful. Traditionally most men prefer to wear a two-piece combination consisting of a *turkia*, a three-quarter length long-sleeved loose shirt, together with a pair of loose-fitting *sirwal*-type trousers. The suit can be made in all types of material, from plain white through many different batik designs and lacy embroidered material. There seems to be no reluctance on behalf of Gambian men to wear bright colours. They will often be dressed in pastel colours or even bright oranges and yellows.

The most characteristic dress of the women is the *granbuba*. This is a full-length dress which sometimes has a highly embroidered neck. It has simple seams down the sides below large sleeve holes. The dress is worn over a simple full-length skirt or wrap in the same material or a contrasting colour. Women will also wear a matching headdress.

Of course when people are at work, especially during hard manual labour, they will not be wearing fine clothes. Upcountry and in the more rural parts of The Gambia, women in the rice fields and vegetable gardens, and men at work in garages and metal workshops will be dressed in their work clothes, wearing a wrap and T-shirt and trousers and T-shirt respectively.

The above is a little indication of the traditional dress worn by Gambians. However, like much of the world globalisation is taking place and many young Gambians can be found wearing T-shirts and jeans. Many men also wear woolly hats, especially during the colder months. Many young women also dress in very tight dresses and trousers, flouting Muslim tradition. In the office setting, suits and Western-style clothes are often worn. However, Friday normally sees everyone putting on his or her special and traditional clothes to come to work. Public and religious holidays are also a time for Gambians to dress up. If you are out and about travelling the country on such a day, it will seem like a continuous fashion parade along the roads and streets.

As varied as the Gambian attire are the ladies' hairstyles. Using hair-straightening lotions, hair extensions, coloured beads and knick-knacks made from plastic, shells and bone, the many different hairstyles are limited only by the imagination. A friend of ours is quite happy to sit for up to six hours every week having her hairstyle changed from one elaborate design to another.

INTERACTING WITH GAMBIANS

Gambians have a reputation for being friendly, and on the whole we think they have earned it. This is a amiable, peaceful country full of convivial, non-violent people who are so laid back that sometimes they can be frustrating to people from the West, who are more used to the 'do it now' syndrome. In The Gambia, it's more like 'do it tomorrow – maybe'. Nothing ever seems to get done on time and people are always late for meetings. In fact the big joke amongst Gambians themselves is referring to GMT, which in this case does not stand for 'Greenwich Mean Time' but 'Gambian Maybe Time'. This relaxed attitude is part of the charm of The Gambia – the fact that life here is much more laid back than in the industrial West. This is Africa and it's either so hot and dry that you could fry an egg on the bonnet of your car, or it's so hot and wet that you need to change your T-shirt every five minutes. In such an extreme climate it is difficult to keep going at a heavy, fast pace for very long, without burning yourself out. You'll probably find when you get here that it will take you a week or so just to chill out and de-stress, but then you'll be able to really relax and enjoy the experience.

The one thing that really annoys tourists in The Gambia is the hassle (see *Bumsters* in this chapter). If you want to walk on the beach, you are constantly hassled, if you walk through Banjul, you are constantly hassled, in fact the minute you leave your hotel you'll be hassled. This is novel in the beginning and the first Gambian to approach you with the famous lines 'Welcome to The Gambia. What is your name? Which country are you from?' etc, will probably get a serious and friendly reply from you. However, after the fortieth person asks you the same questions and it begins to dawn on you that these people are actually only after your money, you'll start getting a little bit peeved with the situation. Some people can take the hassle and give as good as they get, without being ill-mannered. Some people actually enjoy it while others finally get belligerent and rude. But unfortunately most people get so tired of it that they begin to think twice about leaving their hotel grounds (although in some hotels even the staff will hassle you, so there's no escape there). This is a shame because this type of hassle mainly occurs just around the tourist areas and not in the rest of the country.

Time and time again we have seen tourists travelling upcountry who are extremely rude to normal Gambians who are just saying hello. In a way you cannot blame them, because they have been hassled so much and have become so used to constantly being asked for money, that many begin to think that all Gambians are like that. But it's simply not true away from the hotels and the tourist areas. Here Gambians are very keen on greeting people and passing the time of day and are just being friendly. Once you realise this you'll wonder why you ever spent so much time walking along the beach or seeing the sights of Banjul or Fajara, when you could have been really relaxing upcountry.

If you are white, another thing you will have to get used to is being conspicuous. You cannot walk through a village and just be another member of the crowd. You are a *toubab* – which loosely translated mean 'white person', and you'll be reminded of it all the time. Kids will run up to you shouting '*toubab, toubab*' and asking for pens, money or 'minties', and everyone will stare at you in that typically open African way, which can sometimes be a little disconcerting. In these days of political correctness in the west, it can also be disconcerting for a Gambian to come up to you and say 'Hey. White man', but nothing nasty is meant by it, it's just the way it is. We have found that some Gambians will stare at you so intently that you can feel very intimidated. It looks almost as if they hate you. But don't worry about this, just try saying 'Hello' to someone who is staring at you and you will see their face crack into a huge grin and they'll stop and talk to you. 'No problem', as they are fond of saying in The Gambia.

Etiquette

The thing that we really like about The Gambia is that anyone and everyone will stop and say 'Hello' and want to talk to you. Greetings are very important in Gambian society and even if you can't speak any of the local languages, just saying 'Hello' and shaking hands will do the job. If there is one phrase you should learn then '*Salam malekum*' is it, to which the response is '*Malekum salam*'. This is a universal Arabic greeting amongst Muslims around the world and is widely used amongst Gambians, even Christian Gambians. Loosely translated it means 'peace be with you' and 'peace returns to you'. This attitude of greeting everybody is so unlike the West and much more friendly. For example, if you go into a shop in Europe you'll be lucky to get a grunt from the assistant behind the checkout counter, never mind a 'Hello'. In The Gambia, if you say 'Hello' to the assistant

FRIENDS OF THE GAMBIA ASSOCIATION

This UK registered charity (Friends of The Gambia, 12 Bodiam Road, Greenmount, Bury, Lancashire BL8 4DW, UK; tel: 01204 886508; web: www.fotga.org.uk) is run by volunteers and works to help the people of The Gambia. They operate a very successful 'adopt a child' scheme (and are always in need of new sponsors to give needy children the chance of education), provide educational and medical equipment for schools, clinics and hospitals and fund small sustainable projects in schools and villages throughout the country.

you will get a big smile and probably get drawn into a short chat. This type of attitude, if you can relax into it, is so much more friendly and satisfying on a day-to-day basis. For example, think of this: when you walk down a crowded street back home, how many people whom you don't know personally will say 'Hello' to you? Probably no one, right? In The Gambia, you will be assailed by 'Hello' from every direction and many people will want to shake your hand. Even if people are at a distance from you, say working in a field, they will often 'shake hands with you' by clasping their hands together and raising them over their head. Try it for yourself.

There are a few things you should never do in The Gambia, at least if you don't want to cause offence. First and foremost amongst these is walking around only half dressed. Remember that this is a predominantly Muslim country. It may seem incongruous when you often see Gambian women walking around bare-breasted upcountry, but for you to do the same here is considered very, very rude. If you are a woman, then topless sunbathing should be confined to the hotel swimming pool. Topless sunbathing on the beach, or even worse, walking topless around the streets, is considered to be highly offensive. There is also the danger that you may draw unwanted attention to yourself from randy young men. We see many female tourists in the back of Land Rovers, or doing their shopping in the supermarkets, wearing only a bikini top and very short shorts. Many of them just don't realise that this is very offensive too. Even tight-fitting trousers can be seen in a bad light. So when out and about, wear clothes that go down to below the knees and also cover your breasts – something like a cotton summer dress will be fine and will also keep you cool. Men don't escape criticism here, either. We've lost count of the number of male tourists we have seen walking around populated areas wearing just shorts. This is bad for a different reason, as in The Gambia only the 'insane' are seen walking around half-naked and you will immediately be classed as one of these, so at least wear a T-shirt. Covering up is also sensible when out in the sun, and may stop you looking like a boiled lobster. Luckily, Gambians are generally quite forgiving, especially where foreigners are concerned. They know that we have different customs and are tolerant of these, and we're sure that sometimes they even find *toubabs* and the way they dress just a little amusing too.

There are a few other basic rules that you should be aware of. One of these is that you should never ever shake hands with your left hand, only with your right hand. In the same way if you are sharing a communal meal with Gambians, you should only eat with your right hand, never with your left. One reason behind this is that the left hand is used for personal ablutions (we hope we don't have to spell that one out!).

You may find when you are out and about, or if you have made a Gambian friend, that you are invited to join in with a communal meal. It's not rude to refuse if you don't want to join in, but try to be diplomatic and give an excuse such as you have already eaten. If you do join in you may be given a spoon but usually you'll have to use your fingers to eat. Remember to use only your right hand for this and don't be surprised if a woman de-bones your meat or fish for you while you are eating.

When visiting upcountry villages, there are also some forms of etiquette that you should adhere to. One of these is that you should seek out the village *alkalo* and spend a few minutes greeting him before doing whatever it is you came for. It is also a good idea to bring him a small gift. This is usually in the form of kola nuts (you can buy these at most village shops or from street vendors in the larger towns), but if you can't find any then a D5 or D10 note will do (around US$0.50). This is not only polite but may also be very useful, as *alkalos* know everything that is going on in their village and may also be able to provide guides or translators if you require them. Sometimes you may also be introduced to the Muslim *imam* (holy man) of the village. If you enter this holy man's home it is important to remember to remove your shoes and hat first, just as you would if entering a mosque.

Bumsters

If you've never visited The Gambia before, you may think that in this section we are going on a bit about a minor problem. Believe us when we say, the one thing that is most likely to spoil your holiday in The Gambia is constantly getting hassled by bumsters. 'Bumsters' is the local nickname for the young men who hang around tourists. You'll only have to leave your hotel for a walk and you'll meet at least one of them. Most people we have come across feel one of two ways towards bumsters – they either love them or they hate them. One thing is for sure: the never-ending hassle that bumsters give tourists is the root cause behind many people not wanting to ever come back to The Gambia on holiday.

There are a number of classic ways that bumsters approach tourists. Generally they will ask you your name or where you come from, or what hotel you're staying at. More devious than this is the bumster who will come up to you and say 'Hey, remember me? I work at your hotel'. Many people are so embarrassed that they do not remember him that they allow themselves to be drawn into a conversation. Needless to say this is just a con trick and they do not really work at your hotel. Whichever way you are approached, the conversation will probably end up in one of three ways – the bumster may offer you sex, or drugs, or he may tell you how hard it is to get a job or feed his family, and he will ask for money. If you refuse, then it is a rare bumster indeed that will just settle for that and go away. His next tack may be to become rude and intimidating, and if this doesn't work, then he may accuse you of being a racist, in order to shame you into giving him something.

Let's take these options and look at them one by one, starting with sex. The Gambia has recently become a place where many middle-aged, lonely women come to find love and/or sex. A young, very fit, and good looking bumster will take one of these women under his arm, so to speak, during her stay. Often it's just her money he's after, but sometimes he will even propose to her and often this ends in marriage. Of course, most European women do not want to live full-time in Africa, so they will take their young fiancé back home and marry him, or even marry him here during the holiday. Then, after a few months or so he will leave her, after all his 'meal-ticket' has got him where he wanted to go, which is Europe, and he doesn't need her any more. We have heard this same sad story so many times and heard about so many heart-broken women, who have been taken in, yet it still goes on. Of course not all women are that stupid. Some just want to have

HASH HOUSE HARRIERS

The Hash House Harriers has been active in The Gambia for the past 20 years. Their members meet every Monday evening for a run/walk followed by a meal at a restaurant and have raised funds for many projects throughout the country. Details of the Hash House Harriers and how to join in with their fund-raising can be found at the Fajara Club at 12.00 on any Sunday (see *Chapter 7*).

sex with a young virile man, and so they do, and are not taken in by expressions of never-ending love. Fine, if that's what you want, as long as nobody gets hurt.

Now let's take drugs (perhaps we should rephrase that!). It has to be said that marijuana is freely available in The Gambia, though the authorities wage an endless war to stop its production and use. If your idea is to come on holiday and get stoned then you should be warned. Possession of, use of, or dealing in drugs is an offence in The Gambia. If you get caught you will face a heavy fine, and/or a term of imprisonment. At the very least your holiday will be ruined. If you've got any sense you will stay away from drugs whilst visiting The Gambia. Thirdly, there's the question of being asked for money. This in itself can come in many ways, from simply asking for some money for real or imagined services, to many and varied con-tricks. As *toubabs* living in The Gambia for a few years now, we must have seen most of the cons, and even we have been caught out once or twice when we should have known better. You may be told about how poor the bumsters family is and how he can't afford rice for them. Or you may be told that some natural disaster has destroyed his home and he can't afford to repair it. An old favourite is that he has a naming ceremony, or even a funeral, coming up and he hasn't got the money to pay for it. There are so many potential cons, that it would take a book just on its own to list them all.

Be aware that not all con-artists are your classic bumster type. Some are middle-aged, respectable looking people who may tell you that they are a policeman, or a customs officer etc, and that they remember you from when you came through the airport etc. Of course, after a nice chat they will try to sting you for some money. It has even been reported on occasion that real policemen or tourist police have approached tourists and threatened them with being jailed, over some imaginary incident, unless of course, they pay an on-the-spot fine of a few hundred dalasis.

On the other side of the coin, there are some tourists who have made genuine friends out of bumsters and will even come back on a regular basis to visit or to help them out.

Possibly the worst consequence of constantly being hassled by bumsters is when tourists leave the tourist areas and travel upcountry. Here, people will automatically greet you and want to chat, because they are genuinely interested in meeting and talking with all visitors. Unfortunately, after facing a barrage of bumsters, many tourists have become naturally suspicious of being approached by strangers and are either rude or ignore the person making the advance. This is a shame, because the vast majority of the people in The Gambia are OK. It is only the minority that are such a pain, but they tend to colour the view of tourists who have met them.

Again, if this is your first trip to The Gambia, don't let all this talk of hassling put you off from coming here. It's better to be forewarned and forearmed, but remember that The Gambia is a wonderful country, full of wonderful people, and is worth visiting. Here we will give you a few tips on how to deal with bumsters, though they don't all work all of the time. Always make your reply as friendly as possible when a bumster says 'Hello', but never get drawn into a conversation. Instead say something like 'I'm far too busy now, I'll talk to you later maybe' or 'I'm in a hurry, sorry can't stop'. Once you start answering questions, you may just as well give them some money right at the beginning. Never get drawn into following a bumster, especially if he wants to show you his new-born baby child – the chances are it won't be his but he'll still use it to ask for some money. If you're walking on the beach try walking along knee-deep in the water (some bumsters will not want to come in the sea but others will still follow you anywhere). Don't bother swearing at bumsters or threatening them, even though you may feel like it, as it just adds fuel to their fire when they hit you with the racist line. The tourist area now has regular police patrols, so if you are being intimidated try to find one of these and don't hesitate to report the bumster to them. Many of the hotels also employ security personnel. If you can't find a policeman, report the bumster to one of them. If you are a non-confrontational sort of person, you could try another tack, and that is to hire yourself a Gambian 'friend'. If he's big enough he'll keep other bumsters away from you. Or better yet, hire one of the official tour guides that you can find outside many hotels. Then you will not only have someone to keep the bumsters away, but also someone who can help you find out more about The Gambia (see *Guides and tipping* in this chapter).

There are only two guaranteed ways to avoid the attentions of bumsters. One way is to stay in your hotel during your stay. The second is to travel upcountry, away from the tourist areas. The latter option is the one that we would hope that you go for, after all the inside of a hotel in The Gambia could be the inside of a hotel anywhere in the world. If that's all you are going to see of the country you might as well go to Blackpool for a holiday.

Prostitution

Prostitution can be a problem in some tourist areas and if you are a male on your own you may find yourself targeted, especially if you are drinking on your own in some bars and hotels (this sometimes applies even if your partner has just nipped out to the loo). Generally though, prostitutes are only visible on some of the main highways in the larger towns. There are a few places that are also notorious pick-up joints, but we are not going to highlight these in this guidebook, as we do not want to promote this practice in any way. Some people claim that bumsters are just a male form of prostitute, and it's certainly true that they do sell sex for money, but we'll leave that judgement to you as we want to continue living here!

One thing that you should be aware of if you are seeking some sexual company in The Gambia, whether it be male or female, is sexually transmitted diseases. These include not just HIV and AIDS, but the more mundane but just as unpleasant STD's like hepatitis B etc, some of which are prevalent in people active in the sex trade (see *Health* in *Chapter 5*). Our heartfelt advice to anyone coming on holiday here just for sex is to go somewhere else and leave The Gambia alone. The vast majority of people don't want you here.

Begging

Wherever you go in The Gambia, the chances are that someone will ask you for money at some time. This could be a kid walking down the street who will ask for a dalasi, or his mother who will ask for D20. It could be your taxi driver who needs money for repairs to his taxi, or a hotel worker who needs money to fund his education. You will have to decide the merit of each case, but remember that ripping off *toubabs* is a way of life for some Gambians. They are under the mistaken impression that because you are white you are rich. If you happen to be a black tourist the same will apply to you too. If you come from Europe or the USA or wherever, you must be rich, no matter what colour your skin is. In their minds the only poor people in the world are Africans. In this case tourists are their own worst enemy. If no tourist ever gave out money to one of these beggars then after a while the practice would stop and fade away. We know that many people feel guilty when asked for money by someone who is poorer than them, but are they that much poorer? After all, most tourists that come on holiday to The Gambia are just ordinary working people. People who have to work hard for fifty weeks of the year in order to pay for their two-week break in an exotic country. Why should you give out lots of your hard-earned cash to someone just because he gives you a line about how poor he is? He's only trying it on because he's got away with it before with some sucker. This point of view may sound hard, but is vividly illustrated by the crowds of children that follow tourist Land Rovers through villages upcountry, screaming 'Toubab, toubab, give me pen, give me 'mintie', give me dalasis'. They only do this because nearly every landrover that comes through that village has some jerk on the back of it who thinks it's the right thing to do to give poor, little African kids some sweets or some money. In reality, all that this does is perpetuate the misguided belief that all *toubabs* are rich and you can get something for nothing from them. Is this really the way that we want tourists to be seen in The Gambia, and do we really want to be begged for money wherever we go? It's easy to blame the kids for wanting something for nothing, but the real fault lies with the tourists who get off on this type of behaviour. We have seen tourists rip open a bag of sweets and scatter them on to the road behind their Land Rover, so that the kids have to scrabble for them in the dirt. We have even heard one story of a woman from the UK who brought a whole batch of small knitted dolls that she scattered behind her landrover. Can you imagine how these little kids, who have probably never owned a real toy, scrabbled and argued over these dolls? And this woman did it because she thought that the kids were so poor and so cute, and that she was so generous. Do you really want to be a tourist like that?

If you want to help people in The Gambia, and many people genuinely do, then a far better option is to give to an existing charity or directly to an institution like a village school. Many people who have visited The Gambia as tourists in the past, have gone back home and started collecting together money from friends and neighbours, or goods from local businesses, such as books, computers or medical supplies. Then they have come back and passed them on to schools or communities or clinics. This is a far better way of helping out than throwing sweets at kids, and you can be sure that your gifts will not be misused or sold on. For example, many of the village schools have been built and equipped with money raised by such caring people, and are improving the lives of some Gambians in a very positive way (see *Friends of The Gambia Association* on page 52).

What we have taken to calling 'real beggars' are a completely different case. Go to any supermarket or restaurant and you are likely to find someone sitting outside and begging for money. Many of these people are genuinely in need of help and cannot find work (remember there is no social security to fall back on in The Gambia), as they are mentally or physically disabled. Just take a moment to watch what Gambians do, when they are begged for money. Nine times out of ten they will reach into their pockets and give him or her a dalasi or two. Why not take a leaf out of their book and do the same? We leave you to make up your own mind.

Guides and tipping

Outside many of the hotels in the tourist area you will find people who are official hotel tourist guides. Hiring one of these guides is a good way of deterring the unwanted attentions of bumsters; however you may find that some of the guides just ignore the bumsters and let them hassle you. Official guides can also help you find out about Gambian culture first hand, and they often know the best places to buy souvenirs etc.

Unlike many countries that cater for tourists in Africa, there are very few official guides in places such as national parks and museums in The Gambia. Invariably you will be approached by a variety of people who are not official guides. They range from the guy who talks to you in a bush taxi and finds out where you are going (only to follow you and demand payment for taking you there), through to the guy who meets you on the street and talks you into visiting his compound to see his family, then demands money from you for the privilege. When dealing with this type of person you will be placed in a dilemma. Do you pay money to a person who has befriended you simply so that he will get some financial reward, or do you tell him to get lost? Should you, as a tourist who has worked hard and saved up to enjoy your two weeks in the sun, have to pay out your hard-earned money to someone who just happens to be poorer than you and sees you only as some sort of meal-ticket? Then you have to think of all those tourists that will follow after you. The more you give in to this sort of moral blackmail, the more that some people will come to expect it and, worst of all, to rely on it.

Our advice is to only pay someone who has been of real value to you. For example, if you are a birder and you've taken a good birding guide with you who has shown you some good places and good birds, then pay him well. If you've picked up some guy who claims to be a birder but doesn't know a duck from an eagle, then refuse to pay him.

The same goes for tipping in restaurants. If you've enjoyed your meal and the service was good then give a good tip. If the food was awful and the service worse, then don't tip.

When it comes to how much to pay a guide or to how much to tip, then the whole area becomes a little ambiguous. How long is a piece of string? On the whole if you are satisfied with your guide's services, you should pay at least US$1 per hour, US$2 for two hours, or around US$6–7 for a full day. Skilled birding guides should be paid a little more, as often they have years of experience or training behind them. You should pay more if you feel your guide was really good, but be careful not to go over the top, for example US$70 for a single day's work is just way too much. When it comes to tipping, if you are satisfied with the food and service, then between 5–10% of the total cost of the bill is a fair figure.

Birding guides

Many tourists come to The Gambia specifically to see tropical birds and there are many Gambians who have learned to earn their living from this fact, as birding guides. Unfortunately many of them don't know a whimbrel from a curlew, and in some cases don't even know a heron from a stork. As soon as you leave your hotel in the coastal resorts with that dead give-away, a pair of binoculars hanging around your neck, you're bound to be approached by someone offering his services as a birding guide. It's hard to tell at a glance whether or not he is any good. Someone we know coined the perfect term for some of these guides – *Pestiforus gambiensis*!

All is not doom and gloom though, as there is a hard-core of very skilled and dedicated birding guides in The Gambia, who deliver excellent value for money. Not only do they know which birds are which (the sheer number of birds can be

WEST AFRICAN BIRD STUDY ASSOCIATION (WABSA)

WABSA (c/o Atlantic Hotel, PMB 676 Serrekunda, Banjul, The Gambia; tel: c/o WABSA 228601 or 223637; fax: 227861; email: atlantic@corinthia.com – mark for the attention of Lamin Jobarteh) was formed in April 1994 by a like-minded group of young Gambians, who wished to preserve the flora and fauna of The Gambia. It is registered as a charity and non-profit making conservation project. The main objective of the association is to support governmental and non-governmental agencies in formulating policies that will mainstream bird study and environmental protection, and to carry out studies and assessments of the Gambian avifauna.

WABSA has established 22 bird study clubs and bird sanctuaries in schools, with many more to follow. These sanctuaries take the form of small fenced plots of land, that have been planted with seeds and cuttings that are known to attract birds and butterflies. The children in the participating schools are also taught to appreciate birdlife through lessons given by WABSA members, covering topics such as bird identification, feeding and migration patterns. By tackling environmental awareness through educational programmes aimed at school children, the association is gradually involving more people from all sections of the community and has already established two community projects. These are the Meme Agrobiodiversity project and Marakissa Community Bird Sanctuaries. WABSA is also currently engaged in researching the local names of birds in Mandinka, Wolof, Fula, Jola and Sarahulleh.

Recently they have received support from members of Coventry University in England, who have helped them with several small projects. However, like many other projects within The Gambia, WABSA suffers from a lack of resources and skilled personnel. If you are a birder and keen to help conserve the birds of The Gambia in any way, then WABSA would be pleased to hear from you.

quite daunting to a first-timer in Africa), but they know where and when to find most of them. Gambian birding guides also have a phenomenal talent when it comes to calling birds to you, with whistles that mimic the calls of many species. If you want a great example of this, try getting a birding guide to call a pearl-spotted owlet, *Glaucidium perlatum*, on Fajara Golf Course. We have seen some of them whistle one up in just a few minutes, and when the bird answers them it's amazing – almost as though the two of them are having a chat.

There are several places where you can meet birding guides if they are thin on the ground (which does happen when times are busy). The two best-known sites are Kotu Bridge over Kotu Stream, and either the entrance to Abuko Nature Reserve or at the education centre inside the reserve. Also, many hotels now have official birding guides who will take you out and about. If you have any doubts about the guide's skill, then suggest a short excursion for half an hour or so, and test him out on the local birds.

Many of the good birding guides can arrange transport to take you upcountry in search of special birds, often at reasonable prices, though remember you should negotiate for everything here. Don't give them their first asking price or you will end up paying through the nose. On the other hand, remember too that birding guides make their living from guiding and pickings can be very slim during the off-season, so they have to make their money during the tourist season. Please don't be too much of a skinflint. If you are satisfied with the level of bird guiding you have received then pay a reasonable amount for it. In the long term you will be encouraging more Gambians to take up birding, and the more people there are making a living out of birds, the more protection there will eventually be for those same birds.

Below we have listed most of the good birding guides in The Gambia, with contact numbers and addresses. They are not in preferential order but alphabetical order, as we feel it would be wrong for us to say that one is better than another is. Some of them, such as Solomon Jallow, Wally Faal, Mass Cham, Karamba Touray and Clive Barlow are more experienced in leading parties to upcountry sites, but all of them are good birders. If possible, it may be an idea to book their services in advance of coming to The Gambia, as some of them can be very busy. We give sincerest apologies here to any good birding guides that we have not listed, as they are simply not known to us. In other words the list is neither exhaustive nor definitive. Just because someone is not on the list below, it does not mean that they are not good birding guides. On the other hand, if they are on the list, then at least you know that they are good!

Babagalleh Bah c/o PMB 513, Serrekunda, The Gambia; tel: 484100.
Clive Barlow c/o Atlantic Hotel, PO Box 296, Banjul, The Gambia; tel: 228601; fax: 228601; email: business-centre@atlantic-hotel.com.
Momodou Barry c/o 30a Grant Street, Banjul, The Gambia.
Yaya Barry 30A Grant Street, Banjul, The Gambia; tel: 463235 ext 239; fax: 465490; email: kombo@gamtel.gm – all marked for the attention of Yaya Barry.
Sering Bojang Tel: 472140; email: habitatafrica@hotmail.com.
Mass Cham c/o Senegambia Hotel, PO Box 2373, Serrekunda, The Gambia; tel: 462717, 462718 or 467719; fax: 461839 – mark for the attention of Mass Cham.
Mansata Colley c/o Jerreh T. Colley, National Water and Electricity Company Ltd, Customer Relations Department, 10 Street East, Fajara, PO Box 609, Banjul, The Gambia; tel: 372003. Mansata is the only female birding guide we know of in The Gambia.
Bubacarr Daffeh c/o Musa Janneh, Gambia Post Office, Banjul, The Gambia; tel: 373115; email: c/o wildlife@gamtel.gm – marked clearly for the attention of Bubacarr Daffeh.
Pa Darboe Tel: c/o 375888; email: c/o wildlife@gamtel.gm – marked clearly for the attention of Pa Darboe.
Wally Faal PO Box 2555, Serrekunda, The Gambia; tel: 372103; email: wallyfaal@yahoo.com.
Sulayman (Solomon) Jallow Kombo Lamin, Western Division, The Gambia; tel: 472208; email: habitatafrica@hotmail.com.
Lamin Jobarteh c/o Atlantic Hotel, PMB 676 Serrekunda, Banjul, The Gambia; tel: c/o WABSA 228601 or 223637; fax: 227861; email: atlantic@corinthia.com.
Tijan Kanteh PO Box 2090, Serrekunda, The Gambia; tel: 466004; mobile tel: 993294.
Seedy and Gib Saidey PO Box 2239, Serrekunda, The Gambia; tel: 370031 or 392259.
Tombong Sanyang c/o Ebrima Sanyang, PO Box 1209, Banjul, The Gambia; tel: 393767.
Lamin Sidibeh c/o Sani Ceesay, Customs and Excise Department, Wellington Street, The Gambia; tel: 460722.
Malick Suso PO Box 69, Banjul, The Gambia.
Karamba Touray c/o Sainey Kolley, PO Box 2458, Serrekunda, The Gambia; tel: 472147; email: c/o wildlife@gamtel.gm – marked clearly for the attention of Karamba Touray.
Lamin Touray c/o Abdou Sanjo, Gambia Shipping Agency, PO Box 257, Banjul, The Gambia; tel: 472218; fax: 472964; email: dreambird@babarrington.org; web: www.geocities.com/dreambirdsafari.

Bargaining and overcharging

Unlike in the West, haggling over the price of goods in The Gambia is a way of life. There are very few places where goods are sold at fixed prices, and sometimes even here you can still knock the price down by bargaining, though some things cannot be bargained for. It's sometimes difficult to know how much you should pay for something you want but there are a few rules you should stick to if you want to bargain successfully. The first is never to want something (or at least not to let on that you really want something) too much and to be prepared to walk away and leave it if you feel that the price is too high. Secondly, never pay more than what you feel it is worth to you personally. Lastly, never ever accept the vendor's first price, as these are often ridiculously high. As a rule of thumb, if someone offers you a carving etc, for a first price of US$60, then knock down your first offer to at least a third of what you were asked (US$20), and never pay more than half of the original price (US$30). Of course, you will still get ripped off and pay over the odds for a lot of stuff that you buy, but at least you will not have been made too big a fool of. Don't fall for the old trick of 'I haven't sold anything for a month and I really need some money' or 'I have a new-born baby and I need money for the naming ceremony'. This is just a ploy to get you to feel sorry for them and pay a higher price. Be hard when bargaining, as this is the only way to get any respect in this game, and remember – be prepared to walk away if you feel you are being ripped off. A good tip is to get into the market first thing in the morning as many sellers think it's bad luck to turn their first customers of the day away, so you can bargain particularly hard. Bargains can also be had during the rainy season due to the lack of tourists at this time of year.

It's not only the price of goods that should be bargained for, but also the cost of services. This includes just about everything, from the cost of a taxi ride, to the time of a guide, to the price of crossing a river in a *pirogue*. The list is endless. Remember that one of the basic rules is: never to accept the first price offered.

Going back to the theme that most Gambians think that all tourists are rich, you will find that you will be overcharged many times during your holiday. One example we will quote is the canoe crossing to Niji Kajata in Niumi National Park on the north bank of the River Gambia. This is a short crossing over a narrow bolon and takes at most about ten minutes. We have heard of *toubabs* being charged anything up to US$20 for this trip (which by the way is in a canoe that leaks like a sieve). The price that local people are asked to pay for exactly the same trip is less than US$0.50. Is that overcharging or what?

Don't be worried about negotiating a price for a service or for goods. This can be great fun and if you keep a sense a humour you can really get into the swing of things, just like Gambians do. As long as you walk away thinking that you have made a bargain, and the vendor can still rub his hands together and believe that he has made a killing, then everyone is happy.

Theft

Theft is a big problem in the tourist areas of The Gambia, and not always directed solely at tourists. Possibly the worst places for theft are in the crowded markets of Banjul and Serrekunda, where people are constantly bumping into you. If you have valuables or money in your pockets then you will be a target for pickpockets. Even if you keep your money in a shoulder bag or rucksack you are still in danger of being robbed, as a favourite trick is to slash your bag with a sharp knife and take whatever is visible. Thieves often work in gangs and another trick is for one member of the gang to bump into you while another watches your reaction. After the bump it is a natural reaction to feel for your wallet or purse to make sure its still there. In this way you show the second member of the gang exactly where your money is and the next step is for them to steal it.

Car break-ins are also a problem in the built-up areas, and even if your doors and windows are locked, your valuables may still not be safe. A favourite trick is to slash the rubbers holding the windows in and to remove the glass to get access. In some areas there are gangs who go around stealing windscreens in this way to sell them to second-hand car dealers.

Tourists, and residents are sometimes mugged, and even in your hotel your valuables may not be totally safe. It is a big temptation for a poorly paid cleaner, for example, if you leave money lying about.

If all of this talk of crime is putting you off coming to The Gambia, we'd like to put it in perspective a little. There is crime in The Gambia, but compared to most of the cities in the western world it is rare. You have far more chance of being mugged in New York, London, Berlin, Johannesburg or Sydney than you ever have in Banjul or Bakau. You are also extremely unlikely to be threatened with a gun of any sort in The Gambia. In fact we have only heard of one robbery involving a gun and that was a bank robbery that was botched and the perpetrators were caught in the act.

If you are robbed while you are here, it is certain to spoil your holiday, so don't take the risk. Take the following simple, common-sense precautions and you should be fine.

When you are out and about, never carry more money than you need to. Leave the rest locked away in a suitcase in your hotel room, or much better yet, locked away in the hotel safe. Never carry your money in a huge roll in one pocket or bag. Break it up into smaller rolls and spread them about your person or amongst the members of your party, or better yet, carry the bulk of it in a hidden money belt either around your waist, or hanging from your neck, and under your clothes. If you carry the bulk of your money in this way, also carry a smaller amount in a more obvious place so that you can pay for drinks etc, without having to go into your money belt all of the time. Never take money from a money belt in a place where you are open to prying eyes. Never carry money in an exposed and completely obvious place such as a 'bum-bag', as this is the first place a robber will go for. Never leave money in a car unless you have someone to specifically guard it (even then make sure it is someone you can trust, like an official tour operator's driver or guide). If you follow these rules then even if you are robbed, you should only loose a small amount and not all of your hard-earned cash.

If you are carrying expensive gear such as camcorders, cameras, binoculars or telescopes, then keep them out of sight in a rucksack unless you are actually using them. Be extra careful when using them in out-of-the-way and lonely places. Never carry more than what you need and lock the extras away in the hotel safe. Again, never leave them in a vehicle unless they are guarded.

When swimming, be very careful about leaving your valuables on the beach, as people often get their things stolen while they are splashing about, having fun in the sea. Leave them in a prominent place and keep a sharp eye on them while you are in the water, or better still leave at least one person with them at all times.

Our final tip is to avoid walking through the tourist areas in the dark. It's much better to get a taxi, and be very careful when walking in out-of-the-way places, especially apparently deserted beaches. Don't go to these places on your own, or even as a couple. If possible, go as part of a group of people, preferably with several men in the group. There are a few hotspots that you should avoid unless in a large group. These are the beach going south from Bijilo, the beach going north from Calypso Restaurant at Cape Point, and the beach going towards Banjul from

VOLUNTEER WORK IN THE GAMBIA

There are many opportunities to do voluntary work in The Gambia, either on your own or through a volunteer organisation. Normally you have to have a skill (or skills) to be a volunteer and not just want to work overseas, as a major part of your time will be devoted to passing on your skills to a Gambian counterpart and building local capacity. Volunteer work is a good opportunity to see life from a very different perspective and in a new cultural setting, though be warned – it can also be frustrating at times.

The three main organisations that bring volunteers to The Gambia are the British-based Voluntary Service Overseas (VSO), the Irish-based Agency for Personal Service Overseas (APSO) and the US-based Peace Corps. All of them provide in-country cultural and language training, and provide support services for their volunteers.

VSO 317 Putney Bridge Road, London SW15 2PN; UK 24-hour tel: 020 8780 7500; email: enquiry@vso.org.uk; web: www.vso.org.uk

APSO 29–30 Fitzwilliam Square, Dublin 2, Ireland; tel: +353-1-661 4411; fax: +353-1-661 4202

Peace Corps 1111 20th Street NW, Washington, DC 20526; tel: 1 800 424 8580; web: www.peacecorps.gov

Denton Bridge. These are all known places for a particularly nasty mugger who has not yet been caught by the police, and who preys on tourists, especially vulnerable ones.

Follow these rules and you will significantly reduce your chances of having a bad experience. Above all, though, don't let the fear of being robbed ruin your holiday, as the chances of it happening are far less than they are at home. Relax and have fun, just remember to be careful and to keep temptation out of sight.

If, by some unlucky happenstance, you are robbed while on holiday in The Gambia, then please, please, report it to the police, and as soon as is possible. Many robberies go unreported and this is very irresponsible behaviour. If you don't report a crime, how are the police to know about it and to do something to stop it happening again? After we were victims of an attempted mugging we were told by numerous friends and colleagues of similar muggings against *toubabs*, committed by the same person and in the same general area. Yet none of them had been reported. If they had been, then maybe the mugger would have been caught before he had a chance to threaten us. Remember too, that if you want to claim off your insurance you will need a police crime number. Do not be frightened of the Gambian police. They are there to help you and are a good bunch. It may take a little time to write a statement etc, but it's worth the effort on your behalf, and it's the only way that crime will ever be stamped out in this very friendly and peaceful country.

Women travellers

As The Gambia is mainly Muslim, it is appropriate that women travellers, particularly, should dress so as not to cause offence (see *Etiquette* in this chapter). This is a good idea, not only out of courtesy, but also to avoid the attention of men, which at the coastal resorts can be a big problem (see *Bumsters* in this chapter). Even when you are travelling with your partner as a couple, you may get unwanted attention from some men at the beach and outside the hotels, who treat the male partner as if he isn't there. Upcountry you will very rarely have a problem with Gambian men and are much more likely to draw the attention of other male travellers from the Western hemisphere.

Getting hold of tampons or sanitary towels upcountry can be impossible, though it is easy to buy them from any supermarket in the coastal resorts. If you are travelling upcountry it's best to plan ahead and take a supply with you, remembering that when travelling in the tropics it is common for women to have heavier and more irregular periods than they would normally have at home.

Bribery and bureaucracy

Despite what you may have heard about African countries, bribery is not a problem in The Gambia. Undoubtedly it does go on, but only in the same way that it does in Europe, for instance, where someone receives a 'favour' for services rendered. As for bureaucracy, that's the bane of all travellers worldwide and The Gambia is no exception and no worse than many other places. As a visitor, the only times you are likely to come into contact with the bureaucratic machine is if you want to extend your visa for a longer stay, when crossing the border into Senegal, or if you are travelling into The Gambia from another African country. In the latter case you might be asked to produce your yellow fever vaccination certificate, and if you don't have one you may be refused entry (see *Health* in *Chapter 5*).

If at any time during your stay you come up against the wielders of bureaucracy, remember to be polite and courteous. They are people too, and will probably respond to you in the manner that you have approached them. If you behave like a paranoid, arrogant Westerner, then you will be treated as such. However, if you are friendly and patient, and realise that the person you are dealing with may not even speak English and is only doing his or her job anyway, then you will be received much better and treated the same way. If at any time you feel that you are being mistreated, imagine what it's like being an African travelling to the West and how they are treated by our own bureaucrats. It's much worse for them than it will ever be for you.

Asking directions

Finding out directions how to get somewhere can be a problem in The Gambia. Typically Gambian people want to please. Thus if you ask if a certain place is in this direction, nine times out of ten the reply will be 'yes' because they think that is what you want to hear. It is necessary sometimes to be a bit of a detective and double-check the answer to find out its validity. In the same way, if you ask three different people for directions you are likely to get three completely different answers, and if you ask how far a certain place is from your present position, well, in many cases it's simply not worth asking in the first place. There are exceptions to every rule however, and if you are in Banjul or the other tourist areas you will find many extremely well educated Gambians who can probably read a map better than you can. The best way to get somewhere is to find a taxi driver who can speak passable English (or French of course) and get him to take you there.

In many cases you may find some confusion between miles and kilometres, and people often interchange the two quite freely. A good rule of thumb for the independent traveller is that 1.5km is about the same as one mile, and a reasonably fit person can walk around three miles in one hour. The distances quoted in this guide, the vast majority of which we have walked or driven ourselves, are as accurate as we can get them, though the longer a journey, the more likely it is to be out by a small percentage. Remember when planning a journey in The Gambia, everything takes a lot longer than it would in Europe or the USA. A journey of a few hundred kilometres along a motorway will probably take you just a few hours back home. In The Gambia, with the bad state of the roads, irregular public transport, the heat, people stopping to take their prayers etc, it is likely to take considerably longer. It might be a good idea to lay your plans with this in mind, and also better to just relax a little and go with the flow. After all, who wants to hurry? This is Africa.

Photographing people

Always ask permission before taking a photograph of someone you do not know. In the past, many Gambians have found themselves on postcards and calendars and are consequently suspicious of cameras and photographers.

Aside from this it is polite to ask and do not be surprised if you are asked for a small gift (US$0.50–1) afterwards. On the other hand if someone does not want you to take a picture you should respect his/her wishes.

You will probably find that most people love to have their picture taken. In fact the difficult part about taking a picture in The Gambia, and Africa in general is to get a reasonable image before every child piles into the viewfinder as well. It is also difficult to stop your subject smiling inanely at the camera. We have found the best approach here is either getting to know the person first, or taking a picture of them involved in some activity or interest. It doesn't always work, but it is worth trying to get the person to forget that the camera is there.

It's always good to try to get a copy of the photograph to the subject as well. Most people can come up with a postal address and appreciate the effort.

The lighting in The Gambia is best in the early morning or late afternoon for taking pictures of people. At other times it can be very harsh and thus gives little detail in faces unless you skilfully use fill-in flash to compensate. The detail in faces can also be recorded by using the diffuse light that is produced on a cloudy day. If you need to take pictures in the middle of the day it is also worth considering using the shade given by a large tree. The light is often strong enough in these circumstances that a flash is not needed, but not harsh enough to burn out all the detail. Photographs at sunrise, sunset and even in moonlight can also produce unusual and effective results.

Natural History

GEOLOGY AND GEOGRAPHY

The Gambia is a flat country and only reaches a maximum of around 50m above sea level in a few places, mostly inland. The country lies on a vast plateau of sedimentary sandstone that stretches from Mauritania in the north to Guinea Conakry in the south, and is slightly tilted towards the Atlantic. The main feature of the country is the River Gambia, which enters The Gambia about 680km from its source in the Fouta Djallon Highlands in Guinea. The river flows in a general east-west direction until it empties into the Atlantic Ocean and cuts a winding, shallow valley for itself through the surrounding sandstones and claystone. The river has also laid down a series of alluvial deposits such as clay and sand which have partly filled this valley. Some of these deposits have been fairly recent in geological time. The river flats are normally separated from the surrounding plateau by a series of low sandstone hills, especially in the east of the country. In some places, though, extensions of the plateau have formed impressive cliffs that overlook the river.

HABITATS
The coast

For about 40km from the coastline the offshore seas are shallow and lie on the continental shelf, before dropping sharply down into the depths of the ocean. These shallow waters are an important source of fish, not only for people, but also for the numerous birds that feed here. Although the seabed is mainly composed of sand, there are also large outcrops of rocks and extensive beds of sea grass that form huge sun-warmed meadows. The sea grass meadows are grazed by green turtles, *Chelonia mydas*, while dolphins, minke whales, *Balaenoptera acutorostrata*, and Mediterranean monk seals, *Monachus monachus*, hunt the abundant shoals of fish. The coastline of The Gambia consists of a long, recently deposited (in the geological time-scale anyway) sandy beach, which is interrupted in only a few places by low cliffs and associated rock-falls. The top of this beach is clothed with creeping, sand-binding and salt-tolerant plants. Behind the beach is a series of much more ancient raised beaches. They are generally covered with coastal scrub, which is a very rich habitat of small shrubs and grassland interspersed with taller trees such as baobab, *Adansonia digitata*, and rhun palm, *Borassus aethiopum*. Beyond the scrub most of the coast was once lined with moist coastal forest dominated by tall, thick stands of rhun palms and other salt-tolerant trees. This has now largely disappeared from many parts of the country.

Mangroves and banto faros

Mangrove swamp, or forest, covers much of the transitional zone between aquatic and terrestrial habitats around the mouth of the River Gambia. It also extends inland along the edges of the river and many of the *bolons*, as far as 200km from the sea. There are two main types of mangrove trees. 'White' mangrove colonises the edges of the dry land that are rarely inundated by the tides and therefore are less saline. 'Red' mangrove grows right down into the edge of the sea and is very salt-tolerant. The two types are easy to tell apart as 'white' mangrove pokes up aerial roots from below the mud, while 'red' mangrove props itself up above the mud and the water, on curving, stilt-like roots. By the coast the mangrove forests are fairly low in height, while further upriver they can tower to a height of 15–20m. Mangroves grow only in tropical and sub-tropical waters and are an endangered habitat throughout the world. One reason for this is that they are often thought of as 'wasteland', and therefore often cleared for development. This sometimes has drastic consequences because mangroves form a natural barrier against the sea and prevent low-lying coastal land from being eroded and washed away. In fact mangroves actually create dry land by binding mud and sand together. As the mangroves grow they periodically shed their leaves, which gradually builds up the fertility and depth of the soil in which they grow. This continues over hundreds and thousands of years, until eventually the swamp becomes dry land. New mangroves grow further out on the edges of the swamp all the time and the process continues. Mangroves are also of enormous benefit in many other ways, for example many of the fish that are caught as adults in offshore waters, actually spawn amongst the roots of mangroves. The swamps also act as a very important nursery for young fish before they head out to the open sea. In addition mangrove swamps are the only source of mangrove oysters, *Grassostrea tulipa*, which are collected and sold by many Gambian women, as well as being a source of timber for firewood and building.

Behind the mangrove swamps you will find the *banto faros*. These are large flat areas of land reclaimed from the sea by the mangroves and then abandoned. Often these flats can be barren, coated in a crystalline layer of salt crusts. In the less saline parts they are covered in thick mats of low-growing succulent plants.

Wetlands

There are many different types of wetland habitats within The Gambia. These habitats range from coastal salt pans, lagoons and marshes, through mangrove swamps, mud-flats, salt-water rivers and *bolons*, the freshwater stretches of the River Gambia, flooded sand mines, animal watering holes, rice fields and permanent freshwater pools lined with reed beds, to vast seasonally flooded marshes.

Most of these habitats are extremely rich in crustaceans, annelid worms and molluscs which are harvested by vast numbers of wading birds, especially during the dry season when resident species are supplemented by thousands of migrants from Europe and other areas in the north.

Farmland

Much of The Gambia is now covered in land that is managed for agriculture. In the past this was under a rotational regime, where land was once traditionally worked every 20 years or so. During the intervening years it was left fallow and covered in regenerating scrub and woodland. With the recent rapid growth in The Gambia's human population, more pressure is being applied to increase crop production to feed people, and some of the agricultural land is now managed on a much shorter rotation, being left fallow for only two or three years in places.

Much of this agricultural land is used to grow crops such as sorghum, millet, and especially groundnuts. When the land is cleared for crops useful trees such as baobab, figs, *Ficus* species, winterthorn, *Acacia albida*, and African locust bean, *Parkia biglobosa*, are left intact and dot the landscape. After the crops are harvested, the remains of the crops and other vegetables are grazed by herds of cattle and flocks of sheep and goats. During the growing season and into the dry season these animals also range throughout savanna and woodlands.

Savanna and the Sahel

Two types of savanna are found in The Gambia: Guinea savanna and Sudan savanna. In the Western Division (in areas of higher rainfall up to the Bintang Bolon), the type of savanna that is commonly found is called southern Guinea savanna. This type of savanna is made up of a rich mixture of over 50 tree species, which are dense and grow fairly tall.

East of the Bintang Bolon, and covering the whole of the north bank of the River Gambia, Guinea savanna is gradually replaced by Sudan savanna. This type of habitat consists of dry, open woodland with well-spaced trees of moderate height and tall grasses. This type of savanna frequently occurs on lowland soils and the slopes of low laterite hills and ridges, and is characterised by tall red termite mounds that have been formed on the lateritic soils. This woodland is also interspersed with a few taller trees, such as baobab and red-flowered silk-cotton trees, *Bombax costatum*, which are a haven for birds that feed on their nectar-rich, large waxy flowers. In some areas of the Sudan savanna you can find deeper soils which are given away by their much taller, thicker woodland composed of dry-zone mahogany, *Khaya senegalensis*, and African rosewood, *Pterocarpus erinaceus*.

All savanna is subject to bush fires that can occur almost annually in some areas. Some of these are natural fires caused by lightning strikes, etc but people start many of them, either deliberately or accidentally. These fires change the composition of the savannas, favouring fire-resistant trees, eliminating species that cannot cope with fires, and severely reducing the natural regeneration of the vegetation.

In the north of Senegal much of the land is Sahelian in character, with sparse, short grasses and scattered shrubs. The climate appears to be changing around the world, due to the activities of people, and one of the results of this is that The Gambia is receiving less rainfall. This, plus massive deforestation by a timber-hungry population, are the main reasons behind the dry Sahel spreading southward. Already parts of the country north of the River Gambia are showing signs of drying out. It has been noted by a few ornithologists that some birds of the dry Sahel are spreading south into The Gambia. We have noted that animals that are normally associated only with deserts and other arid areas, are also spreading south into the north bank, for example the sand fox, *Vulpes pallida*. Only a massive injection of time and effort can possibly hope to stop the Sahel from pushing even further into The Gambia.

Gallery forest

To the untrained eye, gallery forest looks much like rainforest, like the forest that is found in other parts of West and Central Africa. However, they differ in one main respect. Rainforest is fed from rain, while gallery forest is fed from ground water. It doesn't sound an important distinction, and certainly both types of forest are very moist, especially in the rainy season. In fact, it is quite an important distinction, as a different range of trees and plants prefer the environmental conditions of gallery rather than rainforest, and vice versa, though there is also a considerable overlap in the plant species that are found in both of these habitats. It is a less important distinction to animals, which tend to be more mobile, and therefore the same, or similar species, are generally found in both. Gallery forests are a natural component of the savanna woodlands and are considered to be the vestiges of the closed, moister forests occurring in southern West Africa.

Gallery forest is now a very rare habitat in The Gambia and can only be found in a few places such as Abuko Nature Reserve, Pirang Forest Park and some of the fringes of the freshwater stretches of the River Gambia.

Urban habitats

Urban habitats are widespread throughout the country, though most of the large urban centres are found in the Western Division. Urban habitats range from the smallest of country villages to the vast sprawl of Serrekunda, including everything in between. In some areas these habitats are covered in concrete and tarmac and are devoid of life, except for the usual pest species that can be found anywhere in the world, such as some insects and larger animals such as rats and mice. Other areas contain large open green areas and many trees, especially mango, *Mangifera indica*. These areas are richer in wildlife, with frogs, toads, lizards, snakes (even large ones like the African rock python, *Python sebae*) and birds making their homes there.

WILDLIFE VIEWING

Wildlife is around you everywhere in The Gambia, whether it is sparkling dragonflies or colourful butterflies, noisy frogs, scampering lizards or sleepy crocodiles. Many people think of West Africa as being relatively poor in wildlife, especially when compared with the great national parks of East Africa. Yet there are great national parks in West Africa too. A quick trip through Niokolo Koba (Badiar) in Senegal will turn up hundreds of antelopes, warthogs and monkeys, and possibly more elusive animals such as elephants or lions. Even in The Gambia there are still large mammals such as hippos, leopards and warthogs, as well as dolphins and a range of monkeys. A visit to this uniquely small country will undoubtedly turn up some African favourites to make the trip worthwhile.

Of course the birds are a completely different story altogether and The Gambia is a well known hot spot for birdwatchers. Even a simple walk around the grounds of a hotel will reveal numerous firefinches and cordon-bleus, sunbirds and gonoleks, while a week's steady searching could well let you amass over 200 species, depending on how serious a birder you are and how much effort you are prepared to put in.

Tips for watching wildlife

Successful wildlife watching can be quite an art. Its nearest equivalent is probably stalking and hunting food to eat. It is of course more fun to 'shoot' with a camera these days than to shoot with a gun, and much less damaging to the wildlife as well. If you're an outdoor type then most of the following tips will already be well known to you. For people that are less used to the outdoors and to the rigours of watching wildlife, they may seem a little obvious and archaic. But they are well worth following if you don't want to waste your valuable time in fruitless searches for wildlife. The main point is that if you walk slowly and pause often, your chances of spotting something good will be multiplied.

The one thing that you cannot guarantee is luck. Wild animals are totally unpredictable. You can be in the right place at the right time, with the right clothes and equipment, and follow all the rules for good wildlife stalking, and still not see anything. Conversely you can walk down a busy main street in a town and see something quite unexpected. Luck is the one thing that we cannot help you with. However, you can help yourself by reading and following the advice below.

The right equipment. No special equipment is necessary for watching wildlife although a good set of binoculars can be extremely useful, as getting really close to wild birds and animals is often difficult.

The right clothes. It is important to try and blend into your surroundings as much as possible, but also to keep cool at the same time. A set of khaki safari-type clothes is a good compromise. Remember it is sensible to wear long trousers in the bush, not only because of the small danger of snakes (trousers will prevent most of them from biting into your leg) but also because of the myriad of tiny biting insects such as ants, that just love bare flesh. Tuck your trousers into a good pair of light, stout boots and you are almost snake-proof and can walk around without worrying about stepping on something nasty. It will also stop insects from crawling up your legs. A sunhat with a wide brim is a good idea too, not only to protect you from the sun but also to help break up the outline of your head and shoulders.

The right place. This is fairly obvious. You cannot expect to see dolphins if you walk through a forest, or warthogs from a boat at sea. Animals all have particular habitats that they adhere to, though there are some species, notably birds, which are far more mobile and can be encountered anywhere. It is not always necessary to go for miles into the bush to spot wildlife. Well known sites such as Abuko Nature Reserve can be excellent sites for watching animals at close quarters, simply because so many people visit. The animals have become accustomed to them and do not run off at the first sight or sound of a human.

The right time. This is very important in The Gambia. It gets so hot during the middle of the day that many animals do the sensible thing and have a siesta, normally away from prying eyes. The best times for wildlife watching are from first light to around 11.00, and again from 16.00 to dusk. Of course there are always exceptions. Many butterflies are best seen around mid-day, and some of the larger animals, especially predators, are best looked for during the first and last few hours of darkness. Take a drive upcountry in the dark and you stand a fair chance of spotting animals dashing across the road that you would not normally see during the daylight. Ask permission at any of the protected areas and they will allow you to walk through in the dark and have a torch-lit safari. It is wise though to take a local guide with you – provided you can find one that's not too scared of the dark.

Try and disguise the **shape** of your body, which is a dead give-away to cautious wildlife, even at a distance. The shape that really gives us away as human is our square shoulders with our head perched on top. Wear a floppy hat or scarf and this will go a long way to breaking up your outline.

It is much harder to see things when they are in deep shadow, so try it yourself and use **shade** to your own advantage. For example walk along a line of trees within their shade while you scan adjacent fields, or sit in shade when you rest. It will give you a much better chance of seeing things before they see you. There is also the added benefit that it is much cooler in shade.

Like shape, the human **silhouette** is instantly recognisable to wild animals, so try to avoid standing on skylines where you stand out like a sore thumb. Remember as well, that you can be silhouetted against other plain objects – for example, ploughed fields or bodies of water.

Wearing clothes, or carrying equipment that has a shiny reflective surface is a serious no-no for wildlife watching. The **shine** of such objects can give you away very easily, so go for matt surfaces, and watch those sunglasses.

When searching out mammals, try and walk into the wind so that your **scent** is carried away behind you. This will prevent animals having an advanced warning and disappearing before you can see them. Some wildlife, especially mammals, are more reliant on their powerful sense of smell to pick up danger than they are on their other senses. As humans, with our poor sense of smell, we often forget this simple rule.

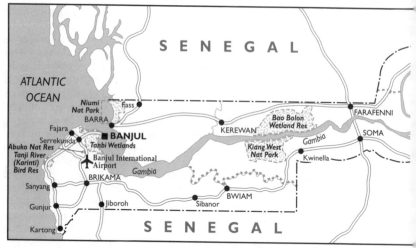

Fast, sudden **movements** betray your presence, so try to move slowly and deliberately. This also helps by allowing you more time to scan the ground around you for those well camouflaged and difficult-to-see species, before they burst away in a cloud of noise and dust. One point that is easily overlooked is that moving vegetation is a dead give-away too, so move carefully through tall grass or bushes so that you don't shake the whole bush and scare everything away. This is perhaps the most important of our tips for watching wildlife.

Wildlife photography

It is difficult to obtain decent wildlife photographs in The Gambia without a good specialist lens, eg: 200mm or 300mm. However, having said this, many birds and animals are highly approachable, especially in hotel gardens and around water bodies towards the end of the dry season. The hides at Abuko Nature Reserve (especially the one that can be rented at the Animal Orphanage) and the sewage ponds at Kotu provide excellent conditions for close up views of many bird species (see *Chapters 7 and 8*).

In addition The Gambia is home to a great variety of plants and insects. Throughout the year both the native flowers and those of the introduced varieties in the hotel grounds can be quite spectacular. However, the first rains result in an explosion of new flowers (eg the scarlet fireball lilies, *Scadodox multifloris*, which can be seen lining the road leading to the airport terminal), and bright colourful insects, including many butterflies and moths.

Lighting is a critical factor in every type of photography and it is especially true of nature photography. The quality and quantity of light vary enormously during the day in The Gambia. Lighting is at its best in the hours just after dawn and before sunset. At this time, the light is not too harsh and allows details to be recorded. The light also comes from a lower angle in the sky and helps provide depth to images due to the shadows that are created.

If you find yourself taking pictures in the middle of the day, you will see that the natural light becomes very intense, making it impossible to record the detail and contrast of subjects. One way to approach this problem is to use a polarising filter, especially if you are taking pictures of water. The filter removes the unwanted glare from the surface of the water, and has the effect of increasing the contrast between any subject and the background.

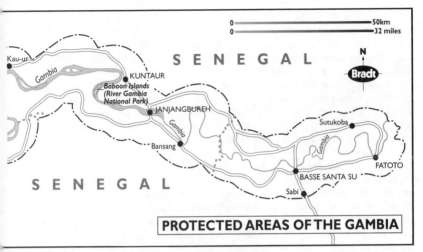

PROTECTED AREAS OF THE GAMBIA

An overcast cloudy sky will always produce a more soft and even lighting, regardless of the time of day. The diffuse light in this situation causes shadows to become indistinct or non-existent, with the result that fine details are revealed.

One more tip to remember is that wildlife photography often requires patience and quite a few hours of sitting or crouching in hot, sticky and cramped conditions. Don't forget to take your insect repellent, sunscreen, hat and plenty of water!

THE WILDLIFE
Primates

At present there are five species of primate that are widespread and relatively common in The Gambia: the western red colobus; patas; callithrix monkey; Guinea baboon; and a bushbaby. The first four are fairly easy to see in the daytime provided you visit the right habitat. The **Senegal bushbaby**, *Galago senegalensis*, is nocturnal, and therefore much more difficult to find, though if you are lucky you may catch a glimpse of its eyes reflected in torchlight during a walk at night. The status of one more species, **Campbell's monkey**, *Cercopithecus campbelli*, is unknown at the present time. This dark, long-tailed, arboreal monkey once inhabited heavily wooded parts of the country and may still be present in the southwest.

The **chimpanzee**, *Pan troglodytes*, occurs in The Gambia at the River Gambia National Park. This is due to the supreme efforts of conservationists, including Dr Janice Carter and Stella Brewer, who have run a chimpanzee rehabilitation project for many years. This project has helped return a large number of orphaned and confiscated chimps to the wild. The chimpanzees live in several troops on forested islands along the river and their numbers have been swelled considerably by natural births among the population. This project has been a fantastic success. The national park is currently off-limits to everyone, tourists and locals alike, except for the staff who run the park (see *Chapter 11*).

Despite being found throughout a large area of West Africa, the **western red colobus**, *Piliocolobus badius temminckii*, is disappearing rapidly. This is due to a variety of factors including the loss of its habitat though the logging of forests and woodland and clearing of land for cultivation.

The colobus is a large monkey, fairly slender and long-tailed with hind legs longer than the arms. The head is small and round, with a short muzzle and flat broad nose. In colour the upper parts are generally dark grey while the lower limbs and under-parts range from a rich red to a light orange. The face is bluish to black and the long, tuft-less tail is dark, though sometimes with an orange tint. One interesting point about this monkey is that its thumbs are virtually non-existent and are reduced to mere stumps.

Colobus live in troops of between 14–32 monkeys. They inhabit various types of forests and woodlands and they are widespread throughout The Gambia. There are large populations present in protected areas, such as in Kiang West National Park, Bijilo Forest Park and Abuko Nature Reserve. Much of the research into this endangered monkey species has been carried out in Abuko.

Of all the monkeys, the **Guinea baboon**, *Papio papio*, must surely be the most impressive in terms of size and ferocious appearance. Females can weigh up to 12kg but a large male can reach 19kg. They are a grizzled, reddish brown in colour, with large dog-like muzzles. Adult males have a sharply defined mane of hair. Baboons are predominantly terrestrial but do visit trees and are quite capable of climbing even smooth palm trunks. The Guinea baboon is fairly common upcountry. However it has become increasingly scarce by the coast, although it can still be seen in the south. One of the few places it can be seen in the coastal region is Makasutu Culture Forest.

Baboons have a very catholic diet, eating virtually all of the edible plants that can be found throughout their range. They supplement this with animal food such as grasshoppers, spiders, scorpions, crabs, fish, frogs, lizards, birds, crocodile eggs, small rodents, hares and even young antelopes. The larger animals are usually only caught by the males who do not share this food with the other members of their troop. The limiting factor in baboon distribution is the availability of large trees (they roost in them away from predators) and the presence of water. Despite the fact that baboons obtain all the water they need to survive from their food and dew, they also like to drink regularly.

The **patas**, *Cercopithecus patas*, is a highly distinctive monkey with long limbs and slender build. Males are large animals weighing between 10–25kg. They have russet-red tails, hindquarters and crowns, while the back and nape are sandy-coloured and the shoulders shaggy and streaked with grey. Females are much smaller, reaching a maximum of 14kg. They are the colour of dry grass interspersed with shades of fawn, russet or grey. In both sexes the limbs are white, the facial skin is pale and the nose is dark.

The long limbs of the patas allow them to travel at a speed of up to 50km per hour when alarmed. Such a great turn of speed has earned them the nickname of the 'greyhound' of monkeys. It is also one of the factors that has made the species very successful.

Patas are widespread and common animals throughout The Gambia. They are found in several vegetation types from open grassland, to dry woodland, including agricultural and fallow land. They are often seen crossing roads upcountry.

The **callithrix monkey**, *C. sabaeus*, is the most numerous of all monkeys in The Gambia and can be found throughout the length and breadth of the country. Once regarded as a mere subspecies of the green or vervet monkey, it has now been upgraded to a full species that is resident only in West Africa.

The callithrix monkey is a long-legged savanna monkey, which is a grizzled golden-green colour. The hands and feet are pale grey, the underside is off-white and the tip of the tail is pale orange. The males have a very pale blue scrotum. A large male can weigh as much as 7.6kg.

This monkey species is adapted to practically all wooded habitats outside of the rain forest. However, being smaller than baboons and lacking the speed of patas monkeys it cannot afford to venture far from the safety of the trees and is also more dependent on trees for food. It is essentially a species that lives in the edge habitat where forests and savanna meet.

Bats

Bats, or *tonso* in Mandinka, are among the most diverse and geographically dispersed group of mammals. Of the 4,300 or so species of mammals that inhabit the world, almost one quarter of them are species of bat. Like other mammals including man, bats give birth to live young and suckle them on milk. They are also able to regulate their own body temperature. Unlike all other mammals, however, they are able to fly, and it is this unique ability that has led to so many species successfully colonising almost every ecosystem on earth. In The Gambia there may be around 30–40 species, although as yet they have been little studied in this country.

Bats come in two main types: there are the large fruit-eating bats and the much smaller insect-eating bats. The fruit bats are commonly seen, as they seem to prefer to roost in places that are both noisy and busy. There are several species but most of them are large, with wingspans up to 75cm. They have large eyes and are quite able to see in the dark as they fly from tree to tree, though their sense of smell is also acute and they often use this to locate their food. Fruit bats eat fruit of course, but also pollen and nectar from flowers. A large roost of **straw-coloured fruit bats**, *Eidolon helvum*, numbered in their thousands during the wet season, can be found in the mango trees behind the mosque in Lamin. The **Gambian epauletted fruit bat**, *Epomophorus gambianus*, can be found just about everywhere. Good sites include the bird garden of the Atlantic Hotel in Banjul, the grounds of the Senegambia Hotel in Kololi and beneath the straw roofs of Makasutu Culture Forest near Brikama.

The insect-eating bats are normally much smaller than the fruit bats. They are amazing creatures and some species have been known to live as long as 30 years. Their eyesight is relatively poor but they more than make up for this deficiency in their use of sound. They hear rather than see their surroundings, using a form of sonar, very similar to that used by submarines. Depending upon the species in question, they emit short sharp sounds from either their mouths or specially adapted noses. These sounds are sent out in waves around them as they fly, and when these sounds hit an object such as a tree branch or perhaps a flying insect they bounce back and are picked up by the bats ears (or again their noses in specially adapted species). The sounds are then processed in the bats brain to produce a 'sound picture' of their environment. These animals are so well adapted that they can hear where insects as small as 1mm long are, and work out the direction and speed that they are flying. This is even more amazing when you think that they do all of this while they themselves are twisting and turning in very fast flight in complete darkness. These bats are very beneficial to man. They eat vast quantities of insects that are pests to farmers and even the smallest species of bat can eat up to 3,000 mosquitoes per night, helping to keep the numbers of these malaria-carrying insects at manageable levels.

Insectivores

This is a group of small insect-eating mammals that to date have been little studied in The Gambia. The **African four-toed hedgehog**, *Atelerix albiventris*, has been recorded at scattered locations around the country, including in Abuko Nature Reserve (though we have lived there for three years and have never seen one). Other species include the giant shrew, *Crocidura olivieri*, and the savanna shrews, *C. nanilla* and *C. lamottei*.

Hares

The **scrub hare**, *Lepus saxatilis*, is a widespread and common species throughout The Gambia. Locals often refer to it as the 'rabbit'. It is generally solitary and nocturnal, living in any area where there is tall grass or scrub.

Rodents

The rodents are a large group of poorly studied animals within The Gambia and contain a variety of species from the very large porcupines to the tiny pygmy mouse, *Mus musculoides*, which weighs between 2–3g. One thing that they all have in common is that they eat vegetable matter such as grass, fruits and seeds, and they all have teeth that are constantly growing and therefore need to be kept worn down by gnawing. The **crested porcupine**, *Hystrix cristata*, is widespread but nocturnal and difficult to see, though probably common. Its relative, the **brush-tailed porcupine**, *Atherus africanus*, has only been recorded by the coast at places like Bijilo Forest Park and Abuko Nature Reserve.

On a walk or drive through the countryside you are much more likely to see squirrels. Two species, the **striped ground squirrel**, *Xerus erythropus*, and the **Gambian sun squirrel**, *Heliosciurus gambianus*, are particularly common. The former is almost always seen on the ground and can be identified by the white stripe along its flank. The latter is found mainly in trees and has a black and white ringed tail. The **red-legged sun squirrel**, *Heliosciurus rufobrachium*, can also be seen at Abuko Nature Reserve, where it is an uncommon resident of the gallery forest. It is slightly larger than the Gambian sun squirrel and can be identified by its red legs. There are also numerous species of rats, mice and gerbils, including the very common (and edible) **giant pouched rat**, *Cricetomys gambianus*, a completely harmless animal that can weigh up to 1.4kg. This species is grey in colour with a long, naked tail that is white for the last half of its length. This is not really a 'rat', in spite of its English name, but belongs to a very old family of rodents found only in Africa. It has large cheek pouches that it stuffs with food, then it carries the food to an underground den where it stores it so that it can be eaten at leisure and in relative safety.

Small carnivores

Small carnivores are common in The Gambian countryside, but you have to be lucky to see any, as they are elusive and mostly nocturnal. The species recorded so far include **side-striped jackal**, *Canis adustus*, which is widespread and **sand fox**, *Vulpes pallida*, which appears to be restricted to the north bank of the River Gambia. **African clawless otter**, *Aonyx capensis*, inhabit many wetlands, especially the mangrove creeks, and this is the largest species of otter found in Africa. The black and white striped **zorilla**, *Ictonyx striatus*, is a skunk-like animal that has been rarely recorded in The Gambia, along with the **honey badger**, *Mellivora capensis*, otherwise known as the **ratel**. The ratel is a small but ferocious carnivore that is well known because of its habit of raiding bee nests for their honey. The shaggy, dog-like, **African civet**, *Civettictis civetta*, with its ornate pattern of blotches, spots and stripes, and a boldly marked face, is said to be common. There are three species of **genet** (looking almost like a cross between a spotted cat and a mongoose) which are very good climbers and feed on fruit, insects, snakes, birds and rodents. The **two-spotted palm civet**, *Nandinia binotata*, is a similar-looking animal that has only ever been recorded in Abuko Nature Reserve in The Gambia, and which may now be extinct. Five species of mongoose are found in The Gambia. These range from the pack-living **banded mongoose**, *Mungos mungo*, which may be seen hunting in the daylight in and around Kiang West National Park, to the nocturnal and very common **marsh mongoose**, *Atilax paludinosus*, which lives a mostly solitary existence. This animal has extremely nimble fingers and survives by capturing crabs at the water's edge. The **African wild cat**, *Felis silvestris*, looks very like a domestic tabby and may be the commonest of the cats in The Gambia. Other species include the rare lynx-like **caracal**, *Caracal caracal*, with a reddish-fawn coat, and the long-legged and beautifully spotted **serval,** *Felis serval*, which are both widespread but uncommon. Identifying any of these species can be difficult. If you are really interested we suggest you invest in Jonathan Kingdon's excellent *Field Guide to African Mammals* (see *Appendix 2: Further Reading*).

Large carnivores

The commonest large predator is the **spotted hyena**, *Crocuta crocuta*. It appears to be fairly widespread, though usually in the more remote regions upcountry.

This animal is a powerfully built, dog-like predator, with high shoulders and long muscular limbs. The body colour varies a great deal and consists of various shades of brown and slate in young animals and pale tawny in older animals. The neck, body and legs are splattered with irregular spots and blotches that become fainter with age. The muzzle is black, as is the tip of the short, brushy tail.

The hyena has a complex social life in which the female plays the dominant role in a clan. Members of a clan seldom assemble together at one place but a communal den shared by up to ten females is a social gathering place for them and their dependent and older offspring. Amongst clan members the ties are very strong, and clans will defend territories and engage in communal hunting. However, individuals also spend much of their time as solitary wanderers searching the landscape for carrion.

Hyenas are normally nocturnal and are seldom seen, though their loud, repetitive and reverberating hoot 'whoo-up' carries for up to 5km.

Often thought of as large animals like their relatives the lions, **leopards**, *Panthera pardus*, are in fact medium sized, with only the largest males reaching up to 2m in length and weighing up to a maximum of 90kg. Females are much smaller, weighing at most around 60kg. They are found throughout Africa and without doubt are the commonest of all the 'big cats' in Africa as a whole.

Leopards can occupy rather small territories of perhaps only 10km², but this is only where food is abundant. In The Gambia we imagine that they probably hold territories that are much larger than this, as prey is scarcer in a country that is so heavily populated in many areas. For most of the time they are solitary animals, living and hunting on their own. Only when a pair of leopards is courting or when a mother is bringing up her cubs, are you likely to see more than one animal together. Leopards are very adept at remaining concealed in dense vegetation, aided by their beautiful colouring, which also provides a very practical camouflage.

Only 40 years ago leopards were so common that they could be watched quite regularly on the outskirts of Banjul, and 30 years ago there was at least one leopard in Abuko Nature Reserve. These days they are much harder to find and seem to have shrunk to small populations inhabiting the most remote parts of the countryside, such as the national parks.

Dolphins

Watching dolphins in the wild is possibly the ultimate wildlife experience. Who can remain untouched by a school of dolphins riding the bow-waves of a boat or leaping out of the water? Several tour operators and hotels offer dolphin-watching trips on The River Gambia.

At least two species of dolphin are regularly sighted – the **Atlantic hump-backed dolphin**, *Sousa teuszii*, and the **bottlenose dolphin**, *Tursiops truncatus*.

The distribution of the two species within The Gambia is unclear at the moment but both are commonly seen off the coast, especially from Jinack Island in Niumi National Park. The bottlenose dolphin is also known to swim upriver as far as Mansa Konko. They are frequently sighted east of the Tanbi wetland complex (south of Banjul) and across the river by Dog Island. They have also been known to enter *bolons* in both Niumi and Kiang West national parks. Apart from specialised boat trips laid on to see dolphins they can also sometimes be seen from the deck of the Banjul to Barra ferry.

The Atlantic hump-backed dolphin is generally the smaller of the two species, with an adult length of 2–2.5m and a weight of 100–150kg. It may be confused with the bottlenose dolphin but can be recognised by the conspicuous, elongated hump in the middle of its back, and a relatively small dorsal fin on top. The dolphin has broad flippers with rounded tips and a long slender beak. The colour is slate-grey on the back and sides, with the underside usually paler. The body may be speckled. This species usually swims in groups of three to seven animals, but sometimes larger schools of up to 40 have been sighted off the coast. They appear to prefer shallow coastal and estuarine water less than 20m deep, especially around mangrove swamps. They are often quite difficult to approach and tend to avoid boats by diving and reappearing some distance away in a different location. They surface every 40–60 seconds but can stay underwater for several minutes. They rarely ride the bow-waves of boats, but in Mauritania they are well known for cooperating with fisherman by driving fish towards their nets.

The bottlenose dolphin can grow up to 3.9m long and weigh anything between 150–650kg. They appear to be a uniform, quite featureless, grey colour with an off-white, light grey or pinkish underside. Their main distinguishing features are their prominent, dark dorsal fin and their inquisitive and active behaviour. They are usually found in groups of one to ten animals but up to 500 have been seen together offshore. They are highly active dolphins at the surface, frequently bow and wake riding and sometimes leaping several metres high out of the water. They are powerful swimmers but their dives rarely last longer than 3–4 minutes.

Aardvarks

The **aardvark**, or ant bear, *Orycteropus afer*, is a strange-looking nocturnal creature that is said to be widespread. It is a large animal with a very long nose, squared-off head and long rabbit-like ears. It spends the day living underground in warrens and even when foraging above ground at night, it is very shy, so seldom spotted. It feeds by digging out colonies of ants and termites and sweeping up the insects into its small mouth with its long, sticky tongue.

Manatees

The **West African manatee**, *Trichechus senegalensis*, is large and cylindrical in shape, reaching a length of up to 3.6m and weighing in at between 350–450kg. It has a dark grey wrinkled skin, which is lighter underneath and is almost entirely hairless except for whiskers on its upper lip. Often manatees can look green as the 5cm thick skin on the back is sometimes covered with a growth of algae. The thick, fleshy upper lip is quite mobile and the head is rounded with very small eyes, no external ears and small round nostrils on the top of the large muzzle. The body tapers into a tail that ends in a rounded tail fin. The front limbs have evolved into short flippers, each with three rudimentary nails. The hind limbs are no longer outwardly present.

The manatee is found far up the River Gambia, from the mouth of the river to at least as far as Baboon Islands, though there has been no recent work to discover just how far or how many there are in The Gambia. The West African manatee is now considered endangered throughout its range.

Manatees are entirely aquatic and cannot come out on to the land at all. They are superbly adapted to an aquatic existence with nostrils and eyes placed on top of the head so that they can remain almost entirely submerged but can still breath and see above the surface. They can dive for up to 15 minutes in an emergency, though an ordinary dive only lasts between 1–2 minutes. To help them dive their nostrils close with the aid of a valve and oily tear ducts allow them to see under the water. Their normal speed is around 10km per hour but when frightened they can swim at considerably faster speeds.

Manatees live mostly in estuaries, coastal lagoons and large rivers and are sometimes encountered in the sea in shallow coastal waters. They are wholly vegetarian, eating a variety of water plants and the leaves of mangroves and other vegetation overhanging the water.

Ungulates

We hardly have to describe what a **hippopotamus**, *Hippopotamus amphibius*, looks like since it is surely well known to just about everyone. Yet here are a few facts and figures about hippos to amaze you: the length of a hippo's head and body can be anywhere between 2.8 and 3.5m; the weight of an adult female can be up to 2,000kg, but large males can weigh in at a staggering 3,200kg.

In The Gambia, hippos can be found upriver from Elephant Island, but they also come closer to the coast and have been seen as near as Kiang West National Park. It is thought that maybe one hundred hippos survive in the country, but we have to say that this is pure conjecture as no recent surveys of the population have been carried out. There are many existing and potential conflicts between people and hippos, not least of which is that hippos cause considerable damage to agricultural crops on the riverbanks, especially rice fields.

Hippos spend the day submerged in deep water and emerge from the river just before darkness falls to graze on grassland nearby for four to five hours before returning to the water to digest the food they have eaten.

The bushpig, more correctly known as the **common warthog**, *Phacochoerus africanus*, is a widespread and common animal upcountry, where in many areas it is the only remaining large wild mammal. On the whole this is because the majority of the Gambian population is Muslim, and therefore does not eat pork. This does not mean to say that Gambians and warthogs live in perfect harmony as these animals can be quite a pest of farmer's crops and are hunted because of the damage that they do. Some warthogs are also hunted to provide meat for restaurants, especially in the tourist areas.

The warthog is a large animal, with males weighing up to 150kg, though females are normally a lot smaller with a maximum weight of 75kg. It is a relatively long-legged but short-necked pig with prominent curved tusks. The skin is almost naked though there is a crest of lank dark hair extending from the crown to the nape of the neck and hanging over the shoulders. The 'warts' are three pairs of thickened pads of skin that protect the jaws, eyes and muzzle. Warthogs prefer to live in lightly wooded, bush and savanna habitats.

There are several species of antelope that are thought to live wild and free in The Gambia. However the status of most of them is uncertain and a few of them may even be extinct within the country now. The two most common species are the bushbuck and Maxwell's duiker.

The **bushbuck**, *Tragelaphus scriptus*, is extremely common and widespread. It is coated with red fur, though mature males become progressively darker with age. It has a white underside to the broad woolly tail, with white flashes above black hooves and white markings on the face and ears. There are a number of subspecies within its range that have differing amounts of markings on the body but nowhere is the animal more prettily marked than in West Africa, with both vertical and horizontal white stripes and numerous spots on the haunches. The bushbuck is rather shy and has a preference to hide by day in deep cover. Because of their beautiful markings and colour, a bushbuck standing still can remain virtually invisible, but when disturbed they will bound off through the vegetation in a blaze of noise and movement, often accompanied by a loud bark of warning to other bushbuck in the vicinity. In Abuko Nature Reserve there is a very large population present. Here, they are also relatively accustomed to people and easy to see.

In contrast **Maxwell's duiker**, *Cephalophus maxwelli*, is a tiny antelope that is often very hard to spot as it makes its way through the grass and trees. Most sightings are made as it crosses open paths. Again it is very common at Abuko and this is one of the best places to see it. They are just over 30cm in height, with a maximum weight of 5.4kg. This is a species adapted to living in forests and they are fruit-eaters in the main, but will also take a variety of leaves and shoots and will even eat ants and other insects. They can often be found following troops of monkeys, waiting for them to drop some half-eaten fruit on the ground.

The **sitatunga**, *Tragelaphus spekei*, is a large but secretive antelope that happily is still present in fair numbers along the banks of The River Gambia. A small population of five animals was introduced to Abuko Nature Reserve some time ago. Sadly, it appears that the sitatunga is now extinct in this reserve. This is not that surprising as the habitat present at Abuko is no longer ideal for this animal. The sitatunga is associated with marshes and other wetland areas, rather than forest. Probably the best site in the whole country for observing sitatunga, as they emerge from cover to feed, is along the southern bank of the River Gambia in Kiang West National Park.

Kiang also proves its worth as the only place that you are ever likely to see a **roan antelope**, *Hippotragus equinus*, in The Gambia. This is one of the largest antelopes in Africa, and is a very impressive and powerful looking creature. Males may weigh up to 300kg with a head and body length of up to 240cm. They are tall, with thick necks and massive arched horns that may reach 100cm in length in males. There is a herd of these magnificent antelopes that frequently wanders into Kiang from southern Senegal during the wet season.

Reptiles

Crocodiles have changed very little in the last 65 million years and are perfectly adapted to living in water. Their eyes and nostrils are located on top of the head and they have webbed hind feet. Their nostrils also have watertight valves and there is a flap at the back of the throat, which allows them to feed underwater.

There are three species of crocodile present in The Gambia. The **African slender-snouted crocodile**, *Crocodylus cataphractus*, has been recorded upriver in the vicinity of Georgetown and the River Gambia National Park. However there have been no reliable reports of this species for over a decade. The **dwarf crocodile**, *Osteolaemus tetraspis*, has fared a little better and survived as a small population at Abuko Nature Reserve. This small crocodile is nocturnal and a forest dweller, where it breeds in pools as small as 1m². It does not visit larger pools, as it is not a very good swimmer. The third species is the **Nile crocodile**, *C. niloticus*. Although widespread along the River Gambia and many of its *bolons*, information on its status is very scarce. Fortunately the future of the Nile crocodile is almost assured thanks to human intervention. A small population of this species is fully protected in Abuko

Nature Reserve where its habitat is carefully managed by the Department of Parks and Wildlife Management. Early in the wet season the crocodiles breed close to the education centre in the reserve. Even more significant than the group at Abuko are the populations present at the three sacred crocodile pools. There is one such pool on the north bank of the River Gambia, at Berending, one in the southern part of the country at Kartung and the most famous of them all at Katchikally, in Bakau. This last pool, although small, has a large crocodile population. Not only do these pools protect wild populations of this species but they may also act as breeding and dispersal centres where excess animals can bolster the wider crocodile population.

Nile crocodiles can live for up to a hundred years in the wild and can attain a length of 6m, with a weight exceeding 1,000kg. We have personally seen a crocodile this large in the Niji Bolon on the north bank of the River Gambia.

Marine turtles are represented by perhaps five species in Gambian coastal waters. All turtles are tied to land for reproduction and must face many dangers as they haul themselves on to the shore to lay their eggs. In the sea they are powerful and elegant swimmers that cover vast distances during their lifetimes. On shore they are heavy, clumsy creatures that must drag their huge weight through soft sand using only the massive strength of their flippers.

Hawksbill, *Eretmochelys imbricata*, **olive-ridley**, *Lepidochelys olivacea*, and **loggerhead**, *Caretta caretta*, turtles are all thought to live along the coast but it is unknown whether they use Gambian beaches to breed. The giant **leatherback turtle**, *Dermochelys coriacea*, which can reach a length of 180cm and an incredible weight of 646kg, is probably by far the scarcest species inhabiting Gambian waters. To date only two specimens have been found on beaches, both of which were dead. This species is easy to identify as it lacks a horny shell, being covered instead with thick, smooth skin that resembles vulcanised rubber. The skin has five long ridges along the back, one each on either side, and five underneath.

The turtle found in greatest numbers along the coast of The Gambia is the **green turtle**, *Chelonia mydas*. This is also a very large species, reaching a maximum length of 140cm and a weight of 300kg. It has a smooth, hard shell, the head is compact and relatively small and both sexes have tails. This species is known to breed on Gambian beaches.

Lizards are the most familiar of the reptiles. There can hardly be a house or compound in the country that does not have a resident gecko or agama. One of the unique features that characterise lizards is their ability to shed their tails when grabbed by a predator. The hunter is then left with a jerking tail in its mouth while the lizard makes its escape to safety. The lizard simply grows a new tail afterwards, though this is seldom as good as the first.

The largest group of lizards in The Gambia is the geckos, and five species have been found here. These common lizards have amazingly adapted feet and eyes. Gecko feet have toe-tips that have groups of scales covered in masses of minute hairs that allow them to 'stick' to seemingly smooth surfaces, even glass. The eyes have transparent eyelids that are fused permanently and thus cover the eye with a 'spectacle 'that protects it. Geckos are found in many habitats, but are best known as living in houses where they happily feed on a diet of insects such as cockroaches, mosquitoes, flies and crickets. Geckos are mainly nocturnal and adapted to living in cooler temperatures than many other lizards. One of the most common species is **Brook's house gecko**, *Hemidactylus brooki angulatus*.

Skinks are another large group of lizards. Four species are found in The Gambia. They look much more like typical lizards than geckos, are mainly ground dwelling and are active during the day. They feed almost exclusively on small insects, which they seize in their jaws after a short rush from cover. The **orange-flanked skink**,

Mabuya perrotetii, and the **brown-flanked skink**, *M. affinis*, both appear to be extremely common and widespread in many different habitats, even in and around urban areas, though the former is normally only active during the wet season. The other two species of skink are much rarer. The **snake-eyed skink**, *Leptosiaphus nimbaense*, has only been found once at Abuko Nature Reserve. **Armitage's skink**, *Chalcides armitagei*, has only ever been found in a small part of The Gambia and nowhere else in the world. Very little is known about the species and it appears only to live in a very short strip of coastal scrub.

The **agama**, or **rainbow lizard**, *Agama agama*, is found almost everywhere in all types of habitat. During the dry season they are generally dull brown in colour, but a month or so before the rains begin the females develop a bight orange patch along their flank and the males become very gaudy in colour with yellow heads and bright blue bodies. You can often see the males displaying to one another, with their front feet planted firmly on the ground and their heads bobbing up and down. The agama is active during the day and feeds almost exclusively on termites and ants.

Chameleons are unmistakable lizards and are famous for their ability to change the colour of their skin to match their background and mood. There are two species of chameleon in The Gambia, *Chamaeleo gracilis* and *C. senegalensis*, which look fairly similar. Chameleons have toes that are bound together and oppose so that they can effectively grip branches. Their tails are prehensile and unlike those of geckos, agamas and skinks they cannot be shed or regenerated. The eyes of chameleons appear to be placed in turrets and move independently of one another as they search for food. Insects form the main prey of these creatures. These are caught with a telescopic tongue (sometimes the tongue is longer than the chameleons body) which can be shot out and has a sticky pad at its tip.

Last but no means least are the monitor lizards. There are two species in The Gambia, **Bosc's monitor**, *Varanus exanthematicus*, and the **Nile monitor**, *V. niloticus*. The latter is the commonest and also the largest of all the monitor lizards in Africa, reaching a maximum length of 2m. They are powerful looking animals, with well-developed limbs and strong claws. They have a long tail and a long flexible neck. These lizards are real predators and will eat almost anything from insects to birds and mice. They will also dig up and eat the eggs of turtles and crocodiles and even catch and eat young crocodiles that have just hatched. The Nile monitor is a great swimmer and therefore is usually found in or near water, while Bosc's monitor is found in more arid areas, mostly during the wet season.

At least 37 species of **snake** have been identified in The Gambia, though most of these are rarely seen or are confined to certain, restricted habitats such as gallery forest. However, some species are widespread, and can be found in the bush, woodlands, gardens and wasteland. The most likely snakes that you may see are the beauty snakes, pythons and cobras.

Only nine Gambian snakes are regarded as being seriously venomous and dangerous to humans. Snakes do not strike at people because they wish to kill them or eat them. Snakes strike because they are stood on by accident or because they are cornered and cannot escape, because they are frightened or because they are protecting their young just as a human mother would protect her children. The ordinary town dweller or visitor is unlikely to even see a snake, never mind being struck by one.

However, if you do see a snake, then do not go near it or attempt to catch it. Back away and leave it in peace and it will do the same to you. Often a snake will see you before you see it, and will rapidly slide away in fear.

Although feared by people, snakes are not the most dangerous animals in the country. To put it in perspective, many more people die from malaria, which is carried by the humble mosquito.

Amphibians

The **square-marked toad**, or **common African toad**, *Bufo regularis*, is probably the commonest amphibian in The Gambia, and the most easily encountered. It is a typical large and compact toad with a warty skin. It is dark olive brown in colour and the skin between the tiny warts on its sides often appears almost black. It is covered by dark patches that are often arranged more or less symmetrically on the back, looking like pairs of dark squares running along either side of the spine – hence one of its English names. In addition younger animals have a light stripe which runs along the backbone, sometimes yellow in colour, though this often fades in older animals.

This toad is encountered in most types of habitats, including coastal scrub and woodland, forest, farmland, swamps and even in urban areas, especially in the irrigated grounds of hotels and gardens. However, its main natural habitat appears to be Guinea savanna. Toads must keep their skin moist in order to survive. They do this by becoming nocturnal, hiding by day beneath rocks and fallen logs, or in holes, and emerging at night to hunt. Their favourite prey appears to be ants, but other insects are also eaten, with termites making up a larger proportion of their diet in damper weather.

Adult toads make up the diet of a lot of other creatures, including Nile monitors, crocodiles, herons and egrets. We once saw a **black forest cobra**, *Naja melanoleuca*, eat three toads in the space of five minutes!

There are at least 21 species of amphibians found in The Gambia, ranging from toads through bullfrogs to reed and tree frogs. During the wet season every pond has its own chorus of singing frogs.

Fish

Fish not only play a large role in the ecology of Gambian waters, but they are also the mainstay of a thriving local industry. Saltwater fishes are common in the shallow seas off the coast. Walk along any beach and you will see dozens of dead fish washed up on the tideline, including stingrays and triggerfish. If you are really interested, a visit to one of the many fishing villages, such as at Tanji, especially when the catches are being brought in, will satisfy even the most ardent of fishwatchers. Commonly caught fish include **bonga**, *Ethmalosa fimbriata*, and **African red snapper**, *Lutjanus agennes*, but even larger species such as sharks are sometimes landed. Along the River Gambia and its *bolons*, there is a small-scale fishing industry that provides much of the protein needs of the Gambian population. The Gambia is also well known throughout the world for its sports fishing, and indeed some of the largest specimens of freshwater fish ever caught in the world have been caught here by keen foreign anglers.

Tilapia and mullets are perhaps the most common fish in the country. The juveniles of these can be found in vast quantities amongst the mangroves, which act as a natural nursery-ground. These fish in turn provide food for huge numbers of fish-eating birds such as herons, egrets, ospreys and fish eagles.

Perhaps the strangest fish of all, and one which you are bound to see wherever there are mangroves, is the **Atlantic mudskipper**, *Periophthalmus papillo*. When the tide is out and the mud is exposed, mudskippers can be seen creeping about using their strong pectoral fins like miniature legs. They are sometimes mistaken for amphibians, but they are true fish, and have developed their walking ability so well that they can even climb up on to the exposed lower roots of the mangroves.

Crabs

The most abundant species of crab in The Gambia is the **West African fiddler crab**, *Uca tangeri*. This species can be seen in huge numbers on the mud alongside mangrove swamps. The males have one small claw and one large claw that they wave around to warn off other males and to attract females.

A walk on the beach at night with a flashlight is the best way to see **African ghost crabs**, *Ocypoda africana*. They inhabit the shore-line and have distinctive eyes on long stalks. They will often scuttle off into the surf and all you can then see is the tops of the eyes looking at you from above the water like miniature periscopes.

Insects

Of all of the creatures inhabiting our world, the insects are by far the most numerous. Science has recognised over one million species in the world so far, and there are many, many more that as yet remain undiscovered and undescribed.

For this reason it is obviously not possible to write about all of the insects in The Gambia in a short section, so we will give a general account that will hopefully give you an overview of this diverse and fascinating group of animals. We have selected some species which are common and therefore more likely to be seen, and those that are particularly interesting or important to people.

Dragonflies and **damselflies** are brightly coloured insects, some quite large, with long transparent wings. They are remarkable fliers, being able to hover with ease and even fly backwards. They live most of their lives as nymphs beneath the surface of ponds, streams and rivers. Dragonflies are voracious predators, both as nymphs, and later, as they emerge, as flying adults. They are very beneficial insects, eating millions of small insects such as mosquitoes, each year. Very common species include the **scarlet dragonfly**, *Crocothemis erythraea*, which is bright red, and the **globe skimmer**, *Pantala flavescens*, a dull brown species that can be found almost everywhere in the tropics. An uncommon species in The Gambia is the **Emperor dragonfly**, *Anax imperator*. This is a large blue-bodied dragonfly that can also be found in many parts of Europe. Altogether there are over 70 species of dragonflies and damselflies in The Gambia.

Stick insects are long and slender, with long very thin legs and antennae. They are coloured brown or green and spend long periods remaining absolutely still, making them very difficult to find as they look just like twigs or sticks. Some species can grow as large as 10–12cm. They are all vegetarian but do not usually occur in large enough numbers to cause damage. They can usually be found hiding amongst grass stems.

Cockroaches are well-known to many of us. Originating in the tropics, they are now found almost everywhere around the world. Although some species are considered pests because they damage books and clothes, and contaminate foodstuffs, many are found only in forests and the bush and cause no harm to man whatsoever.

Mantids always give the impression of being alert and intelligent animals because their long neck allows them to twist their head and follow movement with their eyes, but really they are no more intelligent than other insects. They are beneficial because they prey on many species that are pests. They have well-developed wings and fly mostly at night when they are attracted to lights. Beware, the larger specimens have powerful jaws and can inflict a painful bite. The front legs of mantids are wonderful adaptations for seizing other insects with lightning force before being drawn to the mouth and eaten.

Ants, wasps are bees are all highly social insects, though some species live solitary existences. There are hundreds, if not thousands, of species in West Africa, but some of the most interesting and in many ways most frightening, are the **army ants**, or **driver ants**. This ant travels in dense columns that may be hundreds of metres long. The workers are blind, with large powerful jaws. The queen is seldom seen but is three or four times the size of the workers and is also blind. There is also a soldier caste with very large toothed jaws. They all have a powerful bite and once their jaws are locked into position it is very difficult to make them let go. They were once used to suture open wounds by getting them to bite both edges of the wound together, then twisting off their bodies and leaving the head and jaws in place. Their nest is formed in the ground and colonies can contain hundreds of thousands of individuals. Periodically the nests will move, and this is when the ants form a column. Eggs, larvae, pupa and food are carried by the workers who are flanked and protected by the soldiers. If you happen to step on to a column by mistake you will be instantly subjected to numerous and painful bites! When a nest has moved the ants then spread out and forage over a wide area. They are mainly carnivorous and have been known to kill and devour animals as large as pythons. Chickens and guineafowl have been stripped to the bone by these ants in hen houses where they cannot escape, and there are stories of tethered horses being eaten in the same way. In contrast, the males are large winged insects that are entirely harmless. They are known as 'sausage ants' and are often attracted to lights in the evening. A good place to see army ants is at Abuko Nature Reserve, where columns are frequently seen crossing the footpaths.

A common feature of the countryside are **termite** mounds. These massive castle-like structures have smooth ventilation shafts that keep the inside of the nest at a constant temperature. These are often used as hiding places by snakes, bats and other animals, so never stick your hand down one! Termites are seldom seen during the day and are mostly small and inoffensive, although they can cause considerable damage to wooden buildings. They are highly social insects with a queen, kings, workers and soldiers. The latter caste guard the nests and have ferocious bites.

The rainy season is undoubtedly the best time to see a huge variety of differently coloured **butterflies**, of which there are over 170 species in The Gambia, but there are also many that fly during the dry season. Below we have selected two species that can be commonly seen during the whole year and are fairly easy to identify.

The first of these species is a butterfly that everyone in The Gambia will see at one time or another, for it is extremely common. It is the **citrus swallowtail**, *Papilio demodocus*. This species is large, with a wingspan of between 7–11cm. It is mainly blackish but also heavily marked and dusted with yellow. There is a yellow band across the hindwing and a similar but broken yellow band on the forewing. On each hind wing there are two large blue, black and orange-marked eyespots. The edges of the hindwings are also scalloped. The citrus swallowtail occurs in open country, cultivated areas, gardens and forest margins.

The caterpillar of the citrus swallowtail is very commonly found on cultivated and wild citrus trees such as orange, lime, grapefruit and lemon. They devour enormous quantities of leaves and are sometimes considered a pest.

The **African tiger**, *Danaus chrysippus*, is another butterfly that is very common. It is slightly smaller than the citrus swallowtail with a wingspan of around 7–8.5cm. It is an orange-brown butterfly with black borders to the wings and a large triangular black patch on top of the forewings, which encloses several white spots. The form of the African tiger found in West Africa also has a large white patch on the hindwings. Both sexes are almost identical but the male has four black spots on the hindwing while the female has only three. This butterfly has a foul taste and is mimicked by the females of other butterflies, which apparently taste better, so that they can escape the hungry attentions of birds and lizards etc.

The African tiger butterfly can be seen flying in many different habitats, including open and bush country, gardens, woodlands and the margins of forests. Its flight is very slow and sailing, giving the impression of being very relaxed. Sometimes you may come across small groups of them in the evening as they prepare to roost together for the night. The caterpillars are very distinctive: smooth and ringed with yellow and black bands.

Birds

Birds are a major and vital part of every habitat in The Gambia and can be seen just about everywhere. Unlike many of the 'little brown jobs' that can be found in Europe and North America, Gambian birds tend to be more colourful and confiding, therefore making a birdwatching trip to the country a visit to remember. It can also be a great introduction to many species that can be found elsewhere in Africa. Although thousands of birdwatchers visit The Gambia each year, many of them concentrate on the best known and most easily accessible sites. This means that for the more adventurous amongst you there is still a real chance of adding a new species to the country list, as we ourselves have done on several occasions. At least 540 species of birds have so far been seen in The Gambia, which seems a phenomenal number, considering the small size of the country. Yet there are many reasons why this is so, including the vast array of different habitats, ranging from the coast, through salt and freshwater wetlands, Guinea and Sudan savanna, woodlands and forests, to agricultural land, towns and villages. The Gambia is also visited by hundreds of thousands of European birds during the northern winter, as well as smaller numbers of African birds that migrate from the north and south during the summer.

A visit to each habitat will reveal its own specialised birds. Starting at the coast, there are miles of open, gently sloping sandy beaches where the most common birds are the shoreline waders such as **ruddy turnstone**, *Arenaria interpres*, **sanderling**, *Calidris alba*, and **whimbrel**, *Numenius phaeopus*. These are joined by numbers of **western reef heron**, *Egretta gularis*, **grey heron**, *Ardea cinerea*, **osprey**, *Pandion haliaetus*, and **pied kingfisher**, *Ceryle rudis*. Offshore, and around the scattered fishing centres, **grey-headed gulls**, *Larus cirrocephalus*, are numerous, as are various terns. You may be lucky and spot a few **skuas** chasing the other birds and forcing them to drop their hard-earned food, especially around the port at Banjul. Two rarities that are well worth looking out for include the **kelp gull**, *Larus dominicanus*, which we have recently found breeding in The Gambia, and **Audouin's gull**, *Larus audouinii*, a bird of global conservation concern which winters in moderate numbers along the coast.

The next major habitat along the coastline is the mangrove forest, which stretches far inland along the course of the River Gambia. A canoe trip along a mangrove-lined *bolon* is a relaxing and satisfying way to see some serious birds, including pelicans, spoonbills, **yellow-billed stork**, *Mycteria ibis*, and **goliath heron**, *Ardea goliath*, plus lots of waders, especially at the beginning of the dry season. Others to look out for include **blue-cheeked bee-eater**, *Merops persicus*, and **mouse-brown sunbird**, *Anthreptes gabonicus*. The river itself, and its many tributaries, are good places to spot the magnificent **African fish eagle**, *Hieraaetus spilogaster*, perched on an overhanging tree. Other wetland habitats are sure to provide you with a good list of spectacular species such as **African darter**, *Anhinga rufa*, **white-faced whistling duck**, *Dendrocygna viduata*, **sacred ibis**, *Threskiornis aethiopicus*, **palm-nut vulture**, *Gypohierax angolensis*, crakes, **greater painted-snipe**, *Rostratula benghalensis*, and **African jacana**, *Actophilornis africanus* – the famous lili-trotter, just to name a few of the commonest species.

Inland from the coast are the coastal forests, a prime example of which is Bijilo Forest Park, and a few small patches of gallery forest like Abuko Nature Reserve, Pirang Forest Park and The River Gambia National Park. These forests hold small populations of secretive birds such as **grey-headed bristlebill**, *Bleda canicapilla*, **yellowbill**, *Ceuthmochares aereus*, **ahanta francolin**, *Francolinus ahantensis*, **white-spotted flufftail**, *Sarothrura pulchra*, **western bluebill**, *Spermophaga haematina*, and the beautiful **green turaco**, *Tauraco persa*. Walking around the shady footpaths of these forests is like stepping back into primeval times. There are huge buttress-rooted trees and thick tangles of vines and creepers on all sides and the forests echo to the weird calls of birds.

Next we come to the Guinea savanna, which ranges from open areas of grassland through to thickly wooded patches. This is the habitat that once covered huge chunks of the countryside but has gradually been whittled away. Even here though, you will find spectacular birds such as bee-eaters, **green wood-hoopoe**, *Phoeniculus purpureus*, **blue-bellied roller**, *Coaracias cyanogaster*, barbets, **African golden oriole**, *Oriolus auratus*, and the dinosaur-like **Abyssinian ground hornbill**, *Bucorvus abyssinicus* – a huge black bird that stalks through the grass, seldom taking to the air.

Further inland, and also on much of the north bank of the River Gambia, you will see a gradual transition to Sudan savanna, which is much drier and dominated by massive red termite mounds. Look out for a wide range of birds of prey, especially the large and impressive **martial eagle**, *Polemaetus bellicosus*, plus buntings, coursers and sparrow-weavers. In the far north of the country you can find areas of the dry Sahel, which is slowly encroaching southwards, with its sparse vegetation. Look out here for **northern anteater chats**, *Myrmecocichla aethiops*, which at a distance seem very dark until they open their wings in a short flight and reveal large white wing-patches.

Agricultural land ranges from vegetable gardens and dry fields of groundnuts to vast rice-fields whose roots and lower stems are perched in shallow water. These are the special domain of the weavers, finches, doves and glossy starlings, amongst others. Where cattle graze you are also bound to find flocks of **cattle egret**, *Bubulcus ibis*, and **black magpie**, *Ptilostomus afer*, stalking around the feet of the cows and darting after insects that have been disturbed. You should also keep a sharp lookout for the **yellow-billed oxpecker**, *Buphagus africanus*, perched on the back of cattle. Here, they are providing a good service in picking off ticks and other bothersome parasites.

Surprisingly, one of the best habitats for birds comes from a totally unexpected source. These are the grounds of the many hotels that have sprung up along the coast in recent years. A combination of year-round watering and the planting of exotic flowers in hotel gardens attract many birds to these miniature green oases. These include the **long-tailed glossy starling**, *Lamprotornis caudatus*, **yellow-crowned gonolek**, *Laniarius barbarus*, and many different types of brilliantly coloured sunbird. These are considered by some as the most beautiful of all the birds of The Gambia.

If you are a keen birdwatcher then you will need to get a copy of *A Field Guide to Birds of The Gambia and Senegal* as this is without doubt the best field guide on the birds of the region (see *Appendix 2*).

WILDLIFE AND GAMBIAN LAW

In The Gambia the people are very proud of their rich natural heritage. This pride is manifested in many different ways, including the Banjul Declaration of 1977, the provision of seven protected sites totalling nearly 4.2% of the land area, and through the country's far-reaching and forward-thinking wildlife law. The Gambia is also meeting its international obligations in preserving the world's biodiversity by being a signatory to many international conventions, including the Convention on Biodiversity.

One of the tools that the government uses to prevent over-exploitation of its wildlife is the Wildlife Act of 1977. In essence the law is fairly simple: in order to safeguard the country's wildlife and natural history, *all* wildlife is protected by law, and anyone that is found hunting, selling, importing or exporting, or keeping wild animals as pets, is breaking the law and may be prosecuted, fined and imprisoned. The only exception to this rule is the hunting of a number of species that are considered as pests. These include warthog, giant pouched rat and francolin. Such hunting is licensed and organised by the Department of Parks and Wildlife Management.

The Gambia is also a signatory to the Convention on International Trade in Endangered Species of Flora and Fauna (CITES). Please remember this if you are offered any live, or any part of a dead, wild animal to buy (eg: a skin, horns or turtle shell). It is illegal to export any of these items from The Gambia, or even to have them in your possession while in the country.

If you see an infringement of this law during your visit to The Gambia, *please* inform the Wildlife Department (tel: 375888). All information received is treated as strictly confidential. You can help us to safeguard the wildlife of The Gambia.

Spotted hyena

THE BANJUL DECLARATION

It is a sobering reflection that in a relatively short period of our history, most of our larger wildlife species have disappeared together with much of our original forest cover. The survival of the wildlife still remaining with us and the setting aside of protected natural habitats for them is the concern for all of us.

It would be tragic if this priceless natural heritage, the product of millions of years of evolution should be further endangered or lost for want of proper concern. This concern is a duty that we owe to ourselves, to our great African heritage and to the world.

Thus I solemnly declare that my government pledges its untiring efforts to conserve for now and posterity as wide a spectrum as possible of our remaining fauna and flora.

His Excellency the President of the Republic of The Gambia,
Sir Dawda Jawara, February 18 1977

Above Roots festival, Banjul (AVZ)

Left Woman in traditional dress,
Roots festival, Banjul (AVZ)

Below Yellow-crowned gonolek (AVZ)

Above Marabout house, Toniataba, near Soma (AVZ)

Left Xylophonist at stone circles, Wassu (AVZ)

Below Man playing instrument, Basse Santa Su (AVZ)

Health and Safety

Written in collaboration with Dr Jane Wilson-Howarth and Dr Felicity Nicholson

Many people who travel to Africa for the first time have preconceived ideas about what life out here is like. For example, we remember being asked when we first came to live in The Gambia whether we would be living in a mud hut! It took a long time for this (unnamed) person to be convinced that no, we wouldn't be living in a mud hut, but actually in a rather neat bungalow with running water and electricity. It took even longer to convince her (in fact we don't think we ever really did) that we would do our shopping in modern supermarkets and that we would also be able to watch TV when we wanted, and would even be able to hire the odd video from a video shop to watch in the evenings. Many first-timers also believe that they will be living in the jungle faced with hosts of dangerous animals such as snakes, lions and crocodiles. While this is certainly true for some parts of Africa, nowadays, huge chunks of this vast continent have been converted to farmland or ranches, or covered in concrete and tarmac. Africa is no longer the dark continent as described by Livingstone and other explorers of the Victorian age, but is slowly catching up with the more developed countries of the West.

In the same way, many people also believe that they will be faced by all sorts of nameless tropical diseases during their visit. In a way, this is partly true, as there are lots of tropical diseases here, including malaria. But by taking a few simple precautions you can significantly reduce your chances of contracting any of them, and enjoy a safe, pleasant holiday. This chapter tells you how to take those precautions and you should read it carefully before starting your trip.

By way of reassurance, you have a much greater chance of being hit by a speeding, badly driven car in The Gambia than of being bitten by a venomous snake, standing on a scorpion, or catching an incurable disease. Remember that millions of Africans live long and happy lives here all of the time.

HEALTH
Preparations
Do please read this entire section. There are things you should be doing *well in advance* of travelling to The Gambia. When you read it, consider all the points it makes, but pay particular attention to malaria prevention.

Travel insurance
Our advice is that you should never travel without comprehensive medical travel insurance, especially insurance that will pay for your return home in the event of medical emergency. There are lots of insurance policies to choose from, including those offered by the tour company that flies you over. However, always read the small print thoroughly as not all policies cover the cost of an airfare home. One policy that doesn't cost too much but has a very good reputation is offered by ISIS, available in the UK from STA (tel: 020 7361 6160).

Immunisation

At the time of writing there are no immunisations that were obligatory for entry into The Gambia for travellers from Europe. However, it is a wise precaution to have a yellow fever immunisation, as you may be required to show an international yellow fever immunisation certificate on entry to the country as proof that you have had it. If you are entering The Gambia from other destinations, especially from other African countries that have a yellow fever problem, you are required to have had the relevant immunisation and an immunisation certificate as proof. The certificate is not valid until ten days after your vaccination, so make sure you have your vaccination in good time. If you are intending to travel beyond The Gambia, you need to know that certain countries in sub-Saharan Africa also require a certificate for cholera. In the UK this vaccine is no longer given as it is ineffective, but certificates of exemption can be acquired from immunisation centres.

It is also wise to be up to date on tetanus (ten-yearly), polio (ten-yearly), diphtheria (ten-yearly), hepatitis A and typhoid immunisations. In addition, immunisations against meningococcal meningitis and rabies are also worth considering.

Most travellers are advised to have immunisation against hepatitis A with hepatitis A vaccine (such as Havrix Monodose or Avaxim). One dose of vaccine lasts for a year and can be boosted to give protection for up to ten years. The course of two injections costs about £100. This vaccine can be used close to the time of departure. The newer typhoid vaccines last for three years and are about 75% effective. You should really consider being immunised against hepatitis A unless you are leaving within a few days for a trip of a week or less, when this vaccine would not be effective in time.

Vaccinations for rabies are advised for travellers visiting more remote areas, and for those who are intending to work with animals. Ideally, three injections should be taken over a period of four weeks at 0, 7 and 28 days. The timing of these doses does not have to be exact and a schedule can be arranged to suit you. (see *Rabies* in this chapter).

Hepatitis B vaccination should be considered if you plan a longer trip (two months or more) or if you will be working in situations where contact with blood or children is increased. A course of three injections is ideal and these can be given at 0, 4 and 8 weeks prior to travel or, if there is insufficient time, on days 0, 7–14, and 21–28. The only vaccine licensed for the latter more rapid course at the time of printing is Engerix B. The longer course is always to be preferred as the immunity it confers is likely to be longer lasting. A BCG vaccination against tuberculosis (TB) is also advised for trips of two months or more and this should be taken at least six weeks before travel.

If you feel you need several immunisations then you should visit your own doctor or travel clinic (see below) to discuss your requirements about eight weeks before you plan to travel, so that you have time to complete all of the courses. This is also a good idea as it gives your arms a chance to rest between jabs.

Travel clinics
United Kingdom

British Airways Travel Clinic and Immunisation Service 156 Regent St, London W1; tel: 020 7439 9584. This place also sells travellers' supplies and has a branch of Stanford's travel book and map shop. There are now BA clinics all around Britain and three in South Africa. To find your nearest one, call 01276 685040.

Fleet Street Travel Clinic 29 Fleet Street, London EC4Y 1AA; tel: 020 7353 5678

MASTA (Medical Advisory Service for Travellers Abroad) Keppel St, London WC1 7HT; tel:

09068 224100. This is a premium-line number, charged at 50p per minute.

NHS travel website, www.fitfortravel.scot.nhs.uk, provides country-by-country advice on immunisation and malaria, plus details of recent developments, and a list of relevant health organisations.

Nomad Travel Pharmacy and Vaccination Centre 3–4 Wellington Terrace, Turnpike Lane, London N8 0PX; tel: 020 8889 7014

Thames Medical 157 Waterloo Rd, London SE1 8US; tel: 020 7902 9000. Competitively priced, one-stop travel health service. All profits go to their affiliated company InterHealth which provides health care for overseas workers on Christian projects.

Trailfinders Immunisation Centre 194 Kensington High St, London W8 7RG; tel: 020 7938 3999. Also at 254–284 Sauchiehall St, Glasgow G2 3EH; tel: 0141 353 0066.

Irish Republic
Tropical Medical Bureau Grafton Street Medical Centre, Grafton Buildings, 34 Grafton Street, Dublin 2; tel: 1 671 9200. This organisation has a useful website specific to tropical destinations: www.tmb.ie.

USA
Centers for Disease Control 1600 Clifton Road, Atlanta, GA 30333; tel: 877 FYI TRIP; 800 311 3435; web: www.cdc.gov/travel. This organisation is the central source of travel information in the USA. Each summer they publish the invaluable Health Information for International Travel which is available from the Division of Quarantine at the above address.

Connaught Laboratories PO Box 187, Swiftwater, PA 18370; tel: 800 822 2463. They will send a free list of specialist tropical-medicine physicians in your state.

IAMAT (International Association for Medical Assistance to Travelers) 736 Center St, Lewiston, NY 14092. A non-profit organisation which provides lists of English-speaking doctors abroad.

Canada
IAMAT (International Association for Medical Assistance to Travellers) Suite 1, 1287 St Clair Avenue West, Toronto, Ontario M6E 1B8; tel: 416 652 0137; web: www.sentex.net/~iamat.

TMVC (Travel Doctors Group) Sulphur Spirngs Rd, Ancaster, Ontario; tel: (905) 648 1112; web: tmvc.com.au

Australia and New Zealand
TMVC tel: 1300 65 88 44; web: www.tmvc.com.au. TMVC has 20 clinics in Australia, New Zealand and Thailand, including:
Auckland Canterbury Arcade, 170 Queen Street, Auckland City; tel: 373 353
Brisbane Dr Deborah Mills, Quantas Domestic Buloding, 6th floor, 247 Adelaide St, Brisbane, QLD 4000; tel: 7 3221 9066; fax: 7 3321 7076
Melbourne Dr Sonny Lau, 393 Little Bourke St, 2nd floor, Melbourne, VIC 3000; tel: 3 9602 5788; fax: 3 9670 8394
Sydney Dr Mandy Hu, Dymocks Building, 7th floor, 428 George St, Sydney, NSW2000; tel: 2 221 7133; fax: 2 221 8401

South Africa
There are six **British Airways travel clinics** in South Africa: Johannesburg, tel: (011) 807 3132; Cape Town, tel: (021) 419 3172; Durban, tel: (031) 303 2423; Knysna, tel: (044) 382 6366; East London, tel: (043) 743 7471; Port Elizabeth, tel: (041) 374 7471.

TMVC (Travel Doctor Group) 113 DF Malan Drive, Roosevelt Park, Johannesburg; tel: +27 (011) 888 7488. Consult website www.tmvc.com.au for addresses of other clinics in South Africa.

LONG-HAUL FLIGHTS
Dr Felicity Nicholson

There is growing evidence, albeit circumstantial, that long-haul air travel increases the risk of developing deep vein thrombosis. This condition is potentially life threatening, but it should be stressed that the danger to the average traveller is slight.

Certain risk factors specific to air travel have been identified. These include immobility, compression of the veins at the back of the knee by the edge of the seat, the decreased air pressure and slightly reduced oxygen in the cabin, and dehydration. Consuming alcohol may exacerbate the situation by increasing fluid loss and encouraging immobility.

In theory everyone is at risk, but those at highest risk are shown below:

- Passengers on journeys of longer than eight hours duration
- People over 40
- People with heart disease
- People with cancer
- People with clotting disorders
- People who have had recent surgery, especially on the legs
- Women on the pill or other oestrogen therapy
- Pregnancy
- People who are very tall (over 6ft/1.8m) or short (under 5ft/1.5m)

A deep vein thrombosis (DVT) is a clot of blood that forms in the leg veins. Symptoms include swelling and pain in the calf or thigh. The skin may feel hot to touch and becomes discoloured (light blue-red). A DVT is not dangerous in itself, but if a clot breaks down then it may travel to the lungs (pulmonary embolus). Symptoms of a pulmonary embolus (PE) include chest pain, shortness of breath and coughing up small amounts of blood.

Symptoms of a DVT rarely occur during the flight, and typically occur within three days of arrival, although symptoms of a DVT or PE have been reported up to two weeks later.

Anyone who suspects that they have these symptoms should see a doctor immediately as anticoagulation (blood thinning) treatment can be given.

Prevention of DVT
General measures to reduce the risk of thrombosis are shown below. This advice also applies to long train or bus journeys.

- Whilst waiting to board the plane, try to walk around rather than sit.
- During the flight drink plenty of water (at least two small glasses every hour).
- Avoid excessive tea, coffee and alcohol.
- Perform leg-stretching exercises, such as pointing the toes up and down.
- Move around the cabin when practicable.

If you fit into the high-risk category (see above) ask your doctor if it is safe to travel. Additional protective measures such as graded compression stockings, aspirin or low molecular weight heparin can be given. No matter how tall you are, where possible request a seat with extra legroom.

Switzerland
IAMAT (International Association for Medical Assistance to Travellers) 57 Voirets, 1212 Grand Lancy, Geneva; web: www.sentex.net/~iamat.

Personal first-aid kit

Personal first-aid kits are just that – personal. Everyone who carries such a kit will have their own choice of favoured drugs and treatments, and probably a few little extras as well. We personally carry a range of kits whenever we leave our house to go travelling. We also have a large range of first-aid items in the house. We have kits for the car, for our rucksacks and also a small kit that we carry on our person in case we become separated from our car and our rucksack. The least that you should bring with you is a small kit that can fit in a daysack. One word of warning though: when coming through customs, always make sure that any drugs you carry with you are in their original sealed packages as small, loose, white tablets tend to make customs officers suspicious. If you have prescription drugs, again bring only those that are pre-sealed and always carry your doctor's prescription in the same bag.

A small personal first-aid kit should contain the following items at the very least:

- malaria prophylactics, as well as a malaria treatment and a small thermometer (which is very useful for self-diagnosis)
- soluble aspirin or paracetamol (good for reducing fever as well as killing pain)
- iodine or potassium permanganate crystals (useful in many ways such as for water sterilisation, anti-fungal and antiseptics). Don't take an antiseptic cream with you as it will just be a waste of space, but an anti-fungal cream (eg: Canesten) is a good idea
- antihistamine tablets (such as Piriton) to help against mosquito bites
- water sterilisation tablets (iodine tablets are the best)
- Imodium capsules for controlling diarrhoea (eg: when travelling)
- rehydration sachets
- a few small dressings (Band-aids)
- sunscreen and insect repellent (plenty of these)
- a small eye bath (used with clean drinking water this is useful for washing grit and sand out of the eyes)
- a small pair of scissors and a pair of fine-pointed tweezers (to remove caterpillar hairs, thorns, splinters etc)
- condoms or femidoms

It is also a good idea to carry with you an impregnated mosquito bednet. Even though most camps have mosquito nets they often have holes in them, so its best to carry your own as a backup.

Some people take a range of antibiotics with them, but we don't recommend this unless you are travelling upcountry in out-of-the-way places, or are intending to stay in The Gambia for some time. If you do want to bring some with you, the following are recommended: ciprofloxacin (or norfloxacin) (500mg twice a day for three days) for severe diarrhoea; tinidazole (2g taken in one dose then repeated seven days later) for amoebic dysentery or giardiasis; another broad-spectrum antibiotic like amoxycillin for chest, urine, skin infections, etc if you are going to a remote area. Remember that it can be dangerous to self-prescribe if you are not a qualified medical practitioner. In The Gambia you will never be more than a half a day from a doctor, nurse or health worker, and most antibiotics (and other prescription drugs) are available from pharmacies in the coastal area.

Water sterilisation

It is rare to get sick from drinking contaminated water but it happens, so try to drink from safe sources. Tap water in The Gambia is OK to drink: we have drunk it for a long time with no ill effects. Bottled water is also available just about everywhere, even upcountry. When purchasing bottled water, make sure that the seal has not been tampered with.

However, if you go upcountry the water you are offered may not come from boreholes but from wells. If the wells are open (as most of them are) then they may be subject to contamination. Bats, lizards and snakes often hide in the nooks and crannies in the sides of wells and their droppings fall into the water. We have also heard of freshwater turtles that have deliberately been put into some wells to eat the insects and frogs etc that are found in them. These too defecate into the water. If you have no choice but to drink water from a well then you should purify it first to remove any nasties that may be lurking.

Water purification is done in two stages. The first is to **clarify** the water by removing particles of dirt and other contamination by filtering the water. This is important, as many chemicals that are used to treat water cannot do so if the water is dirty (i.e. has a lot of mud etc, suspended in it). Ready made filters can be purchased from camping shops, etc, and although they are fairly expensive they come in a variety of sizes from huge ones that are capable of treating enough water for a large expedition, to pen-sized filters that will only filter a few litres of water. You can make your own in an emergency – all you need is a piece of fine-woven material such as a handkerchief or the lining of a pocket.

The second stage of water purification is to **sterilise** the water. This can be achieved by bringing the water to the boil, or by passing it through a good bacteriological filter or by adding water sterilisation tablets. If you use the boiling method it is best to keep it at the boil for at least ten minutes to make sure you have killed all the bugs. A better way of using heat is to allow the steam given off to condense in another (clean) container. The resulting distilled water is safe to drink. Today, many of the water filters that you can buy not only include filters for removing large contaminants and dirt (see above), but also the bacteria that can cause problems. Water sterilisation tablets generally come in two forms: chlorine tablets (eg: Puritabs) are adequate, although theoretically they are not 100% effective and taste pretty nasty; iodine tablets (eg: Potable Aqua) are much more effective. If neither are available, putting iodine drops straight into the water is effective but it's difficult to get the dose right. Whichever method you use, always leave the chemicals in the water for at least ten minutes before attempting to drink it, as some bacteria have hard outer shells and the chemicals need time to work on them.

If you are thinking about camping or travelling extensively upcountry in The Gambia, bring a water purification kit with you, as they are not easy to get hold of once you are out here.

Further reading

Self-prescribing has its hazards so if you are going anywhere very remote, consider taking a health book. For adults there is *Bugs, Bites and Bowels*, the *Cadogan guide to healthy travel* by Dr Jane Wilson-Howarth, and if travelling with children it's worth consulting Bradt's *Your Child's Health Abroad: a manual for travelling parents* by Dr Jane Wilson-Howarth and Dr Matthew Ellis (see *Appendix 2*).

Medical facilities

As The Gambia is such a small country you will find that you are never more than half a day away from medical facilities of one sort or another. The main government hospital, the Royal Victoria Hospital (tel: 228223), is located in Banjul, but most people prefer to go to the Medical Research Council (MRC) clinic in Fajara, which is a British-run research station with good African and European doctors. A number of private clinics and doctors is scattered around the coastal resorts. These include the Westfield Clinic (tel: 292213) at Westfield Junction in Serrekunda, the Roland Clinic (tel: 374421) at Churchill's Town, the Lamtoro Medical Centre (tel: 460934) in Kololi, the Swiss Medical Clinic (tel: 392243) along the Sukuta Highway and the Momodou Musa Memorial Clinics in Banjul (tel: 224320) and off the Sukuta Highway (tel: 371683). If you are upcountry, there are hospitals at Bansang and Farafenni, and there are health clinics in many of the villages. Try asking around for the nearest one.

COMMON MEDICAL PROBLEMS
Traveller's diarrhoea

The bad news is that at least half of those travelling to the tropics or the developing world will suffer a bout of traveller's diarrhoea during their trip. The newer you are to exotic travel, the more likely you will be to suffer. Traveller's diarrhoea and the other faecal-oral diseases come from getting other peoples' faeces in your mouth (another good reason for only shaking hands with your right hand - see *Etiquette* in *Chapter 3*). This sounds disgusting (and is), but most often happens when cooks do not wash their hands after a trip to the toilet. However, even if the restaurant cook does not understand basic hygiene, you will be safe if your food has been properly cooked and arrives at your table piping hot. The maxim for safe eating is:

PEEL IT, BOIL IT, COOK IT OR FORGET IT.

This means that fruit you have washed and peeled yourself, and hot foods, should be safe. Raw foods, cold cooked foods, salads and fruit salads which have been prepared by others are all risky. Avoid eating ice cream as some of it is not kept adequately frozen because of power cuts. Also, avoid having ice in your drinks: the drink may be safe but the ice could have been made from contaminated water, touched by unwashed hands or even dumped alongside a road somewhere during transportation and picked up all kinds of germs. In addition, cooked foods that are kept lukewarm in hotel buffets are usually dangerous. If you are struck by traveller's diarrhoea, see the box *Treating traveller's diarrhoea* (page 94).

The good news is that by taking precautions against traveller's diarrhoea you will also avoid typhoid, cholera, hepatitis, dysentery, worms etc.

Sunburn and skin cancer

The incidence of skin cancer is rocketing as Caucasians travel more and spend more time exposing themselves to the sun. It is wise to keep out of the sun during the middle of the day between 11.00–15.00 when it is hottest. If you must expose yourself, build up gradually from 20 minutes per day and do not expose your skin to the sun's rays for more than two hours each day. Be especially careful of sun reflected off water and wear a T-shirt and lots of high factor waterproof suncream when swimming. Snorkelling is a bit of a waste of time in The Gambia as its sandy shores keep visibility down to almost nothing. However, if you do go snorkelling, remember that it often leads to the backs of the thighs and the back being scorched, so wear Bermuda shorts and a T-shirt, or better still a wet suit. Even away from the beaches and the ocean it is easy to get sunburnt. Remember that sun exposure ages the skin and makes people prematurely wrinkly, so cover up with long loose clothes and wear a hat when you can. We've lost count of how many 'lobsters' we have seen walking around the coastal resorts and it must be extremely painful to be so burnt. Why spoil a great holiday by putting yourself in pain?

TREATING TRAVELLER'S DIARRHOEA

It is dehydration that makes you feel awful during a bout of diarrhoea so the most important part of treatment is to drink lots of clear fluids. Sachets of oral rehydration salts give the perfect biochemical mix to replace everything that is pouring out of your bottom but they do not taste nice. Any dilute mixture of sugar and salt in water will do you good, so if you like Coke or orange squash, drink that with a three-finger pinch of salt added to each glass. Otherwise, make a solution of a four-finger scoop of sugar with a three-finger pinch of salt in a glass of water. Another way is to add eight level teaspoons of sugar (18g) and one level teaspoon of salt (3g) to one litre (five cups) of safe water. A squeeze of lemon or orange juice improves the taste and adds potassium, which is also lost during a bout of diarrhoea. Drink two large glasses after every bowel action and more if you are thirsty. If you are not eating you need to drink *at least* three litres a day plus the equivalent of whatever is pouring into the toilet. If you feel like eating, go for a bland, high carbohydrate diet. Heavy greasy foods will probably give you cramps.

The bacteria that induce traveller's diarrhoea normally die out after about 36 hours, so your best bet is to avoid alcohol and greasy foods and just rest up. If you have to travel, take Imodium capsules but remember that this treatment just prolongs the trouble and does not cure it, so only take them if it is unavoidable. If the diarrhoea is bad, or carries on after the 36-hour period, or you are passing blood or slime, or you have a fever, you will probably need antibiotics in addition to fluid replacement and you should seek medical attention. A three-day course of ciprofloxacin 500mg twice daily for three days (or norfloxacin) is an appropriate treatment for dysentery and bad diarrhoea. If the diarrhoea is greasy and bulky and is accompanied by severe flatulence, abdominal distention, stomach cramps and sulphurous burps, then the likely cause is giardia, which is treatable. This is best treated with tinidazole (2g in one dose repeated seven days later if symptoms persist).

Heatstroke

Heatstroke is potentially fatal but avoiding it is easy. Stay out of direct sunlight as much as possible, especially during the middle of the day. If you must go out in the sun, always wear a broad-brimmed hat. If you come from a Western country you will find that you will sweat much more in The Gambia, especially during the rainy season. In order to replace the moisture lost through excessive sweating you must drink more fluids than you normally would. You also lose salt during sweating so if you have a craving for salt put more on to your food than you would back home. Better yet, drink a sachet of rehydration fluid every few days to replace lost salts. If you carry out these simple precautions your holiday will be much more pleasant.

INSECT-BORNE DISEASES AND PROBLEMS
Malaria

It is hard to think that the animals that humans most regard as dangerous, such as lions, tigers, crocodiles and snakes, kill only a few thousand people each year, whereas malaria is passed to humans by mosquitoes, and kills over *one million* people each year in Africa alone. This makes the tiny and otherwise insignificant mosquito the most dangerous animal in the world. Mosquitoes are abundant in

The Gambia, and so is malaria, so take this threat seriously and do everything that you can to prevent yourself from contracting it.

Malaria is a parasite that is passed from person to person in tiny droplets of blood in the mouthparts of some biting mosquitoes. Only mosquitoes of the genus *Anopheles* carry the parasite, and only females of these species bite. The reason that they bite is to collect blood from warm-blooded animals. This blood is broken down in the mosquito's digestive fluids and the resulting constituents are used to produce eggs. *Anopheles* mosquitoes are common throughout the country, but they need stagnant water (places like marshes, puddles and even open sewers) in which to lay their eggs and complete their early development, so there are far fewer of them around in the dry season, while in the rainy season they are much more abundant. Unfortunately, the constant watering of hotel gardens, for example, during the dry season provides many opportunities for mosquitoes to carry on breeding throughout the driest months.

Malaria is also commonest in places where the human population is densest, such as towns and cities. If you live out in the bush with only a few other people within walking distance, you are much less likely to contract malaria than if you live in a bustling area such as Bakau or Serrekunda.

Even if you are visiting The Gambia for just a short period of a week or two, you should take precautions against malaria. We have heard that a significant proportion of holidaymakers from the UK who have contracted malaria, have contracted it while on holiday in The Gambia, so you have been warned. For certain people, such as pregnant women or children, it is unwise to travel in any malarial area as the risk of malaria in many parts is considerable and these travellers are likely to succumb rapidly to the disease.

Malaria prevention

We hear a lot about people who seem to think that they can acquire immunity against malaria. We also hear a lot about homeopathic preventions and cures for this killer disease. We are not convinced by their effectiveness and we believe that the only way to lower the odds of catching malaria is to take proper medically tested precautions. If you want to take your chances, that's your prerogative, but bear in mind that there isn't a month that goes by when we do not hear about a death caused by malaria amongst the families and friends of our friends and colleagues.

There is no vaccine against malaria, but using prophylactic drugs and preventing mosquito bites will considerably reduce the risk of contracting it. Seek professional advice for the best anti-malarial drugs to take. Mefloquine (Lariam) is the most effective prophylactic agent for most countries in sub-Saharan Africa. If this drug is suggested then you should start taking it at least two-and-a-half weeks before departure to check that it suits you. Stop immediately if it seems to cause depression or anxiety, visual or hearing disturbances, fits, severe headaches or changes in heart rhythm. Anyone who is pregnant, has been treated for depression or psychiatric problems, has diabetes controlled by oral therapy, who is epileptic (or who has suffered fits in the past), or has a close blood relative who is epileptic, should not take mefloquine.

Doxycycline (100mg daily) is a good alternative if Lariam is unsuitable and need only be started one day before arrival in a malarial region. It can only be obtained from a doctor. There is a possibility of an allergic skin reactions developing in sunlight in approximately 5% of people. If this happens the drug should be stopped. Women using the oral contraceptive should use additional protection for the first four weeks.

Chloroquine (Nivaquine or Avloclor) two weekly and proguanil (Paludrine)

AVOIDING INSECT BITES

It is crucial to avoid mosquito bites between dusk and dawn. As the sun goes down, don long clothes and apply insect repellent on any exposed flesh. This will protect you from malaria, elephantiasis and a range of nasty insect-borne viruses. Malaria mosquitoes are voracious (just hearing their whine sometimes makes us cringe) and they hunt at ankle-level, so it is worth applying repellent under your socks. Sleep under a permethrin-treated mosquito bednet or in an air-conditioned room. During the day it is wise to wear long, loose (preferably 100% cotton) clothes if you are pushing through scrubby country; this will keep ticks off and also tsetse flies and day-biting *Aedes* mosquitoes which may spread dengue and yellow fevers. Tsetse flies hurt when they bite and are attracted to the colour blue. Local people will advise on where they are a problem and where they transmit sleeping sickness.

Pack a DEET-based insect repellent (eg: Repel) and either a permethrin-impregnated mosquito bednet or a permethrin spray so that you can treat bednets in hotels. Permethrin treatment makes even very tatty nets protective and mosquitoes are also unable to bite through the impregnated net when you roll against it. Travel clinics usually sell a good range of nets, treatment kits and repellents. Insect repellents are extremely hard to get hold of and are expensive in The Gambia, so bring your own with you.

two daily are now considered to be the least effective. They should only be used if there is no suitable alternative.

A new, very effective drug – Malarone – is now available on prescription. It is expensive but has the advantage of fewer side effects than Lariam or doxycycline. It can be started the day before travel and continued for only seven days after leaving.

All prophylactic agents should be taken after or with the evening meal, washed down with plenty of fluids. And with the exception of Malarone, all should be continued for four weeks after leaving the last malarial area.

In addition to antimalarial medicines, it is important to avoid mosquito bites between dusk and dawn (see *Avoiding insect bites* in this chapter).

Malaria diagnosis and treatment

The symptoms of malaria include any combination of a headache, flu-like aches and pains, a rapid rise in temperature and a general sense of being disorientated. There may also possibly be nausea and diarrhoea. Even if you take all of your prophylatics and do everything possible to avoid being bitten by mosquitoes, you may still contract a strain of malaria that is resistant to prophylactic drugs. Untreated malaria may be fatal, but don't panic, as even strains that are resistant to prophylactics respond well to *prompt treatment*. Finding a doctor as soon as possible is the most important thing. Assume that any high fever lasting more than a few hours is malaria regardless of any other symptoms. Remember too that malaria may occur anything from seven days into the trip up to one year after leaving Africa.

You can buy self-administered treatments for malaria, but they all require self-diagnosis and we cannot stress enough that this is dangerous if you are untrained, so seek medical help. If you insist on self-diagnosis, then consult the books mentioned in the *Further Reading* section in *Appendix 2*.

Bilharzia or schistosomiasis

With thanks to Dr Vaughan Southgate of the Natural History Museum, London

Bilharzia, or schistosomiasis, is a disease that afflicts around 200 million people worldwide. It most commonly afflicts the rural poor of the tropics who repeatedly acquire more and more of these nasty little worm-lodgers. Infected travellers and expatriates generally suffer fewer problems because symptoms will encourage them to seek prompt treatment and because they are exposed to fewer parasites. However, it is still an unpleasant problem that is worth avoiding. Symptoms may include a rash around the area of entry, a high fever, abdominal pain and blood in the urine.

When the faeces of someone infected with bilharzia make contact with fresh water, the eggs that they contain hatch and swim off to infect a pond snail. They continue their development inside the snail until they emerge as tiny torpedo-shaped *cercariae*. These are almost invisible to the human eye but are able to disgest their way through your skin when you wade, bathe or even shower in infested fresh water.

The snails which harbour this nasty parasite are about a centimetre long and live in still or slow-moving fresh water where water plants grow. The most risky shores will be close to places where infected people use water, where they wash clothes, or go to the toilet, etc. Winds may also disperse the *cercariae*, though, so they can be blown some distance, perhaps up to 200m from where they entered the water. Going for a swim or wading in still or slow-moving water that is fringed by reeds and near to a village carries a high risk of contracting bilharzia. On the other hand, swimming in the sea doesn't.

Although an absence of early symptoms does not necessarily mean that there is no infection, infected people usually notice symptoms two or more weeks after penetration by the *cercariae*. Travellers and expatriates will probably experience a fever and often a wheezy cough but local residents do not usually have symptoms. You can now have a very good blood test that will determine whether or not the parasites are going to cause you problems, but you need to have this done six weeks or more after likely exposure. While treatment generally remains effective, there are some treatment failures for reasons that are not yet fully understood. Even if the treatment fails first time, retreatment seems to work fine and it is not known if some drug resistance is developing. Since bilharzia can be a nasty illness, avoidance is better than waiting to be cured and it is wise to avoid bathing in high risk areas.

Avoiding bilharzia

If you are bathing, swimming, paddling or wading in freshwater which you think may carry a bilharzia risk, try to spend less than 10 minutes in it. Then dry off thoroughly with a towel by rubbing vigorously. Avoid bathing or paddling on shores within 200m of villages or other places where people use the water a great deal, especially along reedy shores or where there are lots of water plants. Covering yourself with DEET insect repellent before swimming will help to protect you. If your bathing water comes from a risky source, try to ensure that the water is taken from there in the early morning and stored snail-free. In any case it should be filtered and Dettol or Cresol added. Bathing early in the morning is safer than bathing in the last half of the day. If you think that you have been exposed to bilharzia parasites, arrange a screening blood test (your GP can do this) more than six weeks after your last possible contact with suspect water.

Dengue fever

This mosquito-borne disease resembles malaria but there is no prophylactic available to deal with it and it does occur sporadically in The Gambia. The *Aedes* mosquitoes that carry this virus bite during the daytime, so it is worth applying insect repellent even during the day. The symptoms of dengue fever include strong headaches, rashes and excruciating joint and muscle pains and high fever. Dengue fever only lasts for a week or so and is not usually fatal. Complete rest and paracetamol are the usual treatment and plenty of fluids also helps. Some patients are given an intravenous drip to keep them from dehydrating.

Sleeping sickness

Sleeping sickness is carried by tsetse flies, which are medium-sized, long-bodied, dark-coloured flies with a nasty and painful bite. Tsetse flies are common in many areas of The Gambia, especially near sources of fresh water such as in Abuko Nature Reserve, or further upcountry along the freshwater stretches of the River Gambia. If you spot a Nile monitor on your travels, you are bound to see a cloud of tsetses on and around the poor beast. The flies bite in daylight, are much more active away from the shade than in it, and are also attracted to the colour blue. Sleeping sickness itself has a patchy distribution within small parts of the tsetse flies' range and is treatable, so it is only a minor threat to travellers. The symptoms include lethargy and swollen neck glands which may occur several weeks after infection.

River blindness

Minute pestilential biting blackflies spread river blindness in some parts of Africa between 19° north and 17° south. This disease is caught close to fast-flowing rivers since the blackflies breed there and their larvae live in rapids. The flies bite during the day but long trousers tucked into socks will help to keep them off. Citronella-based natural repellents do not work against them.

Tumbu flies

Tumbu flies, or *putsi*, are a very real problem in The Gambia, especially in built-up areas, and it is not only humans that suffer from their attentions. Just look at any local dog and you are bound to find one or two grubs beneath its skin. The adult fly lays her eggs on the soil or on drying laundry and when the eggs come in contact with human flesh (when you put on your clothes or lie on a bed) they hatch and bury themselves under the skin. Here, they form a crop of 'boils', each of which hatches into a grub after about eight days, when the inflammation will settle down. In *putsi* areas always either dry your clothes and sheets within a screened house, or dry them in direct sunshine until they are crisp, or iron them. If you find yourself to be a host for a tumbu fly grub, try smearing Vaseline over the boil or submerging the affected area under water. Both of these methods force the grub to the surface to breath and it is easy then to squeeze the boil and pop it out. Another and perhaps better method is to stick a piece of clear Sellotape over the infected area. When the grub pops up for air you will be able to see it and pull off the tape, hopefully with the grub stuck to the tape. Make sure you do not leave a part of the grub in the wound or it will turn septic and make sure you clean the wound out thoroughly afterwards and then cover it to prevent infection.

Jiggers

Jiggers or sandfleas are another kind of flesh-feaster. They latch on if you walk barefoot in contaminated places, and set up home under the skin of the foot, usually at the side of a toenail where they cause a painful, boil-like swelling. These need to be picked out by a local expert, if the distended flea bursts during eviction the wound should be dowsed in spirit, alcohol or kerosene, otherwise more jiggers will infest you.

Ticks
African ticks are not the prolific disease transmitters that they are in the Americas, but they may occasionally spread disease. Lyme disease has now been recorded in Africa, and tick-bite fever also occurs. This flu-like illness is mild, but still worth avoiding. If you get the tick off whole, and promptly, the chances of disease transmission are reduced to a minimum. To do this manoeuvre your finger and thumb so that you can pinch the tick's mouthparts, as close to your skin as possible, and slowly and steadily pull away at right angles to your skin. This often hurts. Jerking or twisting will increase the chances of damaging the tick, which in turn increases the chances of disease transmission, as well as leaving the mouthparts behind. Once the tick is off, dowse the little wound with alcohol (local spirit, whisky or similar are excellent) or iodine. An area of spreading redness around the bite site, or a rash or fever coming on a few days or more after the bite, should indicate the need for a trip to a doctor.

OTHER DISEASES
HIV and sexually transmitted diseases
HIV, AIDS and other sexually transmitted diseases are extremely common, not only in The Gambia, but also in many other African countries. Having unprotected sex is dangerous and foolhardy. Travelling is a time when we may enjoy sexual adventures, especially when alcohol reduces our inhibitions, but remember the risks of sexually transmitted infection are high. This applies whether you sleep with fellow travellers or with local people. Alarming statistics show that about 40% of HIV infections in British heterosexuals are acquired abroad. Always use condoms or femidoms, preferably ones bearing the British kite mark and ideally bought before you travel, as they offer a high level of protection. If you notice any genital ulcers or discharge seek medical treatment promptly.

Health workers in The Gambia know only too well the dangers of transmitting HIV through infected needles and will only use new sterilised needles on patients. These needles can be in short supply though, so bringing your own with you is a very good idea. If you have not used them during your stay here, then please think about donating them to a hospital or clinic before you go. They are sure to be put to good use.

Rabies
Rabies is carried by all types of mammals (beware village dogs and small monkeys in places like Bijilo Forest Park that are used to being fed by humans) and is passed on to humans through a bite or a lick of an open wound. You must always assume that any animal is rabid (unless personally known to you). The closer the bite is to the face the shorter the incubation time of the disease. But it is always wise to get to medical help as soon as possible and remember that it is never too late to bother. In the interim, scrub the wound with soap and bottled/boiled water then pour on a strong iodine or alcohol solution. This helps stop the rabies virus entering the body and will guard against wound infections, including tetanus. If you intend to have contact with animals and/or are likely to be more than 24 hours away from medical help, pre-exposure vaccination is advised. Ideally, three doses should be taken over four weeks; contrary to popular belief, these vaccinations are relatively

painless! If you are exposed as described, treatment should be given as soon as possible, but always seek help: the incubation period for rabies can be very long. Those who have not been immunised will need a full course of injections together with rabies immunoglobulin (Rig). This product is expensive (around US$800) and may be hard to come by – another reason why pre-exposure vaccination should be encouraged in travellers who are planning to visit more remote areas. Tell the doctor if you have had pre-exposure vaccine as this will change the treatment you receive. Remember that if you do contract rabies, the mortality rate is 100% and death from rabies is probably one of the worst ways to go.

Meningitis

This is a particularly nasty disease as it can kill within hours of the first symptoms appearing. The telltale symptoms are a combination of a blinding headache (light sensitivity), a blotchy rash and a high fever. Immunisation protects against the most serious bacterial form of meningitis (types A and C) that are encountered in Africa. Other forms of meningitis exist (usually viral) but there are no vaccines for these. Local papers normally report outbreaks. If you show symptoms go to a doctor immediately. In the Gambia there is an increased risk of meningitis through the dry season (December until the end of May). Vaccination is usually only recommended for longer trips. However, if there is a specific outbreak it would be wise to take it regardless of the length of stay.

Tetanus

Tetanus is caught from deep, dirty wounds or animal bites, though you can lower your chances of contracting it by applying good first aid and thoroughly cleaning all wounds promptly. Tetanus immunisation gives good protection for up to ten years, so make sure you have received immunisation (or a booster) before you travel.

SKIN PROBLEMS
Skin infections

Any mosquito bite or small nick in the skin gives an opportunity for bacteria to penetrate the body's usually excellent defences. It will surprise many travellers how quickly skin infections start in warm humid climates like that found in The Gambia, and it is essential to clean and cover even the slightest wound. Creams are not as effective as a good drying antiseptic such as dilute iodine, potassium permanganate (a few crystals in half a cup of water), or crystal (or gentian) violet. These are not always readily available in The Gambia so bring some with you in your personal medical kit. If the wound starts to throb, or becomes red (and the redness starts to spread), or the wound oozes, and especially if you develop a fever, antibiotics will probably be needed. Flucloxacillin (250mg four times a day) or cloxacillin (500mg four times a day) are the antibiotics normally prescribed. For those allergic to penicillin, erythromycin (500mg twice a day) for five days should help. See a doctor if the symptoms do not start to improve in 48 hours.

Fungal infections

Fungal infections also get a hold easily in hot moist climates so wear 100% cotton socks and underwear and shower frequently. An itchy rash in the groin or flaking between the toes is likely to be a fungal infection. This needs treatment with an antifungal cream such as Canesten (clotrimazole). If this is not available try Whitfield's Ointment (compound benzoic acid ointment), or crystal violet (although this will turn you purple!), or a solution of potassium permanganate.

Prickly heat

A fine, pimply rash on your trunk is likely to be heat rash. To treat this, take cool showers and dab (rather than rub) yourself dry. Applying talcum powder will also help. If the rash is bad you may need to check into an air-conditioned hotel room for a while. Slowing down to a relaxed schedule, wearing only loose, baggy, 100% cotton clothes and sleeping naked under a fan all help to reduce the problem.

SAFETY
Accidents

Many people who are new to exotic travel often worry about tropical diseases, but it is accidents that are most likely to carry you off. Road accidents are very common in The Gambia, so be aware and do what you can to reduce the risks. Try to travel during daylight hours and refuse to be driven by a drunk (see *Getting around* in *Chapter 3*). Listen to local advice about areas where violent crime is rife and follow the advice given in *Theft* in *Chapter 3*.

Marine dangers

The beaches in The Gambia are great. The sand is fine, the sun is hot and the sea is warm. What more could you want? But remember that this is the tropics and there are a few problems that you should be aware of and take precautions against.

There are a few places along the coast where it can be quite dangerous to swim at certain times of the day. In these places the undercurrent can be extremely strong and the wave power high. Always follow the advice of local people or the staff of your hotel when intending to swim near the coastal resorts. You must never attempt to swim when there is a red flag flying along the beach, but be aware that sometimes the system breaks down and the flag is either left flying all day or is not put up at all. During the rainy season many local Gambian youths drown while swimming off the beach as the sea becomes much rougher at this time of year.

The danger of drowning is not the only threat that you may face when swimming off the beaches, as there are other, less lethal dangers that can be potential problems. These include dangerous fish such as stingrays, well-camouflaged flat fish that sit on the sandy bottom of shallow waters. They have a nasty sting in their tail that is very, very painful. There may also be other fish around that have poisonous spines. However, if you are swimming from a beach that is well-used by other people, the dangers of standing on one of these fish or of getting stung by a stingray are minimal as the disturbance will frighten them away. Quieter beaches are more dangerous so make a lot of noise and splash about when going into the water to scare them away.

Another problem is jellyfish. Sometimes there can be large numbers of jellyfish floating near to the beach and washed up on to it. The most dangerous is the Portuguese man-of-war. However this species is easy to see and recognise, and therefore to avoid. Bright pink and blue, it looks like a small, semi-deflated balloon floating on the surface. The dangerous bits of the jellyfish are the stinging tentacles that stream out behind it underwater. If you are stung by these tentacles, you will find it *extremely* painful. Even when the jellyfish are washed up on to the beach (they soon loose their colour when they dry out) they can still be capable of stinging, so don't be tempted to pick one up.

Other problems that can occur are more mundane and include twisted ankles from underwater rocks and standing on the numerous sea urchins that are sometimes washed up. There are sharks off the coast of West Africa, but as far as we are aware there has never been a reported case of a shark attack on humans along this coast. There is unlikely to be one in the near future as the shark population is being drastically over-fished for its fins.

If you wear old plimsolls or jellies on the beach you will avoid getting sea urchin spines in the soles and you are less likely to get venomous fish spines in your feet. If you are stung by a venomous fish, soak your foot in hot (but not scalding) water until some time after the pain subsides; this may mean 20–30 minutes submersion in all (take the foot out when you top up the water, otherwise you may also scald it). If the pain returns, re-immerse your foot. Once the venom has been heat-inactivated, get a doctor to check your foot and remove any bits of fish spines left in the wound. Urchin spines in the soles of your feet are less painful but can cause infection, so see a local doctor and get them removed and the wounds cleaned.

Snakes

Snakes rarely attack unless provoked, and bites in travellers are unusual. It is likely that you will not even see a snake in your visit to The Gambia (we recently spent a few weeks going around the country and saw only one harmless snake during the entire trip). However, if you walk in the bush, you may come across one. In this case you are less likely to get bitten if you wear stout shoes (or even better, boots) and long trousers. Most of the snakes in The Gambia are harmless and even the few venomous species will only dispense venom in about half of their bites. Even if you are bitten, you will not necessarily have received venom. Keeping this fact in mind may help you to stay calm. Many so-called first-aid techniques do more harm than good. Cutting into the wound is harmful, tourniquets are dangerous and suction and electrical inactivation devices do not work. The only treatment is antivenom, which is available at major hospitals in The Gambia, such as at the MRC in Fajara. If you are bitten by what you think may have been a venomous snake:

- try to keep calm - it is likely that no venom has been dispensed
- prevent movement of the bitten limb by applying a splint
- keep the bitten limb below heart height to slow the spread of any venom
- if you have a crepe bandage, bind up as much of the bitten limb as you can, but release the bandage every half an hour, and
- get yourself to a hospital that has antivenom.

And remember:

- never give aspirin, though it is safe to give paracetamol
- never cut or suck the wound
- do not apply ice packs
- do not apply potassium permanganate

If the offending snake can be captured without risk of someone else being bitten, take it to show the doctor – but beware since even a decapitated head is able to dispense venom in a reflex bite. Alternatively, describe its appearance to the doctor, in detail.

Animal attacks

If you are venturing into the bush remember that it is inhabited by a few species of potentially dangerous wildlife, though The Gambia has far fewer large species than East Africa (or even North America). The most dangerous species are the big primates such as baboons. Leopards are the only 'big' cats we have and these are very rare in The Gambia. Hippos can be dangerous if you happen to frighten them or if you are between them and the safety of their waterhole. So try to watch them from the safety of a *big* boat during the daytime. Probably the most dangerous animals in The Gambia are the semi-tame 'bush dogs' that live in every village, so don't be tempted to try and pet them.

Part Two

The Guide

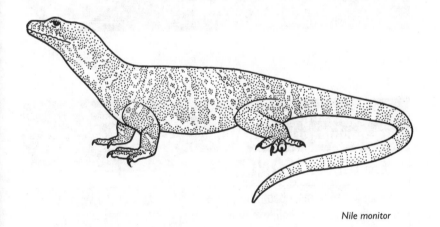

Nile monitor

Banjul

Banjul is the capital of The Gambia, and is one of the smallest capital cities in Africa. It has a population of around 50,000 people and is located on an island jutting out into the mouth of the River Gambia. It is joined to the mainland by a road bridge. As it's situated on an island, the city does not have much room left to expand, so most of the growth in urbanisation is taking place in Serrekunda and Brikama, which are now both much larger than Banjul. However, Banjul remains the headquarters of most of the government departments of The Gambia, and the home of State House, which is the administrative centre for the country.

Banjul is a real hodgepodge of old colonial buildings, shantytowns and modern office buildings, but none of them is more than a few storeys in height and overall, the atmosphere in the city is fairly laid-back, though some areas can be very hectic. There is also a rich mixture of West African cultures here as the city is home to people from all over the region. As you walk the streets, you will see tall Mauritanian Tuaregs in light blue robes, and Berbers in white flowing *burnous*, alongside Gambian businessmen in bright tie-dye shirts and Gambian women in a dazzling array of local costumes. Many of the shops are owned and managed by Lebanese ex-pats, who, with their dark glasses, often dress and look like members of the Italian *mafiosi*. All of these people mix with rastafarians in brightly coloured woollen hats and T-shirts, and male office workers dressed more sombrely in suits and ties, while female office workers wear a selection of Western-style skirts and blouses. It is amazing, but typical of The Gambia, that so many different races and cultures can live alongside each other in peace and tolerance.

HISTORY

Banjul has an unusual history in that it was created by one man, on behalf of the British government, with the foremost intention of preventing the continuation of the slave trade in The Gambia. This man was a captain in the British Army whose name was Alexander Grant, but more of him later.

The River Gambia had been recognised in 1783 by the peace treaty of Versailles as a British possession. In 1807, royal assent was given to the British Abolition Act which stated that from January 1 1808 'all manner of dealing and trading' in slaves in Africa, or in their transport from Africa, was to be 'utterly abolished, prohibited, and declared to be unlawful'. The Royal Navy and the British Army, who were well aware of, and disgusted by, the harsh and inhumane way that slaves were transported and treated, took this law to their hearts. They began a vigorous campaign to stop the slave trade in all of the British colonies in Africa, including The Gambia. They had support from Sierra Leone, another British colony in West Africa, from which The Gambia was administered, where Chief Justice Hogan declared that the River Gambia was henceforth to be considered wholly British and

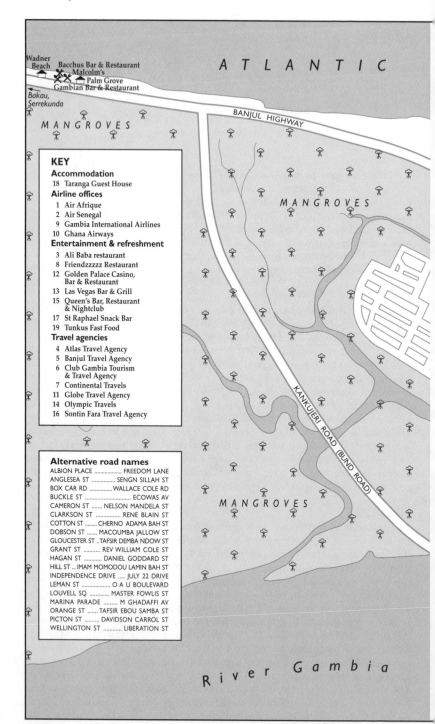

ATLANTIC

Wadner
Beach   Bacchus Bar & Restaurant
           Malcolm's
              Palm Grove
Gambian Bar & Restaurant
Bakau,
Serrekunda

M A N G R O V E S

BANJUL HIGHWAY

M A N G R O V E S

KEY

Accommodation
18 Taranga Guest House

Airline offices
 1 Air Afrique
 2 Air Senegal
 9 Gambia International Airlines
10 Ghana Airways

Entertainment & refreshment
 3 Ali Baba restaurant
 8 Friendzzzzz Restaurant
12 Golden Palace Casino,
    Bar & Restaurant
13 Las Vegas Bar & Grill
15 Queen's Bar, Restaurant
    & Nightclub
17 St Raphael Snack Bar
19 Tunkus Fast Food

Travel agencies
 4 Atlas Travel Agency
 5 Banjul Travel Agency
 6 Club Gambia Tourism
    & Travel Agency
 7 Continental Travels
11 Globe Travel Agency
14 Olympic Travels
16 Sontin Fara Travel Agency

Alternative road names
ALBION PLACE .... FREEDOM LANE
ANGLESEA ST .... SENGN SILLAH ST
BOX CAR RD .... WALLACE COLE RD
BUCKLE ST .... ECOWAS AV
CAMERON ST .... NELSON MANDELA ST
CLARKSON ST .... RENE BLAIN ST
COTTON ST .... CHERNO ADAMA BAH ST
DOBSON ST .... MACOUMBA JALLOW ST
GLOUCESTER ST ..TAFSIR DEMBA NDOW ST
GRANT ST .... REV WILLIAM COLE ST
HAGAN ST .... DANIEL GODDARD ST
HILL ST ... IMAM MOMODOU LAMIN BAH ST
INDEPENDENCE DRIVE ..... JULY 22 DRIVE
LEMAN ST .... O A U BOULEVARD
LOUVELL SQ .... MASTER FOWLIS ST
MARINA PARADE .... M GHADAFFI AV
ORANGE ST .... TAFSIR EBOU SAMBA ST
PICTON ST .... DAVIDSON CARROL ST
WELLINGTON ST .... LIBERATION ST

KANKUJERI ROAD (BUND ROAD)

M A N G R O V E S

River Gambia

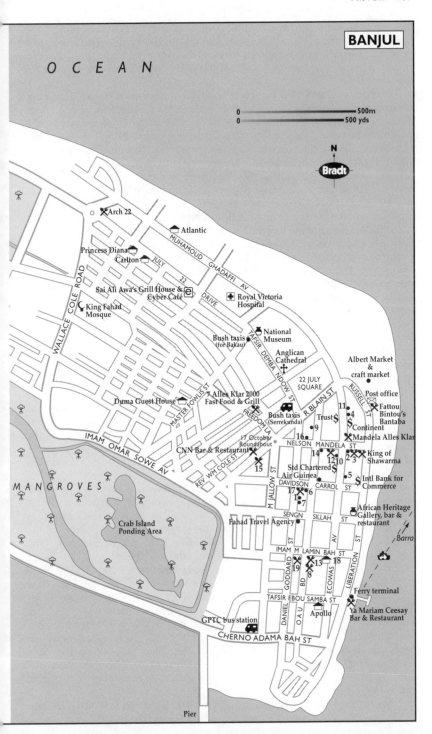

that the river was to be closed to the slave trade forever. However, though the British involvement in the slave trade had ended, the French, Portuguese and Spanish continued to trade in slaves. Even the Americans, who had legislated against importing slaves in 1807, still had ships that were transporting slaves under the Spanish flag.

The British worked hard to prevent slave ships entering the River Gambia but were relatively unsuccessful until 1815. In that year, Sir Charles McCarthy, a senior British administrator in Africa, ordered Captain Alexander Grant to examine the possibility of setting up a military base on the island of Banjul (*banjul* is the Mandinka name for bamboo, which in those days grew all over the island). Captain Grant set off south from Gorée Island, a fortified island lying off the north coast of Senegal, with a detachment of the Royal African Corps, arriving at Banjul in March, 1816. Grant was impressed by the island and the scope that it provided as a base for operations. Consequently, he approached the King of Kombo about the acquisition of the island in return for British protection from slavers. His visit was well-timed as it turned out that the king had recently lost several relatives, who had been taken as slaves by the Spanish ship *Panchita*, only a few weeks beforehand. Grant then proceeded upriver to James Island, whose fort had previously been abandoned. There he met with the King of Barra, Burungai Sonko, and entered into an agreement with him for the reoccupation of the island by British troops, for the annual payment of 300 iron bars. Later, however, the British claimed that the king had reneged on the deal, so they abandoned their plans for rebuilding the ruined fort on the island and withdrew, concentrating their future efforts on Banjul.

In April 1816 Captain Grant, and his superior officer, Colonel Brereton, who had travelled down from Gorée, met with the King of Kombo, and entered into a treaty with him. The king surrendered all rights and title to the island of Banjul in exchange for the annual payment of 103 iron bars to himself, his wife and his retainers. In return the British Government would be allowed to occupy the island and to erect buildings and fortifications upon it. That same day the island was formally handed over to the British and renamed St Mary's Island. That July, the Earl of Bathurst wrote to Sir Charles MacCarthy to officially approve the occupation of St Mary's Island, and Sir Charles and Captain Grant proceeded to name the settlement after the earl.

Captain Grant had begun work on the settlement as soon as the treaty had been signed. He was acclaimed for his personal energy and vigilance, and was well liked by the local people as well as by his own men. This was unusual, as the men he had under his command were the scum of the British Army, being mostly military offenders from other regiments. The army itself consisted largely of ex-convicts who had been given the choice of either joining the British Army or being transported overseas to other colonies, such as Australia. Life in the British Army of the time was hard and discipline was extremely harsh. Offenders in the army were often disciplined by being flogged, sometimes to death, and this was long after English law had stated that whipping slaves was illegal. It is a testament to Captain Grant's strong and likeable personality that such men worked so hard, not only for him, but also towards the cause of stopping the slave trade in The Gambia. It has often been said that he and his men hated the slave trade so much that they almost considered it as a 'holy war' against the traders.

Construction in Bathurst began with a barracks to house 80 men and the erection of a battery of six 24-pounder guns and two field pieces. The battery is still present today in the grounds of State House, but is out of bounds to tourists. The King of Barra facilitated the fort's construction by allowing Grant's men to draw stone from Dog Island in the River Gambia. Colonel Brereton returned to Gorée Island, where he encouraged the growth of the settlement by offering free plots of land to merchants, providing that they built substantial houses of brick or stone within a stipulated time period. Meanwhile, Sir Charles MacCarthy strengthened the garrison at Bathurst, by sending more companies of troops from the Royal African Corps. He also decided that a sergeant's guard would be stationed on James Island whose purpose would be to prevent foreign ships from sailing further upriver.

By the time the rainy season began that year, the commandant's house had been built, a few huts had been erected and the barracks half completed. The garrison had also dug a defensive trench around the whole site. This was because it was known that some local chiefs were against ending the trade in slaves, from which they profited greatly, and that the settlement could therefore easily become a target for attack by these chiefs. Within a few months of setting up their base, Captain Grant and his men had captured five slave ships that had attempted to sail upriver. In those days justice was quick and straightforward: all those found guilty of slave trading were hanged. Slavers therefore resisted capture fiercely and it is easy to imagine that capturing a slave ship was a hard and dangerous task in which many men lost their lives.

During this period there were many British merchants based upon Gorée Island in Senegal. These merchants enjoyed equal status with the French merchants who were also based on the island, but the British feared that this would only be a temporary arrangement. By 1818, many of the British merchants had closed down their operations on Gorée and relocated to Bathurst, whose population had grown to 600, including the garrison. By 1826, the population of Bathurst had grown to over 1,800 people, although only around 30 of them were Europeans. From this time on, the population continued to grow at a phenomenal rate, and people settled in many different parts of the island, forming distinct communities, or wards. Portuguese Town was where the wealthier settlers formed a trading centre and erected their houses. Melville Town (which later became known as Jolof Town), was where the artisans, and the dependants and servants of the merchants were housed. Soldier Town was where the army was based, and the open space separating Soldier Town from Portuguese Town was named MacCarthy Square, after Sir Charles. Mocam Town was where the poorer residents lived, and this later became known as Half Die, a graphic reminder that nearly half of the inhabitants died during an outbreak of cholera. All of these 'villages' were separated from one another by strips of land that were often cultivated. Eventually, as the population continued to grow, these strips of land disappeared beneath buildings until they all joined up to form one town.

The street plan of Banjul today has remained largely unchanged from that laid out by Captain Grant when he founded the city, even though the city has grown in size and now fills almost all of the available space on the island. The public buildings were erected under the supervision of Grant and Captain Kelly of the Second West India Regiment, and the city remains the only example of a comprehensively planned settlement in The Gambia.

Bathurst was renamed Banjul soon after Independence in 1965. MacCarthy Square, originally named after Sir Charles MacCarthy, who played such a large part in the establishment of the settlement, has now been renamed. Grant Street, once named after Captain Alexander Grant of the Royal African Corps, the man who through his personal drive and energy not only founded the city but also almost single-handedly brought to an end the slave trade in The Gambia, has also been renamed. There is now not one single memorial to the man who gave such a large part of his life to making Banjul what it is today.

GETTING THERE AND AWAY

It is easy to get to and from Banjul by using a variety of means, including buses and taxis from the mainland, and ships and boats from the Atlantic Ocean and the River Gambia. Alternatively, it is possible to get there via an organised excursion from the hotels and ground operators along the coast (see *Organised excursions* in *Chapter 3*).

By road

The island of Banjul, which is separated from the mainland by Oyster Creek, can be visited by road by driving along the main Banjul to Basse Highway that crosses Denton Bridge over the creek. The main entrance to the city is marked by Arch 22, which was built to commemorate the military coup of July 22 1994 (see later in this chapter). By turning right from the main road after crossing Denton Bridge, on to the Bund Road, it is possible to circumvent most of the busy streets in the city if you are heading for the ferry.

You can catch a bush taxi to take you to Banjul from anywhere in the country, though of course you'll have to change taxis several times, depending on how far away you start your journey. It should even be possible to take this form of transport from as far away as Fatoto, in the far east of the country, and get to Banjul the same day. From nearer at hand, it is easy to catch one of the regular and numerous bush taxis that run into Banjul and that set off, or pass through, Westfield Junction in Serrekunda for less than US$0.50.

Shared taxis also run regularly from Serrekunda, Bakau and Fajara into the city. Although more expensive than bush taxis they do have the advantage that they'll take you directly to wherever you want to go in Banjul. You'll have to negotiate a price, but it shouldn't be more than around US$0.50–3.50 from any of the areas mentioned above.

Tourist taxis will readily take you from your hotel to anywhere in Banjul but are a lot more expensive, though they do have the advantage that they will wait for you while you do whatever it is you have come for. Even though most hotels display official tariffs for tourist taxis, it is still sometimes possible to negotiate a lower price, so have a go. GPTC buses run into Banjul several times a day from upcountry towns as far away as Basse.

By river

From anywhere on the north bank of the River Gambia, you will have to cross the river by ferry at some point if you want to make for the south bank. The obvious choice if you have a car or taxi is to take the ferry from Barra, but this can be very busy and often only one of the ferries is working. This means you could have a long, hot and uncomfortable wait at the ferry terminal before you get across (see *Chapter 9*). Many travellers from further upcountry prefer to catch the ferry south of Farafenni as it is often much quicker to get across the river. Using this route has the added advantage that the road from Soma to Banjul is tarmac (though full of deep pot-holes in certain sections) and therefore a bit quicker. If you are on foot, you can circumvent all of this hassle by catching one of the *pirogues* that ply the river from Barra to Banjul and vice versa. Many local people prefer to travel this way as it is quick and cheap, but as a *toubab* (white), you may well be charged a much higher rate than the locals, especially in the evening. Our advice is to be hard and don't let them get away with flagrant overcharging of tourists. Be aware that when the river is a little rough, these *pirogue* rides can be fairly frightening, if not dangerous, especially when they are jam-packed to the seams with too many passengers.

The Banjul–Barra ferry is supposed to run between the south and north banks of the River Gambia every hour or so. Unfortunately at the time of writing, only one of the three ferries was in working order. This means that crossing times can be fluid and it is likely that you will have quite a wait for the ferry. The good news is that there are some new ferries being built in the Netherlands at the moment, though it is likely to be at least a year or two before they are delivered and ready for service. The official crossing times of the ferries is from 07.00–19.00, but this is seldom stuck to. If you need to cross the river in a vehicle, you should get to the ferry terminal early. Occasionally, the only remaining ferry also breaks down and there is no way for vehicles to get across at Banjul or Barra, so check with locals for the latest information.

By air

Banjul International Airport is located about 25km from Banjul, at Yundum. It's easy to get there and away by using tourist or shared taxis. Be aware that if you catch a bush taxi, via Westfield Junction in Serrekunda, it will drop you off at the entrance to the airport. It's a long walk from here to the terminal unless you are lucky enough to get a lift.

ORIENTATION

You may be confused by the street names in Banjul, as many of them have been changed recently. Many local people still know and use the old names, but for the sake of consistency, we will use only the new names.

Being a small city on an island, and with its roads laid out in a grid pattern, it is fairly easy to find your way around Banjul. Most tourists that visit Banjul consider Albert Market to be the main attraction, especially the craft market. The roads near here, such as Russell Street and Liberation Street, are also jam-packed with shops and market stalls, as are the pavements around 22 July Square. Apart from the main tourist attractions of the National Museum and Arch 22, though, there's really not a lot more to see.

The main road that leads into Banjul (Independence Drive), is blocked to traffic near Arch 22 and only the President is allowed to drive straight through, though you can walk through if you're on foot. If you're driving, you have to take the second exit off the roundabout with the statue of the soldier on it, on to Marina Parade, then take a right and then a left to bring you out again on Independence Drive. From here you drive straight down to 22 July Square, which you could say is the real centre of Banjul. Away from the main streets are residential streets that consist of compounds with rusty corrugated iron roofs, seldom visited by tourists. When walking, beware of the open sewers that criss-cross the city. It wouldn't be pleasant to fall into one of them.

GETTING AROUND

Getting around Banjul couldn't be easier. If you're on foot, it's possible to walk anywhere you want to go in a fairly short time, especially if you are just visiting the tourist attractions. Alternatively, shared taxis are commonplace and it shouldn't cost you more than US$0.50–1.50 to be driven from one side of the city to the other.

WHERE TO STAY
Midrange: US$100 and under

The **Atlantic Hotel** (tel: 228601; fax: 227861; email: atlantic@corinthia.com) is the only hotel actually in Banjul that caters totally for tourists (although visiting dignitaries and diplomats often stay here as well). This is a very swish place, with two good restaurants, three bars, games rooms, shops, tennis and squash courts and, of course, a very good swimming pool. The beach is right outside the gates but is prone to being washed away by storms and has to be replaced once in a while. It can also be a bit smelly, which is why most of the guests seem to prefer to relax by the poolside. Of course, this also has the added bonus that it's bumster and hassle-free, which the beach most definitely is not. A single air-conditioned room here during the tourist season will cost you US$64.50 per night for bed and breakfast, a twin US$81.50 and a suite US$102. During the rainy season rates are slightly lower, and if you are staying for a longer period you can negotiate a discount with the management.

There is a very good bird garden within the grounds, which was planted by Clive Barlow, who was probably the first European to seriously study the brids of The Gambia, and is still based at the hotel (see *Birding guides* in *Chapter 3*). Here, within a very short period of time, a bare piece of ground has been converted into a miniature forest. There are a couple of small pools in the garden, as well as a raised viewing platform. An amazing variety of birds have visited the garden over the years and there is a resident group of Gambian epauletted fruit bats which hang beneath the canopy and are very easy to see. During the day, especially in late afternoon as the bats begin to get ready for a night of action, you can't help but hear their calls, which sound just like small chiming bells.

The only downside to the Atlantic Hotel is the bumsters that hang around outside. It seems that as soon as you step from the gates someone latches on to you who insists on showing you around Banjul, even if you don't want a guide (see *Bumsters* in *Chapter 3*). Once they are on to you, it's very difficult, if not impossible, to get rid of them. You can cajole, threaten, or abuse them, but it doesn't make the least bit of difference and they can be very annoying if you're just after a quiet stroll to see the sights. Of course they are only after your money, no matter what they may say, but even if you give them some (and many people do - just to get rid of them) they still follow you like a shadow hoping for more. Many tourists give up walking around outside after they have experienced this a few times, and spend the rest of their holiday cooped up in the peace and quiet of the hotel.

Palm Grove Hotel (tel: 201620; fax: 201621; email: palmgrove@gamtel.gm; web: www.gambia-palmgrovehotel.co.uk) is situated on the Banjul Highway about 3km from the city, and is very popular with tourists. It backs on to a salt-water lagoon which is separated from the sea by a vegetated sand spit, making it a very safe area for swimming, with a good beach. There is a swimming pool with a separate pool for children, a pool bar that also serves snacks and meals, a bar, restaurant, gift shop, laundry service, hair salon, massage studio and disco. Activities available at the hotel include tennis, table tennis, petanque, volleyball, windsurfing, canoeing, table football and even karaoke. Accommodation is in single or two-storey buildings and each room has its own balcony or patio. A double B&B will set you back US$73.50 per night, while a single B&B is US$48 per night. This hotel has recently been refurbished and the rooms have en-suite bathrooms, TV, direct-dial telephones and fridges. Upgrades are also available if you want air conditioning or a suite.

Almost next door is the **Wadner Beach Hotel**, also known as the **Laguna Beach Hotel**. This hotel has been closed for a couple of seasons but we have been told it might be open again in the 2001/2002 tourist season. We have no information on prices or the facilities offered but it may be worth while checking it out (the old telephone number is 228236, but we have no idea if it will be the same if the hotel reopens).

Carlton Hotel (tel: 228670; fax: 227214) is in the city and has clean rooms and a pleasant atmosphere. A single room will cost US$11 (US$18.50 with air conditioning), a double room will cost US$13.50 (US$20 with air conditioning) and a triple room US$15.50 (US$21 with air conditioning). Rooms on the first floor are more expensive (a single with air conditioning at US$20.50 and a double with air conditioning at US$24).

Shoestring: US$12 and under

Most of the hotels in Banjul itself appear to be geared more to visiting business-persons than tourists, but are well placed in the city.

Apollo Hotel (tel: 228184) is a little dowdy and is fairly expensive for what you get, at US$8.50 for a single room with fan and US$13 for a double room with fan. The rooms are decent and clean though.

Princess Diana Hotel, also known as the **Kantora Hotel** (tel: 238715) is more full of life, but looks a little run down. It's also more expensive with a single B&B costing US$10 (with fan), a double B&B with fan US$13.50, and a double air-conditioned room for US$17. It's a strange name for a hotel in Africa, but apparently the owner had a thing for Princess Diana.

There are a few places that are seldom visited by tourists but have a more African feel about them, though the facilities are more modern than you'll find in many compounds.

Taranga Guest House (tel: 225641) is a fairly cheap option but not as clean as it could be. A double room will cost you US$5.50 or a little more if you want a room with a fan.

Duma Guest House (tel: 228381) is slightly more expensive, but cleaner. A single B&B is US$5.50, a double B&B is US$7 (US$8 if you want a room with a toilet), and a triple B&B is US$12.

WHERE TO EAT AND DRINK

The **African Heritage Gallery, Bar and Restaurant** is one of a kind. You can eat and drink on the balcony for fairly reasonable prices, whilst watching the hubbub of the street sellers below (you can just see the shoreline of the River Gambia as well). You can also browse in the shop behind the balcony where there is an excellent choice of arts and crafts for sale, all at fixed prices (which are sometimes a bit steep - but it's worth it to take a break from the hassle of the craft market). There are paintings, carvings, jewellery and clothes, just to mention a few of the items on sale. Some of the craft work, in particular, is pretty unusual and different from the normal goods that you will be offered elsewhere. Just to top it all off, the bathroom is almost palatial, and well worth a visit on its own! Don't be put off by the dingy entrance to the restaurant and if you miss it first time (it's just another doorway off the street), keep trying, as it's worth it.

The **Ya Mariam Ceesay Bar and Restaurant** can seem a bit dismal but, then again, it's always been more or less empty whenever we have visited. We imagine that when it's full it can be as lively as they come. Its also very handy if you happen to get stuck at the ferry crossing for a few hours, as it's located right next to the ferry terminal. The **Downtown Restaurant**, which is at the Apollo Hotel, looks fairly drab and nondescript. We've never eaten here, so we can't say what the food is like, but at least it's peaceful. The restaurant at the **Carlton Hotel** looks a lot better, but again we've never tried the food. The **Ali Baba Restaurant** (tel: 224055) is exactly the opposite, and is very popular, with a distinctly Lebanese atmosphere. This restaurant does some wonderful Lebanese food too, such as *shawarmas* and *falafel* sandwiches, that are very tasty and fairly cheap. We heartily recommend Ali Baba's to anyone even though you sometimes get hassled by street sellers while you're eating. Next to Ali Baba's is another good Lebanese restaurant, the **King of Shawarma Restaurant** (tel: 229799). The **Golden Palace Casino, Bar and Restaurant** has recently been refurbished and is worth a try. **Sai Ali Awa's Grill House** (tel: 228748), along Independence Drive, also has a cyber café.

There is also a restaurant and snack bar at the **Palm Grove Hotel** (tel: 201620) about 3km from Banjul along the main highway and a restaurant at the **Atlantic Hotel** (tel: 228601).

There are quite a few places to eat in Banjul that are cheap and cheerful, and the list below is certainly not exhaustive. Don't be surprised if you come across places that are not mentioned here, or if some of those mentioned are not around when you visit. These places tend to come and go, or change their name fairly quickly, as it is often hard for the owners to make enough money out of them to get by. You can also get very cheap food from a number of street vendors, especially around the market area. The best places we have found in this range include **Mandela Alles Klar Fast Food**, **Alles Klar 2000 Fast Food and Grill House, Queen's Bar and Restaurant, St. Raphael Snack Bar, Friendzzzzz Restaurant, Fattou Bintou's Bantaba, Las Vegas Bar and Grill** and **Tunkus Fast Food**. An excellent cheaper place to eat is located opposite the **Queen's Night Club** in Rene Blain Street. This is the strangely named **CNN Bar and Restaurant**. It's an open dining area in a compound, but is full of atmosphere and with some interesting murals on the wall.

There is a small area of bars and restaurants by the craft market near the Palm Grove Hotel, which is 3km out of town along the main highway. The **Bacchus Bar and Restaurant** looks quite good and is located on the beach, while a couple of cheaper places here are **Malcom's Restaurant** and **The Gambian Bar and Restaurant**. Be warned: you will probably face a lot of hassle from bumsters in this area. We did.

LISTINGS
Information for visitors
There is no real information available for visitors, except for a few old leaflets that you *may* be able to buy from the National Museum. If you want to read up on the city or the country as a whole, your best bet is to locate one or more of the books listed in *Appendix 2: Further Information*.

Embassies, high commissions and consulates
As the vast majority of these are in the more fashionable areas of Fajara and Bakau, rather than in Banjul, you will find them all listed in *Chapter 2*.

Foreign exchange
There are numerous exchange bureaux where you can change your foreign currency into dalasis (they take cash or travellers' cheques) throughout the city, but the best places to do this are probably the banks. Some of the banks may charge a small commission on your transaction so it may be worthwhile shopping around to see who offers the best rates. It is possible to draw money using a Visa or Mastercard at all Standard Chartered Bank branches but they do make a small charge on all transactions.

If you want to exchange foreign money for dalasis, you could try the moneychangers that loiter outside Banjul post office. Though it is illegal to change money like this in The Gambia, the police always seem to turn a blind eye to the activities of the moneychangers. If you decide to use them, just be careful to check your money and make sure that no one is watching you from nearby, with the aim of robbing you later.

Banks
There are branches of the International Bank for Commerce, the Trust Bank, the Continent Bank and Standard Chartered Bank in Banjul. All are within easy walking distance of each other.

Hospitals
The Gambia's main hospital, the Royal Victoria, is located within Banjul: it has a casualty department (though it's pretty gory and not for the faint-hearted). If you have not had an accident that requires immediate attention, it is probably wiser to visit one of the many clinics (see *Medical facilities* in *Chapter 5*) in the Fajara, Bakau and Serrekunda areas.

Internet
Sai Ali Awa's Grill House and Cyber Café is on Independence Drive.

Post
The main post office is located on Russell Street. It is open during normal business hours. If you are posting a parcel home, you may find it best to visit the parcel desk first (first on your right as you go in); get them to look at the contents and stick a customs declaration on it. This way you avoid your parcel being opened later by customs officials, who are not always that gentle with your goods. It is also possible (for the stamp-collectors among you) to buy sets of Gambian stamps in the main post office and they actually have a desk that deals just with this.

Telephone
There are several Gamtel offices and private telecentres throughout the city. Remember to ask the call rate in private telecentres before using the telephone, as they are often a lot more expensive than the Gamtel rates.

Travel agencies and airlines
Air Afrique (Daniel Goddard Street)
Air Guinee (tel: 223296)
Air Senegal (tel: 472095, 202117 or 202118)
Atlas Travel Agency (tel: 222171 or 222172. fax: 222280)
Banjul Travel Agency (tel: 228473 or 228813. fax: 225833)
Club Gambia Tourism and Travel Agency (tel: 202218. fax: 226072)
Continental Travels (tel: 224058 or 224059. fax: 224118)
Fahed Travel Agency (tel: 224648 or 201151. fax: 201149)
Gambia International Airlines (tel: 223701, 223703, 223704 or 223705)
Ghana Airways (tel: 228245 or 226913. fax: 225884)
Globe Travel Agency (tel: 224490 or 222144. fax: 224970)
Olympic Travels (tel: 223370 or 223371. fax: 223372)
Sontinfara Travel Agency (tel: 202555. fax: 202544)

Nightclubs
The **Queen's Night Club**, formerly known as the **Oasis Nightclub**, along Rene Blain Street, occasionally has local bands playing and is worth a visit if you like loud music. It has been described as lively and raunchy. The **Palm Grove Hotel** also has a nightclub/disco.

Crafts
Although you may pick up some carvings from street vendors, without a doubt the best places to buy local crafts are the **African Heritage Gallery, Bar and Restaurant** and the Craft Market in **Albert Market**. The shops at the **Atlantic Hotel** and **Palm Grove Hotel** also have a good selection but are more expensive than the market. Between the Palm Grove Hotel and Wadner/Laguna Beach Hotel, which are about 3km from Banjul along the main highway, there is a small craft

market with the usual blend of batiks and carvings etc, but we had a lot of hassle here when we visited.

Casinos

The **Golden Palace Casino, Bar and Restaurant** has recently been refurbished. We have no idea what the casino facilities consist of at the moment but it may be worth visiting if you fancy a flutter.

PLACES TO VISIT

The **National Museum** on Independence Drive is a tired-looking place whose exhibits have been on show for quite a while. However, in spite of this the museum is worth a visit and some of its exhibits are very interesting, especially if you have enjoyed reading the history section of this guide. Some of the exhibits allow to you put a face to some famous names in Gambian history. The museum is open from 08.00–16.00 Monday to Thursday, 08.00–13.00 Friday and Saturday and is closed on Sunday. The entrance fee is US$1 for non-Gambians and less than US$0.50 for Gambians. There are public toilets and a drink shop in the pleasant gardens. The notice board on the wall by the entrance displays some of the museum's recent activities around the country, such as exhibits and shows.

Arch 22 is a very incongruous piece of architecture that somehow just doesn't seem to fit in with the rest of Banjul. It was designed by Senegalese architect Pierre Goudiaby and commemorates the military coup of July 22 1994. It is around 35m tall, with a triangular roof atop a balcony that gives superb views of the city. The entire structure rests on eight massive columns that sit astride Independence Drive; the only person allowed to drive beneath the columns is the Gambian President himself. A lift and stairs lead up to the balcony where there is a coffee shop that is open to the public, a small museum and art gallery. The arch is open from 08.00 to around midnight, seven days a week. The entrance fee is less than US$1.

The **Bund Road** has long been known as a birding hotspot with ornithologists worldwide. The road is adjacent to a large expanse of tidal mud that is exposed at low tide and alive with birds (see *Chapter 8*).

Along the main Banjul Highway, and in the shade of the trees, you will find several groups of ladies that sell oysters. These ladies spend many hours of each day collecting the oysters from the stilt roots of mangroves, both from around Banjul and from within Tanbi Wetlands. They cook the oysters and sell them and many Gambians stop on their way home from work in the city to buy them. We are not too sure how safe it is to eat them as shellfish are notorious for collecting and storing toxins within their bodies, but many people eat them apparently without suffering ill effects. The oyster shells are deposited in huge mounds as waste, though many of them are burnt and crushed to make a lime-based paint that is used in many Gambian compounds.

Patas monkey

The Coastal Resorts and Serrekunda

Many people are surprised at the choice available in the coastal resorts of The Gambia when they first visit. There is a whole range of hotels, apartments for rent, guesthouses, restaurants, casinos, nightclubs, bars, supermarkets and shops. It's almost like a tiny part of a European resort translocated into Africa. The only difference is the hot sun, sandy beaches and palm trees, though there is also a definite flavour of West Africa everywhere you go, whether it is the bright clothes of the women or the gorgeous birdlife flitting around the hotel gardens. If you leave the coastal resorts and go just a few kilometres inland, you will suddenly find yourself in the real African landscape.

One important point to note is that while all of the hotels and restaurants are open during the whole of the tourist season (October to April), many cut down their services or close entirely during the off season, which roughly coincides with the rainy season. It's impossible to let you know which will be closed, or even when, because in many cases this varies year by year. Many of these establishments are owned or managed by ex-pats or foreigners who may go back to their home countries for a week, a month, or even for the whole rainy season. Even the larger hotels often lay-off a significant portion of their staff during this period, so service may well be slower.

GETTING AROUND
This is probably the easiest of all the areas of The Gambia for travelling. There are plenty of tourist taxis available at the many hotels and large numbers of shared taxis ply all of the main roads. Bush taxis regularly take passengers from Westfield Junction in Serrekunda into Bakau and Fajara. All of these except the tourist taxis will cost less than US$0.50. The tourist taxis are more expensive but have the advantage that they will wait for you if you want (see *Tourist taxis* in *Chapter 3* for a rough idea of prices).

CAPE ST MARY
Cape St Mary was one of the first of The Gambia's tourist areas but these days a lot of the cape has been turned over to residential use, though there are still plenty of hotels and restaurants. The beach at Cape Point has been suffering badly from erosion and the government, along with some local businesses, has tried several methods of halting this erosion, with little or no success. Surprisingly, considering its location, if you walk east from Cape Point, you will find an area of long, empty beaches, mangroves and salt marsh, which is fairly undisturbed and undeveloped. Do be careful here though, as many tourists and ex-pats have been mugged on this stretch of the coast, so stay in a group when walking here, the larger the better (see *Theft* in *Chapter 3*).

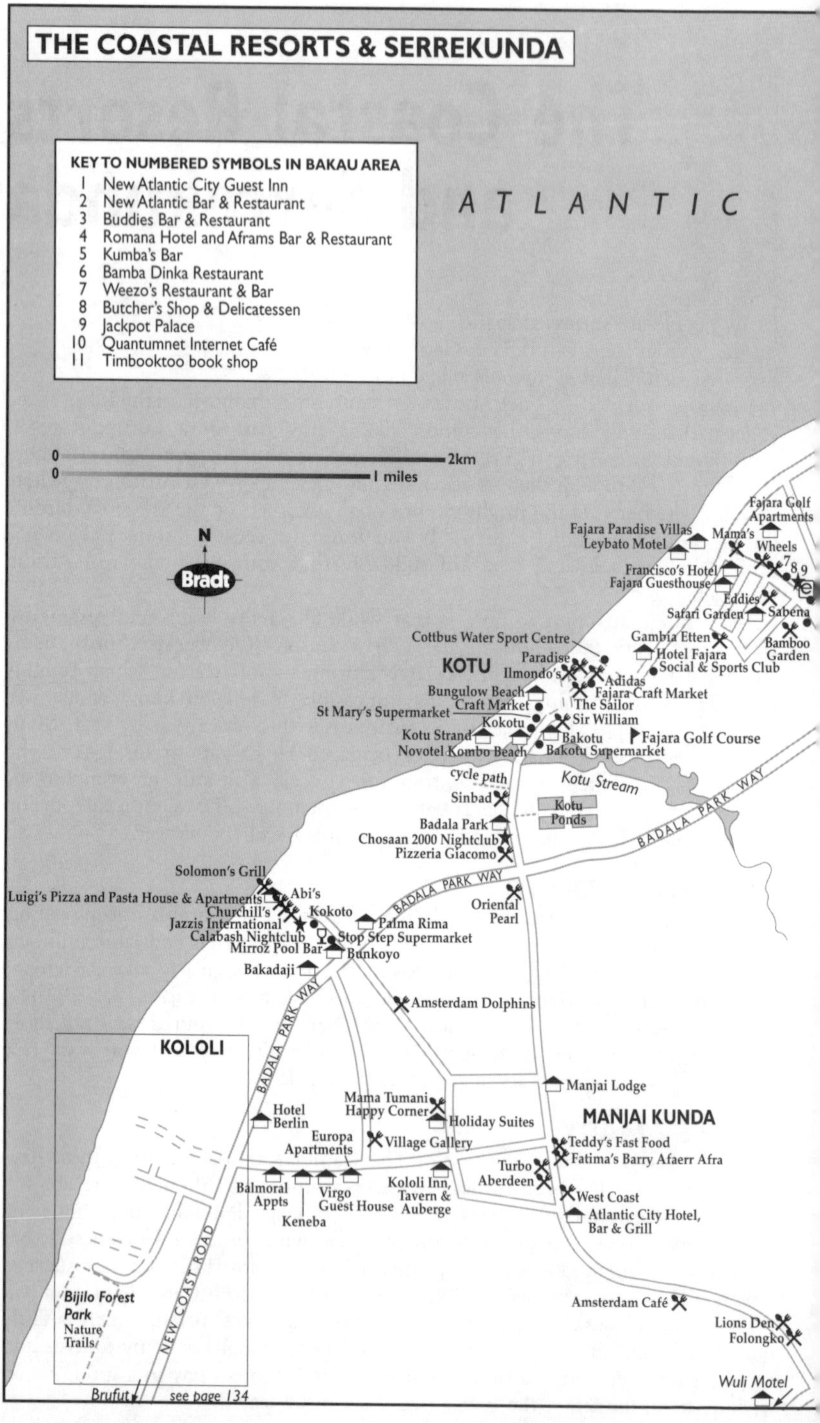

THE COASTAL RESORTS & SERREKUNDA

KEY TO NUMBERED SYMBOLS IN BAKAU AREA
1 New Atlantic City Guest Inn
2 New Atlantic Bar & Restaurant
3 Buddies Bar & Restaurant
4 Romana Hotel and Aframs Bar & Restaurant
5 Kumba's Bar
6 Bamba Dinka Restaurant
7 Weezo's Restaurant & Bar
8 Butcher's Shop & Delicatessen
9 Jackpot Palace
10 Quantumnet Internet Café
11 Timbooktoo book shop

0 _____ 2km
0 _____ 1 miles

N

Bradt

ATLANTIC

Fajara Golf Apartments
Fajara Paradise Villas   Mama's
Leybato Motel   Wheels
Francisco's Hotel
Fajara Guesthouse
Eddies   Sabena
Safari Garden
Gambia Etten   Bamboo Garden
KOTU   Paradise   Hotel Fajara
Ilmondo's   Social & Sports Club
Cottbus Water Sport Centre   Adidas
Bungulow Beach   Fajara Craft Market
Craft Market   The Sailor
St Mary's Supermarket   Kokotu   Sir William
Kotu Strand   Bakotu   Fajara Golf Course
Novotel Kombo Beach   Bakotu Supermarket
cycle path   Kotu Stream
Sinbad   Kotu Ponds
Badala Park   BADALA PARK WAY
Chosaan 2000 Nightclub
Pizzeria Giacomo
Solomon's Grill
Luigi's Pizza and Pasta House & Apartments   Abi's
Churchill's   Kokoto   Oriental Pearl
Jazzis International   BADALA PARK WAY
Calabash Nightclub   Palma Rima
Mirroz Pool Bar   Stop Step Supermarket
Bakadaji   Bunkoyo

Amsterdam Dolphins

KOLOLI

Manjai Lodge

Mama Tumani
Happy Corner
Hotel   Holiday Suites   MANJAI KUNDA
Berlin   Teddy's Fast Food
Europa   Village Gallery   Fatima's Barry Afaerr Afra
Apartments   Turbo
Kololi Inn,   Aberdeen
Balmoral   Virgo   Tavern &   West Coast
Appts   Guest House   Auberge   Atlantic City Hotel,
Keneba   Bar & Grill

Bijilo Forest Park
Nature Trails   Amsterdam Café   Lions Den
Folongko

NEW COAST ROAD

Brufut   see page 134   Wuli Motel

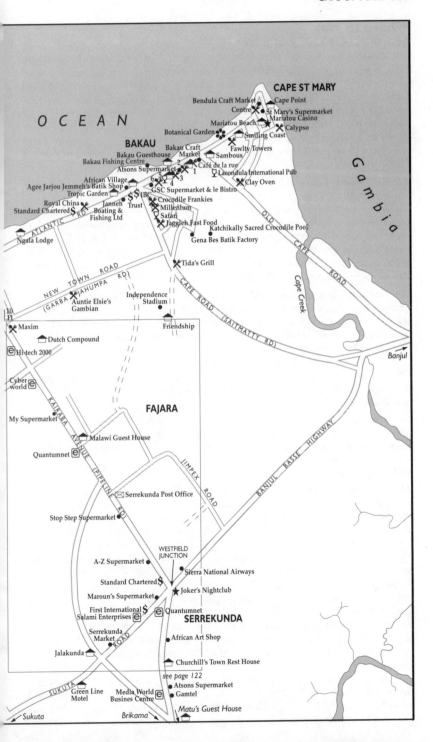

OCEAN

CAPE ST MARY

Bendula Craft Market — Cape Point
Centre — St Mary's Supermarket
Mariatou Casino
Mariatou Beach
BAKAU — Calypso
Botanical Garden — Smiling Coast
Bakau Craft
Market — Fawlty Towers
Bakau Guesthouse — 2 — Sambous
Bakau Fishing Centre
Atsons Supermarket — 1 — Café de la rue
African Village — 6 — 3 — Lacondula International Pub
Agee Jarjou Jemmeh's Batik Shop — 5 — 4 — Clay Oven
Tropic Garden — GSC Supermarket & le Bistro
Royal China — Crocodile Frankies
Standard Chartered — Janneh — Millenium
Trust — Safari
Boating & — Jaggleh Fast Food
Fishing Ltd — Katchikally Sacred Crocodile Pool
Ngala Lodge — Gena Bes Batik Factory

Gambia

ATLANTIC RD

Tida's Grill

NEW TOWN ROAD
(GARBA JAHUMPA RD)
Auntie Elsie's
Gambian
Independence
Stadium
Friendship

CAPE ROAD (SAITMATTY RD)

Banjul

Cape Creek

10
11

Maxim

Dutch Compound

Hi-tech 2000

Cyber
world

My Supermarket

FAJARA

Malawi Guest House

Quantumnet

KARABA AVENUE / PIPELINE RD

LIMPEX ROAD

BANJUL BASSE HIGHWAY

Serrekunda Post Office

Stop Step Supermarket

WESTFIELD
JUNCTION

A-Z Supermarket

Sierra National Airways

Standard Chartered

Joker's Nightclub

Maroun's Supermarket

First International
Salami Enterprises — Quantumnet

SERREKUNDA

Serrekunda
Market

African Art Shop

Jalakunda

Churchill's Town Rest House

ROAD

see page 122

SUKUTA

Green Line
Motel

Media World
Busines Centre

Atsons Supermarket
Gamtel

Matu's Guest House

Sukuta — Brikama

Where to stay
Midrange: US$100 and under

The **Mariatou Beach Hotel** (tel: 497738), which used to be known as **Amie's Beach Hotel**, has a swimming pool (with children's area), four bars, coffee shop, supermarket, three restaurants, shops and a hairdresser. Activities include tennis, table tennis, volleyball, a video room and a disco. The hotel leads right onto the beach and there is often live local entertainment laid on for the guests. Prices start at US$20.50 for a single B&B, US$27 for a double B&B and US$68 for a presidential suite. Each room has air conditioning, en suite bathroom, TV, fridge and balcony. There are also large, one-bedroom self-catering apartments available, with en-suite bathroom, kitchenette, terrace or balcony and lounge, at a cost of US$40.50 per day.

The **Cape Point Hotel and Restaurant** (tel: 495005; fax: 495375) is a fairly small, family-run, friendly hotel. There is a swimming pool, children's pool, bar and restaurant, and you can hire bicycles for a day out. Double B&B costs US$34 (US$40.50 with air conditioning), single-use double B&B costs US$34, and an extra bed will set you back a further US$10. There are also self-catering apartments available for US$47.50 or US$54.50 with air conditioning. If you want a fridge in your room it will cost you a further US$17 per week and air conditioning will also cost you an extra US$17 per day if you don't already have it in your room. Safety boxes can be hired for US$5.50 per week.

The **Smiling Coast Luxury Self-catering Apartments** (tel: 494653; fax: 497653), formerly known as **Fawlty Towers** is a place to stay with a difference. They have 14 apartments in a single block which all have a balcony, though 'self-catering' only stretches to an electric kettle and toaster in the rooms. A room with fan costs US$20.50–24 (or US$27–30.50 with air conditioning) and a family room with air conditioning costs US$32.50 per night, though discounts can be negotiated for longer stays. Continental breakfast costs US$3.50 and an English breakfast US$4. This is a very pleasant place to stay and although there is no integral swimming pool or restaurant there is an agreement that guests can use the ones at Cape Point Hotel, which is not far away.

Sambous Bar and Restaurant (tel: 495237) is a small place that also has some accommodation. There are ten rooms, all with fans, WC, shower, washbasin and mosquito window nets. Although a little old and shabby they are clean. A single B&B costs US$24.

Where to eat

The **Calypso Bar and Restaurant** (tel: 496292) on Cape Point is located in a lovely position right at the sea's edge. The indoor bar is open to the sea breeze and there are tables on small patios next to the water. The food is excellent and the staff always friendly and helpful, giving the whole place a wonderful atmosphere. There is a good range of main courses and omelettes, with a very tasty vegetarian selection and an all-day English breakfast. Meals start at around US$3.50 and the restaurant serves food between 09.30 and 22.00. The **Clay Oven** (tel: 496600) is a very high quality Indian restaurant, though fairly expensive. You can eat either inside or outside and the staff are very friendly.

   Fawlty Towers Bar and Restaurant is a fun place with a good selection of European food. **Sambous Bar and Restaurant** (tel: 495237) also offers a good selection of both local and European foods, starting at around US$3.50. Many of the hotels have restaurants too, including **Mariatou Beach Hotel** and **Cape Point Hotel**.

   There are a handful of cheaper places where you can eat in the Cape St Mary area. Some of them sell only African food, but most can stretch to a plate of chips or a steak as well. One of the best is the **Centre Bar and Restaurant**. Opposite Sambous, along Old Cape Road, is another good place, the **Lancodula International Pub**.

Listings

Crafts
Bendula Craft Market is a large market opposite the Cape Point Hotel.

Casinos
The **Mariatou Casino** is located near Cape Point and behind the hotel of the same name.

Supermarkets and tourist shops
St Mary's Food and Wine Supermarket is opposite Cape Point Hotel, and close to Bendula Craft Market.

Places to visit
The **Botanical Garden** (tel: 495425) was established in 1924 and costs less than US$0.50 to enter. The garden was being renovated in early 2001, with an extension being added at the same time. It is small, but packed with a wide variety of native and non-native plants. The vast majority of them are labelled. There is also a series of winding footpaths, interspersed with benches in shady places. This is a very pleasant place for a morning or afternoon stroll which promises to be even better in the future when present plans are realised. These include a small cafeteria in the garden where you'll be able to sit peacefully in a hassle-free environment and enjoy a drink and snack. In addition the birdlife of this garden is relatively rich considering its size and location, and includes nesting Hamerkop.

Cape Creek is an area of salt marsh, mangroves and open water that is very good for birds. At low tide large expanses of mud are exposed and many waders can be easily seen from the road that bisects the area. They include black-winged stilt, *Himantopus himantopus*, Eurasian oystercatcher, *Haematopus ostralegus*, common greenshank, *Tringa nebularia*, and other wading birds. It is also worth searching the mud and shrubby vegetation for more elusive species. Red-billed quelea, *Quelea quelea*, has been recorded here, as have small Palearctic migrants such as warblers. Further along the road that leads through the area towards the junction with the Banjul Highway, you have a good chance of spotting a yellow-crowned bishop, *Euplectes afer*, among the reeds. In the rainy season these beautiful birds can often be seen performing their strange display flight, looking more like huge, golden bumblebees than birds. In the latter half of the dry season they lose their gorgeous breeding plumage and become just another 'little brown job'. Around the Cape Point area it is also worth keeping an eye open for Armitage's skink, a species of lizard that has only ever been recorded in The Gambia. This small skink, with transverse stripes across its body, is known from only four collected specimens. Nothing is known about its ecology or even the habitats it lives in. On a personal note, any sightings or observations of this rare species would be gratefully received by the Wildlife Department (tel: 375888; email: wildlife@gamtel.gm).

FAJARA AND BAKAU
Fajara and Bakau are cosmopolitan towns with areas ranging from the huge private residences of the rich and powerful, through a range of hotels and restaurants catering for the tourist trade, to the shanty-like town around the area of the sacred crocodile pool. Fajara and Bakau are where you can find most of the large embassies and high commissions and many of the better local business premises. For tourists they are in many ways better than the mainly tourist-dominated areas such as Kotu and Kololi (see later in this chapter), as you can walk around more freely with fewer hassles, though the beach is of course still dotted with bumsters.

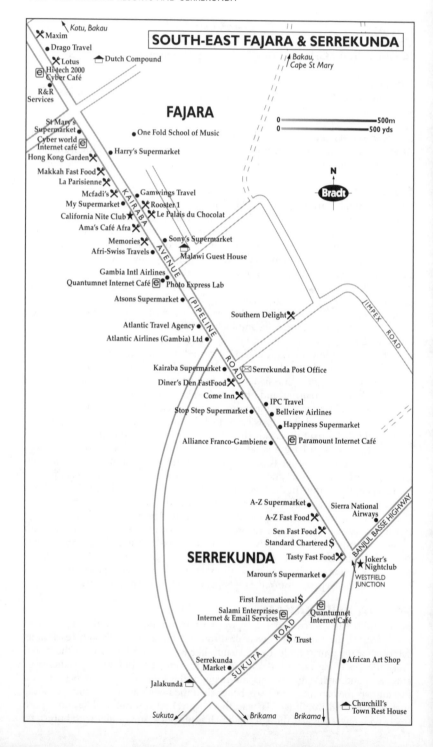

SOUTH-EAST FAJARA & SERREKUNDA

↗ *Kotu, Bakau*
✗ Maxim
● Drago Travel
✗ Lotus ⌂ Dutch Compound
ⓔ Hi-tech 2000
Cyber Café
● R&R Services

↑ *Bakau, Cape St Mary*

FAJARA

● One Fold School of Music

St Mary's Supermarket ●
Cyber world Internet café ⓔ
Hong Kong Garden ✗ ● Harry's Supermarket

Makkah Fast Food ✗
La Parisienne ✗
Mcfadi's ✗ ● Gamwings Travel
My Supermarket ● ✗ Rooster 1
California Nite Club ★ ✗ Le Palais du Chocolat
Ama's Café Afra ✗
Memories ✗ ● Sony's Supermarket
Afri-Swiss Travels ●
⌂ Malawi Guest House

Gambia Intl Airlines ●
Quantumnet Internet Café ⓔ ● ● Photo Express Lab

Atsons Supermarket ●
Southern Delight ✗

Atlantic Travel Agency ●
Atlantic Airlines (Gambia) Ltd ●

Kairaba Supermarket ● ✉ Serrekunda Post Office
Diner's Den FastFood ✗
Come Inn ✗
● IPC Travel
Stop Step Supermarket ● ● Bellview Airlines
● Happiness Supermarket
Alliance Franco-Gambiene ● ⓔ Paramount Internet Café

A-Z Supermarket ● Sierra National Airways
A-Z Fast Food ✗
Sen Fast Food ✗
Standard Chartered $

SERREKUNDA
Tasty Fast Food ✗
Maroun's Supermarket ● ★ Joker's Nightclub
WESTFIELD JUNCTION

First International $
Salami Enterprises Internet & Email Services ⓔ ⓔ Quantumnet Internet Café

$ Trust

Serrekunda Market ● ● African Art Shop

Jalakunda ⌂

⌂ Churchill's Town Rest House

↙ *Sukuta* ↓ *Brikama* ↓ *Brikama*

KAIRABA AVENUE (PIPELINE ROAD)
SUKUTA ROAD
IMPEX ROAD
BANJUL BASE HIGHWAY

N
Bradt

0 ——— 500m
0 ——— 500 yds

The coastline here includes some of the few low cliffs that are found in The Gambia. The cliffs are suffering from coastal erosion and littered at their bases with piles of rocks, making the going difficult, especially at high tide.

Where to stay
Upmarket: US$100 and above

Ngala Lodge (tel: 497672 or 494045; fax: 497429; email: info@ngalalodge.com; web: www.ngalalodge.com) is one of the most exclusive hotels in The Gambia. The lodge was originally a colonial mansion and is proud of the personal service it provides for its guests. There are just eight uniquely decorated and spacious suites, each with many extras including a private balcony or terrace, air conditioning, ceiling fans, en suite shower and WC, bathrobes, slippers, toiletries, hairdryer and minibar. From its cliff-top position the lodge looks out over its own gardens and swimming pool to the ocean. Two suites are available for independent travellers and they are priced at US$250 per night (US$125 per person).

The **Tropic Garden Hotel** is being totally rebuilt and is unlikely to be open before the 2002/2003 tourist season. We had a guided tour of the hotel during the rebuilding and it will certainly provide five-star accommodation to rival any of the other big hotels. Facilities will include a swimming pool, open-air jacuzzi, restaurants, bars, beach bars, games rooms, etc. It also has its own secluded beach at the base of the cliff. The suites are being built to a very high standard and each has air conditioning and en suite bathroom. One de luxe suite has its own private balcony and jacuzzi. We have no idea how much it will cost to stay here but it will be expensive.

Fajara Paradise Villas (tel: 494725 or 460441; fax: 494726; email: fajaraparadise@qanet.gm) are located by Leybato. There are 12 self-catering apartments, all with air conditioning, fridge/freezers, video, CD and mosquito nets and they all overlook the ocean. They range from three bedroom, split level apartments up to penthouse suites and prices start from US$500 per person per week. There is a maid service six days a week, and the maid will even wash and iron your laundry. There is also a garden with private swimming pool and access onto the beach.

Midrange: US$100 and under

Safari Garden Hotel (tel: 495887; tel/fax: 497841; email: geri@qanet.gm) is one of the best in The Gambia and is a special favourite with many independent travellers. It is a small hotel with only 18 double rooms set in a tropical garden. It has possibly the cleanest swimming pool anywhere in the country, with of course a bar and restaurant. The Safari Garden claims to be 'the hotel that gives more than it takes' and certainly lives up to its hard-earned reputation with many environmentally-friendly initiatives, including water and power conservation. It also buys its furniture from a local skill centre and a large proportion of its food from local people. Most telling of all though, is its high-quality and very loyal staff, many of whom have been with the hotel for years and worked their way up into more senior jobs. The Safari Garden Hotel is also one of the few hotels that does not lay off its staff during the off-season. In addition it helps its workers to improve themselves by giving them time off and adjusting duty rosters so that they can attend college courses, sometimes even paying a proportion of their course fees. In fact the hotel was recently awarded a Tourism Training Award by the Association of Small Scale Enterprises in Tourism (ASSET). The hotel guests are treated as members of the 'Safari family' and the staff and the English management are friendly and accessible. Each of the rooms has a fan, shower, washbasin, WC, mosquito window nets and fridge (two of them also have air conditioning, and mosquito bednets are available if required). A single B&B will set you back US$24 and a double B&B US$34 during the tourist season. In the off-season these prices are reduced to US$17 for a single B&B and around US$26.50 for a double B&B. The hotel also has safe-deposit boxes (less than US$1.50 per day, or US$8.50 for a week, with a US$7 (refundable) key deposit. The restaurant has a good selection of food and does some of the best chips in The Gambia. Entertainment includes a *kora* player on Wednesdays and a poolside BBQ on Fridays.

Hotel Fajara (tel: 494576; fax: 494575) is a pleasantly situated hotel right by the beach and adjacent to Fajara Golf Course. It has a swimming pool, children's pool, bar and restaurants. Facilities include a sun terrace, table tennis, volleyball, snooker, mini market, souvenir shop, satellite TV and a cyber café. The accommodation is either located in the hotel buildings or in bungalows. All rooms have en suite bathrooms, a balcony or terrace and a daily maid service. Air-conditioning is available at a supplement. A single B&B is US$44, a double B&B is US$51, and apartments are US$54.50.

Francisco's Hotel, Bar and Restaurant (tel/fax: 495332) is a small place with a very friendly and pleasant character. There are only eleven rooms, all with air conditioning, fan, TV and fridge. A single B&B is US$30.50, a double B&B is US$40.50, and the supplement for one extra person is US$7.

Leybato Motel, Bar and Restaurant (tel: 497186; fax: 497562), one of the oldest and best known establishments in this part of The Gambia, is located at the bottom of a fairly steep cliff, almost on the beach itself. The place is a popular hangout for both ex-pats and volunteers, as well as tourists. Accommodation is in African-style round huts. Each hut has a shower/bath, WC, washbasin, fridge and fan. A few of the rooms also have cooking facilities. A double B&B will cost you US$24. There is no generator here so the electricity supply is unlikely to be constant. The huts are set amongst a little oasis of tropical trees and plants and there are plenty of hammocks to choose from, either in the sun or the shade. The staff can arrange for jeep safaris or a transfer to **Sanyang Nature Camp**, located south along the coast (see *Chapter 8*).

African Village Hotel (tel: 495384; fax: 495307; email: europrop@gamtel.gm) is a lively and friendly hotel situated along Atlantic Road in Bakau. The hotel has a swimming pool, sun terrace, colourful gardens, shop, restaurant and bar. It's on a clifftop and steps lead down to a man-made sunbathing area next to the sea. The rooms are small and simply furnished (the bed is just a mattress on a concrete base), so don't expect too many comforts. A single B&B in an ordinary room will set you back US$27 (US$30.50 for a double), a single B&B in a round hut US$32.50 (US$34 for a double) and a single B&B in a sea view room US$39 (US$40.50 for a double). Apartments range from US$44–51 for a single B&B (US$51–61 for a double) and a mini suite is US$40.50 for a single B&B (US$47.50 for a double).

We were impressed by **Fajara Golf Apartments** (tel/fax: 495800 in The Gambia or 003150 4061401 in the Netherlands), not only by the outstanding quality of its construction and furnishings, but also by its relatively cheap prices. All of this in a very quiet and peaceful compound off-the-beaten-track in Fajara, not far from the restaurants etc. The self-catering apartments (there are only two) each have two bedrooms (with air conditioning), a sitting room (with ceiling fan) and a fully equipped kitchenette. They also have a safe, satellite TV, telephone, radio cassette, en suite bathroom, extra beds and cot (if wanted) and a daily maid service. The power is from the mains but there is also a standby generator, and each apartment has a patio with sunbeds, and faces out onto a tropical garden. During the tourist season the apartments cost US$37.50 per night and sleep four (more if you use the extra beds), but this is negotiable and cheaper during the rainy season. The apartments are about 200m from Kairaba Avenue and signposted.

Bakau Guesthouse (tel: 497460; fax: 396449; email alco@qanet.gm), opposite Atsons Supermarket along Atlantic Road, is far less inviting. There are shabby rooms with fans, WC, shower, washbasin and mosquito window nets, which cost US$13.50 for a single and US$17 for a double, excluding breakfast. There is also a studio, which has a kitchen and balcony with a view of the ocean, for US$22 per night. There is extensive building work taking place here, which includes more rooms and a restaurant, so the standard may be higher in the future.

Shoestring: US$12 and under

Fajara Guesthouse (tel: 496122; fax: 229689) is a pleasant place to stay run by a very friendly chap from Ghana. It is located in a quiet compound away from the main road. There is a bar but no restaurant and each of the rooms has en suite facilities, a fan and a fridge. A single B&B will cost you US$12 while a double B&B will cost around US$20.

The **New Atlantic City Guest Inn** (tel/fax: 494083) along Atlantic Road is one of the cheaper options in Fajara. There are seven rooms, each with fan, shower, washbasin, fridge and mosquito bednets. Some of them also have an en suite WC. A single room costs around US$10 for the night while a double is around US$19. These prices do not include breakfast.

The **Romana Hotel** (tel: 495127; email: romana@qanet.gm or modoubarry@hotmail.com) is cheap and cheerful with 11 rooms. Each room has ceiling fan, WC, shower, washbasin and mosquito window nets. The beds are on solid wooden bases and the rooms are tidy and clean. A double room will cost you US$13.50 per night, excluding breakfast.

The **Friendship Hotel** (tel: 495830, 495832, 495833 or 495834; fax: 497344; email: gnosc@qanet.gm) is a little off the beaten track and is right next door to Independence Stadium. From the outside the hotel looks a little bleak and barrack-like and inside it is showing signs of wear and tear. However, this hotel appears to be ideally suited to younger people, especially those who like sports, and many groups of students stay here when visiting The Gambia. Facilities include a swimming pool, two soccer fields, two basketball courts, two handball courts, two lawn tennis courts, a gymnasium, aerobics centre, synthetic running track and a boxing and judo centre. If you survive all that then there's a restaurant and bar to relax in afterwards. The rooms are fairly basic but cheap, ranging from around US$11 per night for a double room with fan to US$24 per night for a double suite with air conditioning, TV and telephone.

The **Dutch Compound** (tel: 497785; email: tj@qanet.gm) is set in a nice quiet compound away from the main street. There are hammocks for guests in the garden. It's possible to get hot and cold drinks and meals are also available, though they have to be booked in advance. The accommodation is fairly basic but clean and costs US$7 per person with breakfast an extra US$1.50. Double rooms are also available for US$20.50 B&B. Some of the rooms have fans and en suite facilities.

Malawi Guest House (tel: 393012; fax: 392227) is a popular place to stay. Rooms range in price from about US$7–17. There is often live music in the gardens in the evenings so it can be a bit noisy.

Where to eat

Ngala Lodge (tel: 497672 or 494045; fax: 497429; email: info@ngalalodge.com; web: www.ngalalodge.com) is one of the most exclusive places to eat in The Gambia, and is also one of the most expensive, with main courses starting at around US$13–15.50. It is an open air restaurant, perched on a clifftop amid a very peaceful tropical garden overlooking the sea. The atmosphere is wonderful and unlike some other restaurants, you have the time to sit and enjoy each others company and to make a whole evening of it.

The **Royal China** (tel: 497168) is a small but busy Chinese restaurant along the Atlantic Road. It has the usual range of Chinese meals but the choice is not as extensive as at the Oriental Pearl, for example. However, they do some European food as well, including some of the best chips in the country. Meals start at around US$4. **Francisco's Hotel, Bar and Restaurant** (tel/fax: 495332) is located in very luxuriant tropical gardens and serve mainly European food, though the names of a few of the meals such as 'elephant ears' (don't worry this is only thin slices of beef) will bring a smile to your face. Main meals start at around US$4. Remember to wear insect repellent if you come here to eat, as the gardens, pleasant as they are, also encourage mosquitoes - but don't let this put you off. **Leybato Motel, Bar and Restaurant** (tel: 497186; fax: 497562) is right down on the beach. The small restaurant serves a variety of mainly European meals starting at around US$4. The **New Atlantic Bar and Restaurant** (tel/fax: 494083) also offers a selection of local and European food staring at around US$3.50. **Buddies Bar and Restaurant** (tel/fax: 495501) is a newly refurbished establishment that has some very high quality murals by a local artist in the courtyard restaurant. The food on offer is a mixture of local and European meals starting at around US$3 (including a full English breakfast). For the meat-eaters amongst you try 'Buddies special mixed grill' for US$6.50. Buddies also has live music and entertainment every night during the tourist season.

Aframs Bar and Restaurant (tel: 495127) is located in the **Romana Hotel**. It serves both European and local food, with main meals starting at around US$3. It has a happy hour every night between 19.00–20.00 and a live band on Sunday nights. **Le Bistro** is located inside GSC Supermarket and serves a selection of sandwiches and snacks.

Mama's Buffet and à la carte Restaurant, along Kairaba Avenue, is considered a favourite among many of the ex-pats that live in The Gambia. Mama herself has been here for a long time and seems to know everyone. The restaurant opens at 09.00 and serves a different buffet each night. You can also choose your own meals from a selection of good wholesome European food. Meals can be eaten inside or outside in the garden. **Wheels** serves small cuts of meat and portions of chips that you can make into a meal of your own choice. You can eat in the garden or in the bar looking out onto the street. **Weezo's Restaurant and Bar** (tel: 496918) is an excellent Mexican restaurant with main meals starting at around US$7. Its weekday lunches are wonderful. The **Butchers Shop and Delicatessen** serves very tasty lunches with home-made food as well as selling a variety of meats and vegetables.

Maxim Restaurant has only just opened, so we can't pass judgement, but it looks worth a visit. The **Chinese Bamboo Garden** (tel: 494213) is an established Chinese restaurant with a good reputation that serves a good range of food at reasonable prices, as does the **Lotus Bar Grill House** along Kairaba Avenue. The **Hong Kong Garden Chinese Restaurant** (tel: 394669) does a buffet between 19.00–20.00 on Saturdays, priced at around US$6.6. Unfortunately, you often have to wait a long time to be served your meal if you don't go for the buffet. **La Parisienne** serves a selection of cakes and ice-creams at very reasonable prices.

MacFadi's is in a class of its own in The Gambia. It's a little like a Macdonalds but serves far tastier food including pizzas, and in record time for a country where it takes many places up to an hour to serve a meal. Here you can have tasty chicken pieces and chips on your table in around five minutes and at reasonable prices. **Memories Restaurant and Bar** (tel: 396527) is a classy place with a good international à la carte menu and first class food, though quite expensive. The **Come Inn Bar and Restaurant** (tel: 391464) serves good food in a relaxed and cheerful atmosphere. **Sen Fast Food** (tel: 372792), **A-Z Fast Food** (tel: 396467) and **Tasty Fast Food** (tel: 396467) are all located near the junction of Kairaba Avenue and the road leading to Sukuta. They all serve a range of cheap and cheerful meals and snacks, such as chicken and chips. They are all good value for money.

Le Palais du Chocolat is one of our favourite places and *the* place to go if you fancy a treat. It does wonderful cakes and ice-creams and freshly baked croissants, pain au chocolat, waffles and pancakes, all in a very relaxing atmosphere served by friendly staff. Definitely worth a visit whether the heat is getting you down or you need an injection of chocolate in order to keep going. **Malawi Guest House** (tel: 393012; fax: 392227) has cheap food and lots of atmosphere with live music on some evenings. Its buffet is big and it serves first-class roasts on a Sunday.

Southern Delight is a Gambian restaurant that is popular with Gambians and not often visited by tourists. There is a garden bar but best of all it does the best fried pork dishes in The Gambia.

Here are a few of the cheaper places in which to eat in this affluent part of The Gambia, where tourist-orientated businesses thrive. The best of the few include **Café de la Rue Restaurant**, **Kumba's Bar** and **Bamba Dinka Restaurant**, which are all along Atlantic Road. Along Saitmatty Road you can find **Crocodile Frankies Bar and Restaurant**, **Millenium Restaurant**, **Safari Bar**, **Jaggleh Fast Food** and **Tida's Grill Bar and Restaurant**. **Gambia Etten Bar and Restaurant** and **Eddies Bar and Restaurant** are off-the-beaten track close to Safari Garden Hotel. Along Garba Jahumpa (New Town) Road is **Aunty Elsie's Gambian Restaurant** (tel: 494082 or 496255) while **Makkah Fast Food** (tel: 372603), **Diners Den Fastfood, Snacks and Drinks Takeaway** (tel: 372360), **Rooster 1 Restaurant, Pizzaria and Takeaway** and **Ama's Café Afra and Bar** are along Kairaba Avenue. All of these places have lots of character and sell fairly good cheap meals.

Listings
Banks
Standard Chartered Bank has a branch along Atlantic Road in Fajara with a cash machine outside and another branch along Kairaba Avenue. Also along Atlantic Road are branches of the **International Bank for Commerce** and **Trust Bank**.

Internet
There is a cyber café in the grounds of the **Hotel Fajara**. The rates here are US$1.50 for 30 minutes, US$3 for 60 minutes and US$4 for 90 minutes. Other internet cafés include two **Quantumnet Cafés**, **Hi-tech 2000 Cyber Café** (tel: 494940), **Cyber World Internet Café** (tel: 374627) and **Paramount Internet Café** along Kairaba Avenue.

Post
The main Serrekunda post office is along Kairaba Avenue, while the smaller Bakau post office is along Atlantic Road.

Travel agencies and airlines
Sabena (Kairaba Avenue)
Drago Travel (Kairaba Avenue)
Afri-Swiss Travels (Kairaba Avenue; tel: 371762 or 371764; fax: 371766)
Gambia International Airlines (Midway Centre, Kairaba Avenue; tel: 374101)
Atlantic Travel Agency (Kairaba Avenue)
Atlantic Airlines (Gambia) Ltd (Kairaba Avenue)
Bellview Airlines (Kairaba Avenue)
IPC Travel (Kairaba Avenue; tel: 375677 or 375613)
Gamwings Travels (Kairaba Avenue; tel: 372921 or 372922; fax: 372923)

Nightclubs
The **California Nite Club** has its entrance along Kairaba Avenue.

Crafts

There is a large craft market located at the point where Old Cape Road joins on to Atlantic Road. This is one of the best craft markets in The Gambia, with some very good carvings in particular.

Gambling

The **Jackpot Palace** opposite the Butchers Shop along Kairaba Avenue operates a battery of slot machines between 17.00–05.00.

Supermarkets and tourist shops

Atsons Supermarket has one branch along Atlantic Road, another along Kairaba Road and yet another in Serrekunda along the Banjul to Basse Highway. **GSC Supermarket** is at the junction of Atlantic Road and Saitmatty Road. **St Mary's Food and Wine Supermarket, MY Supermarket, Stop Step Supermarket, Happiness Supermarket, A-Z Supermarket, Harry's Supermarket, Sony's Supermarket** and **Kairaba Supermarket** are along Kairaba Avenue. **Agee Jarjou Jemmeh's Batik Shop** (tel: 495980) is located along Atlantic Road in Bakau and sells a large range of batiks and cloth, including ready-made clothes.

Bookshops

Timbooktoo, at the junction of Kairaba Avenue and Garba Jahumpa (New Town) Road is the only good bookshop in the country. It sells a wide range of fiction and non-fiction books plus maps and children's books.

Photo processing

Photo Express Photo Lab (tel: 396795) in the Midway Centre off Kairaba Avenue, is probably the best place in the country to get your photos developed. It is very clean and dependable, and is professionally run by a French ex-pat.

Laundry and dry-cleaning

R & R Services (tel: 497480), opposite the Fajara War Cemetery, offers both a laundry and dry-cleaning service.

Things to do

The **Gena Bes Batik Factory** (tel: 495614 or 495908; email: genabes@hotmail.com) offers you a chance to have a go at designing and making your own batiks for US$20.50 per day and an extra US$3.50 for lunch. The day can last as long as you want (negotiable fee for longer days of course) and you will be shown all the techniques by the proprietress Queen Amie. You will also be involved with the production of your own masterpieces from start to finish (and you get to take them home with you). There is also a shop here that sells a range of batiks, clothing and local textile craft. The factory is quite hard to find but worth persevering over. First find the Elf Gas Station along Saitmatty Road. Go up the smaller road that runs beside it until you reach the defunct Katchikally Cinema. Turn right up the narrow sandy track just before the cinema and the factory is in a compound opposite the Abi Colley Telecentre.

Janneh Boating and Fishing Ltd (tel/fax: 497630), based along Atlantic Road in Bakau, offers a range of specialist boating and fishing trips. These include sport fishing (maximum of ten people in the boat – only four of whom can fish) either offshore or upriver, and creek fishing for four people. They also run sightseeing boat tours to Lamin Lodge (with BBQ) for a maximum of 12 people. These trips are quite expensive at around US$54.50 per person, though they will negotiate, but do include lunch, drinks, fishing equipment and bait, and last for up to eight hours. The company will also consider going far offshore to 'blue water' for fishing trips, or to Dakar or far up the River Gambia. In fact they will consider any reasonable request. You will have to negotiate yourself a deal on these trips.

The **Fajara Social and Sports Club** (tel: 495456) is often known simply as the **Fajara Club**. It is frequented by members of the ex-pat community and is for members only. It is, however, possible to get temporary membership to the club at the cost of US$7 per day or US$27 per week. The club's facilities include a swimming pool, tennis, badminton and squash courts, a restaurant, bar and library. The adjacent golf course is also run from here. This 18-hole course has to be one of the strangest we have seen as the 'greens' are actually brown during the dry season (they are not watered and so there is no grass), but the course is still very popular with visitors. If you fancy a round on the course the green fee is US$7 per day and the caddy fee is US$2.50 per day. If you need to hire equipment then it's a further US$3.50 for five balls and US$5 for the club hire for a day. **Independence Stadium** caters for a range of sports as does the nearby **Friendship Hotel** (see page 125).

One Fold School of Music (tel: 372844; email: onefold@hotmail.com) is located at the rear of Harry's Supermarket and teaches a range of African musical instruments.

Places to visit
Apart from golf, the **Fajara Golf Course** is also renowned as a very good birding spot. There is a range of habitats from open areas to coastal scrub and a few tangled patches of woodland. The course also lies alongside part of Kotu Stream. The course holds lots of different birds, with black-headed plover, *Vanellus tectus*, and wattled plover, *V. senegallus*, on the open areas, Senegal coucal, *Centropus senegalensis*, and African silverbill, *Lonchura cantans*, amongst the scrub and pearl-spotted owlet in the taller trees. Black-shouldered kites, *Elanus caeruleus*, are amongst the birds of prey that are seen flying over the course.

Bakau Fishing Centre is located just off Atlantic Road, and is easily found by following the smell. Although the beach here has suffered recently from erosion (so bad that many of the fishing boats cannot pull up onto the beach anymore) the centre is still a hive of activity. If you are living in self-catering accommodation and fancy a bite of fresh fish, or just want to see some of the local colour, then this is the place to come. There is a remarkable variety of fresh fish for sale, straight off the boats, and at very reasonable prices, though you will have to do some hard bargaining.

The **Alliance Franco-Gambienne**, more popularly known as the **Alliance Français** (tel: 375418; fax: 374172) is a cultural centre that runs French classes and holds exhibitions and shows. It is also a useful place in which to find out what's on culturally in the rest of the country.

KATCHIKALLY SACRED CROCODILE POOL
Katchikally Sacred Crocodile Pool is one of three sacred pools in The Gambia. It is by far the biggest and has the largest population of crocodiles. Other crocodile pools can be found at Abuko Nature Reserve and at Jakoi Sibrik near Bintang Bolon (see *Chapter 8*), but they are not thought to be sacred (see the box *Sacred crocodile pools* on page 130). Katchikally has developed into a bit of a tourist trap these days but is still frequented by local people who come to pray. During the dry season there are more than 30 Nile crocodiles in and around the pool (in the rainy season when the crocodiles breed this can rise to over 70 animals). One of the largest crocodiles here has been nick-named 'Charlie' (reportedly after the first person – an English guy

SACRED CROCODILE POOLS

The three crocodile pools, at Katchikally in Bakau, Folonko in Kartong and Berending in the North Bank Division, are all thought to be sacred. Local people come from all over The Gambia, and also from throughout West Africa, to seek blessings at the pools. They bring with them an offering of kola nuts for the families that are guardians of the pools, and prayers are said to fulfil their wishes. An elder member of the custodian family will bring water from the pool. The water is then blessed, and the visitor will be ritually washed in this water. The ceremony ends with drumming and dancing, and then the visitor is asked to abstain from unbecoming behaviour. Many women come to the pools to improve their fertility, but many other people also visit the pools. These include men who want to reverse their bad fortune in business, parents who are seeking protection for their children during circumcision ceremonies, and even wrestlers who are seeking victory in competition.

Katchikally pool is watched over by the Bojang family, who were the first people to settle in the area. It is said that the family was visited by a woman who tested them to see if they were kind and merciful or troublemakers. They passed the test and so the woman (who was really a spirit who lived in the woods and was called Katchikally) gave the pool into their care and instructed the family to bring two crocodiles to help identify the spot. Ousman Bojang, the present custodian of the pool, says that his father taught him that by doing and saying certain things Katchikally will appear again, but so far he has not tried it as he is too frightened.

The Bambo Folonko ('crocodile pool') in Kartong is looked after by the Jaiteh family. The presiding spirit in this pool is said to be the daughter of Katchikally and so the two pools are closely connected spiritually.

Berending pool differs from the other two in being fed by saltwater, but is still considered sacred.

named Charlie – who had the nerve to touch it) and it often lies on the bank and lets people touch its back and tail while they have their photograph taken. Don't touch it on the legs though as this seems to annoy it and it will snap at you. The pool is often covered in water lettuce, *Pistia stratiotes*, a floating plant that provides shelter for numerous frogs (the staple diet of the crocodiles, though they are also fed bonga fish by the pool's keepers). Around the pool is a small patch of forest with some very large trees in it and plenty of wildlife still, including callithrix monkeys, lizards and lots of butterflies. During the rainy season many of the younger crocodiles disperse into the surrounding town and countryside and we have heard many tales of people waking up to find a crocodile next to their bed. The entrance to the pool is flanked by a large number of craft stalls so expect to be hassled if you walk there. The entrance to the pool is less than US$1 but you may also be asked to make a donation to the 'fish-fund' for feeding the crocodiles.

Getting there and away

The pool is tucked away amongst a labyrinth of small roads but almost anyone will point you in the right direction and you may well be asked again and again by bumsters if 'you have seen the crocodiles', and they will offer to guide you there, for a fee of course. The 'city tour' calls in on the pool as a part of its itinerary (see *Organised excursions* in *Chapter 3*).

KOTU

Kotu is another little enclave of tourist facilities located by the beach and the sea. There's less hassle here than you will find at Kololi, but it still goes on. Kotu is basically a small cluster of hotels, supermarkets, shops, craft markets, restaurants, bars and nightclubs, though there are a few famous birdwatching sites within easy walking distance.

Where to stay
Midrange: US$100 and under
The **Novotel Kombo Beach Hotel** (tel: 465466 or 465468; fax: 465490; email: kombo@gamtel.gm) is a very popular place to stay. It has a swimming pool, beach bar, a choice of restaurants and bars, a clinic, hotel shop, and offers a laundry service and in-room safe facilities. Sports on offer include table tennis, tennis, petanque, volleyball, water polo, billiards, darts, archery and an outdoor mini gym and watersports. The rooms are in three-storey buildings and each has an en suite bathroom, a telephone, air conditioning, radio with piped music and a balcony or terrace. In the winter evenings, entertainment is laid on in the form of a disco, live African music, theme evenings with African dancing and the occasional video show in English. There is only limited entertainment during the summer months. A single will cost you US$68 per night, a double US$81.50 per night and a triple US$92. Single suites are also available for US$88.50 and doubles for US$102.

The **Bungalow Beach Hotel** (tel: 465288, 465623 or 460316; fax: 466180; email: bbhotel@qanet.gm) is a popular destination for many tourists visiting The Gambia. It has a swimming pool, children's pool and playgrounds, beach bar, bar and restaurant, souvenir shop and a mini-market. Evening entertainment is laid on in the winter but not in the summer. The hotel has apartments in two-storey blocks. Each room has self-catering facilities including a modern kitchenette equipped with fridge and electric cooker. De luxe apartments are also available with air conditioning and TV. A single B&B will set you back US$47.50, a double B&B US$61, an extra bed US$8 per day, air conditioning US$7.50 per day and a fan US$1.50 per day. A single in a de luxe apartment is US$64.50 while a double is US$78.50.

The **Bakotu Hotel** (tel: 465959; fax: 465555) is a small family-run hotel that is popular with birdwatchers and has a tranquil atmosphere. It has a swimming pool with sun terrace and a mini-market set amongst attractive tropical gardens. It also has a nature walk that leads to a vantage point overlooking Kotu Stream, which is famous for its birdlife (see page 133). The hotel's guests generally use Sir William's Restaurant and Bar, which is located next door. Each room is individually decorated. A single B&B will cost around US$34 while a double is US$47.50.

Badala Park Hotel (tel: 460400 or 460401; fax: 460402), in contrast to the Bakotu, is loud and brash. It has a swimming pool with children's area, bar, snack bar, restaurants, shop and satellite TV in a public area. Local entertainment is laid on most evenings during the tourist season. The rooms have en suite facilities but are fairly basic, though they should all have fans. A single B&B will set you back US$27, a double B&B US$34, and an apartment with self-catering facilities will cost US$44 per day. A supplement of US$9 per day will get you air conditioning. If you stay for a month or more you can claim a 30% discount on room rates.

The **Kotu Strand Hotel** (tel: 466397; fax: 460950) was undergoing renovations when we visited but was still open to guests. This is a small hotel that has a swimming pool, bar and restaurant, but not much else. A double room will cost US$14.50 a night whether you are staying as a single or a double. Breakfast is an additional US$3 per person. Apartments are also available for US$34 per night, which have a small kitchen, sitting room and bedroom. Most rooms have a free fan (depending on how many are working).

Where to eat

The **Oriental Pearl** (tel: 460428) is set back off Badala Park Way and is one of a handful of Chinese restaurants in The Gambia. It has a huge choice of meals starting at around US$3. The atmosphere is very pleasant, the staff are friendly and the food is served quickly, which is a big plus in The Gambia if you're hungry.

Ilmondo's (tel: 466573) is one of the best-loved restaurants in The Gambia and they do one of the best steaks we have tasted anywhere. The restaurant and bar is located right at the beach and looks a little ragged from the outside. However, there is a very good atmosphere and the staff are extremely good. It's best to book in advance during the tourist season as it can get a little crowded and you may not be able to find a free table otherwise. Unfortunately, by the time you read this guide, the long-standing management will have changed. We only hope that the new management does half as well.

The **Paradise Bar and Restaurant** (tel: 466264) is next to Ilmondo's on the beach. The meals are fairly cheap (main meals start at around US$2.50), but the quality is as good as the atmosphere. The meals range from burgers, chips and steaks through to spaghetti; you have to sit outside, which is no hardship at all really.

The Sailor Bar and Restaurant (tel: 460521) is a little further along the beach than Ilmondo's and Paradise Bar and Restaurant, and is a much bigger establishment. The meals served here are mainly European in origin and very good. Main meals start at around US$5.50. The outside seating is in a very pleasant situation and there are free sunbeds for customers and no hassle.

The **Sir William Restaurant and Bar** is next to the Bakotu Hotel and is used quite a lot by their guests. Snacks start at around US$3 and main meals at around US$6.50. There is a good atmosphere and often there are live bands. The **Pizzeria Giacomo Bar and Restaurant** occupies the building that used to house the now defunct Rendezvous Restaurant, and opened in February 2001. The restaurant is open from mid-day until midnight and serves mainly European food, with main meals starting at around US$5.50. There is a buffet every Tuesday evening (starting at 19.00) which costs US$5 per person. There is both indoor and outside seating. The **Sinbad Restaurant** is located by Badala Park Hotel and has opened very recently.

The **Adidas Beach Bar and Restaurant** is located in front of the Fajara craft market and serves a variety of Gambian meals. This is one of the few remaining Gambian-style beach bars that are still around. Lots of atmosphere.

Listings
Supermarkets and tourist shops

Kokotu is a shop that sells many items that can't be found elsewhere, much as its sister shops do elsewhere in The Gambia. This is well worth a visit if you are looking for something different and of a higher quality. It's located in front of Kotu craft market. Almost next to Kokotu is **St Mary's Food and Wine Supermarket**. This has European goods but don't always expect European prices. **Bakotu Supermarket** is next to the Bakotu Hotel.

Crafts

There are two craft markets at Kotu, selling the usual range of goods. **Fajara craft market** is down by the beach between Kotu and Fajara, and there is also a craft market behind St Mary's supermarket. You will get a lot of hassle in both these markets.

Nightclubs
The **Chosaan 2000 Nightclub** is along the road that runs into Kotu from Badala Park Way. We haven't been but if nightclubs are your thing, why not give it a go?

Things to do
Cottbus Water Sport Centre is based in a small wooden shed on the beach, not far beyond Fajara craft market. This was a brand new venture in March 2001 and the workers and owners seemed full of enthusiasm and hopeful for the future. They have a range of equipment for hire including jetskis (US$13.50 for 15 minutes - a second person for US$3.50), and a 130hp fishing boat with fish finder (US$10 per person, with a maximum of four, for one hour). They will also take you riding on a water-ring (US$7 for 10 minutes), or a giant banana (US$7 per person for 15 minutes - maximum of four people), paragliding (US$20.50 for 10 minutes) or waterskiing (US$17 for 15 minutes). You can even learn to windsurf for US$13.50 for one hour (including the teacher). All children under 12 pay half price. The operation is very hot on safety and the staff speak German, English and Dutch. Only 18 year olds and above can use the jetskis and go paragliding and no drunks are allowed.

Places to visit
Kotu includes a few birdwatching sites that have become famous amongst birdwatchers worldwide. Birders have been visiting these sites for decades now and surprisingly, even though the surrounding areas have become more urbanised over the years, they still retain a good number of birds. One of these sites is **Kotu Stream**, which passes beneath the road at Kotu Bridge before it empties into the sea. Kotu Stream is nearly always one of the first places that birders visit in The Gambia, and the range of common Gambian birds found here is useful for getting your eye in. Amongst the commonly seen birds are some rarer species, including the greater painted-snipe, pied avocet, *Recurvirostra avosetta*, and other waders, as well as the oriole warbler, *Hypergerus atriceps*, and African silverbill. Kotu Bridge is also one of the places for meeting Gambian birding guides (see *Birding guides* in *Chapter 3*). Between the bridge and Badala Park Hotel is a narrow tarmac path that heads off to the west. This is the **Cycle Path**, another famous birding site that has an amazing array of birds along its length and has provided many thousands of birders with new species for their life lists. The really good birds seen occasionally along this track include red-billed quelea and yellow-throated longclaw, *Macronyx croceus*.

Another site at Kotu, though not nearly as famous as the preceding two, is **Kotu Ponds**. In reality this is a series of open sewage pits opposite Badala Park Hotel. The pits are separated from the road by about 50 metres of open woodland and can be reached along a sandy track. The range of birds that can be seen at the ponds is amazing, and the best thing is that they allow you to get fairly close. The only downside is that the smell can be a bit overwhelming sometimes! There are hundreds of waders around the edges of the pools including black-winged stilt, common greenshank, wood sandpiper, *Tringa glareola*, and spur-winged plover, *Vanellus spinosus*. There is also a large flock of white-faced whistling duck, plus grey-headed gull, white-winged black tern, *Chlidonias leucopterus*, kingfishers, parrots, and lots of other species. Rarities here have included red-necked phalarope, *Phalaropus lobatus*, and one of the few recent sightings of tufted duck, *Aythya fuligula*, in The Gambia. The sewage ponds are also a working environment and trucks come regularly to empty their loads of liquid waste, so you have to be a bit careful when walking around. The workers caught on to the moneymaking possibilities of

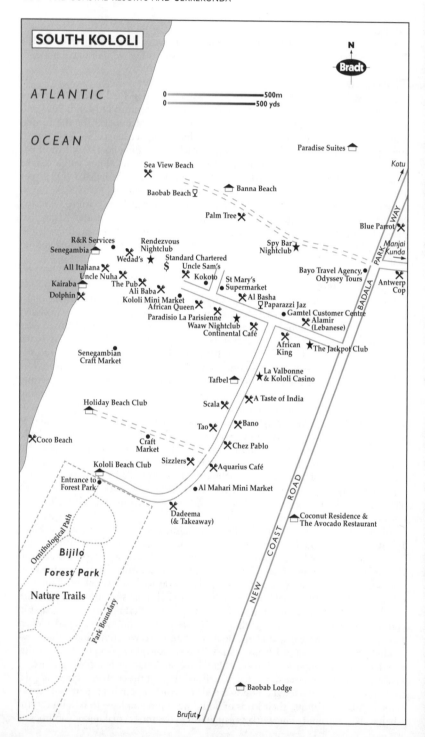

SOUTH KOLOLI

ATLANTIC

OCEAN

N

0 ——————— 500m
0 ——————— 500 yds

Paradise Suites

Kotu

Sea View Beach

Banna Beach

Baobab Beach

Palm Tree

Blue Parrot

R&R Services

Rendezvous
Nightclub

Senegambia

Spy Bar
Nightclub

PARK WAY

Manjai
Kunda

Wedad's

Standard Chartered

All Italiana

Uncle Sam's

Bayo Travel Agency,
Odyssey Tours

Uncle Nuha

Kokoto

Antwerp
Cop

Kairaba

The Pub

St Mary's
Supermarket

Dolphin

Ali Baba

Kololi Mini Market

Al Basha

African Queen

Paparazzi Jaz

Paradisio La Parisienne

Gamtel Customer Centre

Waaw Nightclub

Alamir
(Lebanese)

Continental Café

BADALA

African
King

The Jackpot Club

Senegambian
Craft Market

La Valbonne
& Kololi Casino

Tafbel

Holiday Beach Club

Scala

A Taste of India

Tao

Bano

Coco Beach

Chez Pablo

Craft
Market

Kololi Beach Club

Sizzlers

Aquarius Café

Entrance to
Forest Park

Al Mahari Mini Market

Dadeema
(& Takeaway)

Coconut Residence &
The Avocado Restaurant

NEW COAST ROAD

Ornithological Path

Bijilo

Forest Park

Nature Trails

Park Boundary

Baobab Lodge

Brufut

Above Nile crocodile (AVZ)

Right Royal python (LB)

Below Chameleon (LB)

Above Fireball lilies (LB)

Left Bell-flowered mimosa (LB)

Below Callithrix monkey (AVZ)

the site a long time ago and you will be charged for entry. The fee is less than US$1, which is very little, and though the charge is not official and you don't have to pay, we strongly recommend that you do so as it encourages the workers to keep the place good for birds. This works even to the extent that they will chase off the catapult-wielding Gambian kids who occasionally try and kill the birds for sport.

KOLOLI

Kololi is a small area but is a hive of activity, with hotels, a full range of restaurants, cafés, bars, shops and a casino and craft market, all within easy walking distance of each other and the hotels. This is a real tourist area and is located next to a fine beach with golden sand. Its one main drawback is that it's difficult to leave your hotel without attracting the attention of hordes of bumsters, but once you learn how to handle them, they tend to leave you more or less alone (see *Bumsters* in *Chapter 3*).

Where to stay
Upmarket: US$100 and above

Coconut Residence (tel: 463377 or 463399; fax: 461835; email: coconut@qanet.gm) is in class of its own. Its facilities include two swimming pools, sun terraces, a clubhouse, library and lounge, all set in a wonderfully lush tropical garden. The accommodation is luxurious and arranged in suites and there is 24-hour room service. Prices for the suites range from US$140–320 per night. The highest rate is for a pool villa with a private swimming pool.

The **Kairaba Hotel** (tel: 462940, 462941 or 462942; fax: 462947; email: kairaba@gamtel.gm; web: www.kairabahotel.com) is also one of the best in The Gambia and is located right next door to the Senegambia Hotel. It has a swimming pool, bars, shops, restaurants, landscaped gardens and a beauty salon. The activities available include the only **observatory** in The Gambia (open Wednesdays and Sundays, with an entrance fee of US$1.50), darts, table tennis, squash, archery, boccia (an Italian version of bowls), outdoor chess, lawn games and mountain-bike hire. The hotel also shares the sports facilities of the Senegambia Hotel. In addition, evening entertainment is occasionally laid on. The rooms are mostly in two-storey buildings built in the Portuguese style. All rooms are equipped with air conditioning, mini-bar, telephone (also with an internet connection), in-house video, satellite TV channels, piped music, bath or shower, WC and hairdryer. A single economy room costs US$71 (US$88.50 for a double), a single standard room is US$114 (US$136 for a double), a single de-luxe room is US$129 (US$146 for a double), a single junior suite is US$140 (US$157 for a double), a single executive suite is US$220 (US$249 for a double), a garden suite is US$249 and, finally, a presidential suite is US$341.50.

At the time of writing this guide a new shopping complex was being built in the grounds of the Kairaba, and presumably some of the shops in the main street of Kololi will move there. We know for certain that **Tropical Tours** (see page 142) already has plans to do so. The Kairaba also owns **Sindola Camp** at Kanilai (see *Chapter 8*). Bookings for the camp can be made through Kairaba Hotel.

Midrange: US$100 and under

The **Senegambia Hotel** (tel: 462717, 462718 or 467719; fax: 461839; email: senegambia@gamtel.gm; web: www.senegambiahotel.com) is one of the best hotels in The Gambia. It has a beach with beach bar, swimming pool, bars, snack bars, shops, tailors, a unisex hairdressing salon, restaurants, and provides a laundry service. It also has one of the best tropical gardens in the country within its grounds. This large area has been planted by the hotel management with trees, shrubs and flowers that attract birds and butterflies(the manager is a keen bird photographer while his wife is a very green-fingered gardener). There is even a special 'vulture feeding' event that takes place daily at around 11.00 which attracts not only dozens (sometimes hundreds) of vultures, but also some large Nile monitors which allow the guests to get really close to them. Other activities available include tennis, squash, table tennis, volleyball, mini golf, petanque and archery. There is also a wide range of evening entertainment, including stage shows, African cabaret nights and a weekly barbecue. Most of the bedrooms are in two-storey buildings set in the gardens and they all have ceiling fans, bath or shower, WC and a balcony or patio. A single B&B costs US$54.50 (US$62.50 with air conditioning), a double B&B US$61 (US$69 with air conditioning), and a studio (single, double or triple) with air conditioning upwards of US$95.

Holiday Beach Club Hotel (tel: 460418 or 460419; fax: 460418 or 460023; email: amatagaye@hotmail.com) is located out of the way along a sandy track and is right next to the sea. There is a swimming pool, bars, restaurant and beach bar. The rooms are in two-storey blocks set amongst pleasant gardens. A single regular room costs US$30.50 per night (US$37.50 for a superior room) and a double regular room costs US$37.50 per night (US$47.50 for a superior room). Fans are a further US$17 per week while air conditioning costs around US$9.50 per day extra. Safe boxes are also available for US$13.50 per week.

Tafbel Hotel (tel: 460510/11/12/13/14; fax: 460515; email: tourism@tafgambia.com), which used to be known as the **Tafbel Maisonnettes**, was built in 1994 by a Gambian entrepreneur and is entirely Gambian owned and managed. There is a large swimming pool and separate children's pool, bar, restaurants and sun terrace. Accommodation is in three-storey buildings and you have a choice of standard rooms, studios and suites, ranging in price for a single B&B from around US$30.50–102 per night. The standard rooms are air-conditioned, have a direct-dialling telephone, TV with satellite and movie channels and an en suite bathroom with both tub and shower. There is a laundry service available. The studios also come with a fully equipped kitchenette and in addition each has an electronic room safe. All rooms have private furnished patios or balconies. Five minutes' walk away from the hotel, and also from the beach, is the **Taf Annex**, which is a part of the same complex. Here there are only 14 rooms in a two-storey building, but as with the main hotel all of the rooms are very modern and smart. Each room is fully air-conditioned, has a direct dialling telephone, satellite TV, iron and ironing board and a kitchenette fully equipped with microwave oven, fridge/freezer and gas cooker.

Kololi Beach Club (tel: 464897; fax: 464898; email: kololibeachclub@advsys.co.uk; web: www.kololi.com and www.kololiuk.com) is a clubshare that is run for its members, but it is possible to turn up at reception and book either a one or two bedroom villa if they are available. The hotel is set by the beach, in the midst of well-tended gardens. There is a swimming pool, sun terraces, restaurant and maid service for six days a week, an Atsons supermarket and safekeeping facilities. Activities available at the hotel include croquet, table tennis, petanque, and pool games, and the hotel also has its own nine-hole, par-three golf course (which has real grass, even in the dry season). Each self-contained villa, all of which are located in two-storey buildings, has ceiling fans, three-pin UK sockets, either a balcony or patio with furniture and a well-equipped fitted kitchen. A one-bedroom villa which sleeps up to four costs around US$136 per night or around US$744 per week. A two-bedroom villa which sleeps up to six costs around US$190 per night or around US$1,025 per week. Cots are available on request and air conditioning is an extra US$34 per week. All of these prices are much cheaper if you are a member.

Luigi's Apartments (tel: 460280; fax: 460282; email: luigis@qanet.gm) are smart, clean and very popular. Single rooms have a shower, WC and fridge, while one- and two-bed apartments have shower, WC, lounge and kitchen bar with fridge and cooking facilities. All rooms also have ceiling fans. A single B&B in a standard room will set you back around US$20.50 while a double B&B will cost US$27. In a one-bed apartment, a single B&B will cost US$27 (double B&B US$34). A two bed apartment that sleeps four costs US$61 and a two-bed apartment that sleeps two costs US$47.50. Air conditioning costs an extra US$3.50 per night.

Palma Rima Hotel (tel: 463380 or 463381; fax: 463382; email: palmarima@qanet.gm) is a popular place. Facilities include an enormous swimming pool, pool bar, sun terraces, evening lounge bar, shop and restaurant amongst attractive gardens. There is also a craft market and a theatre with live entertainment. Accommodation is either fairly standard in three-storey blocks or in single-storey bungalows. A double B&B is around US$68 per night while a single B&B is around US$54.50.

Bunkoyo Hotel (tel/fax: 463199) is a small place that has a friendly feel about it. There is a swimming pool and TV lounge and the hotel is only 5–10 minutes walk from the beach. There are ten rooms, including a family room, which range in price from US$24 for a single B&B in a room without air conditioning to US$34 for a double B&B in a room with air conditioning.

Bakadaji Hotel (tel: 462307; mobile tel: 990047) looks a little run-down but is still popular with its guests. There are two restaurants that serve a range of European and African food. Each room has a fan and fridge. Prices are US$24 for single or double B&B. Self catering apartments with two bedrooms are US$44 per night in the tourist season and US$27 per night in the off season.

Holiday Suites (tel: 461075 or 461076; fax: 461077) is a smart place with fully equipped and air-conditioned self-catering apartments. Each apartment also has satellite TV and there is a standby generator in case of power cuts. The prices range from US$40.50 for a single B&B to around US$85 B&B for apartments for up to four people.

Europa Apartments (tel/fax: 460480) are self-catering apartments well off the beaten track. There are eight double apartments with en suite bathrooms, fans, fridge and kitchen with water heater. All apartments cost US$24 per night. The Europa also has a private bar and swimming pool.

Virgo Guest House (tel: 461630; UK fax: 01207 2525897) is not far from Europa Apartments and has a garden and veranda. There are no double rooms, only singles, and these are priced at US$17 for a room with no bathroom and US$24 for a room with en suite facilities. Solar power is available when the power is off and each room has a fan.

Balmoral Apartments (tel: 461079; UK tel for booking during the off season: 01556 650296) is a smart looking establishment with a swimming pool, garden and sun loungers and its own filtered water system. At the moment there are seven apartments but two more are being added. A two person self-catering apartment with cooker and fridge is US$27 per night, while a two bedroom apartment is around US$47.50 per night for four people. There are fans in all the bedrooms and lounges and some of the rooms also have air conditioning.

Hotel Berlin (tel: 463767; fax: 463781) has some tourists stop over but mainly caters for visiting businessmen. This is a small, friendly place run by a German man. There is a bar and restaurant, and the accommodation has en suite facilities, fans and mosquito-netting doors. There is also a standby generator for when the mains power supply fails. A single B&B will set you back US$17 while a double B&B is US$20.50.

Paradise Suites Hotel (tel: 463439 or 463429; fax: 463451) has all the ingredients to make it one of the best hotels in The Gambia. There is a relaxed, friendly and efficient staff with service to suit, and the suites, maisonnettes and villas are well constructed and beautifully furnished. All of this in a well-tended tropical garden only three minutes' walk from the beach and with swimming pool, bar and restaurant. If you're after comfort, what more could you want? Each of the suites has a bedroom (sleeping 1–2 people), living room, kitchenette and en suite bathroom. A suite will cost you only US$54.50 per night. The maisonnettes have two bedrooms (sleeping 4–6), both of them with en suite bathroom, kitchen, living room and either a balcony or patio. A maisonnette will cost US$95 per night. The villas have two floors with two bedrooms (sleeping 4–6), two bathrooms, kitchen, living room, patio, balcony and a small private garden. A villa will set you back US$112 per night. All bedrooms have air conditioning and all living rooms have sofas, easy chairs and satellite TV. The kitchens come equipped with microwave oven, gas cooker, fridge, kettle, table, chairs and all the relevant cutlery and utensils. The hotel is being extended to include more standard rooms and another swimming pool.

Banna Beach Hotel (tel: 461177 or 461255), about 100m from the beach, has a swimming pool, two restaurants and pool bar restaurant. We thought the hotel looked a little run down. There are 100 rooms, each with en suite showers and WC. Three quarters of all the rooms have air conditioning. Strangely we were not allowed to know their room rates; we hope you have better luck as a guest!

Baobab Lodge (tel: 461270; mobile tel: 991831; email: baobablodge@excite.com; web: www.baobab-lodge.co.uk) looks like a top-of-the-range place to stay from the road, but unfortunately on closer inspection turns out to be rather tatty. Facilities include a restaurant and bar and the lodge is only about five minutes' walk away from the beach. There are six octagonal bungalows with two apartments in each, set in a tropical garden. Each apartment has sitting room, a bedroom with king-size bed, a kitchen with gas cooker, fridge and sink, and an en suite bathroom with shower, WC and washbasin. There are ceiling fans and the lodge has a standby generator in case of power cuts. They are planning to have air conditioning in the near future. A single will set you back about US$22 per night (excluding breakfast) while a double costs around US$25.50 per night. The lodge may be open in the rainy season but this is not yet confirmed.

Shoestring: US$12 and under
Kololi Inn and Tavern (mobile tel: 995584) appears to be a friendly place set in a quiet compound about 1.5km from the beach. The accommodation is in huts and ranges in price from about US$11–14 B&B.

The **Keneba Hotel** (tel: 460093) has single and double rooms with fans and en suite facilities. These are priced at less than US$12 for a single B&B and US$17 for a double B&B. There is a restaurant, though it wasn't fully open at the time of writing.

Where to eat
The **Avocado Restaurant** is in **Coconut Residence** (tel: 463377 or 463399; fax: 461835; email: coconut@qanet.gm) and is an exclusive restaurant that caters for people with a taste for cordon-bleu cooking. It is also not too expensive with lunches ranging from US$3–6.50 and main courses starting at around US$5. You can choose to eat either inside or outside by the swimming pool and there is a very relaxed atmosphere where you are pampered just enough to make you feel rather special.

   La Valbonne American Bar and Italian Restaurant (tel: 461068 for a reservation) is a smart but rather cold place where main meals vary between US$5–20.50 a time. Down near the beach beyond the Kololi Beach Club is the **Coco Beach Restaurant** where the staff are excellent and very friendly. The food is very expensive for the size of portions that you get, but tasty. They also serve Chinese and Moroccan buffets on certain nights. There is a beach area (bumster free) and of course a good view of the sea. Other upmarket restaurants in Kololi can be found at the **Senegambia Hotel** and the **Kairaba Hotel**.

   A Taste of India (tel: 460340) is one of the two very high-quality Indian restaurants in The Gambia. The excellent food includes tandooris, curries, vegetarian dishes, biryani, naans, raitas and seafood and a three-course meal will set you back anything from US$9–18. On Saturday evenings there is a buffet that would satisfy any connoisseur of Indian cuisine priced at only US$8. This buffet is a real bargain and very tasty. The **Tao Restaurant** is the place to go if you enjoy Thai food. The staff here are friendly and very efficient and the service is some of the fastest and smartest we've seen in The Gambia, though you don't really seem to have the time to just sit and enjoy your meal before you've finished it. Meals start at around US$4.50. There is a buffet served every Wednesday that costs US$7 per person.

The **Dolphin Bar and Restaurant** is in Kololi, next to the Kairaba Hotel (you approach it through the entrance to the hotel). It's open from 09.00 until late and serves a mixture of homemade British, Gambian and Italian meals. The food is good and cheap and comes in good-sized portions. There is a good atmosphere in the garden restaurant with live music some nights.

All Italiana Bar, Restaurant and Pizzeria (tel: 460063) is located close to the Kairaba Hotel, and serves a variety of mainly Italian dishes, either inside or out on the patio. This is a friendly restaurant serving good food. **The Pub Bar and Restaurant** serves basic food but is a great place to watch people going about their business in the street below. It's good fun to watch the interactions between bumsters and tourists (while not getting hassled yourself of course). There is often African entertainment laid on and it is a lively place that is located on the first floor above **Ali Baba Bar and Restaurant** (tel: 461030). At Ali Baba's you can eat inside, on the patio, or outside in the large garden, where they often lay on local bands and entertainment. Not far from Ali Baba's is the **African Queen Restaurant**, which again is a lively place that serves basic, cheap food. Just along the same street is the **African King** (mobile tel: 992689), which is an Afro-Caribbean restaurant and bar and the **Continental Café**, which serves both English and African food.

Paradisio La Parisienne (tel: 462177) looks a little shabby from outside but the food is excellent, especially the huge choice of different pizzas (cooked while you wait), which you can eat inside or take away and which are some of the best in The Gambia. They will also deliver to your hotel if it's in the Kololi area.

Alamir Lebanese Restaurant (tel: 460860) serves excellent Lebanese food and has a great atmosphere, though the indoor fountain can make conversation a little difficult as it is quite loud. They serve a good hot and cold buffet every Friday evening for US$8.50 per person and advertise it as 'eat all you want', which can't be bad. Nearby is **Al Basha** (tel: 463300), which is another good Lebanese restaurant serving Lebanese and international cuisine.

The **Paparazzi Jaz Bar** is a very popular place with ex-pats. It's rather like a smart European wine bar and closes very late.

Uncle Sam's Bar and Restaurant and **Uncle Sam's Bar and Grill** (tel: 462173) are adjacent to each other, and presumably under the same management. They do a range of food including burgers. Main meals start at about US$2.50, and there is indoor and outdoor seating.

Bano Bar and Restaurant serves Gambian and International food starting at about US$3.50 for main meals. This is one of the few places where they serve authentic *wanjo* juice in the Kololi area. This local drink, made from hibiscus flowers, is delicious. Next to it is **Chez Pablo Bar and Restaurant** where they serve Italian, Chinese and Gambian meals starting at about US$4. You can eat either inside or outside. The **Aquarius Café** has a bar, cafeteria and an ice-cream parlour that serves homemade Italian ice cream. It opens at 16.00 and there is a happy hour every day between 17.30–18.30. There is also a disco every night with

FEEDING THE MONKEYS

Please do *not* feed the monkeys at Bijilo or anywhere else. It may seem like a cool thing to do, but these are wild animals, no matter how cute they look. Feeding monkeys makes them aggressive towards humans, as they come to expect food. If you don't have any food on you then they may attack purely out of frustration. Males can be very large and have a vicious set of teeth. Also remember that these animals may carry diseases such as rabies. Unfortunately, although tourists have been told these facts for years, some local guides have encouraged tourists to feed the monkeys (though of course there are always those who don't need to be encouraged to do something stupid). The result of this is that a large troop of callithrix monkeys now travels along the coast from Bijilo every day, calling in at every hotel and house on the way, causing damage and frightening people with their aggressive behaviour. There will come a point in the not-too-distant future when these monkeys will cause so much trouble that they will have to be controlled in some way, either by trapping and relocation, or by simply shooting them. All because a few tourists think it's cute to feed the wild monkeys.

free entrance.

Sizzlers Restaurant is a good looking place set in its own small gardens. They serve Gambian, European and, unusually for The Gambia, a wide range of vegetarian meals. You can eat inside or outside and main meals start at around US$4. An all-day English breakfast is priced at US$4. **Scala Restaurant** (tel: 460813) is Danish owned and serves European meals starting at around US$7. The food and service is good and the food is also well presented. They have immaculate kitchens that they are only too pleased to show you.

Solomon's Grill is a good beach bar that is popular and, of course, excellent for the beach. **Luigi's Pizza and Pasta House** (tel: 460280) is popular with ex-pats and very smart-looking. This is a great place to get a birthday cake made to celebrate that special occasion. Main meals start at around US$5.50 and there are rooftop tables for those really warm nights. **Abi's Bar and Restaurant** (tel: 464804) has an impressive beach-bar-type menu of African and European food that is fairly cheap, starting at around US$3.

Churchill's Bar and Restaurant (tel: 460830) is the closest you will get to an English pub in The Gambia, and is much loved by tourists. They serve a range of bar meals, snacks and vegetarian food starting at around US$3. Their British roast served on a Sunday is great. The bar also has karaoke and African nights with live music. **Jazzis International à la carte Bar and Restaurant** is a smart looking place which is a venue for live music, including the Chameleon Band on Fridays. Main meals start at around US$5.50. **Mirroz Pool Bar** is located in Farida's Arcade and unsurprisingly has lots of pool tables and is popular with pool players. **Amsterdam Dolphins Bar and Restaurant** (tel: 460590), which serves very good German and some African food, is very popular with ex-pats, especially the English and Dutch. Main meals start at around US$6.50.

The **Auberge** (tel: 460895) is located in the Kololi Inn and Tavern and serves very good food, with an interesting menu. However we have heard complaints of either the TV or the music being too loud and distracting the waiters. The **Village Gallery, Restaurant and Café** (tel: 460369; email: bahs@qanet.gm) is another new venture that combines art (exhibitions), technology (a planned cyber café) and good wholesome food all in one location. The restaurant serves a selection of Gambian, European and vegetarian food starting at around US$2, but specialises in a three-course Gambian meal at US$2, which is excellent value. **Mama Tumani Happy Corner Restaurant** serves a selection of international cuisine. The intriguingly named **Antwerp Cop Bar and Restaurant** (tel: 463005) specialises in Flemish cuisine.

The **Blue Parrot Café, Bar and Restaurant** (tel: 460412) does a good Sunday lunch and is a popular venue for ex-pats. The **Sea View Beach Bar and Restaurant** (tel: 463502) is a very good place to eat, with European and some Gambian food on offer from about US$3.50. As the name suggests, it has a commanding view of the sea and guests have the use of a free sunbed. There is a pool table in the bar and Wednesday, Friday and Saturday nights there is a live band and African entertainment. The staff will even organise jeep safaris for you. **Baobab Beach Bar** serves good value and tasty food, though you'll have to watch your plastic chair as its bound to sink in the sand! The **Palm Tree Bar and Restaurant** would be good but unfortunately you often get hassled here.

Uncle Nuha Restaurant by the taxi rank serves a range of Gambian meals at cheap prices and has lots of atmosphere. The **Dadeema Restaurant and Takeaway** opened just days before we visited and the staff were very proud to show us around their restaurant. This is one of those small places that is worth visiting, not only for the good food but also for its typical laid-back and relaxed Gambian atmosphere. It's also one of those places that could easily go under if not enough people eat there: another good reason to visit. It serves Gambian and European food, though the day-to-day menu is a little restricted, and you can eat either inside or outside. It also serves takeaway sandwiches and Gambian food such as *domoda* and *benichin* (see *Food* in *Chapter 3*), as well as tea and coffee. *Dadeema* means 'good value' in Mandinka, and we think this restaurant certainly is.

Listings
Banks
Standard Chartered Bank has two branches at Kololi, one along the main street and one at the front of the Tafbel Hotel.

Internet
There is an internet café at the **Gamtel Customer Centre**, which also has facilities which allow you to telephone, fax and telex abroad. **Quantumnet** also has an internet café in front of the Tafbel Hotel. The **Village Gallery, Restaurant and Café** (tel: 460369; email: bahs@qanet.gm) is planning to have a cyber café which may be completed by the time you read this.

Travel agencies
Bayo Travel Agency and Odyssey Tours (email: bayodisc@qanet.gm).

Nightclubs
The **Waaw Nightclub** is open from 22.00 until the last guest leaves. The **Rendezvous Nightclub** can be found above **Wedad's** and the very popular **Calabash Nightclub** sometimes has live music. The Calabash opens around 20.00. On Wednesday and Thursday entrance is free but on Friday, Saturday and Sunday it will cost you around US$3.50 to get in. The **Spy Bar Night Club** is one of the most popular nightclubs in The Gambia and is open every night from 21.00–0600. It has pool tables, a bar, and a disco and live music.

Theatre

There is a theatre in the grounds of the **Palma Rima Hotel** that is open to non-guests. Live shows are held on a Saturday evening from 21.00–22.30.

Crafts

The **Senegambian craft market** in Kololi is a large collection of stalls that sell a wide variety of local and traditional craft items and clothes. There are also a few craft stalls away from the market in the Kololi area. There is a smaller craft market located along the sandy track that leads to the **Holiday Beach Club Hotel**. The **Palma Rima Hotel** also has a craft market within its grounds that is open to non-guests. The **Village Gallery, Restaurant and Café** has a small shop on its premises that sells a small range of high quality and unusual crafts.

Casinos and gambling

The **Jackpot Club** caters for slot-machine gamblers while the **Kololi Casino** has roulette, blackjack and jackpot machines.

Supermarkets and tourist shops

There is a wide range of supermarkets in the Kololi area which sell a range of European goods. It's worth visiting them all and shopping around as prices can vary and can be a bit expensive compared to European prices. **St Mary's Food and Wine Supermarket** has a few branches in The Gambia, two of them at Kololi. The **Kololi Mini Market** is located next to the African Queen Restaurant and the **Al Mahari Mini Market** is just beyond the Aquarius Café. An **Atsons Supermarket** is based inside Kololi Beach Club and **Stop Step Supermarket** is based in Farida's Arcade.

At Kololi there is also a number of shops that cater mainly for the tourist market. These include **Kokoto**, with branches in all the tourist areas in Kololi. **Tropical Tours** (which is moving to the shopping complex being built in the grounds of the Kairaba Hotel) and **Wedad's**. The former two shops sell a large range of high quality souvenirs, including some books and very fine T-shirts, and are the places to come if you are tired of the usual goods on sale in nearly all of the craft markets and are searching for something very different. **Wedad's** sells a wide range of western clothes, amongst other things, and is very popular with well-off Gambians.

Laundry and dry cleaning

Clothes can suffer badly in The Gambia from a combination of heat and dust in the dry season and excessive sweating and rain in the rainy season. Some hotels and camps offer a laundry service for guests (look for details in the relevant sections). **R & R Services** (tel: 463505) opposite the Senegambia Hotel offers both a laundry and dry-cleaning service.

Beauty centres

The **Natural Remedy Study** is a holistic therapy centre based next to Ali Baba's.

Places to visit

The **Village Gallery, Restaurant and Café** (tel: 460369; email: bahs@qanet.gm) is a little off the beaten track but worth visiting as it is often the venue for exhibitions, either by local artists or by foreigners with connections to The Gambia. In the future it also plans to host workshops and art lectures and to organise art and cultural trips.

Bijilo Forest Park Nature Trail is located on the coast, adjacent to the Kololi

Beach Club and within easy walking distance of the Senegambia, Kairaba and other hotels. The park covers an area of around 51.3ha and consists of superb coastal forest and scrub overlooking the beach. Coastal forest is now an extremely rare habitat within The Gambia and only a few intact forests remain. Bijilo Forest Park is probably the best of its kind in the country and has been protected as a public nature reserve for close to 50 years because it so uniquely illustrates the original coastal forests of The Gambia. A nature trail has been in place in the park since 1991, when it was set up by the very successful Gambian German Forestry Project which manages a number of forest parks throughout the country.

The nature trail is open to the public from 08.00–18.00 every day of the year. The admission charge is presently less than US$1.50 for all adults but children under 12 can enter free of charge. A guidebook entitled *Some trees, shrubs and climbers of Bijilo Forest Park* is available at the entrance for US$1. The plants and trees mentioned in the book are related to marked specimens along the nature trail. The staff of the park are extremely helpful and friendly to visitors and it is possible to be escorted along the nature trail by a member of the park staff if you want to know more about the park and its flora and fauna.

The nature trail consists of over 4.5km of well-marked and maintained footpaths. Most of it is fairly level though there are a few steeper parts with rough steps. There are shelters and bench seats placed strategically along the way and also some viewpoints overlooking the ocean and the beach. The paths are divided into colour-coded circular routes, so that you can choose how far and in what direction you want to walk. These routes are well-mapped on notice boards located throughout the park; a handy copy of the route map is also printed on your admission ticket. Another straight path which runs through the forest and scrub near to the beach is known as 'the ornithological path'. This path affords excellent opportunities to view many of the park's birds.

Over one-third of all the butterfly species found in The Gambia can be seen at Bijilo Forest Park, which is not bad considering its small size. Butterflies are most common in the scrub along the ornithological path, especially at the end of the rainy season when they can be seen in large numbers. Typical reptiles usually encountered in the park include the agama, brown-flanked skink and Nile monitor. The list of birds found at Bijilo is impressive, and includes a few rarities such as the extremely elusive ahanta francolin, and western bluebill. However the real stars are the common but still beautiful species such as bee-eaters, bishops, hornbills and starlings. Our particular favourites are the small coveys of stone partridge, *Ptilopachus petrosus*, that hustle and bustle like flocks of small chickens ahead of you on the paths, refusing to take flight. Mammals are also well represented within the park, though many of them, such as the African civet, are nocturnal and shy and therefore very difficult to observe. However, no one could accuse callithrix monkeys of being shy and they are often seen, as are the western red colobus, which stay high in the treetops. Other mammals include Gambian sun squirrels, which are frequently seen in the trees, and striped ground squirrels which you can see on the forest floor.

Bijilo Forest Park is a wonderful example of how The Gambian coastline once looked and is well worth a visit at any time of the year. There is plenty of wildlife to be seen in a pleasant, safe environment.

Getting there and away

This couldn't be easier, especially if you are based at the Kololi Beach Club, as you just have to cross the road to get to the forest. It is also only a short taxi ride from anywhere in the tourist area and is well known to taxi drivers.

MANJAI KUNDA

Manjai Kunda is a little off the main tourist trail and consists of an area dominated by local compounds, though its main roads are slowly becoming settled by hotels, lodges, bars and restaurants. This area is bound to become more popular with tourists as the years go by but at present it is visited in the main by the ex-pat community.

Where to stay
Midrange: US$100 or under
Manjai Lodge, Bar and Restaurant (tel: 463414 or 463417; fax: 463415). This is a brand new lodge that was still under construction in early 2001. The facilities here include a swimming pool, stage, bar and restaurant. Accommodation consists of 53 rooms and 22 self-catering apartments, each with shower, WC, washbasin, ceiling fan and mosquito window nets. Air conditioning is planned for the future. Prices had not been set at the time of writing.

The **Atlantic City Hotel** (tel: 463479, 463481 or 463536; fax: 495105; email: sossehkumerra@qanet.gm) has been a lodge for the past three years and is showing signs of wear and tear. A double room costs US$27 per night while fully-furnished apartments range from US$272–341.50 per week (discounts of 10% are available for guests staying more than two weeks). Rooms have shower/bath, WC, washbasin, ceiling fans and mosquito window nets, but are quite tatty (in many cases the window nets are hanging off).

Where to eat
The **Turbo Bar Grill and Restaurant** is newly opened. Close by is the **Aberdeen Restaurant and Bar, West Coast African Bar and Restaurant** and the **Atlantic City Bar and Grill** (tel: 463479). The latter was closed at the time of writing but promises to be open by the publication date of this guidebook. The owners plan to serve a mixture of African and European meals. Also in this area is the **Amsterdam Café Bar and Restaurant** (tel/fax: 461805).

   Teddy's Fast Food and **Fatima's Barry Afaerr Afra and Restaurant** are local restaurants that serve quick, cheap food, as are the **Lions Den Restaurant and Sound** and **Folongko**.

SERREKUNDA

At first sight, Serrekunda seems a hodgepodge of poorly built tin-roofed buildings all crowded together with no rhyme or reason. This is probably because that is exactly what it is. The town has grown enormously over the past 10–20 years, seemingly with no restrictions and to no logical plan. Everywhere there is noise and colour and movement and crowds of people and Serrekunda is now the largest concentration of people in The Gambia. Travelling down the main Banjul to Basse Highway that goes straight through the heart of Serrekunda, you will be amazed at the variety of businesses and shops that line the road. There are bakeries, metalworkers, welders, car repair yards, timber merchants, hair salons and spare part shops. You name it and you can probably find it somewhere along this road. You'll also be surprised at the dirt and dust (or mud in the rainy season) and the constant noise, whether it's metalworkers hammering away or a radio blaring from a shop – and all backed up by the roar of traffic and the never-ending honking of car horns. This used to be the route that the tourist buses drove when delivering their newly arrived passengers to the hotels in the coastal resorts. Many visitors were dismayed at arriving in what they had been told was a tropical paradise, only to find themselves passing through an urban nightmare. Now there is a new road that links the coastal resorts with the airport and passes through open countryside with swaying palm trees, so some tourists may never get to see the other side of life in The Gambia. Even on the new road though, there is now a lot of building going on, so who knows what this area might look like in ten years time?

If you want a taste of the real modern-day Africa, try a visit to Serrekunda market. This is a hive of activity and you can buy anything from traditional African clothes to western platform shoes, rolls of sellotape to music cassettes and hammers. It is crowded and noisy and sometimes smelly (especially near the stalls that sell spice) and is a real culture shock to Westerners who are used to pushing a shopping trolley along sanitised aisles in a spotlessly clean supermarket. This is a good safe place to meet ordinary Gambians and see what their world is really like, though you should keep a wary eye open for the gangs of pickpockets that roam the market; keep your valuables well tucked away. If you are at all nervous about visiting the market, take an official guide or a Gambian friend with you. They'll look out for you and show you around.

Getting there and away
Getting into and out of Serrekunda couldn't be easier. From the coastal resorts it is only a short drive by shared bush or tourist taxi to Westfield Junction, the transport hub of the area. You could even decide to walk it and it shouldn't take you more than maybe 20–40 minutes. GPTC buses (all services though only by request on the super express service) from Banjul also stop at Serrekunda, and bush taxis regularly ply the route back and forth to the capital.

Where to stay
Midrange: US$100 or under
Matu's Guest House (tel: 392925) is a cheap place to stay and is also very friendly, with a smiling and eager to please staff. The rooms are not great but they are clean and fairly comfortable, and also fairly cheap at US$13.50 for a double room, US$17 for a double room with en suite facilities and US$20.50 for a larger room with en suite facilities. All rooms have a fan and air conditioning, though at the moment there is no standby generator (they plan to get one, and install satellite TV, in the near future). There is also a restaurant at the guesthouse that serves a variety of cheap meals from Gambian dishes through to chips and omelettes.

Shoestring: US$12 and under
Churchill's Town Rest House, right alongside the main highway, is a grotty and seedy looking place that is very cheap but with none of the atmosphere of Matu's.

The **Wuli Motel** (tel: 460870 or 461612; fax: 392866), slightly better but still a bit tatty, is located along the Sukuta Highway. All rooms have en suite facilities and fans and cost around US$10 per night. Two rooms also have air conditioning and these cost US$17 per night but since there is no standby generator (they plan to get one in the future) it will not work during the inevitable power cuts. The restaurant was closed during our visit but they assure us it will be open by the time this guidebook is published and they will be offering a selection of fast foods from less than US$1 to around US$4.

The **Jalakunda Hotel** and the **Green Line Motel** are both signposted from the Sukuta Highway but both are pretty tatty and unappealing, though cheap with rooms in the US$8.50–17 range. The Green Line Motel also has a restaurant that serves fairly cheap meals starting at around US$2.

Where to eat
Joker's Bar and Restaurant at Westfield Junction is also a nightclub, but it doesn't really get going until around 23.00 so the restaurant is normally quiet until

then. This restaurant serves great food in a garden setting (their liver and onions is especially good).

A number of fast food restaurants (sometimes known as 'chop houses') along the main highway, Sukuta Highway and the back streets of Serrekunda sell reasonable food at cheap prices. They range in quality from poor to great and while some are distinctly grotty, others are cheerful and full of atmosphere.

Listings

Banks
Trust Bank Ltd has branches along the Banjul to Basse Highway and Sukuta Highway. First International Bank Ltd has a branch along the Sukuta Highway.

Internet
Y.D. Telecentre Cyber Café (tel: 395363 or 395372; fax: 397082), Churchill's Town **Gamtel** Branch (with internet) and **Media World Business Centre Cyber Café and Telecentre** are all along the main highway. **Quantumnet Internet Café** and **Salami Enterprises Internet and Email Services** (tel: 375649 or 391770) are along the Sukuta Highway.

Travel agencies and airways
Sierra National Airways (Banjul Highway; tel: 397551; fax: 397556).

Nightclubs
Joker's is a smart nightclub located at Westfield Junction. The club doesn't really liven up until around 23.00. It sometimes has live bands.

Crafts
The **African Art shop** (tel: 373369) is a large green-painted shop along the main highway. It sells an intriguing collection of beads, necklaces and shells, some of which are from Senegal, Mali and Mauritania. Some of the beads and necklaces are very old indeed. **Serrekunda Market** has a few stalls, especially along the Sukuta Highway, that are orientated towards tourists and sell a variety of crafts such as wood carvings.

Supermarkets
The only supermarkets in Serrekunda are a branch of **Atsons** in Churchill's Town along the main highway, and **Maroun's Supermarket** along Sukuta Highway close to Westfield Junction.

Chimpanzee

Western Division

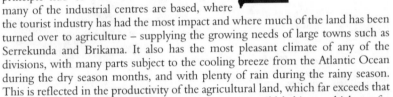

The Western Division is in many ways the principle hub of The Gambia. It is here that many of the industrial centres are based, where the tourist industry has had the most impact and where much of the land has been turned over to agriculture – supplying the growing needs of large towns such as Serrekunda and Brikama. It also has the most pleasant climate of any of the divisions, with many parts subject to the cooling breeze from the Atlantic Ocean during the dry season months, and with plenty of rain during the rainy season. This is reflected in the productivity of the agricultural land, which far exceeds that of many upcountry areas and also in the remaining wild habitats, which are far moister than their counterparts upcountry.

This is also the division where many of the schools are based and you can see this in the way that most people can speak passable English, and also where many of the wealthier people (both Gambian and foreigners) live, which is evidenced by the number and quality of the large houses and compounds, as well as by the high numbers of good quality private cars. Even the transport infrastructure is far better than many areas upcountry, with lots of roads making access to any part of the division fairly easy.

Sadly, this is the only part of The Gambia that many visitors to the country see, which is not to belittle the division since it is highly interesting. It's just that many tourists fail to travel far upcountry, where the real heart of this tiny African country can be found, in the villages and hamlets of the countryside.

THE ATLANTIC COAST FROM KOLOLI TO KARTONG

The coastline in this part of The Gambia is everything that you would expect of a tropical paradise. There are many kilometres of sandy beaches, backed by swaying palms trees in most places, and of course there is the sea – which is warm and for the most part safe to swim in.

In the past the countryside inland was covered in either lush coastal forest or species-rich coastal scrub. Much of this has now been cleared for agriculture or to provide fuel for fish-smoking, but there are still some areas that are virtually untouched and covered in their original vegetation.

The towns and villages along the coast have managed to keep their relaxed and peaceful atmospheres and have not really been influenced by the tourist industry. This is probably because the coastal roads have been in a very poor condition for several years. This has made any journey south along the coast long and tiresome. However, the new coastal road, which was under construction in early 2001, will enable travellers to visit even the remotest parts of the coastline easily and comfortably, when it is completed. Such easy access is bound to have consequences and, despite government controls on building and development, mass-tourism related projects will no doubt spring up all along this as yet unspoiled part of the country.

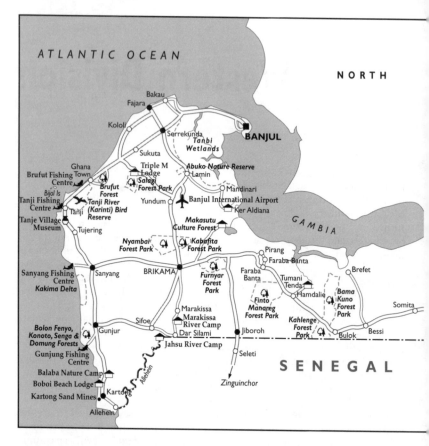

Sukuta and surrounds

Sukuta is almost a suburb of Serrekunda and it is difficult to tell where one starts and the other ends. However, it is quieter in Sukutu and not so busy. Not many tourists go this way, though it has become an important stopping point for overland travellers from Europe and North Africa, and also from the south and east of the region, due to the two camps that are in the town.

Where to stay

Along the new road that has been constructed running from the airport towards the coastal resorts is the **Triple M Lodge** (mobile tel: 994469). This is a brand new venture that at the moment has eight rooms, each with wardrobe, smoke detectors, shower, WC, washbasin, fans and mosquito window nets. The rooms are very smart and clean and a double B&B is around US$13.50, though you can negotiate a lower price for longer stays. The lodge has a standby generator operating from 19.00 onwards and solar power is planned for the lights. During our visit in early 2001 the restaurant and bar were almost completed and the restaurant will offer a mix of African and European food. The lodge is also planning to run excursions in the future and already has a number of mountain bikes for hire to guests (US$7 for a full day hire, US$3.50 for a half day or around US$2 per hour). This is the first of its kind along the new road and is very well placed for the airport, which is about 8km away.

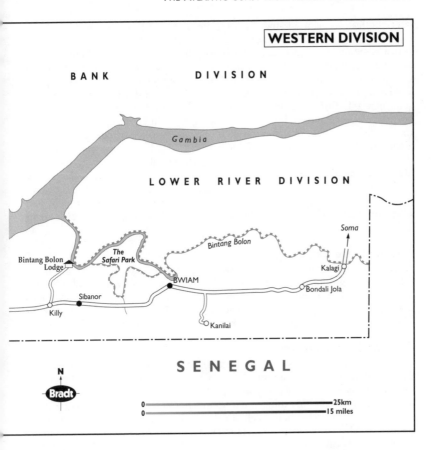

Camping Sukuta (mobile tel: 994149; public fax: 460023 – mark for the attention of Mr Joe Peters, Camping Sukuta; email: campingsukutagambia@yahoo.de) is famous throughout West Africa with overland travellers, though it is also becoming increasingly popular with tourists who are visiting The Gambia. We have had friends who have travelled overland from Europe and tell us that there are signs along the road pointing to Sukuta Camping as far away as Mauritania. Now there's efficiency for you! In fact efficiency, comfort and friendliness are the bywords of this camp. It is set in well-tended and tidy gardens and the accommodation, although not sumptuous, is clean and well maintained. For overland travellers there are camping bays where you can also park your vehicle (US$2.50 per person plus US$0.50 per car or tent each night). It is also possible to leave your vehicle for as long as you want if you need to fly home and then pick it up at some later date. In addition it is often possible for guests to rent or buy cars for local use, and to buy cars to take further afield in the West African region. There is a self-catering kitchen, including BBQ, or you can eat in the restaurant and bar which is available only to guests of the camp (breakfast is priced between US$2–2.50, while main meals are available for US$4–5). There is also a small shop that sells souvenirs, essential spare parts for vehicles and small items for travellers such as toilet paper, milk and sugar etc. Accommodation varies from small bungalows with separate showers and toilets to larger bungalows with en suite facilities. Prices also vary from about US$6 per night for a single to about US$17 per night for a triple room. One word of warning is that some other camps in the country have been known to pass themselves off as Sukutu Camping, because of their good reputation – if it doesn't have Sukutu Camping in large bold lettering near the entrance, it isn't the real Sukuta Camping!

Mustapha's Camping, also known as **Heinz and Monika's Camping** (German tel: 06343 5230; fax: 06343 61339; mobile tel: 991953; email: bormann@gamtel.gm; web: www.gambiacamping – in German) is another camp that is a favourite with overland travellers. This is a smaller operation than Sukuta Camping. There is a self-catering kitchen and four bungalows, each with one double and one single bed, mosquito bednets and a small patio. Showers and toilets are in separate blocks. Although there is no bar or restaurant it is possible to buy soft drinks and beer and there may be a small shop operating by the time this guidebook is published. Prices for camping are US$2.50 per person per night, and US$5 for a room. It is also possible to hire horses here at US$6.50 per hour or US$20.50 for a full day.

Getting there and away
It's best to hire a tourist or shared taxi to get to Sukuta, especially if you are intending to head for one of the camps since they are off the main road and most taxi drivers should know where they are. It is also possible for Sukuta Camping to arrange an airport transfer if you contact them in advance. This is priced at about US$10 per person, though with larger groups this is negotiable.

Brufut fishing centre
This is the first in a series of small artisanal (ie: small-scale and based mostly on traditional methods) fishing centres stretching south along the coast. They are all fascinating places and particularly suited to photographers with lots of opportunity for action shots. The first thing you'll notice after entering a fishing centre (after the sometimes overwhelming smell of fish, of course) is the collection of brightly painted wooden *pirogues* that are anchored just off shore or pulled up high on to the beach. These local canoes vary in size from small one-man jobs to large boats that have crews of half-a-dozen or so and which include shelters for the crew. Many of these larger boats are not Gambian and are crewed by a whole range of nationalities from Senegalese right through to people based as far away as Ghana. French is as commonly spoken as English amidst a smattering of other West African languages and dialects.

Most of the fishing that takes place from these *pirogues* is artisanal. Gill nets are used to catch small quantities of fish, which are then landed and sold at the beach. If you fancy fresh fish, this is the place to come and bargain for it. Some of the catch is bought by local traders, who will then sell it to the coastal communities. Many of these traders sell from large baskets on the back of their bicycles. These traders are a common sight along the coastal roads and we have often wondered just how far they pedal in a day. We often see them starting out well before dawn on old and decrepit bikes that would in Europe or the USA be consigned to the scrap heap.

At the fishing centre most of the catch is either dried in the sun or smoked in the huts by the beach. If you walk around and show an interest, most people will be pleased to show you exactly how the process works. If you keep your eyes open as you walk along the beach amongst the *pirogues* you will see all sorts of discarded marine life, from crabs to the severed heads of hammerhead sharks. Two things that you shouldn't see are dolphins and sea turtles, as these are protected in The

Gambia and it is illegal to catch them or kill them. There are, and always will be, accidents where these species are caught and drowned in fishing nets, and of course there are also unscrupulous people who will break the law but on the whole local fishermen will avoid beaching dolphins and turtles. If you do come across anything untoward then please report it immediately to the local fisheries officer – every fishing centre has one, just ask.

Getting there and away
With the new coast road, which has already reached this far in its construction, it is now easy and quick to get to the fishing centre from the Atlantic resorts. Bush taxis stop all along the road from both directions. The nearest town is Ghana Town (this small town is full of Ghanaian fishermen and their families) and from here it is only a few hundred metres to the beach. From Dippa Kunda in Serrekunda to Ghana Town will cost you less than US$0.50.

Things to do
If you are a brave, adventurous sort of person, you might like to either go out on a short trip on a *pirogue* or even accompany the crew while they are fishing. This will cost you of course, but fishing is a hard life and not well paid, so any other income is always welcome. There are no fixed prices as not many tourists are brave enough to do this, so you will have to negotiate. Be prepared to cough up several hundred dalasis though. A trip like this can be very exciting as you crash out through the surf. You may feel a little unsafe in some of the *pirogues*, which seem to roll about too much or to leak in water just a little too fast, but don't be overly worried. Remember that these fishermen have to go out every day in these same boats, no matter what the conditions are like, and most of them are very good at what they do. However, bear in mind that these trips are definitely not for the faint-hearted. Also remember to watch your camera gear or binoculars, as they are extremely likely to get wet, especially during setting off and landing. We suggest you keep them safely wrapped up in plastic bags during these parts of your trip or better still, don't take them with you at all. Once salt-water gets into your camera or binoculars they corrode very fast and are more or less ruined. You have been warned!

Brufut Forest
Brufut Forest has long been a favourite place for birdwatchers, though it does tend to be ignored in most of the birding literature that does the rounds, such as trip reports. It is quite an open area of woodland where it is easy to see birds, and holds a good selection of species including Verreaux's eagle owl, *Bubo lacteus*, striped kingfisher, *Halcyon chelicuti*, Vieillot's barbet, *Lybius vieilloti*, red-shouldered cuckoo-shrike, *Coracina phoenicea*, yellow-bellied hyliota, *Hyliota flavigaster*, and western violet-backed sunbird, *Anthreptes longuemarei*. Unfortunately, the growing demand for firewood means that the forest is gradually becoming degraded as people from the nearby town of Brufut wander into Brufut Forest to cut down timber. Local birding guides are doing all that they can to try to educate the local people but it's an uphill struggle and they need support.

Getting there and away
This large area of woodland is quite hard to find, as you have to approach it through a short maze of side roads through the town of Brufut. The best way to get there is to hire a birding guide (see *Birding guides* in *Chapter 3*). If you want to find it yourself, the best way to do this is to catch a bush taxi into Brufut and then ask for directions in the town.

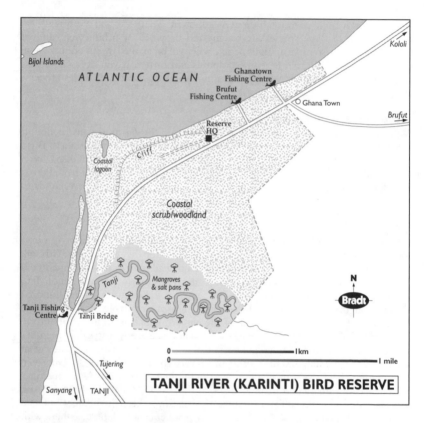

TANJI RIVER (KARINTI) BIRD RESERVE

Tanji River (Karinti) Bird Reserve

Tanji River Bird Reserve, which is in an area known locally as Karinti, is an officially protected area of The Gambia, and is only about 30 minutes drive from the tourist development area. The reserve is just over 6km² and encompasses a wide range of different habitat types, ranging from beach, tidal lagoons, mangrove swamp, barren flats, coastal scrub and dry savanna woodland. The reserve also protects Bijol Islands, which are The Gambia's only offshore islands and lie about 1.5km from the coastline.

Tanji Reserve has been protected by Gambian law since 1993 and received this protection primarily because of the birdlife that abounds in the area. Three hundred and four species of bird, including 34 birds of prey, have been recorded here, over half of the total number of birds found throughout the country. Of the rarities, it is worth looking out for white-fronted plover, *Charadrius marginatus*, Audouins gull, and kelp gull on the beach. Inland you may be lucky and find red-billed quelea or yellow-breasted apalis, *Apalis flavida*. A recently completed 12-month survey of Bijol Islands revealed a large breeding colony of royal terns, *Sterna maxima*, on the smaller of the two islands, together with lesser numbers of breeding Caspian terns, *S. caspia*, grey-headed gulls and western reef herons. There were also up to 700 roosting pelicans in June, July and August, though smaller numbers can be seen there in any other month.

Tanji Reserve is not just good for birds though. Green turtles nest on Bijol Islands and along the beach on the mainland part of the reserve, especially during and around October. The mammals present in the reserve include western red colobus, callithrix and patas monkeys, possibly Guinea baboon, various genets, African civet, spotted hyena, crested porcupine and bushbuck. There are also snakes such as pythons, cobras and puff adders, *Bitis arietans*, though of course you will be extremely lucky (or unlucky, depending on your view) to see any of these. There is also a good selection of butterflies and dragonflies at Tanji. In the sea just off the reserve a number of marine mammals have been spotted, including minke whale, Atlantic hump-backed dolphin, bottlenose dolphin and even the extremely rare monk seal.

The reserve is cut into two parts by the new coast road, and unfortunately the building of this road caused some damage and several large trees were cut down. This is very regrettable but with successive rainy seasons it is hoped that the vegetation will soon be replaced naturally. A more serious problem at the present time is the illegal grazing of livestock and woodcutting within the reserve. To help to control this there is a headquarters building (which is signposted from the road) which houses a small group of rangers employed by the DPWM. These rangers regularly patrol the reserve and the beach, as well as manning the HQ where tickets to the reserve are sold. The entrance fees are standard for all protected areas at less than US$2.50 per adult and US$1.50 per child. You are free to walk anywhere in the reserve except for Bijol Islands, where access is prohibited at all times in order to minimise disturbance. However, a new development at the bird reserve means that the staff have a motorised boat with which to patrol the islands on a regular basis. To help offset the operating costs of this boat the rangers take groups of visitors on boat tours around the islands for a closer look at the birds. The boat is permitted to land on the islands, and there will only be a limited amount of visits per day. The boat will hold four visitors and two crew, and the cost will be around US$10 per person. Please enquire for more information either at the reserve HQ or by phoning the wildlife department (tel: 375888; fax: 392179; email: wildlife@gamtel.gm).

Getting there and away
Tourist taxis or shared taxis are probably the most reliable, if the most expensive, way of getting to Tanji River Bird Reserve. In addition, bush taxis pass on the way to Tanji fishing village and further on down the coast, from Dippa Kunda in Serrekunda and also back in the opposite direction. When the new coastal road finally extends down to the Kartong in the south we will be very surprised if the flow of traffic on this road does not increase dramatically, making transport even easier and cheaper to find.

Camel Safari
The **Camel Safari** (tel: 461083; mobile tel: 990401 or 990402) is in a league of its own in The Gambia. It actually has ten camels that were imported from Senegal and two more that were born in The Gambia. Most people book a safari which includes camel rides, lunch and a chance to relax on the beach through the ground operators (see *Organised excursions* in *Chapter 3* for more details) but it is possible to just turn up and hire yourself a camel. This will cost you just over US$5 per adult and US$3.50 for a child under 12 for half an hour, or US$10 per adult and US$7 for a child under 12 for a full hour). It is also possible to just come and visit the camels for less than US$2 with a free drink thrown in. There is a *bantaba* that sells drinks and a small shop that sells souvenirs, some of which are unusual and of a high quality. The Camel Safari is open every day of the year 08.00–18.00.

Getting there and away
The Camel Safari is prominent on the left as you enter Tanji village along the coast

road. Bush taxis from the south and north stop at Tanji. It will cost you less than US$0.50 to get here from Dippa Kunda in Serrekunda.

Tanji fishing village

This is possibly the largest fishing centre along the coast and is currently being improved with help from the Japanese. The environment around the town has suffered badly over the last decade or so, due mainly to the introduction of smoking as a way of preserving fish. Smoking is a good idea in that it preserves fish that might otherwise quickly spoil, but one negative effect is that huge areas of coastal forest and scrub have been devastated in order to provide fuel-wood for the smoking process. One of the present improvements at the fishing centre includes the building of an ice plant for freezing fish, which we feel can only help in curbing the deforestation. The fishing centre at Tanji normally also has a few boats that are under construction on the beach, and it is fascinating to see how they are put together using methods that have changed very little over generations.

Getting there and away

Bush taxis from the south and north stop at Tanji. It will cost you less than US$0.50 to get here from Dippa Kunda in Serrekunda.

Where to stay

There are a few places in the area that give you a fairly good choice in quality and prices. The first of these is **Nyanya Beach Camp** (tel: 394759), which is located on the beach and along the bank of the Tanji River, immediately on the right of the road as you pass over the river bridge. There are at present three huts that can be hired, which, although basic, are adequate and clean and have mosquito window nets. There is also another hut that includes an en suite WC. Prices are US$7 for a single B&B, US$10 for a double B&B and US$17 for a double B&B in the hut with the toilet. The camp is open all year. The only thing wrong with this site is that it may be a little smelly (and noisy) if the wind is blowing from the fishing village, which is only a few metres along the road.

Next on the list and slightly more expensive, but correspondingly better equipped, is the **Kairoh Garden Bar and Restaurant** (tel: 463456 and leave a message for them to get back to you; email: kairohgarden@hotmail.com; the Dutch contact is Barbara Somers, tel: 070 3548812; email: barbarasomers@hotmail.com). This camp is around 20–30 minutes walk from the beach on the far outskirts of Tanji village. To find it turn left into the village from the coast road just before the immigration post. It was signposted quite poorly during our visit but there are plans to improve this in the near future so hopefully it'll be done by the time you read this. Follow this road into the village and pick up the sign pointing left, just after passing the Bremen Clinic (which is well signposted and easy to find). This camp is fairly new and is open all day, every day of the year. It is located in a huge, bare compound but is presently being planted up with a range of trees and flowers which will make the camp much more pleasing to the eye. There are four rooms, with shower, WC, washbasin and mosquito window nets, and eight rooms without en suite showers and toilets. The latter are located nearby in a separate building. All rooms have electricity in the evenings provided by a generator. The rooms are clean and well-appointed, ranging in price from US$8.50–9 per single B&B, to US$15.50–16 per double B&B. If you intend to stay for two weeks or more you can negotiate a substantial 25% discount on these prices. Pick-ups from the airport can be arranged.

The most expensive but probably the best place to stay in at Tanji is **Paradise Inn** (tel: 996643; web: www.wieringermeer.net/paradise/nederlands.htm). This is fast becoming a very popular site so it's advisable to book well in advance. Here you will find ten huts spread out in beautifully peaceful and lush tropical gardens located right on the banks of the Tanji River and only 10–20 minutes walk from the beach. The camp is open all year except September and is a birdwatchers' paradise. Most of the guests come from Belgium, Holland and Germany, though there are also some English. During the tourist season rooms are priced at US$11 for a single B&B and US$18 for a double B&B. Cheaper rates are available in the off-season. All rooms have a shower, WC, washbasin and both fixed and mosquito bednets. They also have power for a short period in the afternoon and evening provided by a generator. There is a small tourist shop in the camp that sells local goods such as batiks and jewellery etc. On Monday evenings, entertainment is provided by local drummers and *kora* players. To find the inn, turn left off the coast road just before the immigration post and proceed up the road until you come across the first of their signs showing the way. Airport transfers are available if booked in advance.

Where to eat

Along the beachfront there are a few local bars and restaurants in the fishing centre itself, where you can get cheap drinks and meals and as much talking as you want. These include the **Touba Restaurant** and **Gaye's Coffee Shop**. **Nyanya Beach Camp** also has a smart-looking restaurant with terrace overlooking the Tanji River. They have a small selection of cheap meals in the US$0.50–3.50 range. If you're a birdwatcher you'll love this place as you can look at the waders on the riverbank at low tide whilst sitting and relaxing in the shade with a cold beer. **Kairoh Garden Bar and Restaurant** is more sophisticated and offers a wider choice of meals that are a little more expensive at US$8.50–9 for three courses, with a range of drinks available. The restaurant and bar is very pleasant and if you're staying elsewhere in Tanji it would prove ideal for a change of scenery one evening. The **Paradise Inn** also has its own restaurant and bar on site with a good range of snacks from US$2–3 and main meals at between US$2–4.50.

Things to do

The fishing centre is a hive of activity and well worth a visit at any time of day just to watch what's going on. If you fancy a ride in a fishing *pirogue* then read the section on *Brufut Fishing Centre* above as the same rules apply. Boat trips along the Tanji River can be organised at **Paradise Inn**, where you can paddle yourself at US$4 per hour or hire a paddler for a further US$2 per hour.

For those who are staying at Tanji but prefer to occasionally travel further afield, then **Paradise Inn** can organise a wide selection of trips. These include trips to the southern coastal area (US$40.50 per day), Bintang Bolon (US$68 per day), Tendaba (US$54.50 per day), Jinack Island (US$54.50 per day), Janjangbureh (US$68 per day), Basse (US$68 per day) and Dakar in Senegal (US$341.50 for five days). **Kairoh Garden Bar and Restaurant** are also planning to operate jeep safaris in the future so its worth asking there.

With **Tanji River (Karinti) Bird Reserve** being so close to Tanji village, it's hardly surprising that birdwatching is one of the most popular activities for visitors to the area. Apart from the reserve itself, there are other areas locally where the birding is good, including the beach by the fishing village for gulls and terns. A boat trip along the mangrove-lined Tanji River from the **Paradise Inn** is also bound to turn up a few good species, as are walks around the area (you can choose to be guided by a birding guide from the inn at a cost of US$10 per person if you prefer). To find out about newly sighted species and hot spots that may be worthwhile checking out, look through the literature in the restaurant of **Paradise Inn** as there are a few reports here, some of them with sketch maps, from people who have birdwatched in the past.

Tanje Village Museum

Tanje Village Museum (tel: 371007 at either 07.00 or 20.00 as this is when someone is available to answer) is in a class of its own in The Gambia. The site is owned and operated by Abdoulaye Bayo, a former curator from the National Museum in Banjul, who decided to set up on his own and has done so remarkably well. This site is very popular with tourists but is also used extensively by local school groups for educational purposes, and by local craftsmen to sell their wares. The museum is open daily 09.00–17.00 and admission is less than US$2 per adult and less than US$0.50 for under 12s. If you wish you can ask for a guided tour of the museum which is completely free of charge. There is a building with various displays on Gambian culture, musical instruments, etc, and a small selection of unusual gifts for sale. Included here is a display on the wildlife of The Gambia which we won't go on about too much as we wrote it and took the photos! (We've been told it's very good, though!) A dedicated souvenir shop is planned for the near future, which will sell a range of authentic African crafts and materials, as well as examples of all of the musical instruments shown in the museum display.

Local craftsmen use the site and are happy to answer questions about what they do and how they do it. These crafts include weaving and metalwork, and it is possible to buy high quality goods at very reasonable prices compared to the main tourist areas or even to have items made to order if you leave them enough time before the end of your holiday. There is also a traditionally built Mandinka village compound within the museum which contains various styles of huts, furniture and local artifacts that are clearly explained. Future plans here include the building of other compounds in the styles of other ethnic groups such as the Wolof, Jola and Fula, and these should prove to be very interesting.

There is a short nature trail set out around the grounds which contains a good selection of native and introduced trees and shrubs, all numbered and named, as well as several picnic areas with seats and tables. A nature trail guide, available for US$1, describes over 30 of the species found along the trail and how they are used locally. At the end of your exploration of the museum you'll find welcome shade in the *bantaba*, where a selection of cold drinks and food is for sale.

If you want to stay at the museum and explore the surrounding area more fully there are four huts available for visitors. These are built in the local style and are simple. You'll need to bring your own mosquito bednet with you, and don't expect electricity or running water here. Costs are set at US$7 per person for B&B.

Tanje Village Museum is an interesting place to visit and Abdoulaye always has lots of plans for the future, most of which seem to get off the ground, despite a lack of resources. Present plans include helping the local villagers by letting them use a large vegetable garden at the back of the museum for growing their own foodstuffs. He has already had a deep well dug and concrete-lined and is trying to get a pump and irrigation system sponsored. Another idea is to open a craft school for locals and tourists who are interested in learning traditional skills.

Getting there and away

Most people visit the museum during an organised excursion such as the 'four-wheel-drive adventure' (see *Organised excursions* in *Chapter 3*), so check the itinerary of your safari to see if you stop off at the museum. Alternatively, it is possible to catch a tourist or shared taxi from the main tourist areas, or a bush taxi from Dippa Kunda in Serrekunda for less than US$0.50 (ask to be dropped off at the museum, as this is not a regular stop). You can easily walk to the museum from Tanji fishing Village, which is only a distance of about 2km away. Bush taxis are fairly regular in both directions along the coast road.

Tujering Point
At Tujering Point, about 3km south of Tanji fishing village is Suu Berry Beach Bar. This used to be a popular site for tourists and ex-pats but suffered a major fire and is now slowly being rebuilt. It is quite difficult to find from the main road as it isn't signposted at the moment, and anyway the track that leads to the site is suitable only for good four-wheel-drive vehicles. When it's very wet or very dry and sandy, even these may have problems. The best way to check out if the beach bar is operating yet is to walk along the beach, either from Tanji or from Sanyang (at least 7–8km from Sanyang Point).

Sanyang
Sanyang is a small town located about half way between Tanji and Gunjur. It's quite a walk from the beach and so is not a real tourist area, and there are only a few establishments that are tailored to catering for tourists. There is also a small fishing centre on the beach.

Getting there and away
Bush taxis are definitely the cheapest option this far down the coast and run fairly regularly in both directions. A bush taxi from Dippa Kunda in Serrekunda will cost around US$0.50. Airport transfers are available to Sanyang Nature Camp if you book well in advance and transport can also be arranged to the camp from Leybato Restaurant and Bar in Fajara. From the town there are frequent bush taxis to the beach and fishing centre that cost less than US$0.50. Shared taxis will take you on the same route or to Kobokoto Beach Bar and Restaurant for around US$2–2.50.

Where to stay
There are a few places in Sanyang that deal with tourists. Probably the best known is **Sanyang Nature Camp** (tel: Leybayto Restaurant and Bar in Fajara on 390275 or 497186; fax: 497562). This is located in a pleasant area along the dirt road from Sanyang running to the fishing centre on the beach. The camp is open all year round and features 16 rooms in bungalows that will cost you US$7 per person per night (although people staying longer may be able to negotiate a discount on the basic price). The rooms all have a shower, WC and mosquito window nets. The newer rooms also have their own washbasin. At present there is no electricity at the site. The camp is about 20 minutes walk from the beach.

On the outskirts of the town itself is **Rheakunda Camp and African Culture Centre Dance and Drumming School** (tel & fax: 460565 or June-October in Germany, tel: 00 49 7531 57302). This camp is under Gambian/German ownership and is located about two miles from the beach, though donkey-cart transport to the beach can be provided if you don't fancy the walk. Accommodation is based in either three Jola-style mud huts or in a bungalow with four rooms. The rooms are pretty basic with no electricity or running water, but each has a mosquito bednet and their own private bucket-shower out the back. There are also flush WCs and washbasins in a separate block. Rooms are around US$7–10 per night. Lighting is with kerosene lamps and candles and the water is drawn from a well.

THE GUNJUR ENVIRONMENTAL PROTECTION AND DEVELOPMENT GROUP (GEPADG)

GEPADG is a local charity founded by Mr Badara Njie Bayo, following the Earth Summit in Rio in 1992. The group is made up of very enthusiastic people from Gunjur whose current activities include local environmental campaigns, active forestry management and surveillance. They are working in close collaboration with ten local groups (called clans or *kabilos*) covering a total forest area of 145km². Here they are helping to develop community forests and to promote local ecotourism opportunities. Their current sites include Konoto, Senga and Domung Forests, amongst many others, and Bolon Fenyo (see later in this chapter). If you want to explore the countryside surrounding Gunjur or find out more about the local culture here, GEPADG is the best place to start. The group has an office in Gunjur which is signposted from the main road through the town (not far beyond the market area if you are travelling from the south), and will welcome anybody who comes and shows a genuine interest in what they are working hard to achieve. They have very little funds, but have so far done an amazing job in spite of their lack of resources, due mainly to their great enthusiasm and vigour. We really cannot praise them highly enough and urge you to visit them, if only to bolster their spirits (a small contribution towards their efforts would go a long way too!). Members of the group will willingly show you how to get to some of the more interesting sites in the area, such as the turtle nesting ground just along the coast from Bolon Fenyo, or the wonderful coastal forests. They will also introduce you to local guides who help look after these areas and will show you around if you want them to. If you are into protecting the environment, please call in on the project and give them some support.

Kobokoto Beach Bar and Restaurant (tel: 484857 or 990767 between 18.00–19.00 and leave a message with a number and time for the manager to call you back) is located directly on the beach about 10–15 minutes walk north of the fishing centre. This is a very peaceful spot and the management state that bumsters are not allowed to disturb the guests. There are two rooms with their own showers. There are no mosquito nets but with the breeze blowing straight off the sea mosquitoes are probably not a major problem. Bring your own mosquito bednet if you're at all worried. There is a flush toilet in a hut of its own with an outside washbasin. Prices are US$10 per person B&B, but if you're intending to stay longer discounts can be negotiated.

Where to eat

The cheapest place to eat is probably **Osprey Beach Bar**, which is located north of Sanyang fishing centre. The nearby **Sanyang Beach Bar** doesn't provide food but has drinks available. Undoubtedly the best place to eat, and at reasonable prices, is the bar and restaurant at **Sanyang Nature Camp**. There is a range of African and European food priced between US$1–5.50 and a continental breakfast will cost you only US$2. **Rheakunda Camp and African Culture Centre Dance and Drumming School** provides African food for guests and visitors, though if you ask for European food, they will cook it for you.

Kobokoto Beach Bar and Restaurant has a good range of cheap European food including fresh fish every day from US$1.50. Fresh lobster will cost you only US$10, all served in the restaurant looking straight out on to the beach.

Things to do

As we've said before, Sanyang is not a tourist area and therefore there is a limited range of things to do, apart from relaxing on the beach and catching some rays or getting involved with local culture. However, the beach is quite busy here so don't expect to be able to relax in peace and quiet. **Sanyang Nature Camp** does offer a few options including foot safaris with birding guides, which are free of charge, and horse-riding at US$1 per hour, though the two horses (called Bob and Rita Marley) looked very thin and undernourished when we visited.

Rheakunda Camp and African Culture Centre Dance and Drumming School is frequented mainly by people who come to have drumming and dancing lessons. A range of lessons can be taken daily, including dances from Guinea Conakry, explaining *juju* and playing the *kora*, *djembe* and bass drums and the *balafon*, which is a xylophone made out of hardwood. All of these can be in either English or French. Participants get the chance to buy an instrument from the camp and for each one bought the management will plant a tree in the compound. Visitors are also asked to donate up to US$20 towards the camp's local project, which is the primary school in Sanyang. **Kobokoto Beach Bar and Restaurant** can also arrange fishing trips or dolphin watching excursions, though the dolphin sightings are not guaranteed.

Gunjur

Gunjur is another small town set back from the coast and not really set up to deal with tourists, though again there is an active and vibrant fishing centre located on the beach, which is around 4km from the town.

Getting there and away

Bush taxis can be taken from Serrekunda along the coast or inland from Brikama (both for less than US$0.50) to Gunjur. Bush taxis also regularly ply the route to Gunjur from towns further south along the coast road. If you want to go further south you will have to change bush taxis in Gunjur. At the present time the new road south of Tanji is not yet completed while the new road from Brikama is almost done, but this may have changed (for the better) by the time you read this book. **Gunjur Beach Motel, Gunjur Guest House, Rasta Kunda Beach Camp** and **Balaba Nature Camp** will all pick you up if you book in advance.

Where to stay

Falconhurst Guest House (fax: 486026) lies about halfway from Gunjur along the road to the fishing centre. Unfortunately, despite visiting several times we were not able to speak to the owner, though his tariffs are displayed at the guesthouse and are US$5 for a single bed and US$7 for a double. Breakfast is an additional US$1 and it's possible to camp at the site if you bring your own tent. Apparently visitors are encouraged to be self-catering and there are facilities available at the guesthouse for this.

Gunjur Beach Motel (tel: 486065; fax: 486066) is Swiss-owned and managed and is probably the most upmarket place on this part of the coast. At the time of writing the motel was up for sale, so we can't guarantee that its present high standards will be the same when you visit. But it seems that no offers to buy are yet on the table while the owner/manager, Louis, who is exceedingly friendly and proud of his establishment, does not appear to be in a great hurry to leave. The motel is ideally placed right on the beachfront, and all the rooms are literally only a few seconds walk from the Atlantic. Bumsters are actively discouraged from annoying the guests on the beach. There are four single and four double rooms in two bungalows. These are relatively new rooms and are very well furnished and maintained with their own shower, WC, washbasin and mosquito window nets. All rooms also have solar-powered lighting and some of the rooms have their own small balcony. All of the prices quoted here are for B&B: single US$11; double US$18–20.50; three per room US$24 and four per room US$30. It's also possible to camp in the grounds of the motel, which costs US$1.50 per person, less than US$1.50 per tent and the same per car. The motel has one of only a few pool tables in The Gambia, though it is reserved for guests only.

Gunjur Guest House (tel: 486143; fax: 486026.) is an excellent example of a small, family-run tourism project. The guest house is based in a traditional extended family compound and is managed by James Demba, with the assistance of other members of his family, who are all Karoninko. In 2001, the guesthouse won the best new initiative award in a national competition for small businesses. Accommodation is available in double rooms and in a single family room that sleeps four. The rooms are spaced around a small courtyard that is separate from the Demba family compound. The courtyard is filled with a variety of local plants and trees, with several areas where you can relax in a peaceful atmosphere. Prices are US$6 for a single B&B and US$7.50 for a double B&B. The rooms are clean and have fixed mosquito nets and bednets. The toilets and showers are of the local design ie: pit latrines and bucket showers. It is possible to park your car safely in the family compound. The compound is hard to find at the moment and unsigned, although we have been assured that this will change soon with the provision of at least a signboard outside the compound. It is a large white-walled compound on the outskirts of Gunjur on the road to Berending, located about 1.5km from Gunjur gas station. Ask for directions from here, or better yet book a room in advance and be picked up from either the airport or Brikama.

Rasta Kunda Beach Camp (telephone the Netherlands for information; tel: 00 31 (0) 570 622948; fax: 220 486026) was sadly in a state of disrepair during early 2001. However the Gambian owner was on tour in Europe trying to gain financial help to improve the camp, so it may be a lot better by the time you read this. The camp is in a lovely spot set right above the beach amongst the palms, and has a very peaceful and relaxing atmosphere. The accommodation is basic but clean, in traditional style huts. Each bed has a mosquito bednet and the toilets are in one hut and of the local style, ie: pit latrines and bucket showers. There is no electricity and all lighting is by kerosene lamp. The camp is open all year and the accommodation will cost you US$7 for bed and breakfast. Other meals can also be provided at reasonable prices (less than US$2), and there are beer and soft drinks for sale. If you book in advance it is possible to be picked up at the airport.

Balaba Nature Camp (for information from the UK, tel/fax: 01366 501337; to book, fax: 486026) is an excellent locally run project that opened in 1998. The camp's large compound is located in an area of relatively pristine Guinea savanna woodland, about 38km south from Banjul and 4km north of Kartong. It's located off the main coast road and well signposted. This camp is an example of ecotourism at its best, run by and employing local people and involving many different facets of local culture and the surrounding communities. The staff are extremely friendly and helpful to visitors, and will help you to get the most of your stay. Accommodation (for a maximum of 16–20 people) is in simple huts built in the Jola style. They are equipped with bedding (including hand-knitted blankets) mosquito nets and kerosene lamps. There is no electricity or running water and toilets and showers are of the local design with one of each for every hut. Well water is provided for washing and fresh, clean drinking water is transported by donkey cart from the nearest tap. Bottled water is also available to buy. Costs per person for B&B is a very reasonable US$7, or for full board US$11. Discounts are available and can be negotiated if you intend to stay longer. This is one of the places that really impressed us with their attitude, not only towards their visitors but also to their local environment, which they are working hard to preserve. The owners are doing their best to convert their neighbours thinking towards conserving nature as well. The surrounding woodland holds many animals such as monkeys, monitor lizards and even bushbuck which sometimes wander through the compound as well as the occasional hyena.

The list of birds seen by previous visitors is huge and contains many rarities. The camp is helped by the English parents of the owner's late wife, Hazel Isa Manneh. The compound contains a beautiful memorial dedicated to her.

Where to eat

There are a few local restaurants and bars located at the fishing centre where meals and drinks can be bought cheaply and you can mix with the local fishermen. These include the strangely named **Cardiff and South Wales Restaurant** and **Kairabah Restaurant and Beach Bar**.

Gunjur Beach Motel has international meals available at very fair prices ranging from US$1.50–6. The large and airy restaurant boasts the best beef fillet in either The Gambia or Germany and Louis is very much into wines. So if you want to, you can wash it all down with a good vintage, or order a drink from the bar. We found the servings to be huge and could hardly eat all of ours.

Gunjur Guest House has a small restaurant that serves local food at very reasonable prices. Both lunch and dinner are priced at US$2.50 each. Drinks are extra. They also have two bars in the compound, the **Bintu Sambou Memorial Bar**, and the **Jelan Katato's Memorial Bar**, which specialises in local drinks, including palm wine.

Balaba Nature Camp, as well as providing food for its camp guests, also provide meals for day visitors at very reasonable prices, ranging from US$2.50–4. The most expensive item on their menu is fresh lobster at less than US$6. They will provide African or European dishes on request and there is also a bar.

Things to do

If you want to just relax and sunbathe in peaceful, safe surroundings then look no further than Gunjur Beach Motel, which is ideally located and very comfortable. The beach at Rasta Kunda Beach Camp is also very peaceful and quiet.

Gunjur Guest House organises expeditions to Kartong crocodile pool, local villages and to the *Roots* country. They will also take you on birdwatching trips. All prices are negotiable. **Rasta Kunda Beach Camp** can arrange for lessons in drumming and other musical instruments. They can also organise boat and jeep safaris, or fishing trips, at negotiable prices.

Balaba Nature Camp can provide on request a whole range of activities, whether it be art, music, learning new skills or exploring the local countryside. They will also run excursions to places such as the local craft market, Banjul National Museum, Abuko Nature Reserve, the sacred crocodile pool in Kartong and Gunjur's food market and shops. They will also arrange river trips, visits to the local palm wine-tappers or to the fishing centre. Field guides will accompany you if you want at a cost of US$3.50. If you are into birdwatching then they will arrange for an experienced birding guide to take you around for a negotiated fee. Alternatively you can walk to the beach, about 20 minutes from the camp, and catch some sun. If you fancy some local entertainment then the staff will lay on singing and dancing at a nearby village.

Bolon Fenyo and Kakima Delta

The sea front along this stretch of coast is very rich in birdlife. Just by Gunjur Fishing Centre, there is a freshwater *bolon* that manages to retain some water even towards the end of the rainy season. This is the Bolon Fenyo, and it acts as a magnet for a large roost of gulls and an assortment of waders and is worth searching for those more elusive species. The *bolon* used to hold crocodiles but unfortunately they are locally extinct in the area now. It may be possible to

SAND DUNE MOSQUE

Between the Gunjur Beach Motel and Rasta Kunda Beach Camp is the Sand Dune Mosque, or *Kenye-kenye Jamango*, located at the top of the beach and looking out to sea. Although it is only a plain concrete structure, this mosque has a fascinating history and is visited by Muslims and scholars on pilgrimage from all over The Gambia and West Africa. The mosque, rocks and associated ground are all considered sacred.

The site is sacred because of a visit there by Khalifat'ul Tijanniyya Sheikh Umar Taal, who lived from 1793 to 1864, and was the leader of the Tijanniyya Sect in West Africa. Sheikh Umar's pilgrimage to Mecca between 1828 and 1831 and other Islamic centres in the Middle East, made him famous. News of his greatness and erudition preceded him on his return trip from Mecca through Cairo, Bonnu, Sokoto and Madina, before he reached Futa Jallon in 1840. Sheikh Umar fought paganism and challenged the political and social order of the old Muslim theocracies, replacing them with a new branch of Militant Islam. His *Jihads*, or 'Holy Wars', imposed his authority from Senegal to Nigeria, and attracted thousands of disciples from all over West Africa, including the Aku, or freed slaves of African origin, in Sierra Leone. His military campaigns did nothing to improve his relations with the European powers who were colonising the area at the time, and who saw the creation of a vast Islamic entity formed through territorial conquest as a threat. However, Sheikh Umar was very diplomatic whenever he met Europeans, informing them that a large peaceful Islamic state would only improve commerce. Sheikh Umar visited The Gambia during the latter part of his life when he had turned to peaceful Islamisation as a means of attracting more converts. He stayed in several places in The Gambia, including Banjul and Cape Point, before moving further south to Gunjur. Here, he stayed for longer than anywhere else in the country and prayed in the shade of trees and large boulders, thus making the site sacred.

The present custodian of the Sand Dune Mosque is Mr Wasa Jarbang, and he can be found there most days. He has informed us that it is OK for tourists to visit the scared grounds and mosque but you are not allowed to enter the mosque, unless you are a Muslim of course.

reintroduce crocodiles in the near future, especially since the people of Gunjur are very keen to protect and enhance their environment (see the box on the *Gunjur Environmental Protection and Development Group* on page 158).

About 5km further north along the beach from Bolon Fenyo is the Kakima Delta. This is a series of *bolons* that empty into the sea. It is also very rich in birdlife, with huge flocks of terns and white-faced whistling ducks. The land behind the beach is rich in wildlife, though it has been somewhat overgrazed in the last few years. We have heard of both leopard and hyena being spotted here.

Konoto, Senga and Domung Forests

Behind Bolon Fenyo, and stretching north for quite a distance, are the forests of Konoto, Senga and Domung. These are excellent forests, which are receiving very active protection from the local people (see *Gunjur Environmental Protection and Development Group*, page 158). They are full of wildlife, including callithrix monkeys, western red colobus, Guinea baboons, bushbuck, duikers, crested porcupine and, possibly, brush-tailed porcupine, as well as a large range of snakes including green mamba, *Dendroaspis viridis*, royal python, *Python regius*, and African rock python. These forests are at present little explored regarding their birdlife, but just from our brief visits it is pretty obvious that they have great potential. The forests are owned by the local clans, who have placed watchmen in the area to help protect them. The best way to explore this area is to ask for help from the Gunjur Environmental Protection and Development Group, who will be happy to help in any way they can. Both the group and the owners of these forests are very proud of their accomplishments, and rightly so. Between the forests is an excellent example of coastal scrub, that is open grassy land interspersed with low gingerbread plum trees, *Parinari macrophylla*. This too is a valuable habitat for mammals, reptiles and birds. The mammals include marsh cane rat, *Thryonomys swiderianus*, which is a large rodent known throughout Africa as the 'cutting grass' because of its habit of biting off grass stems at the base and storing them in piles. This animal is hunted in many countries for food and is a valuable source of protein to many people. One bird that we have seen here, which is fairly uncommon along the coast, is the pygmy sunbird, *Anthreptes platurus*. This species is much more common in the dry savanna woodland inland.

Kartong

Kartong is in the extreme south of The Gambia along the coastline. Beyond Kartong there is only an immigration post, a small hamlet and fishing centre before the Allahein River and Casamance, in southern Senegal. Kartong is a pleasant town, which has always been famous amongst Gambians because of its sacred crocodile pool. Today it is also the centre of the sand-mining industry in The Gambia.

Getting there and away

Bush taxis can be taken to Gunjur from Serrekunda or Brikama. At Gunjur you catch another to Kartong (all for less than US$1). This is the last stop for the planned coastal road, which may or may not have been completed by the time you read this. If it has been completed, then getting to Kartong will be easy and quick. If not, then be prepared for a very bumpy ride south, as the large numbers of sand-mining lorries that head along the dirt road to the north, have made this a very rough road indeed. Shared taxis will take you as far as Kartong for about US$20.50–24. **Boboi Beach Lodge** will arrange for you to be picked up from the airport if you book in advance. Taxis to the **Follonko Guesthouse** can also be arranged in advance.

Where to stay

Boboi Beach Lodge (web, with email: www.gambia-adventure.com) is located about 8km south of Gunjur and 2km north of Kartong along the coastal road. It is well signposted and it's only a short walk through the bush to the camp from the road. This Gambian/Scottish venture is very eco-tourism orientated and is set in beautiful unspoiled surroundings right on the edge of the beach. This used to be a tented camp but recently the owners have built three double huts to accommodate visitors, though they still have one large tent and there is room for people to pitch their own tents if they want to. The huts are very comfortable, have mosquito window nets and lights that run on solar power. Toilets and washing facilities are in a separate block. Prices are US$7–10 per night, depending on the size of the group, but the management prefers you to haggle over the price to get the real feeling of being in Africa. The large tent is under a grassed roof and can sleep up to five (though it would be a tight squeeze), with bedding provided. Prices are less than US$1.50 per person. Camping costs around US$1 per tent.

Follonko Guesthouse (contact is through the APSO office in Bakau; tel: 495550) is owned by the villagers of Kartong, and all profits go back into the village development fund. There is always someone present at the guesthouse, so it is possible to turn up on spec. The guesthouse is a single building that is well placed on a slight hill, right on the edge of the village overlooking an area largely composed of vegetable gardens. The only thing that spoils the view is the dirt road at the bottom of the hill that is frequently used by the sand-mining lorries from the nearby sand mine. The guesthouse is also perfectly placed to catch the cool breeze off the sea, which is only about 10 minutes' walk away. Consequently it is fairly cool even in the hottest of weather, so make sure you bring something warm to wear in the evenings. There are two double rooms that cost a very reasonable US$5 per person. There is also a flush toilet and a shower in the guesthouse, though there is no electricity, and lighting is by gas lamp. Drinking water is drawn from a well but is put through a water filter so is perfectly safe to drink. If you really want to experience Gambian culture then the guesthouse can arrange for you to stay with a Gambian family in their village compound, where you can join in and work during the day with the family or retire to the guesthouse or the beach. The guesthouse doubles up as a field centre for training Irish and British volunteers and at the time of writing was also used often by a group of British bird-ringers who are carrying out research in the area.

Morgan's Grocery and Restaurant is also planning to build some accommodation, so check him out if you are in the area (see below).

Where to eat
Morgan's Grocery and Restaurant used to be located in the village but has now moved up to the edge of the sand mine. This is by far the cheapest place to eat that caters for tourists and Morgan himself will cook you a range of Gambian food plus omelettes, chips or sandwiches, all priced at less than US$1.50 per meal. He also has a range of drinks for sale at cheaper than normal tourist prices.

    Boboi Beach Lodge has a small but well-placed bar and restaurant looking out over the sea. It serves mainly African food but they will cook European-style meals if you ask them to. All of their vegetables are grown organically and fresh fish tops the menu rather than meat dishes. Meals here are very good value, priced at US$2 for breakfast and around US$2.50 for all other meals.

    The **Follonko Guesthouse** has a really excellent chef who was trained in the hotel trade and who can cook Gambian or European meals on request. Breakfast is US$2 plus less than US$0.50 for a cup of coffee, and main meals are US$2.50.

Things to do and places to visit
It would be quicker to list the things that **Boboi Beach Lodge** *doesn't* offer visitors, than what they do. They will arrange tours and treks to suit your particular requirements, though they make some suggestions just to get your imagination going. These include: walking treks into the bush; mountain biking (they have good bikes for hire or as part of a trek); boating trips along the Allahein River; fishing trips, including night fishing (they have fishing rods for hire); camping expeditions and birdwatching treks (they have binoculars for hire). Alternatively, you can just lie on the beautiful beach, go swimming or use the lodge's boogie boards to roll in with the surf. Another alternative is to go horse riding at negotiable rates, and we must add that the horses here are the fittest and best looking we have seen in the whole of The Gambia. If you want to you can also join in looking after the horses, or learn how to. In addition there are art and music workshops. Just tell them what you want to do, in advance, and we're sure that they can arrange it for you.

The **Follonko Guesthouse** will also arrange jeep, birdwatching, fishing and river excursions for visitors, along with entertainment including cultural dances and music with the people of Kartong. Morgan, of **Morgan's Grocery and Restaurant**, is a birding guide with ten years' experience who will gladly show you around all the local sites, as well as take you south into Casamance. He will also arrange to hire a *pirogue* for a river trip (powered either by out-board engine or paddle).

The local **sand-mines**, found to the west of the village, between the village and the sea, are disliked by some members of the community and liked by others. Among the reasons for disliking the mines is first and foremost the fact that malaria is now more prevalent in the village, and this had led to some deaths that may not have occurred if the flooded parts of the mine (and therefore more mosquitoes) were not there. Another reason is that the lorries from the mine have turned the coast road, which in the south is still at present just a dirt track, into the road from hell. In the wet season it is virtually impossible to travel along the road and the village is often cut off from the outside world. In the dry season too, the road is sometimes difficult to negotiate through thick drifts of sand and dust. The mines do have their good points though.

Firstly, currently it is the only legally controlled place in the country where sand can be removed. The construction industry needs this vital material to build anything, including new roads. Without the Kartong mine, illegal sand-mining would be far more common than it already is, and uncontrolled illegal mining leads to increased habitat destruction, coastal erosion, disturbance etc.

Secondly, the influx of people employed by the mine has led to increased expenditure in some village facilities, such as the market and shops, though not by a great amount.

Lastly, the sand-mines have great potential to increase the tourist trade in this part of The Gambia, especially by **birdwatchers**. This is because after the sand is excavated, the holes that are left are allowed to fill up naturally with rain and ground water. Over the years these huge artificially formed pools have become vegetated around their edges. They are some of the only fresh water pools in the area and there is a very rich bird fauna associated with them. Together with the coastal scrub, which is also very rich in birdlife, these features are fast turning the Kartong area into a region that is going to be increasingly visited by birdwatchers eager to add new species to their lists.

The growing bird list for the area is far too long to reproduce here, but we personally have seen such goodies as European spoonbill, *Platalea leucorodia*, spotted redshank, *Tringa erythropus*, great snipe, *Gallinago media*, and greater painted-snipe at the sand-mines. The British bird-ringers who use this spot have also picked up rarities such as Eurasian wryneck, *Jynx torquilla*, and western bluebill, to name just a couple, and have found new birds for The Gambia such as Baillon's crake, *Porzana pusilla*, and little crake, *P. parva* during their research.

The potential here is huge and this could be, if properly managed, a great boon to the economy of Kartong, if some form of community ownership can be arranged for the area after the sand deposits are mined out.

If you are a birdwatcher visiting this area, then there are a few new pools that have been formed by the road just to the south of **Boboi Beach Lodge** and you should spend a few minutes checking these out. Although these holes had only just been dug at the time of writing, they are sure to develop into good birding sites in the near future. These holes have been formed by excavations for laterite, which has been used in the construction of the new road.

Beyond Kartong the road carries on for a few kilometres until it reaches the

Allahein River, which also forms the border with Casamance. Here there is a small hamlet and fishing centre, and there is also a fishing centre further along the track to the west, located on the beach. The beach area at the mouth of the river is well-worth exploring whether you are a keen birder or just want to find a quiet spot away from it all in which to sunbathe. From here there is nothing but unspoiled, mostly empty beaches, stretching for several miles northwards. Good birds sometimes seen along the beach include white-fronted plover and great spotted cuckoo, *Clamator glandarius*.

The **Sacred crocodile pool** in Kartong, or the *Bambo Follonko* (literally meaning 'crocodile pool'), as it's known locally, is located between the village and the sand-mines to the west. Ask anyone where it is and they will tell you, especially young boys who will want to guide you there for a dalasi or two. We used to direct people to follow the road opposite Morgan's Grocery and Restaurant (see above), but now the whole character of the area has changed due to the road being widened through the village. Even Morgan's place has changed location, so the best way to find it is probably to ask. The pool is fairly small but there is also an associated small area of forest that has received protection over the years, as well as the pool itself. This is not at present a tourist trap like the crocodile pool in Bakau, but may well develop that way once the coast road is completed and more tourists visit the area. The *Bambo Follonko* is still widely visited by many Gambians and Senegalese, who come here to bathe in its sacred waters (for more details see the box on *Sacred Crocodile Pools* in *Chapter* 7). The pool was once the home of several Nile crocodiles. Nowadays some of them have moved out into the flooded sand-mines, where it is sometimes possible to see a large crocodile hauled out on an island. Please remember to remove your footwear before entering the fenced off area around the sacred crocodile pool. This is what the locals do, and though it may not be compulsory for tourists, it does show a mark of respect for local customs.

Allahein River

The Allahein River rises in the Séléti region just south of The Gambia. It then flows west, then southwest before emptying into the Atlantic Ocean at Kartong. For about half its length it forms the border between The Gambia and Senegal. This is a very beautiful river that is full of wildlife, including crocodiles. It starts as small streams with forest-covered banks and gradually opens out to become lined in its final stretches by mangrove swamps.

Getting there and away

There are two main directions to approach the river from. The first is from Kartong itself, or further north along the coast. The second is from south of Brikama, either through Sifoe or Marikissa and Dar Silami. The latter is a pretty route that is lined by wooded areas. These woods are very good for wildlife, especially birds and butterflies, and worth exploring on foot along the way. Birds that have been seen in the woods include red-shouldered cuckoo-shrike and white-breasted cuckoo-shrike, *Coracina phoenicea*, and *C. pectoralis*, long-crested eagle, *Lophaetus occipitalis*, and red-necked falcon, *Falco chicquera*. Most of the good local birding guides (see *Birding guides* in *Chapter 3*) will know where the hotspots are and are worth employing if you travel down this way.

Kartong and the Allahein River can be reached by bush taxi from Brikama, changing at Gunjur (less than US$0.50), though most of the taxis only go to Kartong village and you will probably have to walk the last 3km to the river. You can also catch a bush taxi running south to Sifoe, or Marakissa and Dar Silami from Brikama (US$0.50).

Where to stay and eat

Along the upper reaches of the river are two camps. The first is **Marakissa River Camp**, open all year, which is 2km south of Marakissa by the side of the road. At the time of our visit there were two double rooms, each with their own bathroom, though we didn't manage to get a look inside. Hopefully there will be many more rooms by the time this book hits the shelves. These rooms were priced at US$13.50 for bed and breakfast. The restaurant has some seats and tables on the roof, which overlooks a lovely spot on the river. Local and European food is on offer at between US$3.50–7. We were told that large crocodiles sometimes swim in this part of the river. There is also a pathway along the riverbank that looks promising for birds, including ospreys and waders. Apparently one of the staff went fishing in the river and caught what he thought was a very big fish, but upon closer inspection it turned out to be an even bigger python!

The second camp is a few kilometres west of Dar Silami and has a totally different atmosphere to the one above. This is **Jahsu River Camp**, located on a flat delta of the river (well signposted from Marakissa) and is open only during the dry season. This spot has long been a favourite with birdwatchers and some good species can be seen here including quail-finch, *Ortygospiza artricollis*, yellow-throated long-claw and Eurasian marsh harrier, *Circus aeruginosus*. There are six double rooms on stilts joined by causeways. They are pretty basic and do not have mosquito nets (we were told there were no mosquitoes here, which seems a little unbelievable). Each has an open shower in the room and costs US$7 for B&B. If you stay longer this fee is negotiable. The timber restaurant is on two levels and serves a variety of local and European meals at between US$1–4. There is at least a two-hour wait if you want local food to be prepared. Sandwiches and a range of drinks are also available.

Things to do

Jahsu River Camp organizes boat trips, which can take you out to the Senegalese border for US$3.50–7. Apart from birdwatching there's not a lot else going on in this part of The Gambia. If it's peace and quiet that you're looking for though, in a place that's away from it all, this could be the spot for you.

TANBI WETLANDS

Ask any Gambian about Tanbi Wetlands and they are unlikely to have heard of it. This is despite the fact that this complex of wetlands is one of the largest in the country and surrounded by urban development. This is probably because Tanbi is an infrequently used name for the whole area and Gambians are much more likely to know its constituent parts, such as the Bund Road, Denton Bridge, Oyster Creek, etc.

The Tanbi Wetlands covers approximately 60km^2, encompassing the huge area of mangrove swamp south and west of Banjul, right down to Mandinari Point, and also includes the strip of coast west of Cape Point and south to Camaloo Corner. The whole area has now been designated a Ramsar site which means it is a wetland of international importance. Future plans include designating it as a national park. It includes some very well known sites to birdwatchers, such as the Bund Road, and also parts that are well known to most visitors, such as **Lamin Lodge** (see *Lamin and surrounds* in this chapter) and Oyster Creek. The latter is the creek that many of the organised excursions, such as 'sunset cruise' (see *Organised excursions* in *Chapter 3*) sail on. Even Denton Bridge is one of the best known sites for fishing in The Gambia. Needless to say the whole area is very rich in wildlife. This includes a great variety of birds, the marsh mongoose and the less well-known West African manatee that utilise the many *bolons*.

Getting there and away

This depends on which part of the wetland you want to visit, though most of it around the edge couldn't be easier to get to. Tourist taxis, shared taxis and bush taxis regularly ply the Banjul to Basse Highway which loops around the area. If you want to get into the heart of the wetland the easiest way is to get on an organised excursion (see *Organised excursions* in *Chapter 3*) such as the 'champagne and caviar cruise', though you could also hire a boat from **Lamin Lodge** to take you into the *bolons*. The strip of coast between Cape Point and Banjul is easy to reach from either Cape Point itself or from along the main highway. Be aware that there are many lagoons along this stretch of the coast and you will find yourself back-tracking quite a lot. This is also a favorite area for muggings (see *Theft* in *Chapter 3*) so take care before venturing here, especially if you are on your own or are just a couple.

Where to stay and eat

Lots of places in Banjul, Bakau, Fajara, Serrekunda and Lamin (see the relevant sections in this chapter and *Chapter 7*).

Things to do

There are lots of good sites for watching birds. The Bund Road often gives excellent views of birds, including egrets, pelicans and waders, pied avocet, and African spoonbill, *Platalea alba*, in the bay south of Banjul and along the edge of the mangroves. You will also have to put up with the busy, noisy and fast-moving traffic along the road. This is one of the best sites for picking up rarities in The Gambia. In the past these have included great 'ticks' like saddle-billed stork, *Ephippiorhynchus senegalensis*, European spoonbill and lesser yellowlegs, *Tringa flavipes*. The coastline from Cape Point to Banjul can provide good views of gulls and terns, and the many lagoons are quite good for waders such as black-winged stilts during the winter months. There is also a small patch of woodland at Toll Point, which is a good spot for birds. The marshes around Camaloo Corner are great places to find the magnificently coloured yellow-crowned bishops as they display during the rainy season, but of course they loose their bright plumage during the dry season. These are cracking birds that look like huge, bright yellow bumblebees as they bounce along during their display flights. The rice fields between Lamin and Mandinari are alive with birds and well worth a visit. One way of doing this is to join the organised 'birds and breakfast' excursion from **Lamin Lodge** (see *Organised excursions* in *Chapter 3*).

Fishing is also quite popular here, either from Denton Bridge where there are always some lines dangling in the water or from boats in the *bolons*. Fishing gear and boats can be hired from **Lamin Lodge** (tel: 497603; mobile tel: 996903), Brian (tel: 466573) and **Ganscot** (tel: 373091). Specialist fishing excursions into Tanbi are available from **Pleasuresports (Gambia) Ltd.** (tel & fax: 462125), who also organise very good dolphin-watching trips and general boat excursions and **Janneh Boating and Fishing Ltd** (tel/fax: 497630) in Bakau, who do the same.

If none of the above activities is your thing, then maybe you fancy just relaxing and sun bathing on a boat that cruises slowly through the mangroves, while being pampered just a little along the way. If this sounds good then look no further than the excellent 'champagne and caviar cruise' (tel: 466573); it's easy to book through the various ground operators in the hotels (see *Organised excursions* in *Chapter 3*).

LAMIN AND SURROUNDS

Situated just a few kilometres to the east of Serrekunda, is the small town of Lamin. Unlike Serrekunda, Lamin has a much more rural and friendly atmosphere and is relatively bumster-free. Although there is not much to see in the town itself the surrounding area has a number of tourist attractions including Abuko Nature Reserve and Lamin Lodge. In the mango trees behind the large mosque along the main road, there is a colony of straw-coloured fruit bats which number in their thousands during the rainy season. They make a spectacular sight in the early evening when they leave their roost to raid the fruit trees of the Kombos.

Getting there and away

Getting there could not be easier as Lamin lies along the main Banjul to Basse highway and therefore most forms of transport heading upcountry or back towards the coast pass through the town. A bush taxi can be taken from either Serrekunda or Brikama for less than US$0.50 (ask to be dropped off). Alternatively, a tourist taxi from any of the Atlantic coast hotels can take you to Lamin (at the fixed rate of around US$15–20 for a round trip with a two-hour wait) or a cheaper price can be negotiated as a 'town trip' in a shared taxi. GPTC buses stop in Lamin from Banjul and from upcountry.

Where to stay

The selection of good, affordable accommodation is limited. **The African Zoo Restaurant and Travellers Lodge** (tel: 472900 – this is a Gamtel office so leave a message and a contact number; fax: 390969; email: africanzoo@hotmail.com) is located on the main road just a few yards from the entrance to Abuko Nature Reserve. This is a new enterprise that opened in early 2001 and is ideally situated for early-morning forays into Abuko Nature Reserve. There is a bar and restaurant and the accommodation is in five apartments, which are clean if a little basic. A single room with WC will cost US$13.50 per night B&B. An apartment with one bedroom and sitting room, including bath, WC, washbasin and fan will cost US$24 B&B. A larger apartment with two bedrooms and a sitting room, plus the same facilities as above, will set you back US$30.50 B&B. Future plans include installing air conditioning in all the apartments, five more apartments, a standby generator, horse riding and satellite TV. Traditional entertainment is laid on in the evenings for guests and the managers of the lodge will organise excursions.

The eccentric-looking **Kings Club** (tel: 472148; email: kingsclub@gamtel.gm), built to loosely resemble (of all things) a medieval European castle, is located about 750m from the main road and is well signposted. Prices here start at US$35 for a room in a bungalow. This includes toilet, shower, air conditioning, fan, breakfast and dinner for two. Rooms are also available in 'the castle' for US$50 per night, with extras such as telephone, satellite TV and video, stereo, bath and fridge. All of the castle rooms are different with a waterbed in one, a hanging bed in another and a round bed in yet another. All castle rooms have a balcony with a view of the surrounding countryside. The hotel has a swimming pool, bar, nightclub and restaurant, which serves a good variety of Western and Gambian meals in the US$5–16 range.

Lamin Lodge (see below) is also planning to offer accommodation in the future.

Where to eat

Lamin Lodge (tel: 497603; mobile tel: 996903), about 3km north of the town, is probably the best place to eat, with a good selection of inexpensive, tasty meals in the US$3–10 range. The lodge is built on stilts over a *bolon*, with a wonderful view over the surrounding mangroves. Although the original lodge was accidentally burnt down to the water in 2000, it has slowly raised itself from the ashes and is now fully operational again. The lodge has long been a favourite with many visitors to The Gambia and serves very good food, including Gambian, European and vegetarian meals, starting at around US$3. The **African Zoo Restaurant** offers a choice of European and African food, including Sierra Leonean dishes on request. Main meals start at around US$5.50 and you can eat either inside or outside. They also have the local drink, *wanjo*, on sale.

Along the main road through Lamin there is a selection of grill houses where fairly cheap simple meals can be had for US$2–4. These include **C-Clan 2000 Bar**, **Fila's Hotspot Bar** and **Lamin Edge Grill Bar**. Most of these only have indoor seating and they can get quite hot and sweaty. Often you have to put up with a loud TV set or radio blaring away over the counter. Much more pleasant is **Parks Corner**, situated at the exit from Abuko, which serves cheap simple meals and cool drinks in the welcome shade of a grass roof. This bar is hassle-free and is the ideal place to rest and cool off after a walk in the sun through Abuko.

Things to do

Motorboats and *pirogues* can be hired at **Lamin Lodge** (tel: 497603; mobile tel: 996903), allowing you to explore the maze of mangrove-lined *bolons* that make up the Tanbi Wetlands. The hire prices range from US$10–27 per hour (depending on the size and type of boat), or you can also hire a boat for half a day (US$17–102) or a full day (US$34–170). Several different excursions to Lamin Lodge are organised by the ground operators, including the excellent 'birds and breakfast' excursion. During this trip birding guides will take you on an early morning *pirogue* trip through the *bolons*, followed by a walk through the rice fields and breakfast at the lodge, probably accompanied by a wild monkey or two (see *Organised excursions* in *Chapter 3*). The jetty going across to the lodge is probably the best place in The Gambia to get a close-up view of the strange-looking Atlantic mudskippers (see *Fish* in *Chapter 4*). Another good way to explore the countryside here is on horseback. **Horses** can be hired from Kings Club at US$5 for half an hour.

If the nightlife is more your scene then **Kings Club** nightclub is open to non-guests from Friday to Sunday and features local bands and dance troupes. Alternatively, **Willy's Nightclub** is open at the weekends and is frequented mostly by young Gambians. It's located along the main road opposite the Shell garage in Lamin.

ABUKO NATURE RESERVE

Abuko Nature Reserve was the first area to be given protection in The Gambia purely to conserve its wildlife. Eddie Brewer OBE, who was at that time the director of the Wildlife Conservation Department, initially established it in 1968, following a submission to the central government. Eddie is an almost legendary figure in modern Gambia, and his enthusiasm and endless energy was the driving force that brought nature conservation to the fore in the country. Prior to 1968 the site at Abuko was given some protection. As early as 1916, it was protected as the water catchment area that provided all of the fresh water needs of Banjul at that time.

As a result of this protection, Abuko Nature Reserve contains a pristine and valuable remnant of gallery forest along the banks of the Lamin Stream. This habitat is now one of the rarest in The Gambia and is extremely rich in biodiversity with many thousands of species of fungi, plants, trees, insects and other invertebrates living in and beneath its tall leafy canopy. However, not all of the reserve is gallery forest and as you travel away from the banks of the stream the forest gradually thins out as the ground becomes much drier, eventually changing into Guinea savanna. Although this habitat is not as rare as the gallery forest, it is still an excellent habitat for wildlife, particularly trees and plants and their associated bird life. In 1978 a further area of savanna was given protection and added to the reserve, bringing the total protected area of Abuko to around 105 hectares. This area of savanna is known as the 'bird extension' and is, as its name suggests, noteworthy for the variety and abundance of its bird species. The extension is a valuable addition to the nature reserve and contains a good patchwork of woodland and open grassy areas. In addition there are plans to fence off and protect the existing 'buffer zone' that surrounds Abuko. If these are successful they will double the size of the nature reserve.

The outstanding aspect of Abuko, as opposed to most sites in The Gambia, is that the wildlife at Abuko is very used to humans and therefore relatively easy to see. It's not unusual to have very close views of rare forest birds like turacos and little greenbuls, *Andropadus virens*, or even antelopes. The monkeys in particular are so used to humans that they virtually ignore you as they go about their daily routines. It's only when you leave Abuko and travel upcountry to visit other sites that you realise just how easy the wildlife spotting is in the nature reserve. Of course, the hides at Abuko also help you to get close to the birds and animals too.

The entrance fee to Abuko Nature Reserve stands at less than US$2.50 for adult non-residents and US$1.50 for non-resident children and adult residents. Resident children are allowed in free of charge. As you pass into the reserve from the entrance you immediately enter an area of wooded Guinea savanna. The well-maintained footpath soon leads you under the tall tree canopy of the gallery forest and across a bridge by one of Abuko's famous crocodile pools. There is a small population of around 20 Nile crocodiles that live in and around the pools. They are entirely wild animals and are not sustained by artificial feeding as at other sacred crocodile pools in the country. They survive on a natural diet of fish, frogs, freshwater turtles, birds and mammals and there is evidence of some movement during the rainy season between the crocodiles of Abuko and the crocodile population of the Tanbi Wetland complex across the road just outside of the reserve. A few of these crocodiles reach up to 4m in length, so make sure you stay on the footpath on the right side of the fence. Sometimes you will come across a monkey with a stump for a tail and it doesn't take a genius to figure out what bit the end off! After a short while you will see the public toilets on the left. On the right is the education centre. Here you will find a display on the wildlife in Abuko and the important work that is carried out by the Department of Parks and Wildlife Management in enforcing the wildlife laws of The Gambia, although these displays do change occasionally. If you climb the steps you will find you have a great view of the main crocodile pool. You can spend many happy hours here watching not only the crocodiles but also a wonderful variety of birds, such as hamerkop, *Scopus umbretta*, egrets and herons, black crake, *Amaurornis flavirostris*, kingfishers and birds of prey.

These pools constitute the only freshwater for kilometres around at the end of the dry season in March and April. As such they act as a magnet for many birds including spoonbills, storks, ospreys and even the odd pelican. In the mornings or evenings it is often possible to see bushbucks coming down to the waters edge to feed on the green vegetation. In the rainy season there are fewer water birds here as they tend to go off to their breeding sites, but try sitting in the hide as the evening turns to night. There is a fantastic display consisting of hundreds of straw-

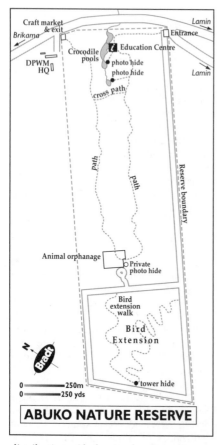

Craft market & exit
Brikama
Lamin
Entrance
DPWM HQ
Crocodile pools
Education Centre
photo hide
photo hide
Lamin
cross path
Path
path
Reserve boundary
Animal orphanage
Private photo hide
Bird extension walk
Bird Extension
N
Bradt
0 — 250m
0 — 250 yds
tower hide

ABUKO NATURE RESERVE

coloured fruit bats. They leave their roost at nearby Lamin and then drop in on the pool for a drink before heading off to their feeding grounds. It really is a wonderful sight and well worth staying just that little bit longer for. Make sure you ask for permission first from the guys on the gate so that they know you will still be there when the reserve officially closes. The entrance gate is always manned so you will not be locked in.

The footpath carries on through the gallery forest for a while, passing two photo-hides that overlook smaller pools on the way. One of the reasons this forest is so important is because it is one of the most northerly projections of the forests that cover other parts of West Africa, like Casamance, Guinea, Liberia, Sierra Leone, etc. There are species found in Abuko that are found in only a small number of other places in The Gambia. Most notable amongst the birds are ahanta francolin, white-spotted flufftail, green turaco and western bluebill. These species are not found north of The Gambia and are on the extreme edge of their distribution. Abuko is also home to some of the birds that are uncommon elsewhere, such as African goshawk, *Accipiter tachiro*, leaflove, *Pyrrhuus scandens*, grey-headed bristlebill, yellow-breasted apalis, oriole warbler, collared sunbird, *Anthreptes collaris*, yellowbill, red-shouldered cuckoo-shrike, and green hylia, *Hylia prasina*. Rare birds and Nile crocodiles are not the only wildlife that Abuko has to offer the visiting naturalist, though. There are over 115 species of plants, over 28 damselflies and dragonflies, over 70 butterflies, 19 amphibians, 37 reptiles, 250 birds (this is the most recent and up to date account) and at least 52 species of mammals. Abuko's monkeys are as famous as its crocodiles and you stand a very good chance of seeing callithrix monkeys and the acrobatic western red colobus. The latter are endangered throughout most of their range in West Africa. You may also be lucky and spot a troop of patas monkeys but these are very uncommon in Abuko.

As the forest thins out you find yourself walking through Guinea savanna and you can see the sky again. The footpath then leads on to an area of Abuko known as the 'animal orphanage'. This is not a zoo, although the orphanage does contain lions and spotted hyenas that have lived all of their lives in captivity. At the moment the lioness that is here was born at Abuko, while the male was generously donated to The Gambia from a captive population at Safari Beekse Bergen, in the Netherlands (a wildlife park with which the wildlife department have had a long

FRIENDS OF ABUKO NATURE RESERVE

It costs a substantial amount of money to operate the protected areas in The Gambia, and of course Abuko is no exception to this. Protected areas do more than just preserve areas of high biodiversity or natural beauty though. They are a much needed resource that help support local communities, especially through tourism, and play key roles in school and community education programmes. By becoming a Friend of Abuko Nature Reserve, you can help to support this valuable work. As a friend you will also receive a quarterly newsletter and regular updates on what's happening with wildlife and conservation in The Gambia. If you are interested in participating, send your name and address (or email) to 'Friends of Abuko', Department of Parks and Wildlife Management, PO Box 2164, Serrekunda, The Gambia, West Africa; email: wildlife@gamtel.gm – marked for the attention of Alhagie Manjang.

and successful association). The hyenas that are bred at Abuko are transported to zoos and parks in Europe. This activity keeps down the number of animals that are taken from the wild in Africa. In return these institutions contribute funds to the further development of Abuko orphanage and nature reserve. The other animals at the orphanage come from a variety of sources. Some are orphaned or injured animals that have been brought in by concerned members of the public while others have been kept illegally as pets and have been confiscated by the wildlife department. The aim of the orphanage is to rehabilitate and return these animals back to the wild. For this reason it is not possible to say what animals are going to be present in the orphanage, but usually there are baboons, patas and callithrix monkeys, antelopes, parrots and parakeets.

Beyond the orphanage is the bird extension walk, which winds through more savanna before returning back towards the orphanage. About halfway along the walk there is a tower hide that allows you to stand above the level of the treetops. This is a very pleasant walk that takes you through woodland, scrub and open areas. Because of the winding nature of the path you feel as though you have walked through a much larger area than you actually have. Rejoining the main footpath at the orphanage leads you through more savanna until you reach the gallery forest again. The path then takes you to the exit of the reserve. Alternatively there is a footpath off the return path, about halfway along. It is well signed and will take you back on to the first footpath and back to the entrance via the education centre.

Getting there and away

Abuko is one of the most popular destinations for visitors to The Gambia and is therefore very easy to get to. Tourist taxis will take you from your hotel to the nature reserve and wait until you have finished your walk, then take you back again for around US$12–15.50. You'll have to negotiate if you want to stop longer than two hours though. Shared taxis will also take you there for less, but may not be happy to wait for you. Negotiation is necessary here again. Bush taxis pass right by the entrance on the Banjul to Basse Highway. These will cost you less than US$0.50 from Serrekunda or from Brikama. There are also organised excursions to Abuko run by the ground operators (see *Organised excursions* in *Chapter 3*). The nature reserve is open from 08.00–18.30. Please note that many local guides will take you to Abuko, but then, instead of offering the option of walking around the reserve, they will drive you straight from the entrance up to the orphanage. This is probably because they get fed up with walking through the reserve so often, but it is *you* that will miss out on a great opportunity.

Where to stay and eat
See *Lamin and surrounds* above for details of places to stay and eat. The nearest place to stay is the **African Zoo and Traveller's Lodge**, which is located close to the entrance to Abuko on the other side of the road. Refreshments can be bought from the stalls that are located within the reserve at the orphanage and also from **Parks Corner**. The latter establishment is a very pleasant little place right by the exit to the nature reserve and run by a very friendly Gambian by the name of Findy Kujabi. He provides a range of drinks and snacks and will cook a meal for you if you give him a little notice. There is also a bar across the road from the reserve called **Eco-friends Drink Stop**.

Things to do
At the exit there is a craft market which purports to be hassle-free, but isn't. Still, there are some very skilled carvers that work here and sell their wares, as well as the normal mix of batiks and necklaces etc and it's worth having a good look around. We have tried to encourage one or two of the wood carvers to start producing carvings of birds and animals that you can't find elsewhere in The Gambia. It's a hard struggle to break with tradition but the kingfishers (and others) that they have carved have sold really well, so perhaps they will continue to expand their range.

Apart from birdwatching and just simply walking through the nature reserve, photography appears to be an important pastime for many visitors, and there is some beautiful scenery to be captured on film as well as the wildlife. To cater for this, in addition to the three hides by the crocodile pools there is also a photo-hide located at the orphanage. This overlooks a small pool that is frequented by many birds and animals, including the odd cobra. It can be privately hired on a daily basis for US$3.50 per day, but you must book and pay for it at the *entrance* to the reserve. You cannot pay for it at the orphanage. Other photo-hides that can also be hired for the day are planned for the near future. Please inquire at the entrance for more information about these.

ABUKO LIVESTOCK MARKET
A livestock market may seem to be a strange place to mention in a guidebook, but this market becomes a focal point for the Western Division in the few weeks leading up to the Muslim celebration of *Tobaski*, one of the biggest days on the Muslim calendar. On this day it is the custom for every family to slaughter a ram. One third of this ram is eaten by the family, one third given away to relatives and one third given to the poor. As you can imagine the buying and selling of rams is big business at this time of the year and Abuko Livestock Market is one of the main centres in the country. In the weeks preceding *Tobaski*, breeders and herdsmen from all over the country flock (if you'll excuse the pun) to the market with their sheep and the place overflows with animals and people bargaining for their *Tobaski* ram. The sides of the main highway are lined with thousands of snowy-white rams and you may well hear your guide or taxi driver lamenting over their high price, as they seem to sell for a lot of money at this time of year. You may also see a ram in the open boot of a car or in the back of a pick-up truck as they are taken home. Often you will even see the unforgettable sight of a ram perched precariously on the roof of a bush taxi as it sways through the traffic!

Getting there and away

As the livestock market is along the main Banjul to Basse Highway it is very easy to get to by most forms of transport. If you come with a taxi and the driver is waiting for you, don't be surprised if you lose your driver for a while amongst the crowds, since he's bound to disappear and start bargaining for a ram.

KER ALDIANA

Ker Aldiana ('house of paradise' in Wolof) is located about 7km from Banjul International Airport, in a beautiful rural spot on the banks of a *bolon*. This is a very pleasant camp and one of the best-kept secrets in The Gambia. There is a swimming pool of course, but also a pool bar and even a yacht-shaped changing room. There is also a grass-roofed restaurant and bar and accommodation in the form of eight double rooms, all set in wonderfully lush tropical gardens. In addition the camp has a boat in which you can have a lazy afternoon relaxing on a trip along the *bolon*. The camp has been there for at least five years and is very popular with visitors.

Getting there and away

This is not easy, as the camp is tucked away, well off the beaten track. Using public transport is almost impossible so your best bet would be to take a taxi or hire a vehicle or a ground operator to take you there. Do make sure that whatever vehicle you use is a four-wheel-drive as the tracks are very sandy when you get close to the camp, and make sure, too, that you have a driver who knows the location of the camp. The best way to reach the camp is taking the track from Lamin to Mandinari and then on to Makumba Ya before turning off towards Kubuni (it's signposted here). Another (and probably much more fun) way is to ask for a boat trip to the camp, perhaps from Lamin Lodge (see page 170) or Makasutu Culture Forest (see pages 177–9).

YUNDUM

Just south of Yundum Police Station is a small fruit market by the side of the road that always has high quality and fairly cheap fruit on sale. Next to this is the **National Bee-keepers Association**, which sells an assortment of cheap but very tasty locally produced honey and items made out of natural beeswax, including decorative candles.

NYAMBAI AND KABAFITA FOREST PARKS

These forest parks straddle the main highway a few kilometres south of the airport entrance. Although large, they consist in the main of non-native gumbar, *Gmelina arborea*, plantations, and hold very little wildlife of any interest. Kabafita is to the east of the highway and is slightly more interesting than Nyambai as it has a strip of savanna woodland running adjacent to the road. This strip is around 100m wide and could potentially hold a fair population of savanna-type wildlife, so it may be worth exploring if you've got time.

BRIKAMA

Brikama is the last large town of the Western Division if you are heading upcountry. However, despite its size and the fact that it is always very busy, there is remarkably little to do here if you are a tourist and most visitors pass through as fast as they can.

MAKASUTU WILDLIFE TRUST

This is a recently formed non-profit-making charity (NGO) that aims to help protect the wildlife and wild habitats of The Gambia, and to encourage a greater awareness, appreciation and participation in all aspects of biodiversity, its conservation and sustainable use, and the environment.

The trust plans to do this by actively involving local people and building their capacity in all aspects of biodiversity and its conservation, promoting education, study and research in the natural sciences and by raising public awareness. It also plans to establish, enhance or otherwise protect representative examples of The Gambia's remaining habitats, flora and fauna and to promote the wise and sustainable use of natural resources.

To this end the trust has signed a 'memorandum of understanding' with the Department of Parks and Wildlife Management, in which it has agreed to help build their capacity through training and to collaborate and provide information about its activities, including research, education, public campaigns, lobbying of government and its other various projects.

It is hoped that Makasutu Wildlife Trust will become the leading independent body within The Gambia concerning the protection of its remaining wildlife, and will become the focal point of all aspects concerning this protection with other NGOs, both local and international, private companies and government institutions.

For more information about membership and the activities of the trust, please contact them c/o PO Box 2164, Serrekunda, The Gambia; email: drumohq@qanet.gm. Their message is that you can help to protect the wildlife of The Gambia.

Getting there and away

This couldn't be easier as Brikama is the transport hub for the whole area, although the Banjul to Basse Highway bypasses the town to the north. GPTC buses from Banjul and from upcountry stop here, as do most bush taxis. In fact this is where you frequently have to change bush taxis to get to your destination, wherever that may be. A bush taxi to Brikama from Banjul will cost you less than US$0.50.

Where to stay and eat

There is only one place in Brikama in which to stay, but unfortunately it wasn't open at the time of writing so we haven't had a chance to check it out. We have been assured that it will be open by the 2001/02 tourist season. This is the **Wuli Resthouse** (tel: 460870 or 461612; fax: 392866 – these are the numbers for the related **Wuli Motel** in Sukuta, who should be able to help you out).

The best place to eat in town is at the **Bantang Bantaba** (see below for directions). They do a tasty plate of chips for around US$1, sandwiches for US$1 and omelettes for US$–1.50. There is also a selection of quite cheap soft drinks and beer. Try the excellent *wonjo* here for a taste experience (*wonjo* is made from hibiscus flowers and very refreshing). Other places to eat in town include **Allah Tentu Noflies Restaurant, Botos Black and White Restaurant** and **Big Bite Fast Food**. All of these cater mostly for local people and are cheap and cheerful.

Things to do and places to visit

Brikama craft market is a typical tourist trap. However, it does have one of the best selections of wood carvings in The Gambia, if you have the patience and energy to sort out the good from the usual stuff that is on sale everywhere. The market is like a rabbit warren inside and we had visions of being trapped there for hours before being able to find our way back out, though in reality it's not that bad. Everyone is on the make here and will try to sell you something, so it is easy to get sucked in and buy everything in sight or to get completely fed up with the hassle and give up before buying anything. Our tip would be to enter the market and stroll around, looking in the stalls without actually entering them, until you see something that you really want to buy. If you go in one stall you will have to go in every stall. Be firm and polite with the vendors, tell them you are just looking for the moment, and hopefully they will soon get the message. Remember to maintain a sense of humour at all times. It can be worth the hassle if you can find that piece that you really want.

A much more relaxing time can be found at the **Bantang Bantaba** (tel: 484853), which is about 400m from the craft market. To find it walk on into town, turn right on to the Gunjur Highway, which at the moment is still a fancy name for a dirt track, then right just after the police checkpoint. The *bantaba* (meeting place) is inside the Methodist mission on your right. Here you can sip a cold drink and eat good food in the shade of this well-appointed bantaba, within sight of a massive silk-cotton tree. You can also visit the preserves factory, where you can sample some delicious jams and chutneys, or walk around the farm and orchards, all in a hassle-free environment. The bantaba was set up by some good friends of ours who worked for the Methodist Missions Agricultural Programme, and we helped to design and cut the short path through the forest that is adjacent to it, so we hope you enjoy it. There are western red colobus monkeys, Nile monitors and lots of good birds such as white-crowned robin-chat, *Cossypha albicapilla*, violet turaco, *Musophaga violacea*, and grey-headed bush-shrike, *Malaconotus blanchoti*. A guide will be happy to accompany you on request (free of charge) and will explain the medicinal and nutritional uses of the various plants, as well as pointing out the flora and fauna. From time to time there are examples of local crafts on display and for sale. It is also possible to take drumming classes if you book in advance.

MAKASUTU CULTURE FOREST

Set alongside a beautiful *bolon* deep in the countryside, Makasutu Culture Forest (email: makasutu@hotmail.com; web: makasutu.com) has become famous as an exceptional eco-tourism centre. It's almost a showcase example of how things could and should be done. Yet when Lawrence Williams and James English found *Makasutu* or the 'big forest' about ten years ago, it was just another piece of 'swamp and bush', typical of most of The Gambia. At the time it was rapidly being destroyed by tree felling and overgrazing. After much hard work and negotiation with local people, they managed to stop this destruction before it became irreversible, and now Makasutu is one of the foremost sites in the country. The big forest is truly a marvellous place to walk through, especially early in the morning, when the bird life is simply stunning. But it's not just the wonderful array of brightly coloured birds like bee-eaters, starlings, rollers and kingfishers that make a day out here memorable. There is also a large range of other wildlife, from Nile crocodiles and the occasional West African manatee in the *bolons*, to beautiful butterflies floating along the forest paths. During most of the year there is even a large troop of wild Guinea baboons that makes its home at Makasutu before moving off to new pastures early in the dry season. It's frightening to realise how easily this forest and its wildlife could have all disappeared from here if it wasn't for James and Lawrence.

Makasutu Cultural Forest is regarded very highly amongst both Gambians and visitors to The Gambia. This is not just because of the wildlife that can be found there, but also because of the way that Lawrence and James have blended so many different facets together. Makasutu provides a lot of employment for local people in an area that had seldom seen many visitors in the past. These are not only people who work at the culture forest such as managers, gardeners, drivers, cooks, guides etc, but also many different craftsmen, such as wood carvers, who utilise the site to sell their wares, and of course the musicians and dancers who entertain the guests. Good, steady employment like this is what is desperately needed in so many parts of The Gambia. Visitors to Makasutu, on the other hand, have a trip that they will long remember and carry home with them in their hearts. Makasutu embodies in one place all the good things eco-tourism stands for. There is also a programme being developed to encourage school visits, so Gambian children can learn about their environment in a fun and positive way.

One other thing that makes a trip to Makasutu worthwhile is the chance to meet and talk to Lawrence and James themselves. They are modest men, who have travelled the world and seen many places and sights that most people have only dreamed about, yet they are happy to sit down and share their experiences with anyone who asks (try to stop them!). They could be regarded as true 'adventurers', yet they have chosen, out of all of the places in the world that they have travelled to, to settle down and plant their roots in the soil of The Gambia. They have also shown real, solid commitment to the country and the people of The Gambia, even when times have been tough for them. For example they were amongst the few *toubabs* who stayed in the country during the coup of 1994, when so many left on the advice of their own governments. James used to work on the oilrigs in Alaska and Lawrence is a qualified architect, which sounds a bit of a mis-match, but that couldn't be further from the truth. It will cost you US$20.50–24 per day to enter Makasutu, but this price includes a welcome cup of tea or coffee, a substantial lunch (with local entertainment) and the use of guides on a nature walk or a river trip around the *bolons* in a *pirogue*.

Getting there and away

If you want to visit Makasutu, it can be easily arranged through the ground operators, who run excursions there (see *Organised excursions* in *Chapter 3*). You can also visit on your own by getting a tourist taxi or a shared taxi to take you there. The culture forest is located in the bush to the north of Brikama and finding it yourself could be tricky and a bit of a hike, so we suggest sticking with the locals who know how to get there. Makasutu is open from 08.00–18.00 unless prior arrangements are made. It may also be possible in the future to get to Makasutu via boat trips from **Coconut Residence** or **Lamin Lodge**. Worth asking about if you fancy it.

Where to stay

Mandina River Camp is an integral part of Makasutu. It is a new venture and will consist of floating accommodation on the *bolon* in as peaceful and beautiful a setting as you could wish for. Each 'houseboat' for want of a better name, will consist of a large room with double bed, shower, WC and fridge. The houseboats can either be moored next to the mainland or out in the *bolons* at a number of designated mooring points, and will come complete with their own 'paddler/guide' and boat to take you to and from the land or around the *bolons* – whenever you want. There will only be a limited number of these houseboats and they will be very expensive, but will provide a specialised and personalised five-star service.

Where to eat

If you're staying at the river camp, meals will be provided at the private quality restaurant in a bush setting, which will serve great European food (BBQ will be a speciality) when completed. This restaurant may also be opened to a limited number of visitors. Day visitors to Makasutu are restricted to the open-air restaurant in the main visitor area. Here the food is cooked in the local style and entertainment is provided in the form of drummers and dancers from the nearby village, making for a fun-filled and memorable meal.

Things to do

You can become involved in many activities at Makasutu. These include taking a canoe trip along the mangrove-lined *bolons* or watching the highly skilled wood carver at work. You can also listen to the excellent entertainment as you eat lunch, go for a walk through the 'big forest' to see some of the wildlife, or simply sit and relax in a totally hassle-free environment. In the reception area there is a gallery which you can have access to for a small fee. This gallery will contain an exhibition of stunning photographs by Jason Florio. This up-and-coming young photographer works at present for a Brazilian newspaper. His exhibition will document the culture and tradition of Makasutu. It is expected that Jason's work will be available in a coffee-table type book that will be on sale at Makasutu in the future.

THE BORDER REGION NEAR JIBOROH AND SELETI

Along the Banjul to Basse Highway at Mandina, about 5km east of Brikama, is a police checkpoint. At this junction another road runs south towards Jiboroh and the Senegalese border about 12km away. Best known as the Gambian border post on the main route to Ziguinchor in Casamance, Jiboroh itself is otherwise unremarkable. However, just south of the border there a few waterholes that normally last well into the first few months of the dry season. These used to be famous for the troops of baboons that visited them to drink, but nowadays the baboons are too persecuted by the local farmers to risk a visit in full daylight. The pools and the woods that spread westward of the first pool are excellent for the range of birds that they hold. These include various birds of prey, waders, sandgrouse, rollers, turacos, cuckoos, woodpeckers, cuckoo-shrikes and exclamatory paradise whydah, *Vidua interjecta*. This is a good spot to spend at least one whole day if you are a birder.

Getting there and away

Bush taxis from Brikama ply the road south to Jiboroh and it will cost you less than US$0.50 to get to there. This is the best way to cross the border if you are thinking of heading south into Casamance (see *Chapter 13* for details about crossing into Senegal). If you are just intending to visit the waterholes then the paperwork involved depends on who is on duty at the immigration post. Some of the immigration officers will insist that you get your passport stamped, while others will not bother, especially as you will not be reaching the Senegalese immigration post on the other side.

PIRANG AND SURROUNDS

Situated just 16km to the east of Brikama, and about 500m north of the Banjul to Basse Highway, is the small village of Pirang. Although there is not much to distinguish this village from hundreds of similar villages in The Gambia, and it has no tourist facilities, the surrounding countryside holds some astounding areas that are well worth exploring. One point of interest in the village is the huge white-flowered silk-cotton tree, *Ceiba pentandra*, which grows there. It is reputed to be the largest tree in West Africa. We don't know whether this is true but it is certainly a huge and magnificent specimen.

Getting there and away

Bush taxis pass Pirang from both directions along the Banjul to Basse Highway. A bush taxi from Brikama will drop you off at Pirang village for less than US$0.50. Another option if you want to explore the forest park, shrimp pools and rice fields is to hire a tourist or shared taxi to take you there from the tourist resorts, as the latter two are a long 4km walk from the road otherwise. Alternatively, you could take a bush taxi and then hire a donkey- or horse-cart from the village to take you. This way you get to contribute to the local economy and to travel in style. GPTC buses (ordinary service) stop at nearby Faraba Banta.

Where to stay

There is only one place in the immediate area that caters for tourists. This is **Fati Kunda**, which is near the village of Faraba Banta. There is self-catering accommodation available (price negotiable but probably very cheap) for a maximum of two people. This accommodation is pretty basic with straw-filled mattresses on a concrete floor, though they did have a mosquito bednet when we visited. If you want cheap no-frills housing for a long stay, or alternatively a one-night stopover, then this place may be ideal for you. To find it travel first into the part of Faraba Banta away from the main highway and turn right at the small market place, heading towards and past the mosque. Fati Kunda is about 1500m along this track, opposite some gardens. Look for the welcome sign in the compound.

Things to do

Pirang Forest Park is about 2km to the west of the village. A track leading to the park is located along the Banjul to Basse Highway just a few metres east of the Radio Gambia sign (a few hundred metres along this track take a left which will then lead you along the edge of the forest). The forest covers about 64ha and is similar in structure to Abuko, though in our experience, not quite so good. There are western red colobus, callithrix and patas monkeys here, but they are unused to people and so are shy and hard to spot. The birds are good, with such forest specialities as African pied hornbill, *Tockus fasciatus*, and white-spotted flufftail, and the edges of the forest in particular hold masses of butterflies, some of which are uncommon elsewhere. Try to time your visit for during the week, as the main path through the forest joins the villages of Pirang and Bonto and there are always plenty of kids along the path at weekends who hassle visitors, making it almost impossible to birdwatch or just to enjoy the peace.

    Pirang shrimp pools are located about 4km to the north of the village (take the left hand fork in the track when leaving the village and park by the shrimp farm buildings). Young children begging for money can be a real pain here and spoil a good day, especially during the tourist season. At the time of writing the shrimp pools were disused and a haven for wildlife. Though there are plans to restore the pools back into a working shrimp farm, we understand that the protection of their wildlife will be a major consideration. We hope that visitors will still have access as this is the only place to see wild black crowned crane, *Balearica pavonina*, in the western division, a small flock of which frequent the pools early in the mornings. There are also good numbers of spoonbills, egrets, kingfishers, waders and other waterbirds including spur-winged goose, *Plectropterus gambensis*, and white-faced whistling duck, especially during the wet season. It is also possible to see yellow-crowned bishop in the sedges, crested lark, *Galerida cristata*, and plain-backed pipit, *Anthus leucophrys*, along the bunds. Ospreys are common during the dry season.

If you return to the village and take the other fork in the track (where you turned left before), this leads on to the village of **Faraba Banta**, through a wonderful area of cultivated rice fields and groves of trees that are rich in birdlife. Apparently the cranes also frequent some of the rice fields – try asking the locals for up to date information on their whereabouts. A boat can also be hired for a trip across the River Gambia to Juffureh from the owner of Fati Kunda (see *Where to stay*) in Faraba Banta (the price is negotiable). From Faraba Banta it is only 1.5km back to the main highway.

INLAND TO KALAGI

In many ways, this narrow strip of countryside, which is never that far from the border with Senegal, is one of the most beautiful to be found in The Gambia. As you travel east along the Banjul to Basse Highway you will pass through groves of African oil palm, *Elais guineensis*. They raise their lofty heads above the surrounding bush and agricultural land, which is bright emerald green during and just after the rainy season. Occasionally you will also pass the southern tips of the many small *bolons* that meander through the land from the Gambia River. These patches of seasonally flooded land are heavily farmed for rice. However, they are still rich in wildlife ranging from herons and kingfishers to dragonflies and frogs. It is also along this stretch of the road that you begin to see the small towns and country villages where many Gambians live.

Finto Manereg Forest Park

This large forest park is well off the beaten track and little explored. Although difficult to enter because of a lack of footpaths and tracks, a day spent here will be rewarding for those who want to see how most of The Gambia once looked before man changed the landscape and began cutting down the forest. We have little information on what wildlife is to be found in the park, except that we have seen a good range of birds and butterflies there, so we would be glad to hear about the observations you make.

Getting there and away

Finto Manareg is easily found. At Faraba Banta there is a track that crosses the main road. Take the southern half of this track and follow it for about 3km. The forest will be obvious when you come across it. Although there is no direct transport to the forest you can get a bush taxi from Brikama to Faraba Banta at a cost of less than US$0.50, or from the opposite direction if you are travelling from upcountry. Then you can either walk to the park or hire a horse- or donkey-cart from the village. Alternatively, hire a tourist taxi or shared taxi for the whole trip. The dirt track to the forest is sandy but not too rough, so a taxi should not have a problem getting there, at least in the dry season. It may be more difficult in the wet season. Personally, we think that walking or carting it would be the better option, as there are lots of birds to see along the way.

Tumani Tenda

Tumani Tenda (also known as Kachokorr Camp) is one of those places that we just cannot say enough good things about (tel: 220 391923; fax: 220 391766). This is a tourist camp, about 20km from Brikama, which is owned and run by the local Jola community from the nearby village of the same name. All the profits from the camp stay in the village and are used to pay for development projects like the new school, wire fences for the gardens etc. In the near future they aim to have their own health clinic in the village as well. The whole village, which has about 300 people, has a strong sense of community spirit and is almost totally self-sufficient, even to the point of selling their excess produce to other communities. Each of the families in the village have chosen one member who works at the camp, and this means that every single family has at least one monthly salary coming in.

Accommodation for up to 32 people is in the local Jola-style mud huts. There are also some grass huts that are used when the camp is full. The mud huts are wonderful constructions that have each been individually designed and built by different families in the village. They may appear basic at first but are very comfortable. The construction keeps the interiors cool in the heat of the day and warm at night. There is mosquito netting on the doors and windows plus an additional mosquito bednet for each bed. The camp itself is situated outside the village in a wonderfully peaceful setting on the bank of the Kafuta Bolon. There is a bar and restaurant, toilets and showers, and of course, a *bantaba*, or 'meeting place', where you can relax in the shade during the heat of the day. Lunches are of local style, eaten communally, while main meals are based on the European style. Prices are based per person and it is US$7 per night for bed and breakfast, plus less than US$2 for lunch and the same for dinner. Bottled water, beer, coffee, tea and soft drinks are available at the bar at reasonable prices.

Getting there and away
To get to the camp using public transport, take a bush taxi from Brikama to a village called Hamdalie (asked to be dropped off) or from Soma if you are travelling from upcountry. From here (it is well signposted along the Banjul to Brikama Highway) it is a walk of around 1.5km to the village. Alternatively, hire a tourist or shared taxi to take you the whole way. If you book in advance you have the option of being picked up at the airport and driven straight to the camp.

Things to do
There are lots of activities that you can become involved with, including a batik workshop (less than US$2 per hour), making soap or salt, fishing, working in the gardens with the village women, or even learning to dance and make music in the Jola style. Some tourist groups come to Tumani Tenda just to learn the skills of dancing and playing musical instruments and end up by giving a concert in Brikama at the end of their stay. Alternatively you can just relax and get away from it all, perhaps taking a guided walk in the community forest (US$3.50 per hour for the guide) or a canoe trip along the *bolon* for US$3.50 per hour. The *bolon* itself is very peaceful and lined with mangroves. The canoe trip takes in an island that is well known locally for its bird life and there is always a remote chance of seeing a West African manatee. If you arrange for a canoe trip in the dark your chances of encountering one of these harmless and rare mammals should be higher – why not try it?

Tumani Tenda is fast becoming popular with birdwatchers, as there are plenty of birds to be seen in the forest, around the camp and along the *bolon*. The highlight of any birding trip to the camp has got to be the brown-necked parrots, *Poicephalus robustus*, that fly across the *bolon* early in the morning from their roosts in the mangroves to their feeding areas in the dry woodland and then back again in the evening. These large and handsome birds appear to be declining in The Gambia for as yet unknown reasons.

Above Pirogues offloading fish, Tanji (AVZ)

Left Fish drying at Tanji fishing centre (LB)

Below Fishing from dugout canoe on the River Gambia, Janjangbureh (AVZ)

Above Colourful batiks (LB)

Right Woman spinning wool, Basse Santa Su (AVZ)

Below Artist's mural (LB)

Bama Kuno and Kahlenge forest parks

These large forest parks (Bama Kuno is 1,092ha and Kahlenge is 406.8ha) lie astride the Banjul to Basse Highway, and cover a narrow strip of land running from the Senegalese border in the south northwards to the mangroves of the River Gambia. They are comprised of Guinea savanna woodland and shrub and have access roads and rides that make them easily accessible to walkers. These are invaluable sites for wildlife and hold a vast array of birds, including fair numbers of helmeted guineafowl, *Numida meleagris*, a wide range of butterflies and lots of mammals. These include baboons and monkeys, jackals, civets, mongooses, genets, bushbuck and most exciting of all – leopards. We have even found hyena tracks along the eastern edge of Bama Kuno and have heard reports of aardvarks in the forest. You would, of course, be immensely lucky to see any of these nocturnal mammals during a daytime walk. It is still thrilling though, to come across a leopard track along the path and to think that somewhere it may be lying up, perfectly camouflaged in the vegetation, and perhaps watching you! A walk in the dark with flashlights may be more profitable, especially if you are looking for owls and perhaps bushbabies. It is hoped that sometime in the future there may be facilities in these forest parks to cater for visitors, but at the moment there are none.

Getting there and away

Bush taxis are regular in both directions along the Banjul to Basse Highway. A bush taxi from Brikama to Bulok, which is about 2km past the forest parks, will set you back less than US$0.50. Or you could ask to be dropped off at the forest parks if you don't fancy the walk back from Bulok.

Brefet trading post

In 1651 a patent granted the right to British merchants to open up trade along the coast of West Africa, and the trading post at Brefet was established by a group of adventurers and traders known as the 'Gambia Adventurers' in 1664. The French built a slave factory across the Gambia River at Albreda in 1717 and the British attacked and occupied this base in 1724. Just a few months later the French retaliated by plundering the posts at Brefet and also at Bintang. The British rebuilt the post in 1779 and it was operated by individual traders, but the French destroyed it again in 1820 and since then it has lay in ruins, its stones used by the villagers for building.

In the days of the trading post the only Africans which freely visited the area were palm oil tappers from Casamance. After the post was destroyed for the last time, Jola people moved into the area and established a village by the ruins. The Jola were then usurped by the Sanyangs, who were Mandinka warriors. The village itself has moved twice since its establishment, as the fresh water from the wells became too salty. The site of the second village is along the path to the trading post, easily recognisable by the stand of large baobab and white-flowered silk-cotton (or *kapok*) trees.

There is very little remaining of Brefet trading post: just a pile of rubble that appears to be the corner of a slave house. But it is in a beautiful setting right on the bank of the Brefet Bolon, and is relatively easy to get to. So if old ruins are your thing you should definitely take the time out to come here. If you are into birdwatching as well then the brown-necked parrots that fly across the *bolon* in the mornings and evenings are another good reason to visit. On the way to the village you pass through a community forest that also looks good for birds. We have seen bushbuck tracks here, and there is talk of warthogs being in the vicinity (this is the westernmost outpost of this species on the south bank of the river). Rumours also abound of Campbell's monkey being found here in the dry season, but as yet we have not been able to confirm this and have only seen patas and callithrix monkeys.

Getting there and away

About 35km east of Brikama along the main highway is a small village by the name of Bessi. A further 6km north of Bessi along a sandy track is the even smaller village of Brefet. The trading post is a walk of another 1km west from the village. Not everyone in the village knows where the post is, so ask at the house of the *alkalo*, Mr Sanyang, for a guide to take you there. Bessi can be reached by bush taxi, as they regularly ply the main highway (less than US$1 from Brikama), tourist taxi or shared taxi. If you use public transport then you could hire either a horse or donkey cart in the village to take you from Bessi to Brefet.

Bintang Bolon Lodge

This lodge (tel: 488055; fax: 488058 – this is a message service, so leave a fax or phone number if you want a reply) is in a beautiful setting amongst the mangroves right on the edge of the Bintang Bolon. Although the site has obviously deteriorated a little since its heyday a few years ago, we found the facilities at the lodge were still in fair working order and that the setting makes up for a lot. Accommodation is in six pleasant huts, four on the rivers edge, each with their own balcony extending almost at the waters level into the *bolon*, and two tucked away in the mangroves. Each of the huts has its own washbasin, WC, shower, electric light and mosquito netting at the windows. Power is drawn from a large generator between 19.00–23.00, which also lights up parts of the nearby village. The huts are joined by a raised walkway through the surrounding mangroves and this also leads to a large and comfortable restaurant/bar (serving Gambian and European meals, shorts, wine, beer and soft drinks) with a balcony looking out on the *bolon*. On the nearby riverbank is a medium-sized swimming pool, with a hill (a rare thing in The Gambia) that gives a great view over the lodge, the mangroves and the *bolon*.

The lodge can accommodate up to 15 people at any one time. Full board costs US$24 per person per night, drinks not included. B&B is US$12. If you are staying for a longer period you can negotiate a 10–20% discount. Both lunch and dinner are three-course meals and cost US$5 each. Their freshly caught ladyfish, with chips, has got to be eaten to be believed. Accommodation and meals can be booked in advance. Apparently the lodge becomes a bit crowded and noisy during the daytime when there is an organised tour visiting, but the evenings can be quiet and relaxing.

Getting there and away

The lodge is open all year and is about 5km north of Killy, which is on the Banjul to Basse Highway just west of Sibanor. You can get to Killy by bush taxi, which will cost US$1 from Brikama, or all the way to the lodge by tourist taxi or shared taxi. Sometimes the lodges own transport can pick you up if you book in advance. Organised excursions to the lodge are arranged by the ground operators, and offer transport, lunch, a boat trip or bush safari (see *Organised excursions* in *Chapter 3*).

Things to do

There are plenty of choices available at the lodge. Boat trips can be organised to James Island, Kemoto Hotel, or to go shopping in Banjul (one hour will cost US$20.50 per group – if you are staying at the lodge you can get a discount on this price). Or you can hire the boat to go fishing in the *bolon* or, better still, fish for free from your own balcony (rods are available). A jeep safari (US$3.50 per person) will take you into the bush where you can visit a natural crocodile pool at Jakoi Sibrik, or you can hire the jeep to take you to Banjul etc. You can also hire guides for a foot safari (tips only for the guides, as there is no set price). Some of these guides claim to be birdwatchers but obviously aren't very good (one told us that there were grey parrots, *Psittacus erithacus*, in the area – we wish – but unfortunately these beautiful birds have never been recorded in The Gambia). If there are enough guests staying at the lodge then dancers and musicians from the local village will provide entertainment in the evenings.

The safari park

This is an exciting project that was in its early phases of completion at the time we were writing this guide. The safari park is located to the northwest of Bwiam in the land between Jurungkumani (Bulanjar) Bolon and Bintang Bolon. The park covers an area of about 60km² and is bounded on the south by a high electrified fence which is intended both to keep poachers out, and large animals, such as elephants and rhino, inside the park. There will be a series of gravelled roads leading around the park that will allow excellent views of a selection of the park's large mammals, including elephants, white and black rhinos, and antelopes, which will be allowed to roam free within the confines of the park. At the time of writing we do not known the final mix of animals to be introduced to the park. It would be great to see some of the large mammals that once roamed freely in the wild state in The Gambia back in the country again. These large mammals include the African elephant, *Loxodonta africana*, which used to be the country's national emblem, but which became extinct in The Gambia in 1913.

A small zoo is also planned within the park to house some of the more obviously dangerous animals such as lions, and in addition a number of camps will be set up to cater for visitors. If all goes well this park could become the biggest tourist attraction in the country.

Getting there and away

When the safari park opens we imagine it will be a popular place to visit and will be easy to reach in either tourist taxis or shared taxis. Bush taxis will also drop you off either near the entrance or at the town of Bwiam, as they regularly ply the Banjul to Basse Highway that runs south of the town. It is uncertain at this stage how you will get around the park, though this will probably be in the park's own vehicles.

Bwiam

Bwiam is a small town that has one dubious claim to fame. This is the *karelo*, or 'cooking pot', which can be found protruding about half a metre out of the ground amongst a stand of white-flowered silk-cotton trees, just outside of town. There are lots of local legends regarding the *karelo*. One states that this pot could swivel to point in the direction of an attack. Another claims that the pot is impossible to move. Unfortunately, despite the colourful legends, it appears that the *karelo* is just the base for an artillery piece, although no one seems to know why or when it was placed there.

Getting there and away

Bush taxis are the most viable option to get this far upcountry and they regularly ply the main highway south of the town. A bush taxi from Brikama will cost around US$1.50. GPTC buses (ordinary service) from Banjul and from upcountry stop at the town.

Sindola Camp

Sindola Camp (c/o Kairaba Hotel; tel: 462940, 462941 or 462942; fax: 462947; email: kairaba@gamtel.gm; web: www.kairabahotel.com) is a new five-star camp located about 75km east of Brikama, close to the Senegalese border at Kanilai. This location is famous in The Gambia as the home village of President Jammeh. Currently there are lots of rumours going around that it is impossible to get to the camp unless you have been cleared by state security. This is untrue and access to the camp is problem free, though it's a long way from the main highway on a laterite road.

The camp has 40 double rooms and is capable of accommodating a maximum of 90 people. The rooms are in rustic looking huts, but if you like your comfort, don't be put off by this, as each room is very modern inside with air conditioning and hot water 24 hours a day. Each standard room also contains shower, WC, washbasin, fridge, ceiling fan and is fitted with mosquito windownets. VIP family suites are larger and contain an extra lounge area. There are plans to fit all rooms with internal telephones so that room service will be available to guests. Standard rooms cost US$24–37.50 for the night with full English breakfast. The VIP family suites cost US$51 per night. Rates are negotiable for those who choose to stay longer. As the camp is new the grounds still look a little like a building site at present, but there has been extensive planting and hopefully if we have a good rainy season during the summer of 2001 it should look a lot better.

The camp is open all year and the facilities available to guests include a swimming pool and pool bar, an excellent restaurant, plus a tennis court, volleyball and basketball courts. Although the accommodation is some of the most expensive (for a camp) in The Gambia, the price of meals at the restaurant, which include pizzas that are cooked on site, are fairly reasonable and the food is very good. There is also an excellent wine list available along with champagne. Accommodation can be booked direct from the camp or through the Kairaba Hotel at the coast. There is transport available to and from the airport.

This is the perfect place in which to relax, and of course your stay is guaranteed to be hassle-free. If just sitting by the pool is not your idea of a holiday though, there are a number of other options being organised by the camp, the first of which is evening entertainment in the form of cultural Jola dances and fire-eaters from local villages. Nearby there is also a traditional wrestling arena under construction, which will hold big contests every 2–3 months plus weekly bouts. In addition future plans include trips to Kanilai Game Park and presumably to the new safari park that is under construction near Bwiam. There will also be donkey-cart safaris into the surrounding countryside, where there are good chances of seeing monkeys and perhaps even bush pigs (warthogs), although the latter are doubtful. We have also been informed that a qualified birding guide will be available to guide guests at the camp in the near future and for birders there will be a photo-hide located over a pool, within the grounds.

Getting there and away

Your best option is to hire a taxi to bring you to the camp. If you fancy a long walk you can always take a bush taxi from Brikama and asked to be dropped off at the police post at the junction of the road to Kanilai for around US$2. Then follow the laterite road southwards for about 6km. Alternatively you can arrange transport through the Kairaba Hotel.

Kanilai Game Park and nature trails

Kanilai Game Park (tel/fax: 483618) is a large temporary park that is being used at present to hold some of the large mammals destined for the safari park (see earlier in this chapter). These include small numbers of Burchell's zebra, *Equus quagga burchelli*, kudu, *Tragelaphus imberbis*, eland, *Taurotragus oryx*, impala, *Aepyceros melampus*, wildebeest, *Connochaetes taurinus*, and blesbok, *Damaliscus dorcas*. Unfortunately not one of these species is native to West Africa, or ever has been. The game park has a number of artificial watering holes that are viewable from a walking trail and a mountain bike trail. The park encloses an area of former Guinea savanna that was once used for farming and as range lands for foraging domestic animals. The area is at present fairly heavily wooded, though there are a few more open areas. Apart from the animals that have been placed in the park there are also naturally occurring troops of patas and callithrix monkeys, scrub hare, honey badger and squirrels, together with a good mix of birds including helmeted guineafowl.

Getting there and away
The best way to get into the park is to organise a tour through Sindola Camp or the Kairaba Hotel, or hire a taxi to take you there. The nearest public transport runs along the main highway several kilometres to the north. Visitors to the park *must* make a reservation in advance and there is a small entrance fee of less than US$2 per person.

Kalagi Park Lodge
Kalagi Park Lodge is a small camp situated by the main Banjul to Basse Highway, in the village of the same name. In early 2001 the camp was still under construction and therefore we do not have any details of accommodation nor prices, but building should be completed by the time this book comes to press and the camp should be up and running. The camp is ideally situated for exploration of the Bintang Bolon and the surrounding countryside and wetlands.

Getting there and away
Bush taxis are the obvious and cheapest choice to get to Kalagi. They run along the main highway in both directions and will cost you around US$2 from Brikama.

North Bank Division

The North Bank Division lies along the north bank of the River Gambia and stretches from the Atlantic Ocean in the west to just past the small town of Ngeyen Sanjal. Here it shares its eastern border with the Central River Division. This part of The Gambia lies within a large belt of Sudan savanna. In the past it was more like the south bank of the river and contained many forests. However, deforestation and the subsequent eroding of the exposed soil through wind and rainfall, together with the generally lower rainfall, have resulted in the dry Sahelian climate encroaching from the north. In consequence, the North Bank Division can look green and lush during the rainy season, but later in the dry season it begins to look more like a desert. Some remedial work is being done to try and stall the deterioration of the environment, such as the setting up of forest parks and community forests by planting trees, but this still has a long way to go to offset the damage that has been done.

The wildlife on the north bank of the river, especially the birds, includes species more commonly found in drier areas, such as wheatears, northern anteater chat, chestnut-backed sparrow-lark, *Eremopterix leucotis*, and Sudan golden sparrow, *Passer luteus*. It is also worth looking out for species that to date have not been recorded in The Gambia, but are known to be present just across the Senegalese border to the north, such as the black-crowned sparrow-lark, *Eremopterix nigriceps*. As the dry Sahel pushes further south it brings with it new species and you stand a real chance of adding to our knowledge as relatively few birders travel on the north bank as compared to the Western Division.

The North Bank Division includes within its borders the internationally famous Juffureh – the home of Kunta Kinte from the 1970s book and TV series, *Roots*, written by Alex Haley. Unfortunately there is some dispute amongst historians as to whether or not Juffureh was the place that Kunta Kinte actually lived, but this has been largely ignored by modern Gambians and visitors. Juffureh has certainly benefited from its fame and is visited by an estimated 80% of all tourists who come to The Gambia, though most of these visits are fleeting and few people stay for any length of time. This is due in no small part to the amount of hassle that visitors get in the village which makes most of them glad to get away for a bit of peace. However, Juffureh has also become the focus for many black people around the world regarding the evils of slavery in Africa, and there is an excellent exhibition in the Maurel Freres building, at the old trading post village of Albreda, near Juffureh. This exhibition is entitled 'Voyage of no return – the Atlantic slave trade and the Senegambia' and is worth visiting.

The main road from Barra to Kerewan is one of the better roads in the country and is also reasonably well signposted. Once you leave this road though, for example, to go north into Niumi National Park or south to Albreda or Juffureh, expect only dirt roads and a rough ride. Beyond Kerewan there are no more tarmac roads until you cross the Trans Gambia Highway at Farafenni. GPTC buses run between Barra and Kerewan, a journey that will cost you less than US$1.

BARRA

As the northern terminal for the Banjul to Barra ferry, Barra is the scene of hectic activity most days. The town itself does not hold much of interest, apart from Fort Bullen. However, the colourful mix of people going to and fro adds life to an otherwise pretty dull scene. As a tourist you are likely to get hassled as you leave the ferry or join the queue of people and vehicles waiting to get on. It can be confusing buying a ticket for a foot passage at the terminal as everyone appears to want to point you in the right direction and be helpful, and not all of the advice is helpful or indeed welcome. The ferry workers don't wear uniforms, except for the security personnel, and sometimes this leads you to do one thing as indicated by one person, while you should be doing another as indicated by a legitimate member of staff. To summarise, *don't attempt to use the ferry unless you have a good sense of humour and the ridiculous*. To confuse matters even more, if you are heading south in a vehicle and want to catch the ferry, you will find that you have to buy your ticket from the poorly signed GPTC office just south of Essau and *not* at the ferry terminal (see *Chapter 6* for ferry times and more information about the crossing).

Getting there and away

Barra can be reached from Banjul using the GPTC ferry crossing or one of the many *pirogues* that carry passengers across the river. Bush taxis to and from upcountry are fairly regular and there is a GPTC bus route between Barra and Kerewan. GPTC also run a bus service to Dakar from the Barra ferry terminal. The bus runs twice daily in the mornings (times are reliant on when the early ferries arrive) and costs less than US$7.

Fort Bullen

Fort Bullen at Barra is unique amongst the many forts that were built along the coast of West Africa in the 19th century, since it was constructed to help put a stop to the slave trade. It was also built as a defence against the local chief, Burungai Sonko, who was known as a troublemaker and disliked the British traders in Bathurst.

The guns located at Bathurst could only cover half the width of River Gambia so in 1826 Burungai Sonko was asked by the British for permission to build a fortification at Barra Point. He initially refused but was then persuaded by the presence of two Royal Navy warships – HMS *Maidstone* and HMS *African* (the *African* was the first British steam vessel to visit the coast of West Africa). The King eventually gave the British possession of a one-mile wide strip of land (known as the 'Ceded Mile') and the right to fortify Barra Point. He also waived the right to collect taxes from traders and received in return an annual subsidy of £100. The commander of HMS *Maidstone*, Commodore Charles Bullen, ordered two cannon to be taken ashore to Barra Point and then took formal possession of the land in the name of King George IV of England. The fort was named after Commodore Bullen, though in reality at this time it was just a cluster of mud huts around the cannon and a handful of men. However, the presence of the cannon finally gave the British full control over the entry to the River Gambia.

The actual date that the present fort was constructed remains a mystery though most historians believe it was in 1833–1834. From then until 1870, when the fort was abandoned, it came under attack only once. This was in the Barra War of 1831,

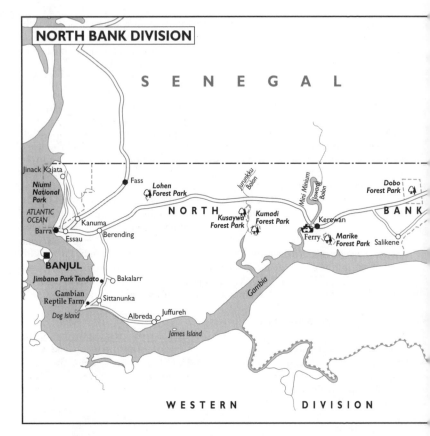

when a small force of British troops and civilians had tried to arrest some people in the nearby town of Essau but was fought off with the loss of several lives. The survivors of the force had then retreated to Fort Bullen, only to abandon it for four months until the following year when the fighting was over.

At the beginning of World War II the Senegalese government sided with the Vichy government in France. This left the British colony surrounded by a potentially hostile enemy, so the British modernised the fort and brought in more weapons, namely a 4-inch Vickers and a 12-pounder. The Vickers can still be seen at the fort.

After the war, the fort was again abandoned until it was claimed as a National Monument in the 1970s. It was renovated in 1996 for the Roots Homecoming Festival. The large, rectangular fort has rounded bastions at all four corners and overlooks both the sea and the mouth of the River Gambia. It is possible for visitors to walk along the battlements. The entrance fee to the fort is around US$1.

Getting there and away
Fort Bullen is within easy strolling distance of Barra, so no problems here.

NIUMI NATIONAL PARK AND JINACK ISLAND
Niumi National Park covers over 49km² and is one of the finest protected areas within The Gambia. Together with Bao Bolon Wetland Reserve, this is one of only

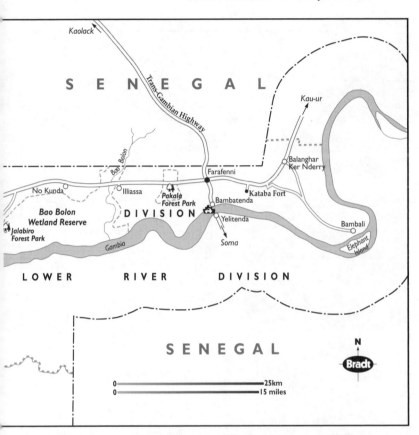

two protected areas to the north of the river. It is also conveniently located at less than an hour's journey from Banjul. Niumi National Park is adjacent to the Parc National de Delta du Saloum (see *Chapter 13*) in Senegal, and shares many of its habitats and wildlife with this much larger area.

Niumi National Park consists of two parts. One part lies on the mainland and stretches north from the village of Kanuma, encompassing a large chunk of bush and woodland savanna and the magnificent Masarinko Bolon with its high escarpment giving splendid views over the *bolon*. The second part consists of the almost legendary Jinack Island, otherwise known as 'Paradise', 'Treasure' or 'Coconut Island'. Niji Bolon separates Jinack Island from the mainland. This *bolon* can be crossed on foot in places when the tide is low, so perhaps it really should not be called an island at all. Yet the Niji Bolon has been the saviour of Jinack, as it is probably the sole reason why the island has never been seriously developed. This has resulted in the protection of an astounding variety of wildlife from over-exploitation.

Jinack has almost 11km of sun-drenched, unspoilt sandy beaches, stretching from Barra Point northwards to the Senegalese border. Compared to some of the beaches of southern Gambia, which have suffered from over-development during the last decade, the beaches of Jinack are a haven of peace and quiet. Here you will not hear the music of ghetto blasters, or the thunder of traffic. On Jinack there are no vehicles and it is possible to walk for miles, with the sea on one side and the

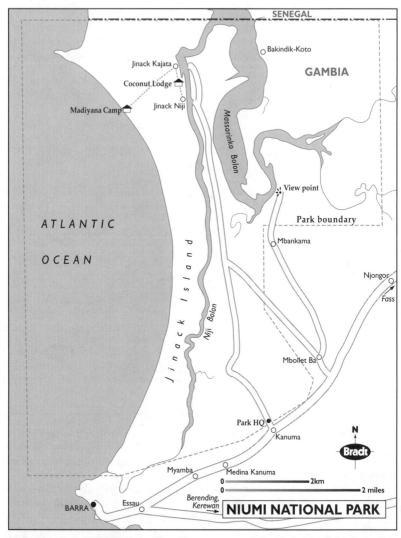

SENEGAL

Bakindik-Koto

GAMBIA

Jinack Kajata

Coconut Lodge

Madiyana Camp

Jinack Niji

Massarinko Bolon

View point

Park boundary

ATLANTIC

OCEAN

Mbankama

Njongor

Fass

Jinack Island

Niji Bolon

Mbollet Ba

Park HQ

Kanuma

N

Bradt

Myamba

Medina Kanuma

0 ━━━━━━━━━━ 2km

0 ━━━━━━━━━━ 2 miles

BARRA

Essau

Berending,
Kerewan

NIUMI NATIONAL PARK

lush greenness of the bush on the other, accompanied only by small birds wading along the tide's edge or the silhouette of an osprey soaring overhead.

The island lies mostly within The Gambia, but the northern part also stretches across the border into Senegal. On the Gambian side there are two villages – Jinack Kajata and Jinack Niji, both of which can be reached by canoe across the Niji Bolon from the mainland. As with most places in The Gambia, the villagers are friendly and welcoming to strangers. From the villages you can cross the island on foot and reach the sea in as little as 20–30 minutes. Be warned though: during the rainy season and early dry season you will probably have to wade in places where the tracks pass through rice fields.

The wildlife of Jinack Island is very rich. A British bird-ringing group has studied the birds on the island at **Madiyana Camp** for several years, and the results of this study have provided a species list of birds that is phenomenal.

Especially prevalent are large numbers of migratory birds that come south from Europe for the winter and either stay in the rich coastal scrub or feed themselves up before travelling further south. At Buniada Point, there are several lagoons and a large sand spit that is only submerged at high tide. Here you will find hundreds of gulls, terns and waders, with perhaps a few pelicans or even a greater flamingo, *Phoenicopterus ruber*. Birds of prey are well represented on the island with dozens of over-wintering ospreys along the *bolons* and the coast, as well as the African fish eagle, shikra, *Acipiter badius*, gabar goshawk, *Micronisus gabar*, African harrier-hawk, *Polyboroides typus*, and even the massive martial eagle. Uncommon birds recorded here include white-fronted plover, bar-breasted firefinch, *Lagonosticta rufopicta*, and European scops owl, *Otus scops*. However it's not only the birds that are well represented on Jinack; mammals are also common and there is an abundance of small rodents and scrub hares living amongst the coastal scrub and tamarisk which provide food for a range of different mongooses and other predators such as genets and perhaps caracal and serval. Hares, guineafowl, francolins and young antelopes, such as bushbuck and duikers, also provide food for the island's top predators – the leopard and spotted hyena. Leopard tracks can be found just about everywhere on the island – even on the beach, though the animals themselves are extremely shy and are rarely seen. There are also some common warthogs, known locally as 'bush-pigs'. The Niji *Bolon* is also home to the largest wild Nile crocodile that we have personally seen in The Gambia. It is a beauty of almost six metres in length that hauls out on mud banks not too far from Kajata. Nile monitors are also common just about everywhere.

One of the highlights of a visit to Jinack has to be the possibility of encountering some dolphins – especially around December and January. Bottlenose dolphins can sometimes be seen on the boat-trip to **Madiyana Camp** as they cavort and play amongst the waves. Sometimes also a large group of Atlantic hump-backed dolphins will swim along only a hundred metres or so from the shore, giving anyone on the beach an excellent view. This last species is a real speciality as they are only found along the coast of West Africa. There appears to be a group of 20 or so dolphins that spend part of their time off Jinack and the rest of it further northwards in the Delta du Saloum.

Jinack Island is certainly worth a visit at any time of year. Since it is a national park, there is a small entrance fee that is payable by all visitors. The price stands at less than US$2.50 for non-resident adults and US$1.50 for children. Obviously any Gambians that are resident in the park can enter free of charge. This rule does *not* apply to Gambian guides from other parts of The Gambia who must pay just over US$1 for entry into the park, just as they have to pay to enter any other protected area. The fee goes directly to the government and part of it works its way back to the wildlife department to help them in managing their protected areas. If you are not asked to pay this small fee on a trip, please ask why.

Where to stay

There are two camps on Jinack Island. The first is **Coconut Lodge**, which is between the two villages of Niji and Kajata and at least 20 minutes' walk from the sea (where they have constructed a basic beach bar). There is accommodation and somewhere to eat here but in our opinion **Madiyana Camp**, though more expensive, is the better of the two camps, with a wonderfully relaxing atmosphere and located right on top of the deserted beach. This is one of our favourite places to stay in The Gambia. Accommodation is in substantial brick huts and there is also a very good restaurant and bar. There is no power or running water but the camp is so pleasant that it's not a hardship at all and just increases the feeling of being castaways on some pleasant tropical island. A single B&B at Madiyana is US$24 while a double B&B is around US$40.50. Lunch is about US$7 and dinner is less than US$11. At the moment the 11km of unspoilt beaches are bumster free – if this was ever to change it would ruin the whole character of the island which would become another tourist nightmare. Luckily the Department of Parks and Wildlife Management has a certain amount of control over developments in the national park, especially those that would damage its integrity.

Getting there and away

If you travel by yourself and are only visiting for just the day, it is quite possible and easy to catch a bush taxi (less than US$1) or a shared taxi (more expensive) from Barra to take you to the canoe crossing at either Kajata or Niji. It would be best to either ask the shared taxi to wait or to come back at a pre-arranged time as the bush taxis that serve Kajata and Niji are very few and far between. You could also bring a tourist taxi across with you from Banjul and retain his services for the day, though of course this would be far more expensive and would require some serious negotiation. In the wet season, the road from Barra to Kajata and Niji is sometimes impassable, in which case it would be better to get a boat across to Jinack from Banjul (this is more relaxing and a lot less hassle anyway). Contact North Bank Tours (tel: 494088; mobile tel: 995950; fax: 495950; email: paradise@qanet.gm) to make arrangements at any time of the year. Alternatively, it is also possible to join an excursion organised by the ground operators. This involves crossing on the Banjul-Barra ferry, a short trip by Land Rover through the bush, and a boat-trip before arriving at **Madiyana Camp** or **Coconut Lodge** (depending on which excursion you take). Be aware that the ground operators call the excursions by a variety of different names, such as 'Paradise Island', 'Coconut Island' and even 'Treasure Island' (see *Organised excursions* in *Chapter 3*).

FASS

This is a small town, near the border with Senegal, that has a large and lively market frequented by both Gambians and Senegalese. We have seen the market held on a Wednesday, but check around, perhaps in Barra, to see if one is being held during your stay on the North Bank. It might well be worth a visit, not only to pick up a bargain or two, but also to experience the market itself which is very loud and colourful and full of life.

Getting there and away

The cheapest option is to get a bush taxi from Barra for less than US$1. An alternative is horse- and donkey-cart since many local people get to the market using this mode of transport. It should be possible to find one of these nearer to the town.

BERENDING SACRED CROCODILE POOL

Berending is a small village about 10km to the east of Barra along the good road past Essau. The only thing that makes this village very different to hundreds of other Gambian villages is the presence of a sacred pool just a short distance to the south. The pool, which is actually a series of three to four naturally linked pools, is a beautiful spot surrounded by good quality bush that contains some large old trees. Of course the focus of the pool is the small population of Nile crocodiles which live there, though they are not always visible. We have been told that the evening is the best time to spot them. There is certainly an abundance of food for the crocs, from fish and frogs through to birds. The latter include herons, egrets, jacanas and kingfishers. Broad-billed rollers appear to be very common and active around the pools.

Most of the villagers at Berending are Mandinka. It is said that when they first arrived in the area and were still pagan, they used to pray regularly at the pools. Now that they have converted to the Islamic religion they still pray at the pools, but much less frequently. The two main reasons for praying appear to be for a good harvest and to increase fertility for women who have trouble conceiving. Those who pray at the poolside normally bring fish for the crocodiles. Unlike the other sacred pools in The Gambia, visitors do not bathe in the pools at Berending (see the box *Sacred crocodile pools*, page 130).

Getting there and away
A bush taxi from Barra costs less than US$0.50. From Kerewan (if travelling from the opposite direction) it is US$1, or you can take a shared taxi from Barra. It's also possible to catch a tourist taxi in Banjul and cross on the ferry with it (an expensive option). The pools can be difficult to find so ask any villager of Berending to point out the way. They are not too far off the good road so you can either drive to them or walk. No fee is charged and locals seem happy to let tourists wander around. We have never encountered any hassle at the pools.

JIMBANA PARK TENDATO
Jimbana Park Tendato (web: www.jimbanapark.homepage.com) – Tendato is Mandinka for 'trading place' – is a little-known place just off the Barra to Albreda road. It is a very new site that lies in a peaceful corner away from the hustle and bustle of some tourist traps. During our visit there were two double rooms available to rent in a small house, or a choice of two-, three- or four-man tents for camping on the site. A small restaurant is planned and should be operational by the time this edition is published. The park is located right by the side of a mangrove-lined *bolon* and there are plenty of potential walks in the area including the nearby village. There are also plans to start excursions from the park. These will include boat trips to Banjul or anywhere else you fancy along the river, and donkey cart trips around the surrounding area. Its possible to swim in the *bolon* where it skirts the camp and the fishing is supposed to be good. Small, local fishing kits are available to hire at the park and as the proprietor told us: 'no fish – no pay', which sounds good to us. There is no electricity and water has to be transported from the village. Local kids can and do hassle you here.

Getting there and away
As with other places this close to Barra, either take a shared taxi from the town or a tourist taxi from Banjul across the ferry. Or get a bush taxi from Barra that is heading towards Albreda or Juffureh and asked to be dropped off (the park is near where the road crosses the Jimbana Bolon and about a 20-minute walk from the village of Bakalarr). This should cost less than US$1. It's not the easiest of places to find at the moment but the owner assured us that it should be well signposted in the future.

GAMBIAN REPTILE FARM
(JERREH KUN KOTO SNAKE FARM)
This is one of those places that is so unusual that it is well worth a visit even if you can't stand snakes (think of it as therapeutic). Luke, a French man who has lived in The Gambia for a number of years, runs the farm. He is very enthusiastic about wildlife and often gets orphaned and injured animals, which he rears under licence

from the wildlife department, before releasing them back into the wild. His main love though, is reptiles, and he is slowly gathering a collection of snakes, lizards, turtles and tortoises. The snake farm is not a tourist trap, though it does welcome visitors, and the income they generate helps to cover the farm's running costs. The farm is licensed by the wildlife department primarily as an educational resource and research centre and is the first of its kind in The Gambia. Many Gambian children visit the farm and learn about wildlife in general, and reptiles in particular. They learn that snakes are not all poisonous and bad, and that they do a great deal of good by keeping down the numbers of agricultural pests. This is a start in the long process of changing attitudes towards snakes in the country. Luke charges less than US$2 per person to visit and will gladly tell you everything you ever wanted to know about snakes but were too scared to ask.

Getting there and away

Not easy. You can get a bush taxi from Barra to Sittanunka for less than US$1, but are then faced by a long walk along a sandy track through the bush (which is not suitable for anything but four-wheel drive vehicles). The forest in this area is pretty exceptional for the north bank of the River Gambia and is full of wildlife, so walking to the farm can have its good points). Alternatively, you can join an organised excursion which also stops off at the farm. You'll have to ask which excursions stop at the farm, as they do tend to change from time to time.

DOG AND PELICAN ISLANDS

These are two small islands in the River Gambia lying just off Dog Island Point. These are Dog Island and the smaller Pelican Island. Dog Island is supposedly named after the dog-like barking of the baboons that inhabited the island when the first sailors visited it. The island was colonised in 1661 by the British, who renamed it 'Charles Island' and then proceeded to build Charles Fort on it. However, because the island was vulnerable to attack at low tide when it is possible to walk across to it from the mainland (though we have not tried this yet) the fort and island were abandoned in 1666. The rock that constitutes the island was used to construct both the early fortifications in Banjul and also on James Island. Today there is no sign of Charles Fort.

Getting there and away

It is possible to hire a boat (from Barra for example) to take you to the islands. However the islands are very rocky and the landing is far from safe, so perhaps your best bet is to travel there overland. The track that goes to the snake farm (see above) goes on further to the river and it is said to be possible to reach Dog Island on foot at low tide (though as we have already stated, we have not tried it ourselves yet).

ALBREDA AND JUFFUREH

These two villages lie so close to each other that it's difficult for a visitor to tell where one ends and the other begins. Albreda is famous for its old trading post and slave factory, which is another name for a fortified trading post. Juffureh is famous from Alex Haley's 1970s book *Roots* in which he, an African-American, investigated his ancestry. Juffureh is the place where Kunta Kinteh, one of Haley's forebears, was taken as a slave around 200 years ago. Both of these villages have benefited immensely from this story and have been visited by tens of thousands of tourists since *Roots* was published. The only trouble is that the vast majority of tourists come on a day trip organised by the tour operators and stop for only a couple of hours before going back to their hotels. The villagers would dearly love for more tourists to stop for longer.

Getting there and away

Most people come on the '*Roots*' excursion (see *Organised excursions* in *Chapter 3*), but it really is quite easy to get to the villages by a variety of means. Apart from the usual tourist and shared taxis, bush taxis ply the road between Barra and Albreda/Juffureh. The journey takes about an hour and costs less than US$1. Perhaps the best way to get here is as part of a self-organised upcountry tour. Or you could stay at either Tumani Tenda or Bintang Bolon Lodge on the south bank for a while, then hire a boat to take you across the river. You could then stay here a few days before hiring another boat to take you upriver to Tendaba Camp. It's a relaxing way to do the off-the-beaten-track bit without killing yourself with the effort (all of these camps are covered in *Chapters 8* and *10*).

Where to stay

The **Home at Last Hotel** behind the museum is where most visiting government officials stay, but they will also put up other visitors, though government staff seem to take priority. The rooms are cheap at US$5.50 for a single and US$7 for a double. Much more interesting is the **Juffureh Rest House** (tel: 710276 and ask to speak to someone from the music school, as it's known, or leave a message so that they can get back in touch with you). This is a village owned compound on the opposite side of the road from the craft market. There are clean, simple rooms, all with mosquito window nets. The toilets are pit latrines and the washroom consists of bucket baths but this is no real hardship and it's how most Gambians live, so it can't be that bad. There is also a very good *bantaba* (meeting place) where you can relax in the shade. At the moment, the rest house is managed by a Frenchman of African origin, Mr Amadou Njie, who is very friendly and is trying to attract more visitors. There is already some collaboration with art and music students in Paris who visit for drumming and dancing courses. We had absolutely no hassle while we stayed here and everyone was friendly. It makes a good base for exploring the villages and nearby countryside. The prices are very cheap at US$3.50 for bed with French-style breakfast, and US$10 for full board. Lunch and dinner are both US$3.50 if required separately. The rest house does not have a fridge at the moment so meals need to be booked in advance, but at least you know the food will be absolutely fresh.

Another camp which was under construction when we last visited, but promises to be a good place to stay, is the **Rising Sun Camp**. Managed by the same man who manages the Rising Sun Bar and Restaurant, Mr Njie Cham, this camp is a few minutes' walk away on the outskirts of Albreda. When completed it will have ten rooms, with shower, WC and mosquito window nets in each. There will also be electricity supplied from a generator. The prices will be about US$5.50 for B&B. All meals are provided at the restaurant.

Where to eat

Without a doubt the best place to eat is the **Rising Sun Bar and Restaurant**. This is close to the river and also acts as the local video cinema, where for less than US$0.50 you can join a good proportion of the village and watch a movie. There is local or European-style food, with sandwiches between US$1–1.50, and meals between US$2.50–4.50. The restaurant has the full range of bottled water, soft drinks, beer, wine and shorts at the slightly inflated prices that you often find on the north bank of the river. We found the food here to be very good and the bar was also open for a good breakfast fairly early in the morning. Meals can also be ordered at the **Juffureh Rest House** but we haven't tried them, so can't pass judgement. There is a *bantaba* next to the museum that serves cold drinks.

Places to visit and things to do

There is a small but thought-provoking museum on the slave trade located in Albreda. This is open between 10.00–17.00 on Saturday and Monday–Thursday, 10.00–13.00 on Friday and is closed on Sunday. The entrance fee is less than US$2 per adult. The ruins of the old slave factory are still standing as is a small church behind the Rising Sun which is said to be the oldest church in West Africa, though we have no idea whether this is true or not. There is also a small shop selling batiks, which is run by the local school, and a large craft market where you can expect the usual hassle.

Excursions by boat to James Island or Bintang Bolon can be set up with local villagers through the rest house or restaurant managers. It may also be possible for them to organise jeep safaris, given some advance warning. Drumming and dancing courses, and possibly other activities like batik-making etc, can be set up with the rest house management in advance. Prices for all of the above are negotiable.

The countryside around the villages contains some good areas, especially close to the river. There are lots of birds and butterflies and it's well worth taking some time out to explore. The jetty and shore line at Albreda often hold good numbers of waders, gulls and terns. Sometimes you'll find a large flock of yellow-billed storks feeding on the riverbank.

JAMES ISLAND

James Island is a small rocky outcrop in the River Gambia which holds the extensive ruins of Fort James, among a small grove of baobab trees. The island is well worth a visit to get a glimpse of The Gambia's past or if you are a history buff. You don't have to plan to stay long though: an hour is more than enough time to see everything the island has to offer.

The island was originally named 'St Andrew Island' after a Portuguese sailor from the entourage of Luiz de Cadamosto, who was buried on the island in 1456. In 1651 the first fort was built on the island by servants of the Duke of Courland, but this was seized by a group with the wonderful name of 'the Royal Adventurers of England' ten years later, who renamed the island 'James Island' after James, Duke of York. The fort was ideally placed to provide strategic defence for English interests along the river and as a staging post for the shipment of slaves. In the following years the fort had a very busy time and was attacked and seized by the French then recaptured again by the English, several times. Often the fort was also destroyed only to be rebuilt again. Other highlights in the garrison's history include the time when it was attacked by pirates in 1719, who carried off all the goods and slaves in it, and an unsuccessful attack on the fort by 500 'Niumi' men in 1768. In 1779 the French, who had seized the island once again, this time without firing a shot, finally destroyed the fort. The island was eventually abandoned altogether in 1829.

The island was so small that it only allowed room for the construction of the fort and had to be extended to provide space for the other buildings that were needed. This was done by creating earth and rock embankments, which were supported by piled stakes. Over the years the stakes have naturally decayed and the embankments have been eroded by the action of the waves. This has been a long process and is still continuing today, though extremely slowly. The island is not sinking, as is often stated, but does require regular maintenance to remedy the erosion that is taking place.

Getting there and away

The easiest way is to join the 'Roots' excursion (see *Organised excursions* in *Chapter 3*). Alternatively, you can hire a small fishing *pirogue* from Albreda to take you across to the island for a negotiable fee.

JURUNKKU BOLON

This is a small *bolon* that crosses beneath the road just after the village of Jamagen. During the dry season, the damp vegetation contains a roost of large numbers of African tiger butterflies. The surrounding bushes are also good for sunbirds and other small birds, including, if you're lucky, yellow white-eye, *Zosterops senegalensis*, which we have seen taking nectar from the flowers of burning bush, *Combretum paniculatum*. A good little spot worth checking out for birds, though it dries up completely towards the end of the dry season.

FERRY OVER MINI MINIUM (JOWARA) BOLON

At present the only way across this large *bolon* is via a car ferry although a road bridge has been under construction for some time and may well be operating by the time you read this book. The ferry runs between 08.00 and 19.30 every day. There is a price list for crossing the ferry on a sign board on the Kerewan side of the *bolon* but we have found that we have paid different prices at different times and have been unable to figure out why. Therefore expect to pay anywhere between US$3–4.50 for a car crossing and but much less than US$0.50 if you are on foot. There are no set times for crossing and the ferry goes when it is full.

Getting there and away

A bush taxi or a GPTC bus from Barra to the ferry terminal will cost about US$1. Cross over the *bolon* and get another bush taxi on the opposite bank. It will cost less than US$0.50 to get you into Kerewan.

Ngara Camp

This is a brand new camp that had not been fully constructed at the time of writing, so we have no information regarding its standard of accommodation and prices, etc. We believe it is located close to the ferry crossing by Kerewan. You could try asking about it at the ferry terminal.

KEREWAN

Kerewan is a small town that has no facilities for tourists. However, it is possible to get a room in the **FORUT Hostel** (tel: 720169, though this number could be redundant as there are plans to change it in the future) run by a local NGO. The hostel is on the right as you enter the town from the west. The staff work normal office hours (08.00-16.00) but if you turn up late there should always be someone on duty that can give you the keys. Failing that, try asking anyone for the assistant director of FORUT, Mrs Isatou Jallow. Isatou is a very pleasant lady who lives in a compound off to the right of the junction along the main road through town. There are two houses with five double rooms. The price for one person for one night is less than US$3.50. Meals are not provided but it should be possible to find someone in the town who is willing to either cook a meal or to share their own. Alternatively bring your own food and find somewhere to cook it yourself.

Getting there and away

A bush taxi or GPTC bus from Barra to the ferry terminal over the Mini Minium (Jowara) Bolon will cost about US$1. After crossing over on the

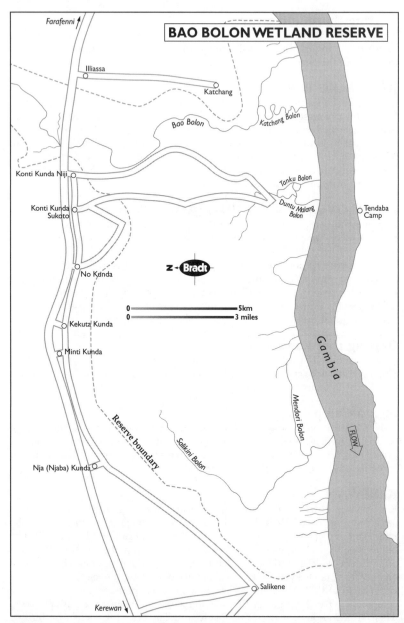

ferry get another bush taxi on the Kerewan side that will cost you less than US$0.50. If coming from the other direction, catch a bush taxi from Farafenni to Kerewan (US$1).

KEREWAN TO FARAFENNI

The road along this route can be pretty rough and during the dry season is intensely dusty. During the rainy season it can be impassable in places and you should check with local people before attempting to travel along it. The countryside is a rich mixture of agricultural land and Sudan savanna though it can look pretty unattractive during the driest months. Every now and again you will see watering holes for cattle along the way and these are usually worth checking out for their birds, especially when the countryside has been without rain for some time. The exotically named exclamatory paradise whydahs are a common feature of these watering holes. The males are striking and look slightly comical as they fly about with their huge, long tail feathers bouncing behind them. This distinctive plumage is that of breeding males whose long tails are commonly present well into the dry season. There are also flocks of weavers, finches and sparrows that contain some pleasant surprises such as the distinctive cut-throat finch, *Amadina fasciata*. The open countryside holds birds such as Abyssinian roller, *Coracias abyssiniica*, European bee-eater, *Merops apiaster*, and Montagu's harrier, *Circus pygargus*. In the early dry season and early rainy season it's also worth keeping an eye open for the uncommon African collared dove, *Streptopelia roseogrisea*. Look out also for the blue pansy butterfly, *Junonia orithya madagascariensis*, also known as the eyed pansy, which seems to frequent this part of the country during the dry season. Travelling along this road gives you the feeling of being in the real African landscape and is also the first place where the rolling laterite ridges begin to appear along the North Bank, adding to the atmosphere.

DOBO FOREST PARK

Dobo Forest Park can be found on the north side of the road, though because of the low height of the trees you may well fail to notice it as you pass. It is worth exploring for its birdlife, which includes four-banded sandgrouse, *Pterocles quadricinctus*, little green bee-eater, *Merops orientalis*, bush petronia, *Petronia dentata*, white-rumped seedeater, *Serinus leucopygius*, and helmeted guineafowl.

BAO BOLON WETLAND RESERVE

Bao Bolon Wetland Reserve is the largest of The Gambia's six protected areas, covering approximately 220km². In 1996 the area was designated a Ramsar site by the Ramsar Bureau and the Government of The Gambia, recognising that it is a wetland of international importance. (The Ramsar Convention is the International Convention on Wetlands.) Just west of Illiassa, the Bao Bolon itself crosses under the road. Here you can see a vast valley filled with salt marsh, which is a haven for water birds such as herons and egrets. The Bao Bolon rises south of Ferlo in Senegal and stretches over 140km before it reaches the River Gambia. Although it is inundated with fresh water during the rainy season, in the dry season saline intrusion from the River Gambia allows mangroves to extend far up the *bolon*. A number of smaller *bolons* flow southwards into the river from the reserve, and here you can find some of the tallest mangrove forests in The Gambia. Their height is attributable to the lower salinity present this far up the river, which exerts a lower osmotic pressure on the trees, allowing them to grow taller.

The reserve does not just contain wetlands, but is also significant because three major habitat types occur together in very close proximity. These are salt marsh, mangrove forests and the Sudan savanna woodland that grows on the higher, drier slopes. The reserve is very rich in wildlife but it is also an important natural resource for the people living around it. The mangroves act as a large nursery for huge numbers of spawning fish, and the fish caught in the *bolons* are an important source of protein in the diet of the local inhabitants. Some of the reserve is also used to grow rice and thatching materials. Building and fencing materials are all harvested from within its boundaries.

Bao Bolon Wetland Reserve is also very rich in wildlife. A number of rare or uncommon species are known to occur here, including large mammals like spotted hyena, jackals, West African manatee, sitatunga, and the African clawless otter. The reserve also holds large populations of reptiles, especially Nile crocodiles and Nile monitors. Birds are very well represented in the reserve with such rarities as white-crested tiger heron, *Tigriornis leucolophus*, white-backed night heron, *Gorsachius leuconotus*, goliath heron, martial eagle, purple swamphen, *Porphyrio porphyrio*, Allen's gallinule, *P. alleni*, African finfoot, *Podica senegalensis*, Pel's fishing owl, *Scotopelia peli*, African blue flycatcher, *Elminia longicauda*, African swallow-tailed kite, *Chelictinia riocourii*, white-fronted plover and brown-necked parrot. The first (and so far only) little green woodpecker, *Campethera maculosa*, to be seen in The Gambia has recently been spotted here in the mangroves along a *bolon*.

The tidally flooded marshes and salt pans are frequented by ibises and waders, whose numbers are seasonally augmented by Palearctic and African migrants. The reed beds on the upper Bao Bolon are used for roosting by mixed flocks of small birds as well as providing feeding and breeding habitats for various water birds.

Getting there and away

The reserve is probably the most difficult of the protected areas in The Gambia to get into, unless you are satisfied with just a look at the Bao Bolon itself where it crosses under the main road. Of course, even this can be difficult in the rainy season as the road often floods at this point. Without a doubt one of the best ways to get a glimpse of the interior of the reserve is to hire a boat at Tendaba Camp or Kiang West National Park (see *Chapter 10*) and cross the river. There are dirt tracks that lead into the reserve from Salikene, Njaba Kunda and Katchang, but they can be impassable to vehicles at times and you will have to go on foot or hire a horse- or donkey-cart from a village. A laterite road leading south from Kontikunda Niji is probably the best option if you have a vehicle or hire a cart, as this goes along the base of the escarpment to the west of Bao Bolon. The escarpment is a good spot to look out for wildlife.

Bush taxis regularly ply the route between Kerewan and Farafenni. A bush taxi from Kerewan to any of the small villages north of the reserve will cost anything between US$0.50–1.

PAKALA FOREST PARK

Pakala Forest Park is located a few kilometres west of Farafenni and again may be hard to spot because of the low height of its trees. Each time we have visited the forest it has suffered from a bush fire (no connection of course!) and has really not been worth exploring in any great detail, though we have seen European nightjar, *Caprimulgus europaeus*, roosting on the fire-blackened soil beneath bushes. These are very difficult to spot though, unless you happen to scare one up by walking too close. Then it will probably only fly a short distance before settling again, thereby allowing you to approach for a better view.

FARAFENNI (INCLUDING THE FERRY ACROSS THE RIVER GAMBIA)

Farafenni lies astride the Trans Gambian Highway, a tarmac road (with plenty of pot-holes) that joins northern Senegal with Casamance, cutting across the middle of The Gambia via the ferry crossing south of the town. This is a busy town with a mix of Gambians and Senegalese, and it is not orientated at all towards tourists. The ferry crossing is about six kilometres south of the town at Bambatenda. Here there is a small bustling marketplace, where you can buy very good *wanjo*, a local drink made from hibiscus flowers. You have to buy your ticket for the crossing from the GPTC office found along the road before Bambatenda. Watch out for the signs. The ferry operates from 08.30–20.30, and crosses every hour. It's US$4.50 to take a car across and less than US$0.50 if you are on foot.

Getting there and away
Bush taxis regularly run from Kerewan and will cost US$1. The taxi should stop at New Town in Farafenni, from where it is a short walk (ask for directions) to Balaguarr (also in Farafenni). From here you can catch a bush taxi south to the ferry over the River Gambia (less than US$0.50 in a four passenger vehicle or in a larger minibus). Balaguarr is also the place to catch a bush taxi to take you further east along the North Bank. If you want to go to the Senegalese border, it is also a short walk from New Town to the market, where you can catch a bush taxi going north (less than US$0.50 to the border).

Where to stay
The only place worth considering is **Eddie's Hotel, Disco, Bar and Restaurant**. Eddie's is located west of the crossroads in the town, south of the police station. It is not signposted from the main road, but we have found that almost everyone knows where it is and will point it out to you. The rooms are large and clean but fairly old and have ceiling fans, WC, washbasin and shower, though the power doesn't usually come on until 18.00. There is a protected car park for guests which it is safe to leave your car in, though in the morning you may find it washed by the night watchman (whether you wanted it to be or not), and he will expect to be paid for doing it. Unfortunately this is not a place in which to get a sound night's sleep as the town is pretty lively at night and the music can be loud and intrusive from the disco. A double room will cost between US$12–13.50 per night.

Where to eat
There are a few cheap places in which to eat in town, including **Balanghar Fast Food** and **Sunu Yai Fast Food**. Undoubtedly the best place though is **Eddie's Hotel, Disco, Bar and Restaurant**, though you will have a long wait for your food to appear, so you should order it well in advance. There's not much of a choice, foodwise. Continental breakfast will cost US$1, breakfast with eggs US$1.50 and chicken and chips US$2. The restaurant is in a pleasant shady courtyard beneath some trees, with lots of tropical plants growing around you. Look closely and you will recognise several plants that are grown only as *indoor* house plants in Europe. As evening closes in you may well be joined by several yellow-winged bats, *Lavia frons*, which fly around your head picking insects off the tree leaves. You may also get some hassle as you try to relax so be prepared.

KATABA FORT
This is a place that is quite hard to find but if you are interested in history or archaeology then it is worth taking the trouble. About 10km east of Farafenni along the main road, turn south (there is a large concrete square on the side of the road at the junction) on to a dirt road towards a small village called Katabatata. In fact there are now three villages here that grew from the original one. Go through the first village and into the second and ask to see the *alkalo*, or chief of the village there. He is a very pleasant man but unfortunately speaks no English, though he should be able to find someone to interpret for you. It would be a good idea and very polite to take a few kola nuts with you to give to the *alkalo*, as a sign of respect, and also to tip your guide for showing you around the fort, or *tato*.

The *tato* was built in 1841 by the Wolof king, Sefo Kanni Touray, apparently with the help of the British, though it is unclear exactly how they aided him. The design of the fort is typical of *tatos* of that time. It is relatively small, covering an area of approximately one acre. It is made of laterite boulders and concrete, though there would also have been a stockade of logs and thorns. When it was first constructed the function of the fort was to fend off the Fula troops enlisted by the neighbouring king who had made several threatening gestures towards the village. At the time the Fulas and Bambaras were raiding villages in the area and stealing cattle and slaves.

Unfortunately the fort today is nothing more than a series of broken foundations on a slight rise just outside the village, but it is full of atmosphere. There is also a large and deep dry well by the fort that apparently was used only by the king. We found the nest of a small raptor in the side of the well a few metres down from the edge, but were unable to identify the species, as the single chick was very small and covered in down. Perhaps you'll have better luck if the nest is still in use when you visit (please let us know!). Don't go too near the edge of the well though, as it looks pretty unstable. This is a place that could really benefit from more visiting tourists and would be ideal for some interpretation and protection if the resources became available. There is also another fort nearby at Kumbijae but we haven't visited that one.

Getting there and away

Bush taxis are fairly regular between Farafenni and Kau-ur. A bush taxi from Balanguarr in Farafenni to the stop for Katabatata along the main road will cost less than US$0.50. From here your best option is to walk to the villages. It is quite rocky but downhill all the way and not more than 2km. At the village you can hire a horse or donkey cart to bring you back to the main road.

BAMBALI AND ELEPHANT ISLAND

Bambali is a small village that is about 20km south of the main road along a series of laterite and dirt roads. Most of the way is easy but there are occasional soft spots that can often be impassable except for four-wheel-drive vehicles. The village is like many others in The Gambia, but is surrounded by good woodland savanna that holds plenty of wildlife. The reason that most tourists go so far off the beaten track at this point is that there is a very real possibility of spotting a hippopotamus in the river around Elephant Island. The village is not set up for tourist activities but the people are very friendly and helpful. When you enter the village ask anyone for the *alkalos* compound. Although he cannot speak English he should be able to find an interpreter. The *alkalo* will find you lodgings in a village compound. Although the price for accommodation is negotiable it should not cost more than around US$3.50 per person per night. The *alkalo* will also help in providing guides to show you around. Possibilities include a long walk down to the river or a trip in a *pirogue*, either very early in the morning or late in the afternoon, to see the hippos. It's also possible to be taken out during the night by a local hunter who will try his best to spot hyena and warthog (known as 'bushpig' in The Gambia) for you. Although nothing is guaranteed this is an experience not to be missed if you're a real wildlife buff. Another good point is that we have been told that black crowned cranes frequent the area, though we have not seen them there ourselves.

Getting there and away

A bush taxi from Balanguarr in Farafenni, to Bambali, will cost you less than US$1, though they are not very frequent.

Lower River Division

The Lower River Division spreads east from the Bintang Bolon to the Sofaniama Bolon, and occupies only the south bank of the River Gambia. As you head eastwards from the Bintang Bolon, the road is at times very heavily pot-holed and pretty uncomfortable to travel along, though there are some clear patches. The traffic also begins to thin out along this stretch. If you look closely at the surrounding vegetation as you go you will see that it is getting drier. The area immediately east of Bintang Bolon comprises the transition zone between the Guinea savanna that is prevalent nearer the coast, and the Sudan savanna which is the main vegetation type east of here until you reach the far borders of the country. Sudan savanna is generally lower in height than Guinea savanna and made up of a rich mix of small savanna tree species. You will also begin to notice that African oil palms are a less common feature of the countryside from this point on, except for tall groups clustered around wetter areas, such as where *bolons* cross under the road.

The Lower River Division is less crowded with people than the Western Division and there are some huge tracts of land that have few people living in them. One of these areas is Kiang West National Park, and it was this lack of people and the subsequent wildness of the countryside that led to Kiang being established as a national park in 1987. The only large town in the division is Soma. The north-south Trans-Gambian Highway runs through Soma after crossing the River Gambia south of Farafenni. This is a major highway which links northern Senegal to- the Casamance in the south.

THE ROAD EAST TO DUMBUTU

This stretch of road is where some of the worst patches of pot-holes are located so be ready for a bumpy ride. This is also the stretch of road where, for the first time, you get the feeling that you are stepping back into the real Africa, with small villages made of mud-walled and grass-roofed huts lining the way.

Sankandi

Although there is nothing to mark the site, this small village is where two British commissioners were murdered in 1900 during a local uprising. In retribution the British razed the native settlement to the ground in nearby Dumbutu the following year.

Getting there and away

Bush taxis are frequent along the main Banjul to Basse Highway. A bush taxi from Brikama will cost about US$2 to get to Sankandi.

KIANG WEST NATIONAL PARK

Kiang West National Park is located about 145km from Banjul. The entrance is well signposted from the village of Dumbutu, along the main highway, and is

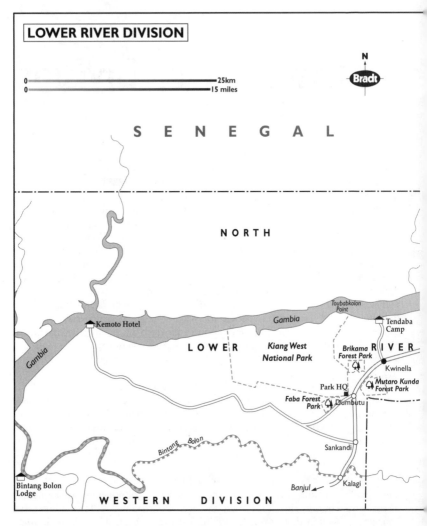

approached along a dirt track from the village. The park was established in 1987, primarily because the area has suffered little from human activities and is probably the best remaining example of wilderness in The Gambia, as well as being a very important reserve for wildlife. The park is huge, covering approximately 110km², and almost all of the major animal species remaining in the country can be found within it.

The park stretches along the southern bank of the River Gambia, taking in some large areas of mangrove forest, creeks, salt pans and tidal flats, but the majority of the protected area consists of dry woodland savanna. Other habitats that are well represented include relict forests, baobab forests and raphia palm, *Raphia palmapinus*, swamps. One outstanding feature is a laterite escarpment running close to and overlooking the river bank. This landmark indicates the past course of the river and provides some marvellous views and wildlife watching.

The wildlife of the park is rich and varied, but it does take some effort to see it,

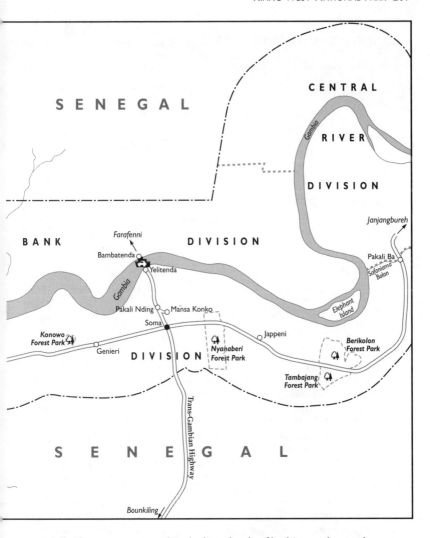

especially if you are more used to the large herds of herbivores that can be seen on the open savanna reserves of East Africa. The most easily seen species are of course the birds and Kiang boasts a range of large and impressive birds of prey with 21 species recorded, including ospreys and African fish eagles along the banks of the river. This is one of the best places to see the enormous and rare martial eagle, long-crested eagle, and the colourful bateleur, *Terathopius ecaudatus*, which has been adopted as the official symbol of the national park. In total over 300 species of birds have been recorded within the area, which is a pretty impressive total and over half of the Gambian bird list. It is worth searching amongst the 'little brown jobs' for the plaintive cisticola, *Cisticola dorsti*, which is very local in the more open parts of woodland. At Kiang, you also have a very good chance of coming across one of the strangest looking birds in The Gambia, the Abyssinian ground hornbill. This is a huge and unmistakable bird that seldom flies. When walking the species looks entirely black but on the few rare occasions when it takes to the air you will see a

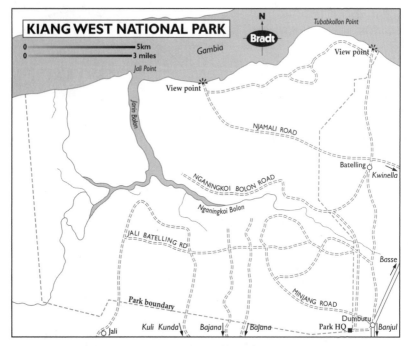

flash of prominent white primary feathers on the wings. The male has bare blue skin around the eyes and bare red skin on the throat and neck, while the female is similar but with blue skin on the face, throat and neck. Usually you will find this species in pairs or small parties, stalking about in open country like some ancient dinosaur. Occasionally they can walk quite close towards you though usually they are fairly shy. In addition there are several Gambian birds that have their strongholds in Kiang West, including white-rumped swift, *Apus caffer*, red-winged pytilia, *Pytilia phoenicoptera*, and brown-rumped bunting, *Emberiza affinis*, and the brown-necked parrot which is listed as a red-data-book species by the International Union for the Conservation of Nature (IUCN).

Mammals are also well represented at Kiang, but not so easily seen as the birds. In fact to the casual visitor they may seem to be very thin on the ground, except of course for the monkeys. The park has numerous troops of callithrix and patas monkeys, western red colobus and Guinea baboons, and these are all active during daylight hours so it shouldn't be too difficult to see them, especially the patas and the baboons. Senegal bushbabies are also common and easy to see during the night. If you are a dedicated mammal-watcher the park can be very productive if you pick the right spot to sit and wait either early in the morning or in the hour or so before it gets dark. One of the best places to do this is along the escarpment that overlooks the river or near one of the watering holes in the park, but check to make sure that it holds water first! This may sound obvious but often you can't tell until you have a close look. A number of species can be observed this way, ranging from the scrub hare, crested porcupine and warthog to antelopes such as bushbuck, various species of duiker, and even the rare and elusive sitatunga. The park also offers a significant natural refuge for carnivores such as genets, banded and marsh mongoose, serval, side-striped jackal, caracal, spotted hyena and leopard. Don't be too disappointed if you don't see any of them though, as all carnivores, especially the larger ones, are extremely shy and very good at remaining hidden from watching eyes. We have heard of only two sightings of leopard in the park in recent years. The last one was in 2000, yet they are certainly resident there and most sightings are not (of course) reported. Still, there's always a chance ….

The River Gambia and the *bolons* that meander through the park are also home to some large mammals including West African manatee, African clawless otter and bottle-nose dolphin. Occasionally even a hippopotamus may stray down to Kiang from the freshwater parts upriver, though this is a rare event. Nile crocodiles are fairly common wherever there is water. In the recent past a herd of large roan antelope has been spotted in the park during the rainy season and it is thought that this herd strays from across the border in Casamance to feed upon the tall grasses that are abundant here.

It is harder to spot wildlife during the rainy season as the grasses are often so tall that you cannot see over them, while all the bushes and trees are covered in leaves. As the dry season sets in, the vegetation gradually dies back or is struck by the park's major problem: bush fire. Probably the best time to visit Kiang is towards the end of the dry season when the ground and trees are mostly bare and you have a far better chance of seeing things, although a visit at any time of the year is sure to produce something of interest.

As we mentioned earlier there are some good spots in the national park that overlook the river. One of these is Toubabkolon Point, which is well signposted from the road leading to Tendaba Camp. It is not on the escarpment but there are a few seats and shelters here from which you can just sit and relax and enjoy the view, in the shade. Following the track westward from Toubabkolon will lead you on to the escarpment and to other viewing places.

As with all the nature reserves and national parks in The Gambia, there is a small entrance fee for visitors (less than US$2.50 for adult non-residents). This should be paid at the park's headquarters along the track from Dumbutu. Here you may also be able to pick up a park ranger who will show you around the park and act as a birding guide.

Getting there and away
It is possible to get to Dumbutu using a bush taxi from Brikama (about US$2.50), or from Soma if you are travelling from upcountry, but from here it is quite a walk to the national park headquarters. An alternative to walking would be to hire a horse- or donkey-cart in Dumbutu to take you the rest of the way. This is also a good way to get local people involved in the park and for them to get something out of your visit, which of course encourages them to help protect the area. In addition **Tendaba Camp** organise jeep excursions into Kiang West National Park, and also to Toubabkolon Point (see later in this chapter for more information). A good idea would be to hire a bird-watching guide and vehicle from the coastal resorts. Then you would have the freedom to explore this large wilderness area more fully.

Where to stay, eat and drink
The headquarters of the national park has modern bungalows that are used to house researchers and volunteers. They can also be hired out to visitors to the park (ring the wildlife department tel: 375888 for more information, ask for the manager of Kiang West or a wildlife conservation officer attached to the directorate, or email: wildlife@gamtel.gm). The construction of a restaurant has stalled due to lack of funds, though it may well be finished by the time you read this book. If you want to camp in the park this can also be arranged through the wildlife department.

The only other sites that are nearby are Tendaba Camp and Kemoto Hotel (see below).

KEMOTO

The **Kemoto Hotel** (tel: 460606; fax: 460252) is in a lovely position on the edge of the river, in a remote and undisturbed part of the country. Unfortunately the hotel was undergoing extensive renovation at the time of writing and its opening date was unknown. Worth a phone call to see if they are up and running.

Getting there and away

It's not possible to get to the Kemoto Hotel using public transport. Your first option is to hire a taxi or car to drive you there, though the access tracks are not tarmac so you will need a four-wheel-drive vehicle. Alternatively, you can go by boat from Bintang Bolon Lodge (see *Chapter 8* for details). But check first to make sure the hotel is open before attempting such a journey.

THE ROAD EAST TO SOMA

The road eastwards begins to get a little better along this stretch, with fewer potholes, though there are still some bad spots. However, the countryside now starts to get both a little drier and more wild looking. This is where you should really start looking out as you drive along for those big birds of prey, either perched in trees by the roadside or soaring overhead.

Kwinella

This small village, apart from being on the junction of the laterite road that leads to Tendaba Camp, is also famous as the site of a fierce battle in 1863 during the Soninke-Marabout wars where about 500 people were slaughtered during the battle.

Getting there and away

Bush taxis are regular along this stretch of the main highway. A bush taxi from Brikama will cost about US$2.50 to Kwinella. GPTC buses (ordinary service) from Banjul and from upcountry stop here.

Tendaba Camp

Tendaba (tel: 465288. Fax: 466180.) is probably the most famous and most frequented of all the camps in The Gambia. It is also the oldest, having been established during the 1970s by a roving Swedish sea captain who used to sail up the river and bring visitors with him. Today it is Gambian owned and can accommodate around 150 people. It sometimes gets very busy during the tourist season, so large groups are advised to book in advance, while small groups and couples will probably find room if they want to risk just turning up. Many people use the camp as a convenient stopover on their way further upcountry.

The camp is situated in the heart of the small village of Tendaba, right on the banks of the River Gambia. Accommodation is simple but clean and well looked after. You have a choice of accommodation, with a bed in a simple bungalow costing US$10 per person. The toilets and showers are located in blocks. If you fancy stepping up a bit in price, then you can stay in the VIP rooms, which have en suite WC, washbasin and shower, plus a TV and video. Video cassettes can be hired for a small charge by asking for the list from the restaurant bar. A VIP room will cost you a little more at US$11.50 per person. You can go one step more and stay in a riverside VIP room. This has the same facilities as a VIP room but additionally has a small balcony looking out on the river. The latter VIP rooms are generally the most peaceful on offer and will cost you US$12 per person. Family suites are also available for US$40.50 per night.

Tendaba Camp has an excellent restaurant where a full range of both European and local dishes is served at reasonable prices. There is also a small bar along a jetty butting out into the river. The bar is called the Bambo Bar, *bambo* being Mandinka for crocodile. This is quite relevant, as there is a small enclosure within the camp where you can see two Nile crocodiles, which are held in captivity. In addition the camp also has a small swimming pool and lounge area for guests (no crocodiles in this one you'll be pleased to note). Entertainment is provided on some evenings by local villagers who come for some music and a dance, which you are free to join if you dare.

The camp organises both boat and jeep excursions. The jeep excursions will take you into nearby Kiang West National Park (see earlier in this chapter) and cost US$7 each for a minimum of six people. We highly recommend the boat trip, especially for keen birders, but also for anyone who fancies a quiet peaceful trip into the mangroves, as this is possibly the best way to see another of The Gambia's protected areas, Bao Bolon Wetland Reserve (see *Chapter 9*). The boat crosses the River Gambia and takes you deep into the *bolons* of the reserve. Here you have a chance of seeing some of the rarest birds in the country, such as the finfoot, which is a small water bird that likes to skulk amongst the roots of the mangroves. White-backed night heron and goliath heron, the largest heron in the world, can be seen along the *bolons*, along with Pel's fishing owl, mouse-brown sunbird and perhaps even a stunning African blue flycatcher. Of course, seeing these species is not guaranteed but you should be able to see at least one of them on every trip. The boat excursion costs US$7 per person for a minimum of four people.

There are also some excellent bird-watching areas around the camp and within easy walking distance. These include the airfield, where birds such as Abyssinian ground hornbill, bateleur, African hawk eagle, *Hieraaetus spilogaster*, four-banded sandgrouse, white-throated bee-eater, *Merops albicollis*, and the highly endangered brown-necked parrot are regularly seen. Rarities here have included saddle-billed stork. There are a few Gambian birding guides based loosely at the camp who will gladly take you around the area and show you the best spots, for a small fee of course.

Getting there and away
Tendaba Camp is easily reached by private taxi from the coastal resorts and every driver knows where it is. Alternatively you can catch a bush taxi from Brikama and ask to be dropped off at Kwinella, for around US$2.50. GPTC buses (ordinary service) also stop at Kwinella from Banjul and from upcountry. From here it is a long, hot walk of about 5km to the camp, so your best option is to hire a horse or donkey cart in Kwinella to take you the rest of the way. Many ground operators also do excursions to the camp, including Gambia River Excursions (see *Organised excursions* in *Chapter 3*).

Genieri
This small Mandinka village has a very interesting history. The village itself was established 900 years ago but the interesting part of its history comes from the Soninke-Marabout wars of the 19th century. This is not so long ago when you consider that the present *alkalo's* grandfather was alive during this period. At this time the village was under fierce attack by Muslim invaders who were led by a man named Foday Kaba. Foday Kaba besieged the village for about 12 months in an effort to get the villagers to convert to the Islamic faith, but they constantly refused

to give up their animist beliefs. At the end of the 12 months most of the villagers were smuggled out to nearby villages, but the elders remained on, adamant that they would fight and would not be taken as slaves. This was despite the fact that they knew the end was inevitable because of the superior forces that they faced. The eventual attack lasted a whole day and the elders defending the village were down to the last of their ammunition, so they killed themselves. All except one old man named Chombai Sanneh.

When the victorious forces of Foday Kaba surged into the village they found this old man sitting inside his compound facing the east. He refused to talk to the conquerors for a while but then told them that he had stayed to wait for them so that he could talk to them. He told them that the other defenders had killed themselves not because they were afraid of the attackers, but because they did not want to become slaves. After delivering this message the old man was killed. The village is today, ironically, a predominantly Muslim village.

During the siege it was said that the villagers threw into the village well their valuables including silver, jewellery, clothing, and according to some accounts, even their children. The well is in the process of being excavated and so far some very exciting finds have been recovered, including gold and silver jewellery, a Queen Victoria shilling, pots, kettles, weapons, tools, *jujus* and extremely high quality carved bone hair-pins. If you want to see the well, you should approach the village *alkalo*, who will be happy to provide a guide and perhaps even regale you with the story of his grandfather.

Getting there and away
A bush taxi from Brikama to Genieri will cost about US$3. If you're travelling in the opposite direction, from Soma, a bush taxi will set you back less than US$0.50.

SOMA AND SURROUNDS
Soma is a busy town located at the junction of the Banjul to Basse Highway and the Trans-Gambian Highway that connects northern Senegal to Casamance. It is basically a large truck stop and there is little of great interest here for tourists, except the large market. It is also a good place to buy food, drink and fuel, and to get those punctured tyres repaired.

Getting there and away
If you're travelling from the west, a bush taxi from Brikama to Soma will cost you about US$3. If you're coming from MacCarthy Island in the east a bush taxi will set you back around US$2. Bush taxis also run north to Pakali Nding (less then US$0.50). A shared taxi from Soma to Palaki Nding is more expensive at US$1–1.50. To go further north to the ferry terminal on the south bank of the River Gambia, at Yelitenda, a bush taxi from Soma will still cost less than US$0.50. If you are thinking of going south into Casamance, a bush taxi to the Senegalese border will also cost you less than US$0.50. All GPTC bus services stop at Soma from Banjul or from upcountry.

Where to stay, eat and drink
There are two establishments where you can find rooms and they both seem pretty clean and well maintained. The first is **Moses Motel** (tel: 531462) in Soma, situated on the left of the Banjul to Basse Highway as you approach the junction. Here you can rent a room for US$4.50–7 per night, and they also cook a range of European and local meals at reasonable prices. Just over 3km north of Soma is the small town of Pakali Nding, and here you can find another small hotel, the

TransGambia Highway Lodge (tel: 531036, 531294 or 531388). The lodge has rooms and huts for US$5-7 per night and again provides a range of European and local meals at reasonable prices.

There is one tourist attraction in Soma and in our view it's definitely worth visiting if you are passing through. This is **Fil's Bendula and Demba's Art Paradise Shop**. *Bendula* is Mandinka for 'meeting place', and the place is owned and managed by Filip de Clerck, a Belgium national who will be happy to chat with you and tell you about his interesting past, which includes running a café in Belgium, living in Senegal and now in The Gambia. The *Fil's Bendula* is a café that sells a variety of African meals, including fish and chicken dishes at very reasonable prices, and of course cold drinks. The café is decorated and furnished in a unique and original fashion and has a good atmosphere, but you'll have to visit it to understand exactly what we mean. Filip is very friendly and it won't take much asking to get him to show you around the place and his garden, with its orchard and home-grown vegetables. He uses the vegetables and fruits from the garden in his cooking and also has fresh mango juice for sale during the mango season. Apart from the café, he also has a small selection of local goods for sale, which he hopes to expand. Located within the compound is **Demba's Art Paradise Shop** which has a variety of wood carvings for sale. Many of the organised tours that pass through Soma stop off at Fil's Bendula.

THE ROAD EAST TO SOFANIAMA BOLON
There's not much of interest along this stretch of the road that you haven't seen already getting this far. You will notice that bush fires are more regular the further east you travel, and that the vegetation is more characteristic of Sudan savanna, with much lower trees than in the moister Guinea savanna.

Pakali Ba
This small village is the last along the main highway before you pass out of Lower River Division and into Central River Division. There used to be a small camp here but it was not operating during our visits through the village, though it may be worth inquiring about in the future. The border between these two administrative divisions is marked by a bridge over the Sofaniama Bolon. The area is worth a brief stop to search for water birds.

Getting there and away
Bush taxis are regular along the main highway. A bush taxi running east from Soma to Pakali Ba will cost around US$1. GPTC buses (ordinary service) from Banjul and from upcountry also stop at Pakali Ba.

African civet

Central River Division

The Central River Division is the first of the administrative divisions to cover both the north and south banks of the River Gambia. On the north bank it extends from Balanghar Ker Nderry in the west, through the larger towns of Kau-ur and Kuntaur to Sami Wharf Town in the east, where it shares its border with Upper River Division (URD). On the south bank it extends from the Sofaniama Bolon through Kudang and the larger town of Bansang to Santantu Buba, where again it shares its border with URD. In the middle of the River Gambia lies the old trading town of Janjangbureh, still known by many as Georgetown, or MacCarthy Island. The division covers a large area of contrasts. In the north the land is dry, very hilly and covered by Sudan savanna, where it has not been cleared for agriculture. There are no tarmac roads linking towns and the roads consist totally of either laterite or sandy tracks. These are very dusty in the dry season, and sometimes difficult to navigate, even in four-wheel-drive vehicles, during the rainy season. The land on the south bank is dry too and also has a covering of Sudan savanna, though it is heavily farmed in places. However, the transport situation is much better and the main road through the countryside is tarmac and in good condition. In contrast to the general dryness of the land the River Gambia dominates the central strip of the division. In the west, upriver to Kau-ur, the river is affected by salt water intrusion from the Atlantic Ocean, but east of Kau-ur it consists of fresh water flowing from the east. This is not a hard and fast rule as the limit of saline intrusion varies between seasons, for example in the rainy season the greater volume of fresh water flowing downriver from the east pushes back the salt water further to the west. There are also many large areas of low-lying land along the river valley that become flooded during the rainy season, and a few of these keep their water through the dry season, though they do tend to shrink in size. Some of these swamps have been turned over to rice growing but a few remain almost pristine.

The freshwater stretches of the River Gambia are very different from the salt water stretches. Mangroves do not survive in fresh water and are replaced here by patches of gallery and swamp forests along the river banks, although much of these forests have been cleared for firewood and to make way for agriculture. However there are a number of large islands in the river, and although a few of them have been cleared and are used for growing various crops, some of them (in particular the Baboon Islands and Kajakat Island) have retained their covering of dense gallery forest and are havens for wildlife. The rarity of this type of habitat has been recognised by the government and the Baboon Islands now form a national park and receive high protection.

There is also a lot of history in Central River Division, extending from the old trading post of Georgetown, which had been a collection point for the transportation of slaves to the New World colonies, to the stone circles that dot the landscape and whose origins are lost in the distant past.

KAU-UR AND SURROUNDS ON THE NORTH BANK OF THE RIVER GAMBIA

This is a large village that again does not cater for the tourist trade in any way, but does have a few points of interest for visitors in the surrounding countryside.

Getting there and away

Fairly regular bush taxis run east from Balanguarr in Farafenni to Kau-ur, and will cost you less than US$1 for the journey, or run west from Janjangbureh for about US$1.50.

Belel Forest Park

This small forest park is probably the best example of Sudan savanna woodland on the whole of the north bank. Located south of and adjacent to the main road, about 5km to the west of Kau-ur, it is easily accessible and worth a visit at any time of the year. The forest is made up of a wonderfully rich mixture of small savanna trees and bushes with the occasional huge baobab tree dotted amongst them. During the dry season it is easy to wander about between the trees though this will be harder in the wet season when the ground flora is growing. The birdlife in this forest is phenomenal. We have seen many kinds of raptors, francolins, black-headed plover, doves, white-faced scops owl, *Otus leucotis*, striped kingfisher, *Halcyon chelicuti*, rollers, bee-eaters, parakeets, parrots and various glossy starlings here: the list is almost endless. Though we haven't seen them ourselves, Savile's bustard, *Eupodotis savilei*, and the chestnut-crowned sparrow-weaver, *Plocepasser superciliosus*, have also been recorded here. The former was first added to the Gambian list in 1994, which just goes to show that the north bank of the River Gambia can still hold some pleasant surprises for birders.

Kau-ur stone circle

About 2km west of Kau-ur is a sign along the main road that shows the way to Genge Wolof School. Go north along the small dirt track and pass through the first two small hamlets. About 100m past the second hamlet and about 75m east of the track is a small stone circle beneath a tree, though you have to be alert to spot it (we passed it a few times without seeing it). This is the first easily found stone circle along the road but it is not as big or well-known as the circles at Ker Batch or Wasu (see later in this chapter). Local folklore has it that this stone circle was formed from a wedding party that was turned to stone.

Kau-ur swamp

About 1km west of Kau-ur, where another small *bolon* crosses beneath the road, is a small swamp that keeps its water throughout most of the dry season. It is worth looking at this site, especially early in the morning, to see what birds are about. We have seen white-faced whistling ducks, little bittern, *Ixobrychus minutus*, greater painted snipe, malachite kingfisher, *Alcedo cristata*, and a variety of waders here. One special bird that sometimes makes an appearance at the edge of the swamp is the magnificent purple swamphen. This site has had some very rare birds turn up at it, including Egyptian plover, *Pluvianus aegyptius*, and large flocks of collared pratincoles, *Glareola pratincola*.

BETWEEN KAU-UR AND KUNTAUR

The main road between Kau-ur and Kuntaur is a continuation of the laterite road which passes through a mixture of agricultural land and yet more Sudan savanna. The road heads steadily northeastwards towards the Senegalese border that in

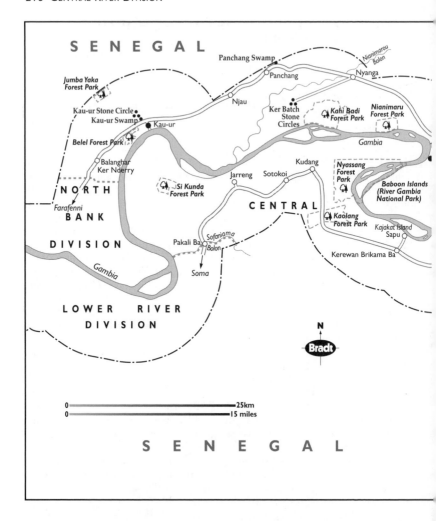

places is only a short walk away. In the villages along the way there is a mixture of Gambian and Senegalese who regularly cross the border in both directions. This is reflected in the languages that are used here, with French even more commonly spoken than English.

Panchang swamp

About 25km east of Kau-ur and 1km east of the village of Panchang is a wonderful swamp where yet another *bolon* crosses beneath the road. There is a large pool here at the side of the road that usually keeps its water throughout the dry season. This is a great place for birdwatching and it's worth spending some time here to search for elusive species amongst the vegetation. The pool holds populations of herons and egrets, African jacana, long-tailed cormorant, *Phalacrocorax africanus*, white-faced whistling duck and black-winged stilt. If you are lucky you may even spot some delightful African pygmy geese, *Nettapus auritus*, whose stronghold is in the swamps and pools of Central River Division. This species can be found here all

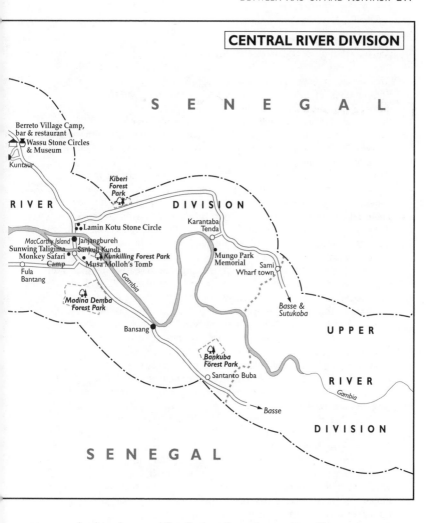

CENTRAL RIVER DIVISION

SENEGAL

Berreto Village Camp, bar & restaurant
Wassu Stone Circles & Museum
Kuntaur

RIVER

Kiberi Forest Park

DIVISION

Lamin Kotu Stone Circle

Karantaba Tenda

MacCarthy Island — Janjangbureh
Sunwing Taligima — Sankuli Kunda
Monkey Safari — Kunkilling Forest Park
Camp — Musa Molloh's Tomb
Fula Bantang

Mungo Park Memorial
Sami Wharf town

Gambia

Madina Demba Forest Park

Basse & Sutukoba

UPPER

Bansang

Bankuba Forest Park
Santanto Buba

RIVER

Gambia

Basse

DIVISION

SENEGAL

year round, though especially during the rainy season. You may even see uncommon gems such as Allen's gallinule.

Getting there and away

Bush taxis from both directions are fairly regular along the main road that runs through the site. A bush taxi from Kau-ur to Panchang will cost less than US$1.

Ker Batch stone circles

About another 15km further east, after crossing the Nianimarou Bolon, you come across the village of Nyanga where there are two signposts pointing the way southwest towards Ker Batch stone circles. One sign says the circles are 7km away while another says they are 9km. We found that the latter was closer to the truth. The way is along a sandy dirt track that is soft in places and would be best travelled in a four-wheel-drive car or a cart. It is well signposted all of the

GAMBIAN STONE CIRCLES

Gambian stone circles extend from Farafenni in the west to beyond Basse in the east, and are part of a much larger complex of stone circles that extends northwards through Senegal to the River Saloum. The number of stones in the circles varies from ten to 24 and the diameter of the circles varies from 4m to 6–7m. The area within the stone circles normally displays a slightly domed rise, usually constructed of sand, though a few mounds are topped with laterite pebbles, presumably to stop erosion. A common feature of many of the circles is a line of pillars set away from the circle on the eastern side. In the case of the site at Wassu, where the circles form a line from south to north, these alignments of stone form a line that is continuous to the east. In some sites there are no circles but only single pillars. In others there are just single circles while in still others there are large groups of circles. In general the circles appear to be associated with either single or multiple burials. In Senegal some of these burials seem to have been made from bodies simply thrown into pits, perhaps after a battle or an epidemic disease. In other sites it looks as though the people were buried alive as sacrifices. Generally the bodies are poorly adorned, often with only a bracelet for decoration and with a weapon, usually a spear, laid beside the body. Sometimes there are also some pottery vessels found by the bodies, usually turned upside down. The stones were cut from quarries close to the sites and set vertically into pre-dug pits. Most stones are fairly small, ranging from only 0.75m, but some are much larger at 3m tall. Carbon dating has aged the stone circles from AD400 to AD1000 in the Iron Age. This is in comparison to 1200BC, which is the latest date for the very much earlier stone circles of Europe. It is interesting to note that the Senegambian stone circles all flank freshwater rivers and *bolons*, suggesting that the people that erected them were probably farmers who lived on the fertile plains by these water courses. At the present time it is unknown who the builders of the stone circles actually were, but some historians believe it to be the Jola people, who are also thought to be the ethnic group that has lived the longest in The Gambia. Certainly the stones were laid prior to the arrival of Islam in the country.

way. There are quite a few impressive stone circles at Ker Batch, all close together, and one stone in particular, the lyre stone, is the only one of its kind in The Gambia, though others are found in Senegal (see the *Gambian Stone Circles* above. This stone is shaped like a large 'V' but has broken in the past and has now been repaired with cement. There are also a number of dilapidated buildings on site which seem to hold promise of interpretation although it turns out that they are completely empty, save for some toilets that are still operational. The buildings have become home to a single slit-faced bat that allowed us to get a pretty close look at it, although we couldn't identify it down to species level. The watchman at the site lives in the nearby village, but although he was very friendly he unfortunately couldn't speak a word of English (we later learned from the guide at Wassu that he is from Guinea Bissau). We also found that visitors appear to be the entertainment for the local kids who arrived in droves to follow us quietly

STORIES CONCERNING THE GAMBIAN STONE CIRCLES

There are many stories concerning the origins of Gambian stone circles, ranging from them being built by giants, or being the burial places of kings. Many people imagine that the circles are the home to spirits, either benign or evil. Others think that because Europeans visit the circles they must know what they contain. If you want to learn more about these interesting monuments and stories then you should get hold of a copy of *Historic Sites of The Gambia – an official guide to the monuments and sites of The Gambia* (see *Appendix 2, Further Information*). This is an excellent and well-written guide that contains many fascinating insights into the history of the stone circles and many other Gambian sites as well.

around the stones. They were also a very friendly bunch who did not hassle us but were merely curious to see the *toubabs*. There is a small fee payable (US$1) for entrance to the site.

Getting there and away

A bush taxi to Nyanga from Kau-ur will cost US$1. From here it's either a long walk or you can hire a horse or donkey cart in the village to take you the rest of the way to Ker Batch. Bush taxis from Janjangbureh are also fairly regular along the main road.

WASSU STONE CIRCLES AND MUSEUM

The stone circle site at Wassu is the most famous in the whole country and contains some very impressive stones. One of them is at least 3m in height. There are a lot of circles in the grounds and they are accompanied by a good museum that is laid out very well with models, photographs, paintings and plenty of interpretation. This makes all the difference and really helps to bring the history of the stone circles to life. The official guide at the site stays on until late in the afternoon as he knows that it is a long journey to get there and that visitors often turn up later than office hours. He was very friendly and helpful; he has his own interesting theories on the origin of the circles and their spiritual meaning.

Getting there and away

This site is now well known in the area, and just about everyone will be able to show you how to get there. Many of the camps at Janjangbureh organise excursions to Wassu (see later in this chapter for details). Alternatively you can catch a bush taxi from Kau-ur, if you are travelling from the west, which will cost around US$1.50. If you are coming east from Janjangbureh, a bush taxi will cost you US$0.50 from Lamin Koto on the north bank of the river. The museum and stone circles are well signposted from the main road.

Where to stay and eat

The only accommodation appears to be **Berreto Village Camp, Bar and Restaurant** which is signposted from the museum. This camp has rooms for a very reasonable US$3.50 per person per night, though they do not have any electricity. At the time of writing the camp was in the process of being developed, and the restaurant had not yet been constructed, so meals were only available if booked well in advance. However, by the time you read this the restaurant should be up and running.

BABOON ISLANDS (RIVER GAMBIA NATIONAL PARK)

Baboon Islands (also officially known as the River Gambia National Park) is a collection of five islands in the River Gambia, south of Kuntaur and around 300km from Banjul by road. The islands cover about 5.85km² and are densely cloaked in gallery forest with some open patches of swamp and moist savanna. The national park was gazetted in 1978 and is jointly managed by the Department of Parks and Wildlife Management (DPWM) and the Chimpanzee Rehabilitation Project (CRP).

The wildlife of the islands is not that well known except for the mammals, which include warthogs, baboons, callithrix monkeys, western red colobus, aardvark, ratel, serval, genets, bushbuck, Maxwell's duiker and common duiker, *Sylvicapra grimmia*. In the freshwater of the River Gambia around the islands live good populations of African clawless otter, West African manatee and Nile crocodile. Snakes and lizards are also well represented and a small satellite island is the nesting site for thousands of birds, especially herons, egrets, cormorants and sacred ibis, *Thrskiornis aethiopicus*.

Baboon Islands' main claim to fame is that they are home to nearly 61 chimpanzees that have been rehabilitated to the wild and released. These chimpanzees were originally illegally-held captive animals confiscated from international traders all over West Africa and overseas. The captive chimpanzees (many of which were babies) undergo a complete retraining course in foraging for wild food, building nests and responding to predators etc. This retraining is a long-term process, needing much time, care and perseverance by the staff of the CRP, which is headed by Dr Janice Carter and Stella Brewer. This project has proved to be a resounding success and has led not only to the rehabilitated animals adapting successfully to living in the wild, but also to the birth of over 37 young and totally wild chimpanzees. Indeed the project has done so well that even chimpanzees of a third generation have now been born into the population.

Unfortunately for tourists (but fortunately for the chimps), the Baboon Islands park is not open to the public and permission to visit the national park must be sought first from the director of the DPWM. There are several reasons for this. The most important is protecting the welfare of the chimpanzees, which can be undermined by exposure to humans. Secondly, there is a very real danger that they will contract illnesses from humans for which they have no natural immunity. Finally, these apes are several times stronger than people and due to past mistreatment, some of them are liable to become aggressive and potentially very dangerous when over-stressed by the presence of humans. Even the staff of the national park do not set foot on the islands, but are based on the bank of the river.

The CRP, as another integral part of its work in saving chimpanzees, operates a successful education programme in the surrounding villages. They not only teach about the chimpanzees but also raise general awareness about conservation of the environment.

Getting there and away

Although the River Gambia National Park (including part of the river itself) is closed to all visitors, there is a navigable channel that passes a few of the islands. Boat trips to view the islands are available from several camps (see *Janjangbureh, MacCarthy Island and surrounds* in this chapter), but it has to be stressed that your chances of seeing any of the chimpanzees are very slim and the boats are not allowed to approach the islands. In fact they *must* (by law) stay in the centre of the navigable channel and the River Gambia National Park has guardboats stationed on the river to make sure that this rule is adhered to.

All things considered you are probably better off visiting other and closer islands, such as Kajakat, on boat trips (see below), rather than paying out a large sum of money for a long boat trip with little chance of seeing chimpanzees at the end of it.

KAJAKAT ISLAND

This is a large island, like many others along the river, with intact forest cover that has never been cut down. The reason for the island's escape from deforestation is that local folklore has it that spirits inhabit the island. If you get a boat from Janjangbureh and pass the island you will see that it looks pretty impenetrable. You also have a very good chance of seeing the family of hippos that live in the river around the island and also some of the rich birdlife in the area. Sometimes a large flock of knob-billed duck, *Sarkidiornis melanotos*, roosts in the trees on the south side of the island. Please do not try to land on Kajakat as it would be a shame to see it put under undue pressure from visitors. Be happy that it still exists and with the view you can have of it from a boat.

Getting there and away

Boats can be hired from nearly all of the camps at Janjangbureh (see later in this chapter) to take you around the island to see the hippos. Small fishing *pirogues* can also be hired from Sapu on the south bank of the river for negotiable prices.

JANJANGBUREH, MACCARTHY ISLAND AND SURROUNDS

Janjangbureh used to be known as Georgetown and this is still a commonly used name for the town. The town is located on a large island in the River Gambia known as MacCarthy Island. It was once a busy and thriving centre for commerce when big ships still used to sail as far upstream as the island, but it is now rather a sleepy place with a very laid back atmosphere. One good thing that will please visitors to Janjangbureh is that you can walk the streets here with very little hassle, especially compared to the tourist areas on the coast. You may get a few children asking for pens or sweets but even these tend to give up after only one or two tries. This is in spite of the fact that the town, the island and the surrounding area is perhaps the most popular place for visitors to stay when they are travelling upcountry. One exception to this lack of hassle is a large dilapidated warehouse near the northern ferry terminal on the island. This is fêted as a former slave house and for a small 'donation' local youths will show you around the place, including the damp, dark cellars where slaves were chained and fed through holes in the walls. Unfortunately this is probably all a scam, as it seems likely that the warehouse postdates the slave era. It can be intimidating when large well-built young men take you down into the cellar and hassle you for money, so be warned. More research is needed to ascertain whether the 'slave house' really did house slaves. Certainly the chains attached to one wall of the cellar are obviously new and are not very convincing, even though Georgetown was definitely used as a staging post at one point to hold slaves.

Getting there and away

Approaching Janjangbureh on the north bank of the river from the west, you can take a bush taxi from Kau-ur, which will cost you around US$2 or from Kuntaur for US$0.50. On the south bank of the river a bush taxi from Basse in the east will cost US$1. GPTC buses (ordinary service) from Banjul and from upcountry stop

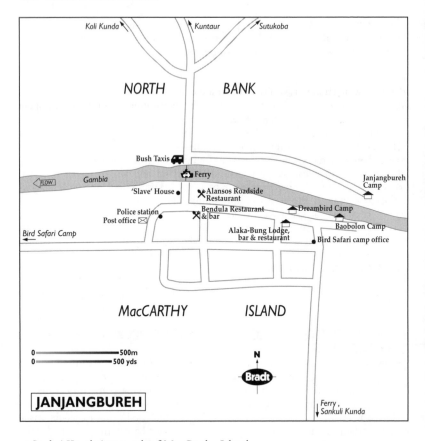

Koli Kunda   Kuntaur   Sutukoba

NORTH   BANK

Bush Taxis

Ferry   Janjangbureh
Camp

FLOW   Gambia

'Slave' House   Alansos Roadside
Restaurant

Police station   Bendula Restaurant   Dreambird Camp
Post office   & bar
Bird Safari Camp   Baobolon Camp
Alaka-Bung Lodge,   Bird Safari camp office
bar & restaurant

MacCARTHY   ISLAND

0 ━━━━━━ 500m
0 ━━━━━━ 500 yds

N

Bradt

JANJANGBUREH   Ferry ,
Sankuli Kunda

at Sankei Kunda just south of MacCarthy Island.

The ferry from MacCarthy Island to the north bank of the river runs between 08.00–18.30. It costs US$3 to take a car across but much less than US$0.50 if you cross as a foot passenger. The ferry from MacCarthy Island to the south bank of the river runs at the same times as the northern ferry. It is slightly cheaper for a car to cross at US$2 on this ferry and again is very cheap for a foot passenger. It will cost you less than US$0.50 in a bush taxi from the town to the ferry. There is also a small foot ferry that runs from the western tip of MacCarthy Island to Tumani Fatty on the south bank of the river.

Where to stay

There is a large choice of camps and lodges in which to stay at Janjangbureh. Probably the best camp in the area is the **Bird Safari Camp** (tel: 676108; fax: 674004; email: bsc@gamtel.gm; web: www.bsc.gm). This is a British-owned camp located about seven minutes' drive from the town (according to the accurate signposts which mark the way). The office for the camp is located on the eastern side of the town, while the camp itself is located near to the western tip of the island, hidden in the bush and right by the river. This is a friendly and relaxed camp and the staff are very helpful and do not give you the hassle that you may receive at some of the others. Accommodation is in 12 very good cottages, each with a double and single bed, ceiling fans, locally made furniture, shower, washbasin and WC. An innovative feature of the cottages is a lockable stowaway closet beneath each bed in which you can store away your more expensive items of luggage in safety. Power is from a generator that provides electricity from 19.00 to midnight. You can have your laundry done here for between US$0.50–1.50 per item, which includes washing and ironing. There is even a 12m swimming pool that may seem strange as you're in the middle of the bush but take our word for it, it is very refreshing to take a swim in the pool after a hot morning spent birdwatching. A single B&B will cost you US$19, a double US$32.50 and a triple US$42.50. Alternatively, you can sleep in the camp's one-man tents for US$10 per night (including bedding), or pitch your own at about US$5 per person. The last two prices include access to a shower and toilets plus free access to the swimming pool. All volunteers, such as APSO, VSO or Peace Corps members get a 10% discount. The camp does not accept credit cards, but any international currency or travellers' cheques are welcome, though they do admit that their exchange rate is poor compared to the rate at the coastal resorts and they advise you to pay in the local currency. The camp is aptly named as they have a wide variety of birds living wild in the camp, including up to seven species of owl, which is quite remarkable. Special birds include swamp flycatcher, *Muscicapa aquatica*, yellow-throated leaflove, *Chlorocichla flavicollis*, and Wilson's indigobird, *Vidua wilsoni*, which differs from the common village indigobird, *V. chalybeata*, by having white instead of red legs. They used to burn their rubbish at the camp until they realised that it was attracting some large Nile monitors, so now they leave the rubbish in a tip a short distance away so that the monitors can scavenge what they want from it. At the time of our visit here there were at least five large monitors that visited regularly. Hippos, Nile crocodiles and even West African manatees have all been seen around this end of MacCarthy Island, though you have to be extremely lucky to spot any of them. One animal that you have a much better chance of seeing is a roosting yellow-winged bat in the trees by the river. Ask a member of staff to show you where you can find these wonderful orange-yellow and blue-grey bats.

Janjangbureh Camp (tel: 495526) on the north of the river opposite Janjangbureh, has a different atmosphere from Bird Safari Camp, although this too is a very relaxing place. The accommodation is of a lower standard and is more local in origin, but still comfortable, though we found the huts to be rather dark and dingy inside even during the day. Each bed comes with a mosquito bednet. There is no power here and lighting is from kerosene lamps. The staff are still helpful but we found that some of them are quite prepared to hassle you for extra money which can be very annoying when you are just trying to relax. However, prices here are very reasonable at US$7.50 per person for one night. The camp is just a short walk away from the northern ferry terminal and again is ideally placed right on the river bank. One feature of the camp is the troop of callithrix monkeys which hang around the restaurant. These monkeys are quite fearless and will readily try to steal the food off your plate so take care and keep a good eye open. There is a sign asking visitors not to feed the monkeys around the restaurant area but unfortunately the monkeys can't read. On our visit to the camp we saw a single western red colobus in the trees with the callithrix and presumably there are more around.

Dreambird Camp is located on the shore of MacCarthy Island opposite Janjangbureh Camp and is owned by the same people. Accommodation and prices are similar at this camp though there is no restaurant and you have to be ferried across the river by the camp's boat to take your meals in the main camp. This is not an unpleasant journey and so is of no real inconvenience.

Baobolon Camp (tel: 676133 or 676151; fax 676120 – mark for the attention of Baobolon Camp) is located on the eastern edge of Janjangbureh and is completely different in atmosphere to the previous camps described. This camp can accommodate around 80-90 people in good clean huts with shower, WC, washbasin, stand fan and mosquito window nets (rooms are also sprayed every day to kill any mosquitoes that get in). They have VIP rooms that are larger and have their own fridge. Ordinary rooms cost US$7 per night and the VIP rooms cost US$20.50. Power is from the town but they also have their own generator. Water is from a bore-hole and is said to be drinkable though you should be careful and drink bottled water. For large groups entertainment is laid on with local dancers.

Alaka-bung Lodge, Bar and Restaurant (tel: 676123) is located in the heart of the town and again is very different in character. There are five double rooms with shower, washbasin, WC, fan and mosquito window nets. Power is from the town but there is also a standby generator. Five more single rooms were under construction when we visited the lodge. Its best to book a room in advance but you can turn up and get a room if they are available. Double rooms cost US$11 per night and the singles will cost US$5.50 per night when completed. This lodge also lays on cultural entertainment from various different ethnic groups such as Mandinka, Fula and Wolof, and can provide training in drumming, dancing and some local crafts.

Where to eat and drink

There are a couple of cheap places to eat in Janjangbureh, namely **Bendula Restaurant and Bar** and **Alansos Roadside Restaurant**, where meals can be had for around US$1–3. Other restaurants are found in the various camps around the town. **Bird Safari Camp** has a pleasant restaurant that offers breakfast at less than US$3, lunch at around US$4 and dinner at around US$6. There are fixed meals when there is a group for dinner, when there is always a vegetarian alternative. You should also be able to order something else if the set meal is not to your taste. **Janjangbureh Camp** and **Dreambird Camp** both use the restaurant in Janjangbureh Camp on the north bank of the river. Breakfast costs US$3.50, salads, sandwiches or chips US$1.50–2.50, and a choice of western or Gambian main meals between US$2.50–5. You also have a choice of joining in the buffet dinner, if there are enough people in the camp, for US$6. Remember to watch out for those thieving monkeys though.

Baobolon Camp (see above) has a large indoor restaurant, or you can eat outside around the *bantaba* (meeting place). A continental breakfast with eggs and omelette will cost less than US$3, sandwiches are US$2, European or Gambian main meals are US$3–3.50 or you can join the buffet dinner for US$5. Desserts are US$1–2, and, just in case you are suffering from withdrawal symptoms, there is a TV in the restaurant. **Alaka-bung Lodge, Bar and Restaurant** also has a pleasant indoor restaurant where you can have breakfast for less than US$3, with tea or coffee costing a little extra, and European or Gambian main meals at between US$2–4.50.

Things to do

From MacCarthy Island it is very easy to take a boat trip. **Bird Safari Camp** offers trips around MacCarthy Island for US$51 (for the boat). They also offer a 2–3 hour trip down the river to Kajakat Island (see above). Here you have a very good chance of seeing the hippos that live around the island, or even a Nile crocodile hauled out on to the river bank. The birdlife along the way is also rich. This trip costs US$51 for the hire of the boat and crew. They can also organise a trip even further upriver to Baboon Islands but you need to get permission from the wildlife department first (see *Baboon Islands* in this chapter). **Janjangbureh Camp** also hires out boats. A small motorboat per day costs US$54.50, or US$12 per hour. A larger *pirogue* costs US$205 per day or US$24 per hour. Trips around MacCarthy Island cost US$30.50, to Baboon Islands US$68–205 depending on the size of the boat, and to Sankuli Kunda between US$26–51. In addition they hire out kayaks for US$17 per day or US$3.50 per hour. **Baobolon Camp** also organises boat excursions at US$34 for four hours. In addition they have an evening boat excursion to the end of the island where you stay and have tea or coffee. **Alaka-bung Lodge, Bar and Restaurant** will organise any of the above-mentioned boat trips at negotiable prices, plus trips to local villages to sample the culture.

Birdwatching is one of the main reasons why tourists visit the island, and most of the camps run birdwatching trips on foot with local guides. With **Bird Safari Camp** this will cost you US$13.50 per group for a two hour walk. **Baobolon Camp** is managed by two very enthusiastic local birders, Laurence and Abdoulie. They do a night walk to see owls and nightjars, which they attract by playing a tape of their calls. Several species have been seen on this walk including Pel's fishing owl, though the latter is only rarely encountered. Prices for this walk vary. If there is a large group of ten people it will cost US$3.50 each. If there are as few as two people it will cost them about US$5 each. They also run birdwatching trips to Sapu rice fields that cost US$13.50 for the guide, plus you have to pay for your transport (which can be by boat or vehicle, or a mixture of both).

MacCarthy Island is also a convenient stepping stone for a trip to see the stone circles and museum at Wassu. **Baobolon Camp** will give you a guide for US$1 who will help you catch a bush taxi to Wassu, which should cost around US$0.50 each. **Bird Safari Camp** can also arrange tours to Wassu, Mungo Park Memorial or into Janjangbureh. **Alaka-bung Lodge, Bar and Restaurant** will take you to Bansang to exchange money there for no fee except the guide's fare. You only tip the guide if you want to.

Alaka-bung Lodge, Bar and Restaurant is managed by Mr Sulayman Faal, a local artist. You can buy some of his excellent work from the adjacent art gallery. He will readily organise workshops in tie and dye, batik making or printing. He also offers training on playing local drums. All of these workshops are at negotiable rates depending on your length of stay and the number of people wishing to attend.

Places to visit
Lamin Kotu Stone Circle is a small stone circle that is within easy walking distance (about 1.3km) of the north ferry terminal at Janjangbureh. It is along the road leading to Wassu, on the eastern edge, under a big tree. If you've already seen the stone circles at Wassu, you probably won't want to bother with this one, which is pretty small by comparison. If you don't fancy the long drive to Wassu, but still want to see a stone circle, then visiting Lamin Kotu could be a good compromise.

Sunwing Taligima Monkey Safari Camp is a new venture set up by local entrepreneurs, but we're not sure whether it will attract enough visitors to survive. You will find it signposted on the south bank of the river, and it is about 1km away in the countryside. When we visited there was nothing but a grass-roofed *bantaba* in the bush, almost, but not quite, overlooking a small *bolon*. The proprietor is Mr Konko Trawally, who will lead you on guided walks through the bush, where he says you have a good chance of seeing a range of monkeys and perhaps a warthog. Prices for his services are negotiable. This is a small operation but worth supporting if you have the time, as it's a good way for local people to make money out of the wildlife around them and to encourage them to look after it.

MUNGO PARK MEMORIAL

Close to the village of Karantaba Tenda, about 30km east of Janjangbureh, is a memorial pillar erected to the memory of Mungo Park. He was a Scottish explorer who stayed close to this spot in 1795, while he learned several local languages and prepared for a trip into the interior to search for the source of the River Niger. After he set off, with just a few donkeys and servants for company, he had a fascinating journey and faced many hardships, including being captured and then escaping, but he failed to find the source of the river. When he eventually returned to Britain, he wrote a book entitled: *Travels in the interior of Africa*, which was an instant best seller for its time. In 1801, he returned to The Gambia and set off again, this time with a large force of army deserters. Many of his force died along the way and he and the remainder of his men later died in eastern Nigeria. The pillar commemorates the spot from which he set out on his last ill-fated expedition. For a small fee local children will be happy to guide you to the pillar, which is within walking distance (about 1.5km) of the village.

Getting there and away

A bush taxi from the north bank of the river at Janjangbureh to Karantaba Tenda costs about US$1. Alternatively, many of the camps in Janjangbureh will arrange either a boat or vehicle-based trip to see the memorial.

THE ROAD EAST TO BANSANG
ON THE SOUTH BANK OF THE RIVER GAMBIA

This road is tarmac but less pot holed than the road through Lower River Division. The section from Janjangbureh eastwards is very good apart from a bad part going through Bansang. There is little of great interest here apart from a few forest parks and *bolons* that sit astride the road, though one or two places are worth stopping at, the first of which is the village of Jarreng.

Jarreng

Jarreng is about 14km east of the Sofaniama Bolon, which marks the border between Lower River Division and Central River Division. This is a small village well-known for its market, which deals mainly in furniture made from cane and raffia. Some real bargains can be had here though transporting a cane bed base on the airplane home might be difficult. Still, even if you're not buying, it's very interesting to watch a craftsman at work and to see how the furniture is made. From the village it is only about 2km north to the River Gambia, where it is possible, after some hard bargaining, to hire a *pirogue* and boatman to explore the part of the river lying near to Papa Island. There is always the chance of spotting hippos along this stretch of the river but do not try and get your boatman to go too close. Remember that these animals are wild and particularly big, the males sometimes reaching weights of over 3,000kg. In January 2001 there was a horrific accident at Kuntaur, about 35km further upstream. The accident involved a hippo and a canoe that held 13 people. The boat overturned and seven of the occupants were drowned.

Getting there and away

Compared to the main road on the north bank of the river, bush taxis are more frequent on the Banjul to Basse Highway on the south bank. A bush taxi from Soma to Jarreng will cost about US$1. GPTC buses (ordinary service) from Banjul and from upcountry stop at Jarreng.

Kaolang Forest Park

This large forest park lies astride the road around eight kilometres east of Kudang. It is typical of the Sudan savanna woodland that was once the natural vegetation cover of all of this region but suffers badly from bush fires in the dry season. It's worth exploring if you have the time.

Sapu rice fields

About 23km east of Kudang is a road-sign for Sapu Agricultural Station. The site itself is about another three kilometres northwards along a laterite track. This area has long been known as one of the birding hotspots of this part of The Gambia, and has a rich mixture of habitats including agricultural land, rice fields and gallery forest along the riverbank. There have been some good birds recorded here, including the rare and elusive Pel's fishing owl, and during the rainy season this is also a good place to find the black coucal, *Centropus grillii*. Other species to keep an eye open for are swamp flycatcher in the trees bordering the river and African finfoot. White-backed vultures, *Gyps africanus*, often fly overhead.

Getting there and away

Organised trips to the area are operated by **Baobolon Camp** in Janjangbureh (see this chapter). These trips are by boat, vehicle, or a mixture of the two. Alternatively, bush taxis from Soma to Kerewan Brikama Ba, which is the nearest village on the main highway, will cost about US$1.50. To reach Kerewan Brikama Ba from MacCarthy Island in the east will cost less than US$0.50. From the highway it is 3km to Sapu, which you can either walk or travel in style on a horse- or donkey-cart hired from the village.

Where to stay

Sapu Rest House (tel: 678073 – ask for Mr Sulayman Jallow) is a government rest house that will also let tourists stay. It's situated close to the agricultural station and the river, so just ask for directions. The rooms are clean and cost US$7 per person per night. The power is on nightly from 19.00 to midnight and the water is on from 07.00–09.00 and 17.00–20.00. There is a shared lounge area and kitchen where you can cook your own meals.

Fula Bantang

This village is much the same as many others that you have passed and will pass as you travel upcountry, though at the time of writing it was the site of a large group of nesting Marabou storks, *Leptoptilos crumeniferus*. These birds, along with yellow-billed storks, nest high in the tops of baobab, white-flowered silk-cotton, and mango trees. Marabous nest between October and April and yellow-billed storks during the rainy season. However, do not be surprised if they are not there when you go through Fula Bantang, as these species regularly move their nesting sites by a few kilometres to other villages. Therefore it's worth searching the tall trees at all of the villages you pass through in Central River Division.

Getting there and away

Bush taxis regularly ply the main highway through the village. A bush taxi from Soma will cost less than US$1.

Musa Molloh's Tomb

A Muslim Fula, Musa Molloh Balde, was a famous and renowned warrior and leader of his people, as well as being capable of skilful diplomacy when dealing with both the British and French colonial powers. Born in the 19th century, he was the son of Alfa Molloh, the founding king of the Empire of Fulada, which stretched southwards from the River Gambia into Guinea Bissau. In 1884 he himself became king of the empire, after the death of both his father and uncle, and fought many wars against exiled Soninke Marabouts (see *Chapter 1*). In 1902, after he had handed over control of British Fuladu to the government of The Gambia in the previous year, the British part of his empire was incorporated into the colony. At the time he was still engaged in the slave trade which was banned by a British ordinance in the same year. He settled in Kesser Kunda in 1904 but was exiled by the British to Sierra Leone in 1919, because they did not appreciate his continuing autocratic behaviour. In 1923 he was allowed to return to The Gambia, though he was not allowed to hold any political power, and he died in Kesser Kunda in 1931. In 1971 his tomb was renovated and in 1974 it was declared a national monument. The present tomb was built in 1987 in collaboration with the Government of Senegal.

Getting there and away
About 1km east of where you turn off the main highway towards Sankuli Kunda and Janjangbureh is the village of Boraba. About 2km northwards from this village is another called Kesser Kunda. Here you should visit the *alkalo* of the village who can find a guide to take you to the tomb. You can take a shared taxi from Janjangbureh, walk, or hire a horse- or donkey-cart from local villagers.

Madina Demba Forest Park
This is another large forest park that lies adjacent to the main highway, about 5km east of the turn off to Janjangbureh and Sankuli Kunda. This forest suffers badly from bush fires during the dry season, as does most of the countryside around it. We have seen plenty of evidence of warthogs in the park but you stand little likelihood of seeing these animals during the daytime.

BANSANG
Bansang is a large town with a large and impressive hospital being built next to the town. It is however not a very interesting place from a visitor's point of view. Most people, except keen birdwatchers, simply pass straight through on their way upcountry to Basse. Birdwatchers, of course, know the town very well, because this is the spot where they are almost guaranteed to see red-throated bee-eaters, *Merops bullocki*, which nest in a quarry in the surrounding hills. It is often not even necessary to go out and search for these beautiful birds, as a close look at any of the telephone and power lines south of the town is bound to yield a few sightings.

Getting there and away
From the ferry on the south bank of the river at MacCarthy Island, a bush taxi will cost you less than US$0.50 to get to Bansang. If you're travelling westward from Basse, regular bush taxis cost about US$1 to get you to Bansang. There is a small car ferry that operates between Bansang and the north bank of the river. This costs US$1.50 to take across a car, but much less than US$0.50 for each foot passenger. It can be hard to find when you are driving through the town so look out for the main police station, it is 20–30m west of the station on the north side. All GPTC bus services from Banjul and from upcountry stop at Bansang.

Where to stay, eat and drink

There is only one place catering for tourists in Bansang and this is **Carews Bar and Restaurant**, which is west of, and next to, the police station. The rooms are clean and fairly cheap at US$3.50 for a single, US$7 for a double or US$10 if you fancy a bigger room. A fairly wide selection of cheap meals and drinks can also be purchased in the restaurant and bar. This appears to be a pleasant place and the manager certainly speaks fairly good English, though we noticed that they do like to have the music in the bar quite loud.

Upper River Division

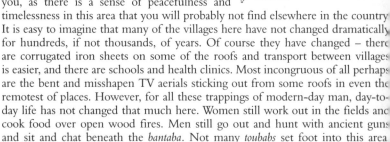

If you enjoy getting off the beaten track, the Upper River Division could be the place for you, as there is a sense of peacefulness and timelessness in this area that you will probably not find elsewhere in the country. It is easy to imagine that many of the villages here have not changed dramatically for hundreds, if not thousands, of years. Of course they have changed – there are corrugated iron sheets on some of the roofs and transport between villages is easier, and there are schools and health clinics. Most incongruous of all perhaps are the bent and misshapen TV aerials sticking out from some roofs in even the remotest of places. However, for all these trappings of modern-day man, day-to-day life has not changed that much here. Women still work out in the fields and cook food over open wood fires. Men still go out and hunt with ancient guns and sit and chat beneath the *bantaba*. Not many *toubabs* set foot into this area except to visit Basse, and the people are extremely friendly, though English as a spoken language is uncommon.

Basse is totally different, full of bustle and noise. It's rather like a frontier town in some old cowboy movie (minus the cowboys of course, though there are still plenty of cows). This is the easternmost outpost of urban Gambia and tries to make the most of it.

There are few officially gazetted forest parks and no national parks in this part of the country but there are some great seasonal swamps that are a haven for birds and dragonflies (see *Eastern swamps* in this chapter). The wildlife of the Upper River Division is much the same as that found elsewhere in the central and eastern parts of The Gambia, with the same mixture of Sahelian and Sudan savanna species, though there are a few specialities to be found here.

THE NORTH BANK OF THE RIVER GAMBIA

The north bank of the River Gambia in Upper River Division is peaceful and quiet, without the bustling crowds and hassle that you find in the western part of The Gambia, especially near the coast. This part of the country is well away from the tourist areas and the people are genuinely friendly and helpful to strangers.

The dry conditions found here throughout the larger part of the year make this the most likely place to find two rare Gambian birds, the sun lark, *Galerida modesta* and the rufous scrub robin, *Cercotrichas galactotes*.

THE ROAD EAST TO SUTUKOBA AND BRIFFU

The road running east from the border with Central River Division up to the end of the country is a continuation of the laterite track from Janjangbureh, with a similar scenery of low hills, Sudan savanna woodland and agricultural land. There is little to say about this part of The Gambia from a tourist's perspective, as there are no facilities for visitors, apart from **Fullada Camp**, located on the north bank of the river near Basse.

The ferry north of Basse
The ferry from the north bank of the river across to Basse can easily accommodate a couple of vehicles. It operates officially from 08.00–18.00 hours, but will only cross the river when enough vehicles have arrived to make it worthwhile, so be prepared for a long wait. The price is US$2 for a car and less than US$0.50 for foot passengers. However, if you are on foot and want to get across quickly, there is a busy trade in small metal boats that ply the same route across. You may have to share a boat with a motorbike or two, and sometimes so many people crowd aboard that the boat looks fairly unsafe and probably is. We have even seen a cow taken across by one of these boats by the simple expedient of dragging it by its halter and forcing it to swim the river. Needless to say, this was not a happy cow!

Fullada Camp
Fullada Camp is situated on the north bank of the River Gambia not far from the ferry across to Basse. This is a new camp with excellent facilities for visitors. The rooms are spacious and comfortable. There is a restaurant and bar, and of course, even here out in the bush, there is a large swimming pool. We found that the organisation during our visit to the camp left a little to be desired, but this is not unusual in a new place and the staff, though still being trained, were exceedingly friendly and helpful. In January 2001 there were enough rooms, with four rooms to a hut, to cater for at least 65 people, but more rooms were being added and should be in place by the time you read this book, extending this to a maximum of 120 people. Each room has two beds, with mosquito bednets and mosquito window nets. They also come equipped with shower, WC, washbasin and standing fans. Eight of the new rooms will have air conditioning. Prices are US$11.50 per person per night, though the air-conditioned rooms will be more expensive. These prices include free transportation across the river into Basse in the camp's own boat. Power comes from a generator, of which the camp has three, though two of them were not working when we visited. Water for the shower and washing is pumped from the river and should not be drunk. Unfortunately the water supply is reliant on the generator, so at the moment is only certain from 19.00 to midnight when the power is on, though 24-hour power is planned in the future. The staff do try to keep the water tanks full all of the time but didn't succeed during our visit. However, do not hold this against them as we are hopeful that this and other problems will be ironed out as the staff become better trained and the number of visitors increases, as surely it will.

The restaurant had collapsed during the previous rainy season but is being rebuilt. However, there is an outdoor restaurant by the swimming pool which is very pleasant. The restaurant offers international and local food. A standard breakfast is US$3.50, lunch is US$6 and buffet dinner is US$6. Other main meals on the menu cost from US$3.50–5. When large groups are present, live entertainment is provided either by local dancers from a nearby village, or by traditional Fula fire-eaters. The camp has plans for a large licensed crocodile pool and a snake farm, so that visitors can get as close as they want, to these often elusive creatures.

The camp runs boat trips upriver to Tambasensan, where you stand a chance of seeing wild hippos, though this is not guaranteed. The trip lasts about three

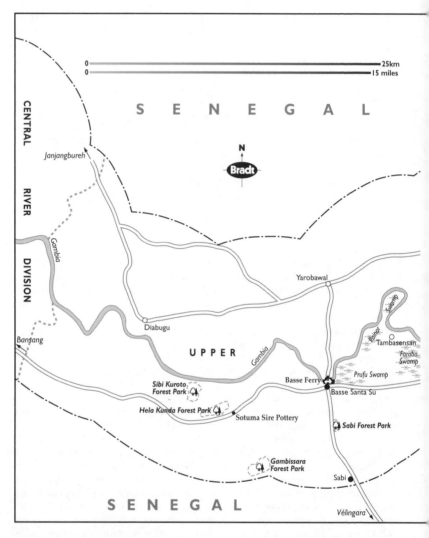

hours and costs US$6.50 per person, with a minimum of four people. They can also organise jeep excursions around the surrounding area or into Senegal. They advertise safaris into Niokolo Koba (Badiar) National Park, about 2–3 hours' drive away in neighboring Senegal, but again, at the time of our visit, two of their three vehicles were in for repair and their remaining car was in our view unsuitable for the trip. Hopefully, this is another problem that the management will have ironed out by the time you read this book. The price for this two-day trip is US$51 per day for the vehicle and driver. However, remember that you will have to pay for the fuel and also for your accommodation and meals whilst in the park (see *Chapter 13*), though the driver's food and accommodation is included in the fee.

This camp is ideally situated, and is probably the best accommodation available so far upriver. As time goes by it is bound to become more popular and busy,

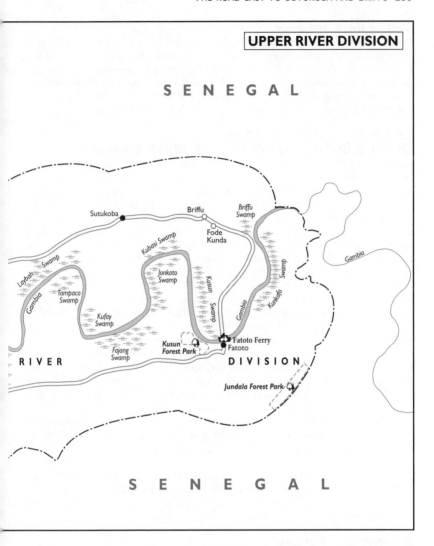

and it provides good employment opportunities for local people from the tourist trade.

Getting there and away
A bush taxi from the ferry terminal on the north bank of the river near MacCarthy Island to Basse will cost you about US$1. All GPTC bus services from Banjul stop at Basse. Some ground operators organise excursions to Niokolo Koba (Badiar) National Park, which stop at Fullada Camp for the night before going into Senegal.

THE FERRY NORTH OF FATOTO
A small ferry capable of taking a car operates across the River Gambia from the north bank to Fatoto. This ferry has no motor and is pulled across by cable – a job that you are expected to help with.

Getting there and away

Bush taxis run (but not that regularly) from the north bank of the river by Basse, eastwards through Sutokoba and Brifu, to Fode Kunda, just south of Brifu (for less than US$0.50). From Fode Kunda it is necessary to make your own way south to the ferry crossing north of Fatoto if you want to return to Basse via the south bank. This is most easily done by hiring a horse or donkey cart in the village, or by cadging a lift, though vehicles this far east are few and far between.

THE ROAD EAST TO BASSE
ON THE SOUTH BANK OF THE RIVER GAMBIA

Having reached this far on the main highway eastwards, you will have had enough of pot-holes to last you a lifetime. So you will be happy to note that the road from here (in fact all the way from Janjangbureh, except for a rough patch through Bansang) is smooth and pot-hole free. This means a quick and bump-free ride all the way to Basse. If you are visiting later in the dry season, one thing you are bound to note is that much of the woodland, bush and agricultural land on either side of the road has been burnt. This is caused by the numerous bush fires that afflict this area and much of the rest of The Gambia. Some of these fires will have started naturally or as the result of accidents, such as drivers throwing their cigarette butts from car windows, but most are set deliberately for a whole variety of reasons. These range from clearing land for crop planting or firewood collection to making the bush safe for children to walk in. Whether or not you agree with any of these reasons, the fact remains that the regeneration of woodlands is severely impeded by these fires, usually to the advantage of a handful of tree species that actually benefit from periodic burning. Apart from aesthetic reasons, ie: woodlands look far better than masses of exposed, ash-covered ground, there are many other reasons why these random acts of arson should be discouraged. Among them are the resulting soil erosion which lowers the fertility of the land and the fact that many villages, compounds and domestic animals are caught unawares by these fires, with a resultant loss of property and probably, in some cases, even life. Many government departments are actively trying to educate farmers and others against this annual destruction, but it is a long uphill struggle that may never be won.

There is little else to catch the eye along this stretch of road apart from the usual collection of small villages and hamlets scattered along the way, although there are a few places where small *bolons* cross under the road which may be worth looking at for their birdlife.

Sotuma Sire Pottery

About 12km west of Basse is a small village along the road called Sotuma Sire. This is much like many other villages except that here there is a small pottery industry. It's easy to find as you will normally see a batch of various pots placed next to the road. This pottery has benefited greatly from the help and advice of **Traditions Café and Boutique** in Basse (see *Basse Santa Su and surrounds* in this chapter), and some of their material is relatively original and unusual, including some enamelled candlesticks. If you see something you want to buy, simply ask the potter and negotiate a price. The potters are not usually far away but if they are absent the man who runs the nearby store will negotiate a price on their behalf.

Getting there and away

Although a small village, Sotuma Sire is easy to get to as it lies across the Banjul to Basse Highway. Travelling from the west a bush taxi from MacCarthy Island or

Bansang will cost less than US$1. From Basse in the east a bush taxi will cost you less than US$0.50. GPTC buses (ordinary service) from Banjul and Basse stop at Sotuma Sire.

BASSE SANTA SU AND SURROUNDS

Basse Santa Su, or simply Basse as it is widely known, is the last large town in the east of The Gambia. It can be a bit of a shock when you enter the town, especially if you have expected it to be a sleepy sort of place, being so far upcountry, because sleepy it definitely is not. This is a busy, noisy, thriving town, with a large market and lots of people. Many of them are Senegalese who are passing through. This is also the ideal place to base yourself if you are intent on exploring this end of the country as there are several places to stay of varying quality and price. It's also a good base from which to set off towards Niokolo Koba (Badiar) National Park in southeast Senegal (see *Chapter 13*). Basse is also home to two banks, the Trust Bank and Standard Chartered Bank. Although credit card facilities are not available here, you should be able to cash travellers' cheques and/or exchange foreign currency if you need to.

Basse is famous amongst birdwatchers visiting The Gambia, as it is just about the only place in the country where you are almost guaranteed a close-up view of one of the country's most beautiful birds, the Egyptian plover, which is known locally as the 'crocodile bird'. This fairly small, but strikingly coloured bird is frequently seen from June to February, with numbers peaking between September and December. In Basse they often forage along the river's edge adjacent to the town, and the wharf is also a good place to spot them if it is quiet. Probably the best place to see them is from **Traditions Café and Boutique** (see *Where to eat and drink* below).

On your way into the town look out for the roadside sign that says 'Go slow – hunches ahead'. We'd be grateful if anyone who has any idea what this means would let us know!

Getting there and away

Bush taxis from MacCarthy Island or Bansang will cost less than US$1 for the trip. All GPTC bus services from Banjul stop at Basse. The Basse ferry can easily be reached by walking from where you are dropped off as it's not very far. Ask for directions if you're not sure which way to go. If you want to travel to the Senegalese border at Sabi, a bush taxi going south from Basse will cost you US$0.50. Here you normally have to change to Senegalese transport if you want to continue across the border. Remember to watch out for those hunches on your way into Basse!

Where to stay

Fullada Camp, just across the river to the north of Basse, is probably the most comfortable place to stay in this area (see *Fullada Camp* above in this chapter). Apart from this there are a few places that are very cheap but quite rough and ready. These are the **Plaza Hotel**, where a room will cost you about US$4 per night per person, and **Basse Guest House**, where a room will also cost you US$4 per night per person (if there is no power from the power station) or US$5 if you're lucky enough to have power. There is also the **Traveller's Lodge**, which is US$3 per night and the **Apollo Hotel**, which will cost you US$3.50 per night. Do not expect to get a decent night's sleep in any of these places as they are located in noisy and busy streets. Also, the accommodation leaves a little to be desired if you're used to your comforts. However, they are very cheap, so as usual you get what you pay for.

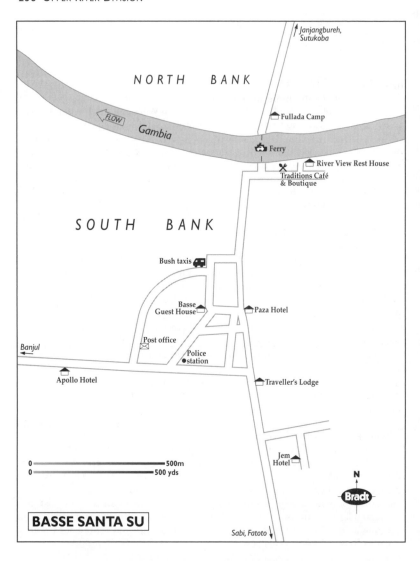

Janjangbureh, Sutukoba

NORTH BANK

FLOW

Gambia

Fullada Camp

Ferry

River View Rest House

Traditions Café & Boutique

SOUTH BANK

Bush taxis

Basse Guest House

Paza Hotel

Post office

Police station

Banjul

Apollo Hotel

Traveller's Lodge

0 ———————— 500m
0 ———————— 500 yds

Jem Hotel

N

Bradt

BASSE SANTA SU

Sabi, Fatoto

A step upmarket is the **Jem Hotel**, a larger establishment away from the busy main roads in the town, which is fairly well signposted. This is a very quiet and tranquil hotel in spite of the fact that they have a large disco room on site, which is apparently only used for special occasions. It's worth checking out this room just to have a look at some of the strange and oddly out-of-place murals that cloak the walls. All rooms have a shower, WC and ceiling fan, with power supplied either from the local power plant or by the hotel's own standby generator. The rooms are clean and comfortable and face on to an enclosed courtyard, though they are more expensive at US$10 for a single and US$20.50 for a double room. There is also one single room with air conditioning available for US$20.50, just in case the heat is getting to you. It can get *very* hot at this end of the country, especially towards the end of the dry season and during the rainy season.

Another alternative rest place that's cheaper than the Jem Hotel is **River View Rest House**, also known as the **Four Aces Bar**. This is a small place run by two very friendly Lebanese Gambians, Michael and George Nahra, who speak excellent English and go out of their way to make you feel welcome. At first glance the place may seem a little dilapidated but do not be put off, as the rooms are contained in three new huts (some more were being built in early 2001) and the location is great, with a fine view overlooking the river, hence the name. Each room has two single beds though there are only local pit latrines and bucket showers for your ablutions. One night out of three they have power from the local power plant. A single B&B will cost US$5, or just US$4 with no breakfast, and a double B&B will cost US$7, or US$5 with no breakfast. In our view this is by far the best of the cheaper alternatives to stay in at Basse.

Where to eat and drink

Traditions Café and Boutique (Ann Slind, General Delivery, Basse, Upper River Division, The Gambia; tel: 668533; fax: 668004) is a very special place. It's open from 09.00–18.00 and you can either sit in the shade in the quiet compound or sit out on a balcony with a great view of the river and wharf area. This has got to be one of the very few places that you can sit and have a cold coke while watching Egyptian plovers wander about on the side of the river. We've been told that these magnificent birds actually come up on to the balcony at times, which must be a very special treat for birdwatchers. Traditions also provide a choice of food at very reasonable prices.

Next door, **River View Rest House** will cook lunch or dinner at a negotiable price, though as with many places in Basse, you have to book your meals in the morning. This is because of the lack of constant electricity in the town, so food cannot be kept cold in refrigerators and has to be bought fresh from the local morning market. There are also a few fast-food places in Basse that deal with local food at cheap prices, but apart from those and **Fullada Camp** across the river, the only other place to eat is **Jem Hotel**. An English breakfast with fried eggs will cost around US$2.50, lunch is US$4 and dinner is US$4. The hotel bar is also open between 08.00 and midnight.

Things to do

Traditions Café and Boutique (see above) is one of those places that you come across now and again and instantly take a liking to. The boutique unfortunately burned down in 1999 and is in the process of being refurbished, although the owners have done such a good job so far that you don't really notice. The boutique is situated in a lovely old warehouse on the banks of the River Gambia and has a marvellous atmosphere. Most of the goods that are for sale are made locally in the region. For example, there is some excellent weaving from a nearby village, pottery from Sotuma Sire (see *Sotuma Sire Pottery* in this chapter), decorated calabashes from Janjangbureh and even hats from Mali. Many of the artists have also benefited from the advice and help given by the café owners, who have introduced things like spinning and pottery wheels to the local artists. There are plans to hold workshops for the different crafts here, so if you are art-minded this could be a wonderful way to spend part or all of your holiday in The Gambia. The owners can even arrange tours along the river or into Senegal and Niokolo Koba (Badiar) National Park (see *Chapter 13*).

Apart from looking around the town and the market, or birdwatching along the river banks (hoping especially for the famous Egyptian plover), there is not a lot else to do in Basse. It is possible, however, to talk to local *pirogue* owners about hiring them and their boats for a trip along the river. Of course you'll have to negotiate your own price.

EAST FROM BASSE TO FATOTO

Travelling east from Basse you'll find that there is a decent laterite road from the town all the way to Fatoto. Like its equivalent on the north bank of the River Gambia, this area is seldom visited by tourists and there are no facilities for visitors. We feel it's worth the short drive east, as it's here that you get a feeling for the *real* Africa. There are no large towns here, no traffic to speak of, and certainly no large, bustling crowds. It's a very peaceful region with grass-roofed compounds in small villages dotted around the farmland, and, of course, smiling people. Birdwatchers should definitely make the trip as there are birds here that you would be unlikely to see anywhere else in The Gambia, such as the African swallow-tailed kite, a dainty tern-like bird of prey that hovers effortlessly above your head while it hunts for insects. Even a drive up this road in darkness will give you a good chance of seeing a rarity like the spotted thick-knee, *Burhinus capensis*, a nocturnal bird that often forages along laterite roads in this area. Other good species that you might come across here include adamawa turtle dove, *Streptopelia hypopyrrha*, along the vegetated banks of the river, the little green bee-eater and the beautiful northern carmine bee-eater, *Merops nubicus*.

Getting there and away

Bush taxis run between Basse and Fatoto, but are not that frequent. From Basse a bush taxi will cost less than US$1 for the trip.

THE EASTERN SWAMPS

During the rainy season, and for a short while afterwards, many large low-lying areas of the Upper River Division are covered in shallow swamps along the course of the river. These are good places for birdwatching and you should really make the effort to get here if this is your reason for visiting The Gambia, as very few people visit these swamps and who knows what goodies you may discover?

Leopard

Side Trips into Senegal

Senegal is much larger than The Gambia and surrounds it on three sides. Senegal was administered by the French during the colonial era, and therefore everything has been influenced by the French, rather than the English influence that is prevalent in The Gambia. This is in spite of the fact that many ethnic groups of the same origin share both territories. This means that a Wolof from The Gambia can communicate in his local language to a Senegalese Wolof, even though they might not be able to communicate together in the official languages of their respective countries, ie: English and French. Having said this, most people in the Senegambian region are proficient in several languages including English and French. All of this adds up to the feeling of stepping into a very different country just by crossing a simple border, which may not even be marked on the ground in many places.

Senegal is a lovely country with a wealth of different habitats, ranging from arid, almost desert-like habitats in the north to lush, heavily forested belts in the south. Being such a large country it takes a long time to travel between most places, so in this chapter we have concentrated on a few sites that lie close to The Gambia, within a few hours travelling time. Luckily, there are two national parks lying close to our borders that are rich in wildlife and worth visiting. These are the Parc National de Delta du Saloum and the Parc National de Niokolo Koba. A third national park, the Parc National de Basse Casamance, is also within fairly easy travelling distance. Due to local fighting in this region, however, we have not visited this park, and would not recommend anyone to visit until the troubles are over.

The currency in use in Senegal is the West African CFA, known as *seefa* (see *Money* in *Chapter 3*). This is also the currency that is most widely used in most countries in West Africa, excepting of course, the anglophone countries. It is relatively easy to change US dollars, English pounds sterling or Gambian dalasis into *seefa* at most banks and bureaux de change in The Gambia. Also any of the street money-changers (for example at Westfield Junction in Serrekunda, outside the post office in Banjul, or at any border crossing post) will only be too happy to change your money for you. If you are intending to use the street money-changers see *Money* in *Chapter 3* first to prevent being cheated. A word of warning about Senegalese money-changers at the borders. Many of them are young, good-looking Senegalese women who use their charms to great advantage on unsuspecting male travellers. You'll see what we mean if you cross the border, but you have been warned.

For the purposes of this guidebook we have converted CFA into US dollars at the exchange rate of CFA 732 per US$1.

TRAVELLING TO AND FROM SENEGAL

Visitors from the UK, Ireland, USA, France, Belgium, Germany, Italy, Luxembourg, the Netherlands and Denmark do not require **visas** to enter Senegal,

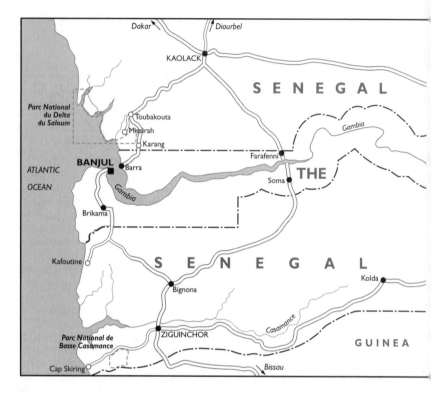

but citizens of all other countries need them. Tourist visas valid for one month's duration cost US$20 and are available from most Senegalese embassies and consulates (see *Chapter 2* for details of the Senegalese consulate in The Gambia).

Senegalese **customs** officials at most **border crossing points** are fine to deal with, although they can seem a little dour on occasion, but then don't they everywhere? Most, of course, do not speak English, so a little spoken French and a friendly attitude will take you a long way. When crossing the border either way remember to visit both the Gambian and Senegalese border posts. Sometimes finding these posts can be a little confusing, but there are always local people willing to help. There should be no charge for crossing at most points but for some reason, that we have never been able to fathom, you will be charged a small amount for crossing the border at Sabi, near Basse Santa Su. On the Gambian side this is US$1 per person and on the Senegalese side less than US$1 per person.

Another confusing fact is that sometimes, when using public transport such as bush taxis, you can cross the border and use the same vehicle to complete your journey. At other times you have to leave one bush taxi at the border and catch another on the other side of the border. It seems that there is an agreement between the Gambian and Senegalese taxi-drivers union that only Gambian drivers ply the Gambian routes and only Senegalese drivers ply the Senegalese routes, but this agreement is often flouted. Occasionally there have been violent disputes between the drivers of both countries. If you are travelling north towards Kaolack or Dakar from Banjul and Barra, then there are two GPTC buses that do the trip daily. The full trip to Dakar costs less than US$7 and takes about five hours. If you hire a vehicle during your stay in The Gambia and intend to take it across the

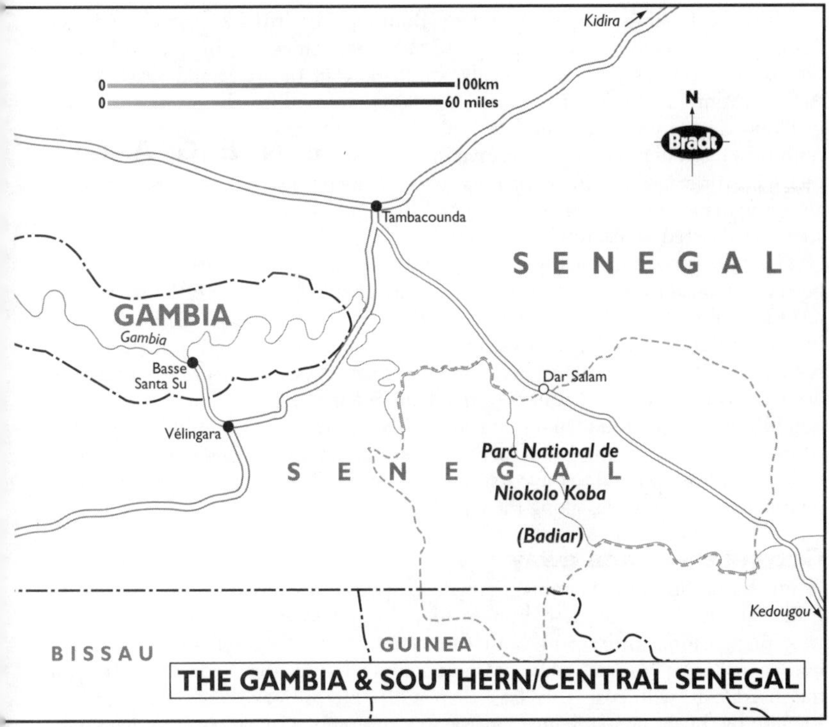
Kidira
0 100km
0 60 miles
N
Bradt
Tambacounda
SENEGAL
GAMBIA
Gambia
Basse Santa Su
Vélingara
Dar Salam
SENEGAL
Parc National de Niokolo Koba
(Badiar)
Kedougou
BISSAU
GUINEA
THE GAMBIA & SOUTHERN/CENTRAL SENEGAL

border, make sure that the vehicle is correctly insured by having a green card. Vehicle registrations and insurance are checked thoroughly by customs on both sides, including even the chassis and engine numbers. If you do not have a green card you will not be allowed to take your vehicle into Senegal.

It all sounds like a lot of hassle, but really it's not that bad and well worth the effort to visit some of the most beautiful countryside and see some of the best wildlife left in West Africa. Just remember always to be polite and above all patient, and you will get through relatively easy. One more reminder: don't forget to take your passport with you.

PARC NATIONAL DE DELTA DU SALOUM

The Siné-Saloum Delta occupies the land immediately north of The Gambia along the length of the coast. This huge area, covering 760km^2, is one of the most beautiful in Senegal and contains the Parc National de Delta du Saloum, the fourth largest protected area in the country. The national park is adjacent to Niumi National Park in The Gambia (see *Chapter 9*) and together they protect an area that is rich in both scenery and wildlife.

The park is located around the river Saloum, where it meets the Atlantic Ocean, and is a wonderful mix of habitats. These include barely vegetated sand islands lying just off the coast, extensive and impressive mangrove forests, tidal *bolons*, lagoons, and huge mud flats that are exposed at low tide, and open Sudan savanna woodland and forests. The park is especially noted for its fabulous bird life which includes all the usual mix of species for this part of Africa, such as pelicans, egrets, herons, fish eagles and ospreys, gulls, terns and waders. One specialty of the delta that is worth looking for is its flamingos. Both the greater flamingo and the lesser flamingo, *Phoenicopterus minor*, can be found here, sometimes in flocks of many thousands. Another bird occasionally found here in the river and *bolons* is the African skimmer, *Rynchops flavirostris*. This fairly rare bird has the interesting habit of flying very low over the surface of the river, with its lower mandible actually trailing in the water; whenever this mandible strikes a fish, the bird's bill snaps shut on it. The drier parts of the park are also worth spending some time in as there is always a chance of coming across species that are not common in The Gambia, such as helmeted guineafowl.

The delta is not particularly noted for its mammals, perhaps because they have been overlooked by many authors, yet there are plenty of them here. These include terrestrial species such as leopard, warthog, spotted hyena, bushbuck, patas monkey, callithrix monkey and western red colobus, but also rare aquatic species such as the West African manatee and the African clawless otter. Atlantic humpback dolphins also occur in the waters of the delta in fair numbers. This is a species of dolphin that is only found along the coast of West Africa, geographically separated from its near relative the Indo-Pacific humpback dolphin, *Sousa chinensis*, whose nearest population is along the coast of South Africa. The park also holds breeding populations of sea turtles along the coastline.

Getting there and away

From Barra, in The Gambia, it will cost you less than US$1 to get to Amdallai on the Senegalese border in a bush taxi. Here you will have to visit the customs offices on both the Gambian and Senegalese sides of the border in order to get your passport stamped. On the Senegalese side of the border it will cost you less than US$0.50 to make the short hop to Karang by bush taxi. Change at Karang to catch a bush taxi to Missirah, which will cost US$1 for the trip. If you are intending to stay for one or more nights you will probably have to walk from Missirah to the **Gîte du Bandiala**, unless you are very lucky and find one of the rare shared taxis that service the village. Ask for directions in the village to the Gîte. Most of the inhabitants know where it is. Once you leave the village it is well signposted along the road and about 2.5km from the village. Alternatively find a shared taxi in Karang to take you all of the way to the Gîte, though this will be more expensive than using bush taxis.

Where to stay, eat and drink

The nearest camp, both to The Gambia and to the national park, is the **Gîte du Bandiala** (tel: 9487735 or 9412341). This is an excellent, if slightly expensive, camp located in a very peaceful woodland setting, about 2.5km from the small town of Missirah. There are ten rooms, all with shower, WC, washbasin, ceiling fan and mosquito window nets, and there's lots of space in each. Prices are US$24 per person for full board (less than US$18 for a child over eight years), about US$17.50 per person half board (less than US$14 for a child over eight), or about US$8 per person for the night. In addition to this you have to pay tax at less than US$1 per person per night. The single supplement per day is below US$3. Children under eight years of age stay free of charge. The camp is surrounded by a low wall, presumably to keep out some of the larger animals inhabiting the area, such as warthog, and there is a pleasant bar and restaurant on site. Meals are very French, with two or three courses, even for lunch, and are of excellent quality. If you are a beer drinker, try the Gazelle Beer that is brewed in Senegal. Its hard to get hold of in The Gambia but is worth trying (we were tempted to buy a few extra bottles to take home with us). The couple who own and manage the Gîte are very friendly and helpful, though their English is a little limited.

There are other camps and hotels in the delta, the closest of which are at Toubakouta, about 12km further north, but be prepared, as these are more expensive than the Gîte and not located as near to the national park. There is also a small camp on the northern, Senegalese end of Jinack Island, called the **Plage d'Or**, which may be worth having a look at. This is within easy walking distance along the beach from **Madiyana Camp** (see *Chapter 9*) on the Gambian side of the border, but once you've settled at Madiyana, which is in our view the closest you can get to a peaceful paradise along the Gambian coast, why move?

Things to do

One option at the **Gîte du Bandiala** is to stay in the camp and do nothing. This is not as boring as it sounds, especially if you are into wildlife spotting, as the wildlife will often come to you. There is an artificial waterhole close to the camp that can easily be watched while you sit in the restaurant and sip a cold beer. There is also a hide overlooking the pool, but it was in a sad state of disrepair when we visited, and the view from the restaurant is almost as good. A wide range of mammals visit the pool, the only source of freshwater close to the camp. These mammals include warthog and spotted hyena, though we didn't see them during our stay. However, we did see both patas and callithrix monkeys drink at the pool and also a white-tailed mongoose, *Ichneumia albicauda*, which stayed for several minutes. The pool is floodlit during the evening to improve your chances of seeing things. Birds abound in the woodland around the camp and we were awoken one morning by the pleasant sound of a large flock of helmeted guineafowl foraging amongst the dead leaves below our window.

A walk in the woodlands is very satisfying, with plenty of birds and a troop of western red colobus not too far away. A night walk can also be good. We were directed to a spot about 1km away where we had fantastic torch-lit views of Senegal galagos (bushbabies). They are fairly easy to spot as their eyes reflect the torchlight, seeming to glow like little red rubies. It was a simple matter to get closer to them and to watch them jump from branch to branch. On this walk we also saw a warthog and heard hyenas whooping very close to where we were. Don't forget to take a torch or flashlight with you.

Another option is to ask for a boat trip through the *bolons* or a Landrover safari into the surrounding countryside. The boat trip is very pleasant, with a short stop-off on a small island where there is a shelter and a tiny village. Prices are around US$22 for a half-day boat trip for two. For a trip in a *pirogue* to visit Bird Island, which lies just off the coast, expect to pay US$75 for ten people. The Landrover safari will cost US$34 for six people. You should also have to pay the standard entry charge for the national park, which is less than US$3 per person, on every excursion you take.

Another option available here is to go fishing, and judging from the selection of photographs in the camp, it can be pretty rewarding, with large catches of fish like barracuda. A day's fishing will cost you around US$57.50 for two people or US$30 for half a day. Fishing holidays are a specialty here. Six days at the camp with five of them spent fishing will cost in the region of US$260 per person, with a slight discount for non-fishing people who accompany you, during the low season (July 1 to October 31). The same deal during the high season (November 1 to June 30) costs more at around US$324. Fishing materials can also be provided at around US$54.50.

PARC NATIONAL DE NIOKOLO KOBA (BADIAR)

Niokolo Koba National Park in southeastern Senegal covers an area almost the size of The Gambia, with 9,000 km² of uninterrupted wilderness. Recently the park has been allied with the Parc National de Badiar, across its southern border with Guinea, protecting the whole area as a transfontier park. This is the premier site in both Senegal and The Gambia for large mammals and has been designated as a World Heritage Site and an International Biosphere Reserve, reflecting its global importance for wildlife. If you are into wildlife in a big way then a visit to this park is a must. It's also the nearest African national park to Europe that contains big game.

In the west of the park the ground is relatively flat and heavily wooded, although there are many low-lying plains that become inundated with water during the rainy season. In the east the ground is more open with huge expanses of grassland and a few low hills, the highest of which is Mount Assirik. The River Gambia flows through the park from south to north, along with two other smaller rivers, the Niokolo Koba and the Koulountou. The banks of the rivers, which are very steep in most places, are clothed with patches of gallery forest.

The main centre of the park is at Simenti, where there is a visitors' centre and the park headquarters, as well as a hotel. This is where most visitors head and there is plenty of wildlife around the area, though you will find a greater selection of the larger mammals further east. During the 1980s and early 1990s the park went through a period of neglect and there was a lot of poaching and human encroachment. Thankfully there was a massive injection of cash into the park in the mid-1990s and these problems are mostly a thing of the past.

Walking is not allowed within the boundaries of the park, except at Simenti, where you can walk a short distance to a hide overlooking a flat area of grassland that floods during the rains. This holds a good selection of large mammals that are easily seen. There is also a short guided walk that you can take with a park ranger as guide, where you will be told about the various trees along the way and their local uses. This is a handy place to point out that none of the rangers that we came across could speak a word of English. Unless your French is passable or you have a Gambian driver or guide that can speak in Wolof and translate it into English, forget the guided walk. In the box opposite we have included a short list of some of the animals you are likely to see and their French names, so at least you'll be able to decipher some of what you are told. The tracks around the park are suitable only for four-wheel-drive vehicles and driving at night is also not allowed within the park, because of the likelihood of breaking down and being stranded.

The park is open all year around but we suggest that it is really only worth visiting in the dry season, from December to May, because in the rainy season the vegetation is just too thick, and the grass too tall, to see much of anything. The roads can also be impassable at this time of year. The entrance fee to Niokolo Koba is payable for each 24-hour period you intend to stay. For a car this is about US$7, with a further US$3 for each person. All visitors must take a park guide with them, unless you come with your own vehicle and driver. The guide will cost a further US$8 per day. If you do not have a car, then it is possible to take an organised half-day safari from Simenti Hotel for around US$8 per person (minimum of four people). Morning and evening boat trips along the river are offered by the visitor's centre and will cost you around US$5 per person (minimum of two people).

The wildlife of Niokolo Koba is simply astounding, and very easy to see, being almost, but not quite as good, as many of the national parks in East Africa. Most of the large mammals that can be found in West Africa inhabit the national park. The only species that you will not find are normally those that are associated with high rainforest habitats. The antelopes present include bubal, *Alcelaphus*

WILDLIFE IN FRENCH

The following are the French names for some animals you are likely to see (and a few rare ones):

african buffalo	*buffle*
african wild dog	*lycaon or cynhyène*
banded mongoose	*mangue rayée*
bohur reedbuck	*cobe rédunca*
bubal	*bubale*
bushbuck	*guibe harnaché*
callithrix monkey	*singe vert*
common duiker	*sylvicapre de Grimm*
common warthog	*phacochère*
defassa waterbuck	*cobe defassa*
Derby's eland	*elan de Derby*
guinea baboon	*babuin de Guinea*
hippopotamus	*hippopotame*
kob	*cobe de buffon*
léopard	*panthère*
nile monitor	*varan du Nil*
oribi	*ourébie*
patas	*singe rouge*
red-flanked duiker	*céphalophe*
roan antelope	*hippotrague*
side-striped jackal	*chacal à flancs rayé*
spotted hyena	*hyène tachetée*
striped ground squirrel	*écureuil foisseur*
western red colobus	*colobe bai d'Afrique Occidental*

buselaphus, roan antelope, defassa waterbuck, *Kobus ellipsiprymnus defassa*, kob, *K. kob*, oribi, *Ourebia ourebi*, bohur reedbuck, *Redunca redunca*, bushbuck, common duiker, red-flanked duiker, *Cephalophus rufilatus*, and the speciality for the region, the massive Derby's or giant eland, *Taurotragus derbianus*. Other large herbivores include African buffalo, *Syncerus caffer*, and the ubiquitous common warthog, which you can see just about everywhere you look. The African elephant is also present, although there may now be as few as 20 animals left due to poaching in the past. We have, however, been reliably informed (by the park director himself) that there could be as many as 80 left. Along the rivers live all three species of African crocodiles, the slender-snouted, dwarf and Nile crocodiles, as well as good numbers of hippos. Monkeys are extremely common, especially Guinea baboon, which is estimated to number around 100,000 animals throughout the park. Other species include all those found in The Gambia: western red colobus, patas and callithrix monkeys, along with the nocturnal Senegal galago (bushbabies). In the east around the area of Mount Assirik, there is a small but thriving population of wild chimpanzees, though you have to be lucky to see them.

Other animals inhabiting the park, which you also have to be lucky to see, because they are naturally thinner on the ground than the herbivores, are the carnivores. These include an apparently growing population of African lion, *Panthera leo*, leopard, side-striped jackal, and many mongoose, including banded mongoose. A great rarity among the carnivores, that appears to be just hanging on

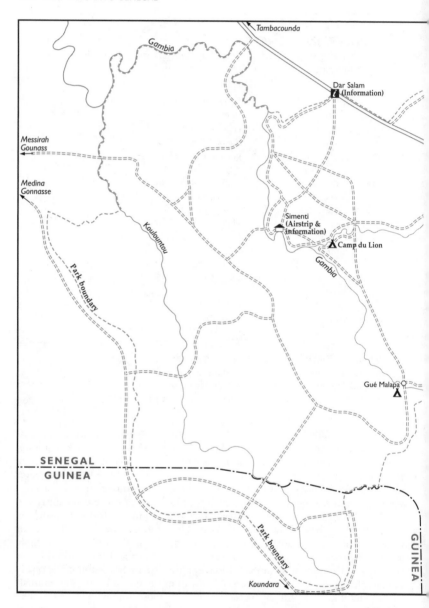

at Niokolo Koba, is the African wild dog, *Lycaon pictus*, which is still sighted occasionally by visitors to the park.

Other animals that are present (which you will probably not see during a short visit to the park) are red river hog, *Potamochoerus porcus*, African civet, genets and the nocturnal ant-eating aardvark. All in all, over 80 species of mammal have been recorded at Niokolo Koba, and it's quite easy to see over a quarter of them during a stay of only two days' duration.

Over 350 species of birds have been recorded in the national park and there are

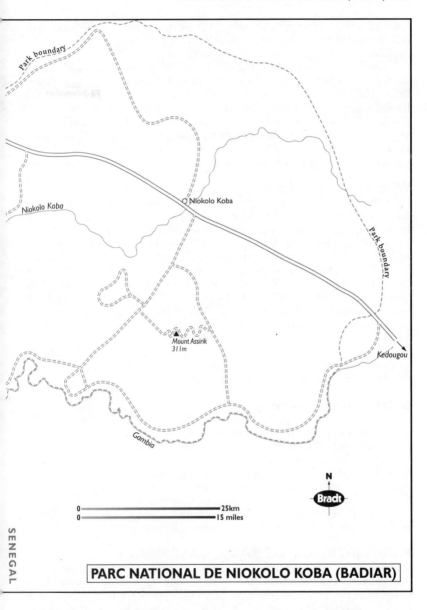

PARC NATIONAL DE NIOKOLO KOBA (BADIAR)

some birds found here that you are unlikely to see anywhere else in either Senegal or The Gambia. These include saddle-billed stork, green-headed sunbird, *Nectarinia verticalis*, secretary bird, *Sagittarius serpentarius*, adamawa turtle dove, shining-blue kingfisher, *Alcedo quadribrachys*, sun lark, magpie mannikin, *Lonchura fringilloides*, and Ethiopian swallow, *Hirundo aethiopica*. Other common species include helmeted guineafowl, African pied wagtail, *Motacilla aguimp*, white-crowned plover, *Vanellus albiceps*, red-throated bee-eater, bateleur, Abyssinian ground hornbill, hadada ibis, *Bostrychia hagedash*, black-crowned crane and, of course, Egyptian plover, which is very common and approachable, in some areas near the rivers. Other wildlife that you might see include many different species of amphibians and reptiles, dragonflies and butterflies.

To aid you with your animal and bird identification there is a park guidebook entitled *Niokolo-Badiar. Guide à l'usage des visiteurs du complexe écologique du Niokolo-Badiar*. Unfortunately, it is entirely in French and there is no English translation. It's still useful as it contains several maps of the park and a few colour drawings detailing many of the common species you are likely to see, as well as a small visual key to the parts of the park where you are most likely to see them. The guide makes a neat souvenir of your visit even if you don't use it much in the field. There is also a selection of gifts, such as T-shirts, usually available at the entrance to the park.

Where to stay and eat

Most visitors to the park stay at the **Hôtel de Simenti**, although on first glance this looks a bit of a dump, with lots of car wrecks and untidy huts around it. However, the accommodation is at least comfortable and the view over the balcony to the river below is great. A room here will cost you US$20.50 per night. The restaurant is close to the balcony (but not close enough) so you might want to drag your table and chairs over to the edge where you can look down while you eat. Breakfast is around US$1.50, lunch and dinner are around US$6 each. A far cheaper place to stay is the **Camp du Lion**, not far from Simenti, where there are local-style round huts which cost about US$8.50 per night. This is in a beautiful location by the River Gambia and is often visited by a troop of baboons that wander around. You can also buy basic meals here for around US$4. If you bring your own tent then this will cost you about US$4 per night. There is also a camp further south near **Gué Malapa**. We haven't visited this yet though a fair guess would be that the facilities and prices are similar to Camp du Lion.

Getting there and away

If you are visiting The Gambia and want to take a short visit to Niokolo Koba (Badiar) National Park, then undoubtedly your best option is to join an organised excursion – several of the ground operators run them (see *Organised excursions* in *Chapter 3*). This will cut down on the time spent travelling, and even on the time spent getting through customs at the Senegalese border, which can take the best part of several hours on some occasions. This will also mean that you will be in a four-wheel drive vehicle, which is a must for travelling on the park's dirt tracks.

It is possible to hire a vehicle and driver from **Fullada Camp**, near Basse, but read the section on the camp first (see *Chapter 12*).

PARC NATIONAL DE BASSE CASAMANCE

We have thought long and hard about writing about visits to the southern part of Senegal, known as Casamance, and in all honesty we cannot recommend that tourists visit this area at the present time. This is a pity as Casamance holds some of the most beautiful countryside in the region and still has plenty of wildlife. However, recent conflicts between the Mouvement des Forces Démocratique de la Casamance (MFDC) and the Senegalese government, heavily represented in the region by the Senegalese army, has made Casamance an unsafe place in which to travel, even for tourists. The MFDC is a separatist movement which wants independence for Casamance and at times its struggle has developed into outright civil war, while at other times it seems almost to have been forgotten. There have been recent casualties from land mines planted on the roads just a few miles from the regional capital, Ziguinchor, and several incidences of random killings. Many local people have been forced to cross the border into The Gambia to escape the fighting. Tensions run high in the area in which there is a large and obvious military presence. Many ceasefires have been negotiated between the MFDC and the Senegalese troops but most have been broken with each side blaming the other for committing occasional atrocities on the civilian population.

The Parc National de Basse Casamance is a large area of high forest, grassland and mangrove forest. However, according to the latest rumours that have reached us, it has been more or less abandoned by its staff for several years. In the recent past separatist MFDC fighters from Guinea Bissau have moved across the border through the park and there has been some heavy fighting around the area, and no doubt a lot of poaching of the larger mammals that are found here, such as African buffalo. The birds that inhabit the park have probably fared better than the mammals and they include some forest species that are not found in The Gambia. If you still wish to visit the park, even after our warnings, your first step is to get to Ziguinchor, which can be reached by taking a bush taxi from Serrekunda.

We hope that the dispute over independence for Casamance will be peacefully and finally resolved in the near future. Only then will we feel able to include it more fully in future editions of this guide.

Appendix 1

LANGUAGE

English is the official language of The Gambia and most people around the coast and the tourist areas can speak it to some degree or another. Many of them speak it very well. The further upcountry you go, however, the fewer people you will find who can speak English. This is where learning a few words in a local language will come in handy if you intend to spend any of your holiday away from the tourist areas. The trouble comes in deciding which language to learn, as there are several that are in everyday use throughout the country. When we were trained in a local language it was Mandinka, and this seems to make sense as the majority of the population are Mandinka so we have concentrated on this language in this section. But we have found that people of other tribes respond very well if you can at least greet them in their own language, such as Wolof, Jola or Fula, so we have also added the commonest greetings in these languages. It feels good to know that someone has gone to the trouble of learning a few phrases in your language and just a few words will make many people happy.

You'll also find that a smattering of French will get you a long way as there are many francophones living in The Gambia who have moved from other countries such as Senegal and Guinea, etc. French will also be of great use if you decide to visit Senegal, where it is the official language.

Note that the foreign words given below are spelt phonetically, ie as they are pronounced.

The importance of greetings in The Gambia cannot be over-emphasised. Everybody greets one another, either verbally or through handshakes, and sometimes these greetings can take several minutes. It's just another manifestation of the friendliness of the Gambian people. Even people who are too far away to talk or to shake hands will clasp their own hands above their head to greet you at a distance.

Universal greeting

The universal greeting is in Arabic because most of the population are Muslims. The greeting is: *Salam malekum* (loosely translated as 'peace be with you'), to which the response is: *Malekum salam* (peace returns to you).

Basic Mandinka words and phrases

Good morning	*Esama*
Good afternoon	*Etinyang*
Good evening	*Ewulara*
How are you?	*Kori tanante?* (response *Tanante*, which means 'I am fine')
How is your family?	*Sumoole?* (response *Ebebeje*, which means 'they are fine')

How is your wife/husband?	*Ila muso/kemo le?* (response *Ebebeje*)
How are your children?	*Ding ding olule?* (response *Ebebeje*)
How is your work?	*Do kwo be nadi?* (response is normally *Domanding, domanding*, which means 'slowly, slowly')
No	*Hani*
Yes	*Haa*
Thank you	*Abaraca*
Thank you very much	*Abaraca bake*
Good	*Abetiata*
Very good	*Abetiata bake*
Water	*Jio*
What is your name?	*Etondi*
My name is ...	*Nto mu ... le ti*
Where do you come from?	*Ebota minto le?*
I come from ...	*Nbota ... le*
How much (money)?	*Jelu lemu?*
Where is ...?	*... le?*
White man	*Toubabo*
Black man or child	*Mofingo*
Go away!	*Acha!*

Wolof greetings

Good morning	*Naka subasi*
Good afternoon	*Naka bekeck*
Good evening	*Naka ngosi*
How are you?	*Naka nga def?* (response *Jamarek*, which means 'I am/they are fine')
How is your family?	*Naka wa kerr?* (response *Jamarek*)
Thank you	*Jere jeef*

Jola greetings

How are you?	*Kesume?* (response *Kesume kep*, which means 'I am fine')
How is your family?	*Kissindi?* (response *Cocobo*, which means 'they are fine')

Fula greetings

How are you?	*Nambata?* (response *Jamtan*, which means 'I am fine')

Serer greetings

How are you?	*Nafio?* (response *Memehen* or *Jamarek*, which means 'I am fine')

Mandinka numbers

1	*kiling*	20	*Muwang*
2	*fula*	21, etc	*Muwang ning, muwang kiling* etc
3	*saba*	30	*Tang-saba*
4	*nani*	40	*Tang-nani*
5	*lulu*	50	*Tang-lulu*
6	*woro*	60	*Tang-woro*

7	*worowula*	70	*Tang-worowula*
8	*sei*	80	*Tang-sei*
9	*kononto*	90	*Tang-kononto*
10	*tang*	100	*Keme*
11, etc	*tang ning, tang kiling, etc*	1000	*Wili kiling*

Bushbuck

Appendix 2

FURTHER INFORMATION
Further reading
History
Meagher, Allen (Editor) *Historic Sites of The Gambia – An Official Guide to the Monuments and Sites of The Gambia.* National Council for Arts and Culture and roc International, 1998. This is an excellent little book that is very readable and contains lots of information not only on historic sites but also on the culture of the country.

Faal, Dawda *A history of The Gambia – AD1000 to 1965* Edward Francis Small Printing Press, 1999. This is quite a detailed publication relating the history of the country and dealing with it from the perspective of a West African.

Natural history
Edberg, Etienne *A Naturalist's Guide to The Gambia* JG Sanders, 1982 (English edition). Original edition in Swedish. Although quite dated now, this is still the best of the guides available for naturalists who are visiting The Gambia. It includes an introduction to the country, places to visit and a section on common animals and plants. This is a gem of a book with some very good black and white illustrations. Worth getting hold of.

Department of Parks and Wildlife Management *A Guide to the Protected Areas of The Gambia, West Africa* DPWM 2000. This is a useful little guide to the national parks and nature reserves of the country.

Project Niokolo Badiar *Niokolo-Badiar: Guide à l'usage des Visiteurs du Complexe Écologique du Niokolo-Badiar* Project Niokolo Badiar, 1995. Although this guide is in French throughout, it is still very useful as it contains a number of maps to this wonderful national park and some very informative illustrations. It also makes a good keepsake of your visit. Only available from the national park.

Kingdon, Jonathan *The Kingdon Guide to African Mammals* Academic Press, 1997. This is undoubtedly the best field guide on African mammals and all the known land species are covered with the most up-to-date classification. Colour illustrations throughout and easy to use.

Haltenorth, Theodor and Diller, Helmut *A Field Guide to the Mammals of Africa, including Madagascar* Collins, 1980. This is the next best book to get if you can't get hold of a copy of the *Kingdon Guide*, despite its age. Though it does not deal with the smaller species such as bats, the colour illustrations are not too bad.

Dorst, Jean and Dandelot, Pierre *Collins Field Guide: Larger Mammals of Africa* Harper Collins, 1970. Like the other Collins field guide, this book is only worth taking if you can't get hold of the *Kingdon Guide*. This deals only with the larger species.

Carwardine, Mark *Eyewitness Handbooks: Whales, Dolphins and Porpoises* Dorling Kindersley, 1995. If you're into dolphins and their kin then you probably have this book already as it is an excellent field guide to identifying species. Although there are only a few species of dolphin in The Gambia this guide will be useful on those dolphin-watching trips.

Barlow, Clive, Wacher, Tim and Disley, Tony *A Field Guide to Birds of The Gambia and Senegal* Pica Press, 1997. This is *the* field guide on the birds for The Gambia and Senegal. Most species are illustrated in colour, though in our opinion a few of the illustrations are not quite accurate. However, the text is authoritative and up to date and this book is definitely a must if you're into birds.

Serle, William, Morel, Gérard and Hartwig, Wolfgang *A Field Guide to the Birds of West Africa* Collins, 1977. This is the only field guide to cover the majority of West African birds available currently, though it is quite old now. It's still a useful backup to have on birding trips.

Barnett, Linda, Emms, Craig and Camara, Amadou 'The Birds of Bijol Island, Tanji River (Karinti) Bird Reserve, The Gambia'. *Bulletin of the African Bird Club* 8: 39-43. 2001. This short paper covers the latest information on the birds to be found on Bijol Islands (see *Tanji River (Karinti) Bird Reserve* in *Chapter 8*).

Rödel, Mark-Oliver *Herpetofauna of West Africa: Volume 1 – Amphibians of the West African Savanna* Edition, Chimaira 2000. This new book covers all of the toad and frog species likely to be found in The Gambia and has a good selection of colour photographs. It is a little technical.

Barnett, Linda, Emms, Craig and Santoni, Christina 'The Herpetofauna of Abuko Nature Reserve, The Gambia' *Bulletin of the British Herpetological Society, No.77* (Autumn, 2001). This short paper covers all the amphibians and reptiles that have been found in this species rich nature reserve.

Larsen, Torben *Butterflies of West Africa – Origins, Natural History, Diversity, Conservation* In preparation. When this book finally makes it to press it will see the end of a monumental achievement by Torben, who is a great friend of ours. He has spent many years amassing a great deal of data but has that easy way of getting it across to people that have made all of his other books a treat. If you're into butterflies this will be a must.

Williams, John *A Field Guide to the Butterflies of Africa* Collins, 1969. Although this field guide deals with only a small selection of the total African butterfly fauna, it does enable you to identify some of the more common species to be found in The Gambia. Colour and black and white illustrations throughout.

Kasper, Phyllis *Some Common Flora of The Gambia* Stiftung Walderhaltung in Afrika, 1999. This is a very useful illustrated guide to the common plants found throughout the country.

Jones, Michael *Flowering Plants of The Gambia* AA Balkema, 1994. Although describing only 10—12% of the flowering plants found in The Gambia, this book is still very useful and beautifully illustrated with colour photographs.

Overland travel

Scott, Chris *Sahara Handbook* Trailblazer, 2001. An essential read if you're bringing your own vehicle overland.

Shackell, Charlie and Bracht, Illya *Africa by Road* Bradt Travel Guides, 2001. A very useful guidebook to travelling by road throughout Africa and a very useful read when you are planning your trip.

Health

Wilson-Howarth, Jane *Bugs, Bites and Bowels* Cadogan Guides, 1999. A guide to healthy travel for adults.

Wilson-Howarth, Dr Jane and Ellis, Dr Matthew *Your Child's Health Abroad: A Manual for Travelling Parents* Bradt Travel Guides, 1998.

Culture
The following is a selection of locally produced booklets. They can usually be found in Timbooktoo Bookshop along Kairaba Avenue in Fajara, Tanje Village Museum or in many of the supermarkets and tourist shops throughout the country.

Bayo, Abdoulie *Traditional Crafts in The Gambia.*

Sidibe, BK and Galloway, Winifred *Wrestling in The Gambia* Occasional Papers of The Gambia National Museum, 1976.

Sonko-Godwin, Patience *Ethnic Groups of the Senegambia: A Brief History* Sunrise Publishers, 1985.

Language
Many locally produced booklets on Gambian languages are usually available in Timbooktoo Bookshop along Kairaba Avenue in Fajara, as well as in many of the supermarkets and tourist shops.

Websites
The official website of the Republic of The Gambia can be found at www.gambia.com. There is tourist information on the site, including details on obtaining visas. A good birding site is www.Gambiabirding.org. Details of the Drum Doctors drumming courses can be found at www.africandrums.net.

MEASUREMENTS AND CONVERSIONS

To convert	Multiply by
Inches to centimetres	2.54
Centimetres to inches	0.3937
Feet to metres	0.3048
Metres to feet	3.281
Yards to metres	0.9144
Metres to yards	1.094
Miles to kilometres	1.609
Kilometres to miles	0.6214
Acres to hectares	0.4047
Hectares to acres	2.471
Imperial gallons to litres	4.546
Litres to imperial gallons	0.22
US gallons to litres	3.785
Litres to US gallons	0.264
Ounces to grams	28.35
Grams to ounces	0.03527
Pounds to grams	453.6
Grams to pounds	0.002205
Pounds to kilograms	0.4536
Kilograms to pounds	2.205
British tons to kilograms	1016.0
Kilograms to British tons	0.0009812
US tons to kilograms	907.0
Kilograms to US tons	0.000907

5 imperial gallons are equal to 6 US gallons
A British ton is 2,240 lbs. A US ton is 2,000 lbs.

Temperature conversion table

The bold figures in the central columns can be read as either centigrade or fahrenheit.

°C		°F	°C		°F
−18	**0**	32	10	**50**	122
−15	**5**	41	13	**55**	131
−12	**10**	50	16	**60**	140
−9	**15**	59	18	**65**	149
−7	**20**	68	21	**70**	158
−4	**25**	77	24	**75**	167
−1	**30**	86	27	**80**	176
2	**35**	95	32	**90**	194
4	**40**	104	38	**100**	212
7	**45**	113	40	**104**	219

Index

*Page numbers in **bold** indicate main entries: those in italic indicate maps*

Nile monitor